ROBBIE

WITH DAVID MADDOCK

FOWLER

MY AUTOBIOGRAPHY

PAN BOOKS

First published 2005 by Macmillan

First published in paperback 2006 by Pan Books
an imprint of Pan Macmillan Ltd
Pan Macmillan, 20 New Wharf Road, London N1 9RR
Basingstoke and Oxford
Associated companies throughout the world
www.panmacmillan.com

ISBN-13: 978-0-330-43763-9
ISBN-10: 0-330-43763-1

9 8 7 6 5 4 3 2

A CIP catalogue record for this book is available from
the British Library.

Typeset by SetSystems Ltd, Saffron Walden, Essex
Printed and bound in Great Britain by
Mackays of Chatham plc, Chatham, Kent

To Kerrie, who I truly adore,
for her love and support, and to
Madison, Jaya and Mackenzie, our pride and joy.
Without them, I would be nothing.

To my family, especially my mum,
who I love to bits and who has always been there for me,
and my dad, who was with me every step of the way,
and taught me everything I know.

To Lisa, Anthony and Scott, the best
sister and brothers anyone could ever have.

To you all, I am so grateful.

Contents

PROLOGUE

I remember being told at the time it was an important moment, but I don't recall the day I was supposed to have written a little bit of history as being different to any other at Melwood. It was 1 November 1994, not exactly pissing down but it was damp as usual, a grey Liverpool day that made you glad you weren't on the building sites like some of my mates, or on the railways like me dad. It was training, with Ronnie Moran barking orders and making sure none of us got too carried away. Fat chance.

Training was a right laugh when I joined Liverpool – plenty of messing about and seeing what you could get away with. I was never the greatest trainer, but I always loved going in then. And afterwards, before I got in the bath, Roy Evans, the gaffer, came over and said they were ready for me, that Peter Robinson had come down with Tom Saunders so we could get it done. They had to wait a while until I washed the mud off, I then strolled in, jeans and a T-shirt on. A little casual maybe, for what they said afterwards was a big step for football.

I was nineteen, and just into my second season in the first team. I wasn't bad either. A few weeks before, I'd scored a hat-trick against Arsenal in four minutes and thirty-two seconds, which was supposed to be the fastest of all time in the Premiership. Already by then, I was getting used to making history, even if deep down I've always known it means fuck all in the scheme of things. I had been offered my first proper contract by Liverpool, and today I was going in to sign. The funny thing is, I didn't even know how much it was for. George Scott, who has looked after me since I was a kid, had negotiated everything on my behalf with the club secretary Peter Robinson, and I wasn't there when they met. In fact, I don't think I even knew that I was supposed to sign it that day. George had rung me and said it was all right, told me how much a week it was, but at that age, you don't think about money, you can't even work out how much it all adds up to, with the clauses and bonuses and all that.

So I went into the manager's office, this tiny little dark room at the training ground with a desk and a TV on the wall and a few books, and the three of them were crammed in there waiting, smiling and giving it the usual stuff. There was no press, no Sky TV, just the four of us, and I think Tom Saunders was only there because he had been present to witness everything when me dad took me up to Anfield to tell them that I would sign Schoolboy forms for them, about five years after they first asked me. He was a great bloke, one of the legends of the club and someone we all respected. He was an auld fella, a director who had been mates with Bill Shankly, and was part of the club's fabric, so I suppose the fact that he was there maybe should have said to me it was a big thing. There were a few pages that I didn't bother to read, and then the part where I had to sign, which they turned to pretty quickly. I grabbed the pen, said thanks a lot, and stuck me name down.

As I did it, one of them – I'm not even sure which one now – was gabbing on about Liverpool and how this was an important moment, and how I could be as big as some of the biggest names in their history, and he goes to me: 'Enjoy the moment, Robbie son, you've just won the lottery.'

My first thought was, What the fuck is he on about? The national lottery had started that year, but winning it for me was a couple of years back when I signed for Liverpool, YTS forms with a promise of a professional contract afterwards. I know it sounds like another footballer talking bullshit, but I was a kid from Toxteth, who had been dreaming of playing football since I was six years old, and, since I was ten, had aimed my life at being a professional. So the day I signed that first YTS contract, in 1991, was the day that I thought I'd hit the jackpot. The money didn't mean anything to me at that stage. I got £29.50 a week on my first deal, and I thought I was the luckiest person alive. At that age, it was proving yourself, getting into the team and staying there. It was all about getting there, making it, being a pro, the holy fucking grail – and the only thing that interested me about the contract was that it was for five years, which meant I had done something right and I had something of a future.

I always had a belief in my ability, and I knew if I could prove it to the manager, then the money would come anyway. But what they meant when they said that I'd won the lotto was that I was a millionaire. It was Roy Evans who told me later that the deal I had signed had guaranteed me a million. I was the first teenage footballer in the country to have been given a contract that size. The first teenage football millionaire. It wasn't actually that much a week – by the standards when the TV money really kicked in later – but over five years with bonuses and appearances and signing-on fees, it probably was worth close to a million. Me dad still reckons it should have been a lot more.

I've been told enough times in my career that I came into the game at exactly the right time. I arrived just as the Premiership was formed, and they signed the first big contract with Sky. From then on, players could earn big money. Nowadays, even your journeyman pro can earn a million quid a year, and most Premiership players can be set up for life by signing one decent contract.

When Wayne Rooney was eighteen, I read in the *Echo* that Everton announced they had offered him a basic salary of £3 million a year, even before bonuses. You don't want to discuss anyone's wages, but he would hardly need an agent to know where his starting point in negotiations with Manchester United should be. A decade ago, though, wages were nowhere near the same levels, even though most people tend to assume that footballers have always been on outrageous salaries. Massive stars like Ian Rush and John Barnes were on decent money, but it was peanuts compared to what they could earn today. Rushie had an incredible career at Anfield, and was one of the greatest strikers of all time, but the biggest contract he ever got was when he left Liverpool right at the end of his career, and played at Leeds and then Newcastle.

When you were a kid you didn't earn the big money, it was a YTS for spends, and then a small contract until you had served your time, and proven your worth. By the time I came along, players like Steve McManaman, Ryan Giggs, Lee Sharpe and Nicky Barmby had all burst onto the scene and done it as these incredible teenagers who were taking the league by storm, and being treated like pop stars. According to the boss, though, they were into their twenties by the time they signed decent contracts. Paul Scholes, David Beckham and Gary Neville were about the same age as me, but they got into the United side a season or so after I was doing it. So even though I didn't know it, I drove out of Melwood that day, in my little beige Escort with the brown interior, as the first of a new breed of footballer. They're not my words, by the way, it's something I read a lot later and at the time it made me laugh. But it's not bad for a kid from Toxteth.

Money's not an easy thing for a footballer to talk about, even if the press lads are always banging on about it, always plucking a figure out of the air and doubling it. I'm not moaning, because it's not such a difficult thing to have, and I'm bloody grateful for what football has given to me. When you talk about it, though, you always get criticized, and come across as greedy. I don't think I'm greedy, even if I know that I'm paid money that most people can't even dream about. Some of the players I know, they're always talking about it, saying how much they're on and how good that makes them, and it makes you laugh, because it seems that's all they're interested in. I've never bothered about it. I've never been involved in a contract negotiation in my life, and most of the time, whatever was put in front of me, so long as George said it was okay, I knew I could sign it and get on with the football.

To be honest, if Liverpool had asked me to pay to play for them at the start, I'd have said yes. I'm embarrassed to talk about money, and I don't think I'm flash with it, either. I've got decent cars, but when I'm out, I don't think people would know that I'm a pro footballer, if they didn't recognize my face. My mate Calvey reckons that I look like a tramp, cheeky git. What he means, I hope, is that I don't like to show off, to have all the fancy stuff that some footballers like to surround themselves with. You can't argue when people say we're paid too much, although I don't know anyone in the game who would offer to give some of his wages back, and as one of the players, I'm bound to think that we deserve the money that's sloshing around the sport, rather than a lot of the other characters who seem to make a pretty tidy living on the back of us.

It might not be the fairest example, but who would the fans of Manchester United rather have seen get their money, the shareholders or Eric Cantona? The point is, the money's there, and when you're a teenager from inner-city Liverpool, and you win the lottery, you don't have any training on how to deal with it. You're not prepared for it, or for the adulation, fame and demands that come along with it. I've made plenty of mistakes, I know I have, and during my time as a footballer, things have changed so that the spotlight is even more intense, and you have to be even more of a role model, a sensible, mature, intelligent professional, even if you're a cheeky little lad who's come from an inner-city council estate, and put football before his studies. I was one of the first who had all this.

Ten years ago, I went through what Wayne Rooney has to go through now, and what David Beckham went through just a bit after me although he got it much worse, obviously. Somebody who interviewed me recently said I was a guinea pig, which is a bit harsh, because I look nothing like one. But I know what he means. My story is not about going through the system as a promising talent, making the grade and living happily ever after. It's about a kid from Toxteth who wanted to play football, and got a whole lot more than he ever, ever imagined could be possible when his dream came true.

One thing I've noticed about the game – for all the changes that have happened, for all the money and the media interest and the outrage now when a footballer fucks up – is that they still get the players from the same place. Which is basically a council estate. Me, Rooney, Stevie Gerrard, Jamie Carragher, Beckham, Scholes, Macca, Joe Cole, Rio Ferdinand, whoever. Just go through the England squad. London, Liverpool, Manchester, wherever, the players who get through are generally from the same sort of areas, and I guess it's probably the same with the foreign players who come into the game, too.

It doesn't mean you're thick, or a thug, but it does mean you have a certain outlook on life to begin with. What happened to me is that I signed YTS for a year, played a few reserve team games and was straight into the first team, so I got the money almost straight away. I was a boy, suddenly treated like the men and expected to act like them. And Liverpool had a tradition of their players working hard and playing hard, back before the nineties and through all the glory era. When I got there, all the pasta and science stuff hadn't quite caught on in England – things that were perfectly acceptable then wouldn't be tolerated now. We had some characters too, some lively boys who could teach a wide-eyed little kid a thing or two. So I had an introduction into the old way of doing things, just as the whole mentality began to change in football.

Nowadays, the kids get a bit of training, have a longer education and are coached on how to deal with the media, with the money and the fame stuff. I didn't. I didn't have a fucking clue. I once made a joke about not having an education, saying the only brains I had were in my feet, and that quote still gets dragged up now, trying to show I was some wrong 'un from this part of Liverpool that was almost a ghetto, who had come from the gutter. I wasn't thick. I went to school, did my lessons, learnt what I needed to know, and was pretty streetwise as it happens. And the place I come from might not be the smartest area in the world, but it wasn't all bad, certainly not back when I was a kid. The fact is though, everything that has happened to me started from a maisonette in Toxteth. It was a journey on a bus from the inner-city council estate, through the city centre up to Anfield because we didn't have a car. Then, suddenly, when I was still a boy, I had enough money to buy a hundred cars. I live on the Wirral now, in a fantastic house with my beautiful family. But to understand my story, and my journey, you have to know where I came from.

TOXTETH (1)

Before I became 'God', the media tried out the nickname of the 'Toxteth Terror' for me. I know they always try to come up with those corny-sounding names with the same letters at the start of each word, but I always think deep down it was a little dig in some way, suggesting I was this scally who had crawled out of the gutter. When you think about it, it kind of puts Toxteth down, because I'm sure it's meant to imply something negative about it being a terrible place, and about me being a bit thick.

When I first played for Liverpool, I wasn't exactly Bamber Gascoigne, but I wasn't Paul Gascoigne either (only kidding, Gazza). Nobody wanted to see past the cliché, it was always about this kid who had come from Toxteth, the ghetto that was famous because the riots had been on the telly, and it looked like Beirut because all the buildings were burnt out. If there's one thing that does my head in, it's all the stuff banging on about Toxteth being this shit-hole, the inference being that it was miraculous I managed to claw my way out of there. Just about every top-flight footballer comes from an inner-city council estate, but Toxteth is somehow portrayed as being much worse than all the rest. Toxteth is the bogey-man of the inner cities, because of the riots.

The God's honest truth is, it really wasn't that bad for me. There was the usual sort of stuff that goes on in cities, there were the kids who went nicking cars, and probably those that did the drugs – although you didn't see it out in the street like you do these days. But I remember it as being a safe enough place to grow up, and I don't remember ever having much trouble as a kid. There were always places you shouldn't go, and people you should avoid, but the fact is, you didn't go far at all anyway, stuck to your street and the ones just beyond, where everyone knew you, and the people you knew looked out for you. I'm not trying to say that it was all that 'working class look after their own' stuff, because there were plenty of people you'd want to avoid, and places yer mum would say were out of bounds. It was like this, though, at one end of my road was the school, and at the other end was an all-weather football pitch, and for me, that was the extent of my world. Everyone I saw there I knew, and they knew me and my family.

There was nothing scary or particularly rough about that. The problem has always been the image that the television pictures of the riots gave to the rest of the world. I think people were shocked because it was happening in England, and not Belfast or some place like that. People still talk about 'the Toxteth riots' as though it was yesterday, but in fact, it all blew up in the summer of 1981, when I was six years old. I don't remember much about it, because I was too young, and me mum shielded us kids from it, wouldn't let us go out, and we were too little to understand what was being shown on the telly. I suppose it's funny that had I been old enough, I could have put the telly on and seen all these pictures of civil war, and then opened the curtains and watched it live. Me mum and dad have told me a lot since, and I've read about it, and how it is an important moment in English social history. I don't know much about that, but I do know it happened right outside our front door.

Toxteth is about a mile away from Liverpool city centre, to the south, and if you drew it on a piece of paper it would be a sort of a triangle. At the north, which is at the top of my old road, is Upper Parliament Street, which runs down into Smithdown Road on one side, and Sefton Street on the other, which is down by the river. Growing up, Toxteth was one of the few properly multiracial areas in Liverpool. When I was a kid, there were all sorts of different ethnic groups who lived close by.

There was a strong community of Somalians, and we used to go down to the all-weather pitch at the Sports Centre on the corner of our road, and play footie matches against the Somali kids who lived in the area. We'd start off at eight a side, and by the end it would be about thirty-two onto eight, all of their team playing in their shoes, and their dress kecks, because they just rolled up and joined in. It was a great laugh.

There was a large black population, mostly families who had lived there for generations, and I don't remember any real trouble between any of the ethnic groups. What did happen, though, according to me dad, was that the police used to stop the black lads all the time, and harass them. It was what was known as the 'sus laws', and what they did was called 'going farming' round our way, basically planting things on the kids they picked up. It wasn't a no-go area by any means, not *Mad Max* or *Precinct 13* or anything like that, but there was serious unemployment, not much money around, and obviously plenty of the roads were run down. I remember that we were always a bit wary of going over to Granby Road, which was only a few streets away, because it was supposed to be rough. You were always told not to go there. I suppose it was a pretty poor area, nobody had any money, and there was some unrest because of the poverty and deprivation. But if you live there, you're used to it, and you hardly notice it, do you?

In that summer of 1981, there was a lot of unrest around the country, and it all came to boiling point in Toxteth on the night of 3 July. It started, so I've learnt, when a young black man was arrested on Selbourne Street, a couple of hundred yards away from where I lived. It all kicked off, and three policemen were injured when the lad's mates tried to help him, because they thought he was being done over. Whatever the reasons, and I think people now accept that it was a reaction against the conditions and the oppression, that incident was enough to ignite – literally – nine nights of rioting, which have always been described as race riots, but me dad says that plenty of the young white lads got involved, because everyone was pissed off.

From what I've read since, the Toxteth rioting was the worst case of civil unrest in Britain in the twentieth century, worse than Brixton, worse than the miners' strike. It was a war: pitched battles breaking out all over the place. More than 500 people were arrested, about 1,000 policemen were injured, and about 150 buildings were burnt down. There were these incredible stand-offs with the police at night, with bricks and bottles and every weapon you can imagine being used, and looting, cars overturned and burnt out, and buildings destroyed.

Every night, for more than a week, people poured onto the streets, and the pictures that were on the telly, the ones that people still remember now, made it look like World War Three. I just remember the charred, blackened remains of so many buildings. There were loads of them around the area, and you used to walk by them on the way to school, on the way to the all-weather, or the youth club. The thing is, I remember them, but I didn't think it was anything unusual, because they were just there. Around the corner from the top of our road, on Upper Parliament Street, was the Rialto, which was an old cinema and dance-hall where the Beatles once played, according to me mum and dad. That was set on fire, and my nana told me that it had one of those green copper roofs, which glowed for days afterwards. It was a massive building, and it ended up as a burnt-out shell, which stood there for years before they rebuilt it. The Co-Op supermarket that a lot of the local families used over on the corner of Lodge Lane was also burnt down, and plenty of buildings on Upper Parliament Street and Princes Road, all of them not far from our house.

The funniest one was a place called the Racquets Club, which was a sort of private club where the circuit judges used to stay when they were sitting in Liverpool. That was looted before it was burnt to cinders, and some people who lived near the club had all these old oil paintings on their walls of these crusty old judges in elaborate gold frames! Me mum's memory of the rioting was pretty frightening, because the police station was right down opposite the very end of our road. One of the nights early on, the rioters charged down the road, putting through a lot of the windows in the maisonettes, and headed off towards the police station, where they laid siege to the place. She said that they brought police in from Manchester because the local plod were completely overrun and couldn't cope, and they were in battalions down the bottom of the road, and then they started banging their shields and doing all that stuff you see on the telly. They also fired CS gas into the crowds, and the rioters responded by pelting them with petrol bombs.

Every night, for over a week, it would be the same. As darkness fell, the police would be getting ready down by the police station, and gangs of young lads would start to gather around the top of our road, more and more of them, until it all exploded into carnage. The two sides would charge at each other, meeting down the middle of our road. Mum says that there was no way we were going out, and she remembers that when she went out, to check on me nana, she was walking right through the middle of it, with bottles flying round her head, and all these incredible battle scenes around her. We were lucky because our windows weren't put in, but twice me nana – who lived across the road then – had people running into her house, and she sheltered them to stop them getting a pasting. Me dad said that when he went out in the morning to go to work, there was a stench of burning on the air still, the gas catching in the back of your throat.

Me nana remembers great big tins of ham and corned beef rolling down the road after the rioting one night, and all the shops being looted, with fellas just running down the road with tellies, radios, all sorts of stuff in their arms. She also remembers the roads littered with odd shoes, either where the rioters had lost theirs or dropped looted ones. Me mum says that one night, she saw someone come down the road with a milk float, all loaded up with stuff that had been looted. This all happened on the pavement right outside my front door, about ten feet away from where I was watching the telly . . . and I can't remember a thing about it!

At the end of it all, Mrs Thatcher said she felt for those poor shopkeepers, and they planted a few trees down on Princes Road, and called it a garden city. Nothing much changed, except that Toxteth was now twinned in people's minds with the Lebanon. But it's funny, I lived there, right in the middle of it all, and I didn't notice anything different. I didn't even know about the place being this infamous ghetto until I was much older, when I kept getting the same reaction whenever I said where I was from. Even now, people can look at you like you've got two heads if you say you're from Toxteth. I go back often enough still, and maybe it has got worse now because all the money that was promised to do it up hasn't arrived and so it's got more broken down over the intervening twenty years. But back then, it was a good enough place to live, the streets where I roamed just a pretty small local community, which generally looked out for each other.

Toxteth was one of the poshest bits of Liverpool in years gone by. There are still some massive houses around Canning Street; they used to be owned by sea captains and rich merchants, as well as bankers and judges. It was once countryside until Liverpool expanded, with the rich people who made money from the busy port living in their grand houses with lots of servants. Even before the Second World War, it was an upmarket suburb, with loads of huge Georgian and Victorian houses, and a lot of money around. After the war, it began to change, with the merchants and bankers moving out as they lost their servants and couldn't run the big houses any more, and gradually, those houses were split up into flats. With the terraced housing as well, and lots of building after the war, it gradually became more of a working-class area, according to me nana Louie anyway, me dad's mum, who has lived there all her life, and she's eighty-four now.

Her family were the Devonports, and they were well known in the area, going back years and years, to when it was a fairly upmarket suburb still, her mum and dad coming from the area, and living in Hislop Street. When she was fourteen, her dad carried her hat and coat for her down to the Pen Works, where she got her first job, before she went to work for a drum-maker on Upper Parliament Street. At eighteen, she went to the Grand National meeting at Aintree where she met me grandad, John Fowler, who was from the north end of the city, up by Paddy's Market. They were married soon after, and lived with nana's parents on the Dock Road, before they got a place on Caryl Gardens.

Me grandad John was supposed to be a bit of a character. He went off to the war in 1939, and survived Dunkirk, came back and had seven kids. I don't know too much about him, because he died just before I was born, but I'm told he was a mad Liverpool fan, and used to go out and celebrate after a victory by dancing on the piano in the local pub. When I played my first game for the club, everyone on me dad's side of the family said that Grandad would have been incredibly proud, and he would have been looking down on me with a huge smile across his face.

Me dad Robert, or Bobby as everyone still calls him, was born on 27 June 1950, third of the seven kids, and was delivered by the local midwife in the house where they lived on Caryl Gardens. Before him were Norma and John, and then came Delores, Bernard, Julie and Tony. Dad was a bit of a rascal when he was younger, getting up to the same tricks that I got up to later, one time being rushed to hospital when he climbed a drainpipe that collapsed and fell on top of him as he crashed down. Funnily enough, he went to the primary school that I was to attend all those years later, although it wasn't at the same location, because they moved it when it started to fall down! He was a tall, good-looking fella, which is probably where I get my handsome profile from, and when he left school at fifteen, he got jobs working as a labourer in the area, before he moved onto the railways.

I was close to my mum's family obviously, because we lived with her mum and dad, me nana and grandad, for years. Me nana, especially, I adored, and it was a terrible loss to the whole family when she died early in 2005. I was really close to her, and she did so much for me, and for the rest of the family. She was the rock that the family was based on, and she gave us all the right sort of attitude. Me mum was the same. People go on about where you come from, and how that makes you, but me nana brought her kids up the right way and so did me mum, so we turned out fine.

Grandad died only a few months before me nana, and not long before that, me Uncle Alan also died, which made it a horrible time for me mum and all the Ryder family. They were also a well-known family around Toxteth, and went years back in the same area, not moving far from the streets where we lived as children. We are a big family, and we've lived in the same place for decades and decades, and so it is not surprising that people will remember the Ryder family in Toxteth.

Nana was called Mary, and she was actually from Shaftesbury Street, which is just off Warwick Street where me dad lived. Interestingly, when she married me grandad Johnny, they first got a place down by Caryl Gardens, by where me other nana and grandad lived. Me mum was one of nine, the third daughter of six, behind Pat and Cathleen, and before Joan, Eileen and Jacqueline. She had another sister too, Josephine, who sadly only lived for half an hour after she was born.

Me mum had three younger brothers, John, Alan and Tony. She was born on 23 March 1952, in Sefton General Hospital, where I was also born, and she has some wonderful memories of this large, close family living on Tavistock Street, off Park Road, being brought up by me nana to respect each other and look out for one another. Mum says Grandad was a real character. Even though they were a good Catholic family, who used to go to church every Sunday, Johnny would get a few drinks down him on 12 July when they had the Protestant marches, and he would then go out and lead the parade! He was a funny fella, and I think I get my sense of humour from him. Mum was a character too. When she was little, nana would make all the kids go to Mount Carmel church, but Mum would sneak off and go to the Protestant church instead, because all her friends went there, and she didn't want to miss out.

Nana never went out to enjoy herself, because she gave everything she had for the family. She worked in a bingo hall cleaning, and then she worked for fifteen years down at the Polytechnic on Hope Street. Grandad Johnny was a foreman with Guinness on Stanhope Street for years, and apparently the two of them weren't happy unless they were arguing.

There was real drama in the family when me mum was eleven, because – and it must run in the family, this – she was climbing on a roof and went through, falling forty feet down onto the concrete. Everyone thought she had died, but she was incredibly lucky, because she didn't break anything, just damaged her back and a lot of the muscles. Mind you, she didn't escape scot free, because she couldn't walk for a long time, and was off school for six months. She remembers being taken in an ambulance every day to get physio at the Southern Hospital, and she had to learn how to walk properly again. She went to St Malachy's primary, and then St Finbar's secondary, and she remembers getting caned by the teacher if she didn't get the church service exactly right.

Mum eventually lived in Windsor Street, and at the bottom of that road, forming the T-junction, was Upper Warwick Street, where me dad moved to when he was eight or nine. So they were neighbours since they were kids, but they were hardly childhood sweethearts, because they didn't meet until they were in their twenties, and that's when they started going out.

Dad was best mates with me Uncle John, and also knew Alan, and that's how they met. John and me dad started going to the footy together, watching Everton all over. It was a romantic first date too . . . they went down to the Bankhouse, the pub on the corner of my road, and had a few bevvies.

My parents never married, and they never really lived together either. I know some people will find that surprising, but for me, it has never been a problem. When I was a kid, I never thought about it, and as I got older, I was so used to the idea that I never gave it a second thought. It wasn't even an issue as far as I was concerned. I never got any stick about it from other kids at school or round our streets, because plenty of their mums and dads weren't living together. It's just that mine kept seeing each other. They've always been friends, and they still get on now, but for whatever reason they say that they weren't compatible living in the same house. Me dad did move in across at Windsor Street for a short time, but Uncle

Bernard got cancer, and so Dad moved back across the road to help out. Uncle Bernard died at the age of twenty, which was a terrible time for the family, especially me nana, and so me dad stayed put over there with her, and he never moved back into Windsor Street again.

Eventually my parents separated, or it's probably more accurate to say they went their separate ways! The thing is, there was never a moment when I came in from school and me dad wasn't there, never a time when he walked out or there was a big barney or a breakdown or whatever you like to call it. It might sound funny, but I never noticed that they were no longer together, and I couldn't even tell you when it happened. I always saw Dad at night, or the weekends or whenever, so when they drifted apart and were no longer a couple, it didn't make any difference to how us kids saw things.

So I can't say I've got any hang-ups about me mum and dad not being together, and I can't claim I was a product of a broken home or any of that shite. I have a great relationship with Mum and Dad, and we're all close in the family. I reckon I was brought up the right way by me mum, who gave us everything, made sure we were always all right and showered us with affection. What makes me laugh about the Toxteth thing is that we were never deprived, even if we weren't loaded. If I'm honest, until I got married I was always at me mum's, even when I had my own flat, and she carried on cooking and washing and ironing for me. And Dad was always there. I reckon he watched every game I ever played from the age of about ten, and he always took me down to play football and practise, practise, practise. I used to go over the road on Saturdays, watch *Match of the Day* and fall asleep, and then come back over the next morning. It was a laugh really, having two homes – there was always somewhere to go. In fact, all me family lived close by on both sides. That's why I say I never had a problem living in Toxteth, even though people think I must be this great survivor, or this incredible scally, to have come from there.

If you ask me whether I would have liked my parents to stay together, then yeah, I suppose so, but not if it makes them unhappy. I'm quiet, really, outside my own little sphere, and maybe I'm not as confident as people think. I'm not the sort of person to think too much about it, but maybe I'm more insecure than people would imagine an England footballer to be, and I sometimes think I've needed a bit of an arm around me in my career – which I've not always got from certain managers and coaches who didn't understand me.

When I'm in my own circle, then I'm pretty loud and outspoken. Everyone says that when I was a kid I always had to have the last word, and I've not changed much now. I like a joke, and as I got older I was probably always one of the jokers in the dressing room, although there are plenty worse than me around! That's what happens when you're a lad, you join in, take the piss, act up, and hide away any weaknesses. Dressing rooms haven't changed much in football, probably not in 100 years. You used to whistle down the pit, and now you set up your academies in the inner city. All these working-class kids in the dressing room, from similar backgrounds and with all that peer pressure to conform, to fit in. You don't get a university debating society. Mind you, there is usually plenty of a different kind of debate when Gazza or Incey are in that dressing room. Or me, for that matter. But outside that, I'm quiet, God's honest truth.

I see these kids now, coming into the game on this incredible amount of money, and not always with the record to justify it, and fuck me, they're cocky. I was cocky, but not in that way, not being flash and showing everyone how much money you earn, and going round saying you're the bee's fucking knees, when you've done fuck all. I look back, and the most outrageous thing I did in that way was to dye my hair blond, and that was just a laugh when I was on holiday with a few mates. People say I copied Gazza, by the way, but did I bollocks. It was me, Dom Matteo and Calvey and a few others on holiday, and we just went for it for a laugh because we were a bunch of daft lads away from home. I reckon Gazza saw us on the telly when we got back, and went for it himself.

I made a video when I was a kid about my life story, and when they were speaking to me, I was wearing this old grandad shirt, and a pair of crap jeans, and I didn't give a monkey's. I have never been interested in the flash stuff – apart from the cars. I've always liked a decent car since that beige Escort I bought from me Uncle Phil, Jackie's husband, for £800! – and I've always had this idea that you only shout your mouth off when you've got something to shout about, if you do it at all. Later in my career, I've been in England sides in warm-up matches and these kids have come in, and acted like they own the fucking place, and played as though everyone should give them the ball, and they'll never give it back because they're so good. None of them can pass a ball three yards any more, because they just want to beat twelve men and shoot every time. And you're thinking, they couldn't lace the boots of some of the other players.

It strikes me that these days, clubs don't even want players who can truly play any more, they just want athletes, quick guys who don't have a football brain, can just run and run, and keep running all the way down to the Dock Road if they opened the fucking doors. Rooney's a top man, and from what I've seen of him, he's like the other Scousers who came into the England squad in my time, pretty low key and unpretentious. But some of them, Jesus. I can never imagine acting like that. Have a laugh, yeah, dick about, but don't give it the Charlie Big Bollocks. It's inevitable, I guess, because of the money and the fame now, because everyone is a superstar, even if they're just an average player, and maybe that was part of the process set in motion when I signed that contract in 1994.

I've got confidence in my ability, and I think I've got something, but just because I'm a footballer, I don't think I'm perfect. In fact, I'm bloody certain I'm not. Things have changed over the past decade. The kids now, they're from the same places as me, but they have a different attitude to it all, like it's their right, even before they've kicked a ball. Maybe that's just the way we are though, these days, not just in football but the whole of society.

About a year or so after Mum and Dad were a proper item, my sister Lisa was born, in 1974. I love Lisa, we've always been close and she was a brilliant big sister to me. We went to the same primary school, and there was only a year between us, so she really looked out for me. When we were kids we used to play together and all that, because she was a bit of a tomboy. She went off to an all-girls school, and when I went to secondary, it was all boys, but before that, we'd stick together, a really close pair, because Anthony was five years younger than me, and Scott is only sixteen, so he's fourteen years younger than me and, obviously, a gap like that means that I had a different relationship with them.

When we were kids me mum used to make us be in early every night, and we'd moan like mad as you do, saying that it wasn't fair because all the other kids around could stay out as long as they liked. And she said that must mean their parents didn't love them. I look out for me brothers, and I love the bones of them, but me and Lisa being so close together, we had a special bond. We fought like mad, and argued all the time, but we had a special bond all the same. I remember we used to race each other to school every morning and have a laugh about that. Well, I say race, because by the time she'd got going I'd already be there because I was so quick. They used to call me the whippet in our family, because I was always racing around everywhere (I don't know what happened later), chasing really fast the whole time, and never stopping. That was me, always on the go, always doing something to keep meself occupied.

On 9 April 1975, I came into the world. I was christened Robert Bernard Fowler, after me dad and me uncle who died. Me nana Mary was there with me mum in hospital, and me dad came in to be there when I was born. I had jet black hair, quite a bit of it, and it was long and curly. Me dad said that he went out onto Smithdown Road and got bevvied to celebrate. There was hardly the rich promise that I would be a footballer, because I was born with a problem with my hips, and at first they thought I might be disabled. I had those 'clicky' hips, and it was a worry for a long time, but apparently, it all cleared up as I grew, and I didn't need operations or anything like that. I did have an inhaler though, because I had bad asthma when I was a kid, and so I was hardly the epitome of the perfect athlete. I used to have bouts of being unable to breathe, and I had to take it easy and suck on that inhaler thing until it passed.

But like everything you get used to it, and even though it might look a bit dramatic to someone when you're having an episode, it's not even an issue. That cleared up too, before I got too serious about football, so I didn't have too much of a struggle with it, although I did get tight chested and short of breath sometimes when I was playing . . . and not just because I was out of condition.

When I was a kid I wasn't Robbie, but Robert, and my family still call me that now. It's only when I got to Liverpool that I got called Robbie – it's a Scottish thing, apparently, and there were a lot of them around. And I wasn't Fowler either. Because I lived with me mum, I was automatically called Ryder, which was her name, of course. Even now, when people talk about me as a kid, they remember little Robert Ryder, because I was about two foot nothing until I was fifteen, a tiny little kid who could play football and natter like a scratched record.

When I was selected to play for Liverpool Schoolboys it was Robert Ryder who was on the team list. Even when I went to my secondary school, Nugent, I was called Ryder until the second year. It was only when I took my birth certificate to show them that I was Fowler, that my name got changed, and everyone knew me from then on as Robert Fowler. It didn't bother me either way and me mum didn't mind, so that was that. I had a new identity. It was like being James Bond.

I remember when we made the video about me and my life about three years after I broke into the Liverpool team – three years, for fuck's sake, now there was a cash-in if ever there was one, but hey, yer learn, don't yer? – me dad had all these videos from when I was a kid playing for Liverpool Schoolboys in a big final at Goodison, and he gave them to the producer to sort through, to see if we could use any of the clips. Anyway, the fella goes away with them, and rings up George, who was looking after me by then, and says he scanned all the video looking for Robbie Fowler, but there was no sign, and was he sure I was playing in that match? Then he goes, 'There was this tiny little kid playing though, called Robert Ryder, and he was pretty good, even if he was only about three inches tall!'

Dodgy hips, asthma and Ryder not Fowler, it could have been a very different story for me. By rights, it should have been a very different club as well, because I was an Everton fanatic as a kid. Me dad's parents were Reds, but when he started seeing me mum, all her brothers were massive Evertonians, and so he went along with them to the match, and started supporting the Toffees. So that was that then, me dad and me uncles on me mum's side made sure I was a Blue right from the start. I even had a little baby Everton bob hat, and a royal blue romper suit, which must have looked pretty tragic . . . no wonder Calvey calls me a tramp. I was a proper Everton fan, I went to the games with me auld fella and me Uncle John from as young as I can remember, and when I was older, I used to go up there with me mates. It was such a laugh. There was that pub on the corner of our road called the Bankhouse, and on a Saturday morning Dad would take me down there, and I'd go around all his mates and me uncles at the bar scrounging the money to get into the game. It worked as well, sometimes I would get so much that I could afford to go up to Goodison in a taxi. I could do it even when me dad wasn't there. Those were the days.

Dad took me a fair few times, but the first game I can remember properly me Uncle John took me. Even though I know it wasn't my first it stuck in the memory. It was hardly a classic because Everton got stuffed by Tottenham 4–1 on the opening day of the '84–85 season, and Clive Allen got a couple, I think. Adrian Heath scored a penalty for the Toffees, but it was his partner up front that I used to idolize, Graeme Sharp. God, he was a ledge. Everton won the title that season, even after that bad start, and they got ninety points, which was a record. They were bloody brilliant, and I remember going to see games like the 3–1 win over Bayern Munich in the semi of the Cup Winners' Cup, which was a mind-blowing experience, and I still count it as being one of the best games

I've ever seen. Going up to Goodison on the packed bus (or in a taxi!), that little church on the corner, that sea of people washing along, gathering everything up, the smell on the air of takeaway food and raw excitement, the family paddock, amazed faces and that roar of the crowd, terror and aggression all rolled together.

People have said that was the best atmosphere ever at Goodison Park, and as a ten-year-old kid, believe me, that noise, that incredible emotion straight from the gut is a powerful feeling, and it left such a lasting impression. I used to sit there and think, I wanna do that so much, please let me be like that. You know where you're a kid and you're out in the street doing the commentary thing? Well, I was always Sharpie, beating the first man, beating the third . . . and the fifth . . . and about the fifteenth, the way I was then . . . and smashing it into the net. I liked Trevor Steven too, but Sharpie was the man.

Years later I used to bump into him in town and he's a great lad. He asked me if I could get one of my Liverpool shirts for his lad Chris, and I said no problem . . . so long as he gave me one of his old Everton shirts! He did as well, and I've still got it at home. In fact, I've given Chris one of my shirts from all the clubs I've played for, and an England one too, which is a nice connection.

I remember walking up to Goodison, which was three or four miles away, and never thinking twice about it, except that when I went along with me dad, he walked that fast I used to have to jog behind him to keep up. We lived in me nana's house at first, and then we moved over the road to number 96a in the upstairs maisonette – Mum, Lisa and me together, until Anthony came along. By the time Anthony arrived we had moved to a house on Hughson Street, where we lived with Nana and Grandad Ryder again. We actually moved once before that, not too long after I was born, but we hardly had to get the removal men in, because we just went from the upstairs maisonette to the one downstairs at number 108a.

As I mentioned, me mum had a terrible bad back from that fall, and eventually she had to have an operation, which meant her movement was restricted, and the council allowed us to move to make things easier. It was a bad time for us, because me mum was in hospital for a long time, and I remember bunking off school and going up to the hospital to be with her, even though she'd chew me out for missing my lessons.

It was a hard time for all the family because me mum couldn't work, and that meant we really didn't have any money at all. Me nana, bless her, went out and got a job cleaning, and she came back and handed over her entire wage packet to me mum, just so we could get by. Life in Windsor Street wasn't exactly regal, but I have fond memories of growing up there. My earliest memories are of little things: me mum making us hot chocolate and hot buttered toast when we came home from school on cold winter evenings, snuggled around the gas fire, and of playing out round the houses with me mates from the primary school I attended, St Patrick's, which was just at the end of the road.

As I said, Lisa and me were close, always played together and always looked out for each other. We played the usual games, all the army stuff, and I was a bugger for climbing. I was only little, but I had a head for heights, and I used to scramble up everywhere. I remember when the maisonettes were being refurbished, they had all this scaffolding up, and I used to get up there and climb about the roofs, looking out over my little kingdom, towards the Anglican Cathedral, which was basically at the top of our road.

Me mum went fucking hairless, because it was over 100 feet high. But she could talk. There were some garages down the road, two blocks of them with a gap in between, and we used to run across the roof of one, and jump the gap onto the other one. I don't know what was more dangerous, falling in the gap, or going through the asbestos roof. There was another time I remember when I was a kid, that might have prevented the Robbie Fowler story from going beyond a few pages. Windsor Street is a cross-street that runs between Upper Parliament Street and down beyond Upper Warwick Street, right down running into Admiral Street, and eventually Belvedere Road, a main road out of Liverpool. Running parallel to our street were lots of smaller cross-streets, all with terraces, and closely packed together.

One day, when I was still a little lad, only about eight or nine, I came out of the shop on the corner and ran right out into the road. God I remember it, shitting meself as I saw this car heading straight for me, an Austin Allegro, and it slammed its brakes on, and was coming and coming, and I had one of those moments where me life should have flashed before me. It didn't like, I just thought, Oh Christ, and the car stopped right in front of me, so that I had my hands on the bonnet like you see in the films. And it was later that I thought, that could have been me done for, like a couple of kids who got knocked down from our school. It was fucking morbid too. We used to have this big chart in the school hall about road safety, and my mind might be playing tricks with me, but there was this kid, not anyone I knew, who got knocked down and killed, and so in the middle of all these gold stars for the kids learning their road safety and all that, there was this big black triangle. Tasteful. I remember there were some red stickers too, but I can't remember what they were for – maybe it was me running out in the road, no gold stars for that one.

It was the usual games with me mates from school, and football was the game we played the most. Morning, noon and night, and in those days, it was with a couple of mates from St Pat's, Kevin Ellison and Paul Fox, whose dads were mates with me dad, so we kind of knew each other from the start. But most of all when I was a little lad, I played out with Lisa, and with me cousins who all lived close by – Vincent, Roysan, Kieron and Jamie.

As well as the Toxteth Sports Centre, there was also the Davey Lewis youth club where we often went as primary school kids, and another club up on Stanhope Street, that ran across our road, where again we went and played pool and footie and all that, so there was always plenty to do, if you could be arsed. I could be. From as young as I can remember, me dad used to take me up to the all-weather, and we would practise. Wind or rain, snow or shine, we'd be there, even if I wasn't feeling all that. I wore this kind of windcheater thing with no sleeves, a body warmer type thing, and me dad would say, come on lad, off we go. His mate Mick gave him a little solid ball that we used to improve my right foot. He said I only ever used my right for standing on when I was a lad, but practising with that little ball soon got me out of that. It was fucking murder.

Me dad wasn't a bad footballer himself, he briefly played for a local Sunday side from Liverpool called Nicosia who won the FA Sunday Cup a couple of times, and got into a few finals when he was with them, but he'll tell you himself that he wasn't anything special, and he wasn't a striker, either. Played in midfield. In fact, there's no football in my family at all, anywhere down the line. Me mum was good at sports, she loved gymnastics, and was always running around, but her dad and her brothers weren't footballers. I wonder sometimes about where my football talent comes from. People say it must be in the genes, but it's not in mine, I just came out of nowhere and surprised everyone. I learnt a lot when I was a kid from me dad, and all that practice paid off, but I don't think I'm a manufactured footballer, because it's always been instinctive with me, and yet the funny thing is, there's no indication where that instinct comes from. That's me, a freak of nature.

I was a spirited little kid, always chirping back. I can remember vividly we'd have arguments in the house, and I'd go outside, shout the last word through the letterbox, and then leg it as fast as I could up the path and down the street before anyone could come out and say anything! I was quite a funny kid, chatty and cheeky, but not rude or obnoxious, and – despite everyone's image of me – not a bad lad at all. Me mum's biased, but she has always said I was no problem as a kid, never got into any real trouble, and was never one to show her up, because I always knew how far to go. I could always stick up for meself though, not exactly a scrapper, but I could handle meself.

I've got a scar over my eye from when I was hit with a brick that was thrown when I was six or seven on a raid against another gang. Me mum came to meet me at school, and I was there, pouring with blood and smiling. We went to the hospital and I needed stitches, and apparently I didn't cry because I loved it. It's a good job, because a week later I was back there having stitches over the other eye – I'd been running in the street and fell down directly onto a big piece of glass. I've got matching scars. I got into a few scrapes, sometimes because other kids would have a go when they thought I was a bit cocky as the lad who thought he was great because he could play football. I didn't, but I always knew I was a decent footballer, one of the best around our way, and I always stood out. I had a confidence from that, and in my own environment, when I was comfortable, I was very lively.

Me mate Stephen Calvey remembers the first time he really heard of me was when I was supposed to have punched one of the lads that he hung around with, and he and his gang were going to get me for it. They never did, even though they were supposed to have looked out for me for two years.

When I was about twelve, I was already training with the Liverpool academy kids and Calvey was up there having a trial with them. He'd heard about this Robert Ryder kid from round his way who was supposed to be decent at football, and anyway, when we were jogging around the pitch he got talking to me because we were from the same place, and we looked out for each other. He reckons he had this pair of boots that were the dogs', and I was going on about them, saying how boss they were, but I don't remember at all. He didn't make it with Liverpool, but he played non-league with Marine for a while, or with Marine reserves anyway, which was about his level.

We became mates after I went to secondary school, when I went to Nugent on Smithdown Road, and he was at St John Almond. We met through another mate of mine when I started to venture a little further afield than Davey Lewis. All these stories that have always kicked around about me when I was a kid from big bad Toxteth, and this is what it really used to be like. There was a group of us, me and Calvey, Tony Smith and Gary Brown, Jamie McCafferty, and a few girls hanging around the group. No drugs, never even noticed it, not like now when it seems to be so obvious with the kids smoking in the streets, no getting bevvied because I was playing football all the time, just hanging out down on the benches down by ours, and also around a phone box down there.

That phone box was a laugh. We'd just dial random numbers and take the mickey out of people. One day we rang this woman and said we were from the *Echo*, the local paper, and that in conjunction with the Renault garage in town, she had won a prize draw her name was entered for. She didn't believe us, so we gave her the telephone number of the box, and said to ring back and verify the prize. When it rang, one of us said, Hello, *Liverpool Echo* switchboard, and she asked to be put through to Mr Stephen Calvey, competitions editor. A bit of a pause, and then she was talking to Calvey, and saying how she'd never won anything in her life and how incredible it was, oh my God. He told her to get down the garage the next day to pick up the keys. We were pissing ourselves, but we didn't have the bottle to bunk off school the next day, to see her face when she found out she'd been done. What we'd do was go down the benches or hang around the phone box, and then go off to the youth club down by Park Road, called St John's, or maybe to a place that was called the Buford Street pitches. After that, it was down to Mick's Chippy on Mill Street, and then home. Always the same, always the same order, although as we got older, and we had a little bit more money, we could splash out a little bit more.

When we were kids, it was pitta bread and crisps, then we could afford chips to go in the bread, and when we got really flush, it was pitta with kebabs. Gordon Ramsay, eat your fucking heart out. St John's used to charge 20p to get in, and we'd go there between six and eight. There were pool and snooker tables and a tuck shop, as well as an indoor pitch, so it was footie and snooker, and sometimes we'd play pairs and if you kept winning then you stayed on until the older lads came in at eight o'clock. As we got older, I got closer and closer to Calvey and we formed a friendship that has lasted through everything that has happened to the pair of us. His family and mine are great friends, and I'm really close to his mum and dad, Betty and Lennie. Lennie's always looked after me and he's a top man, just like Calvey.

With the gang, we'd go out most nights in the week, but never on Friday, because I always had a match on the Saturday, so they'd come around and knock at ours and stand on the doorstep talking, until it was time for me to get some kip. Other nights, we'd go round to Tony Smith's house, because his ma and da would go out and let us have the run of the place. I remember one time, we were dead chuffed because we were shopping in town, and in Top Man we entered a draw, and won some tickets to get into one of the big cinemas in town and watch *Naked Gun 2½*, which was a bit of a moment for us.

Calvey and me, we were so close, we went to the Liverpool show at Wavertree, and we had on the exact same gear, trackies, trainers and tops, and when we got back to school the next Monday, some lads asked how we managed to get jobs as stewards at the show, because we were spotted wearing uniforms. As we got older, we ventured further afield, and we even managed to get away for a holiday. Calvey and me arranged to meet up with me mum at a caravan she hired at Presthaven Sands, which is by Prestatyn in north Wales ... Scouse on Sea. We went down there full of expectation because we'd heard stories about there being a pretty wild night life, with discos and birds and all that, but we spent the whole fucking time chasing rabbits in the camping field, because there was absolutely nothing there. I reckon I was quick enough back then to catch them, as well.

We were lads, inner-city lads, so it wasn't all innocence. But at the same time there wasn't any delinquent behaviour, we weren't a criminal under-class going round robbing people and nicking cars. There was one lad – they all used to tease me, saying he was me cousin – who nicked the lead off roofs, and you know, you'd get the knock-off stuff on sale in the pubs, but nothing too dodgy. I sometimes wonder if I've got this idealized view of when I was a kid, but you have to remember it was different for me – from a very young age I stood out at football. I never got near the dodgy stuff ... maybe if I'd not been able to kick a ball it would have been different, but I doubt it because all my mates are decent blokes now, just normal fellas with families.

I get the impression it's worse now, with no real sense of community, definitely no investment in the place, and lots more crime and drugs. When I lived in Toxteth, there used to be seven boozers down by us, now there are three. Loads of places have been boarded up or knocked down and there's no building to replace them.

We didn't even get bottles of cider and sit down the benches and drink like most of the kids, probably because we were all so into football all the time. Mind you, Calvey and me did a bit of exploring with the bevvy when we got old enough, like most kids do. There was this pub called Black George's where we used to go and hang around outside, probably because we thought we'd be able to sneak in. That's the place we first started to go in and get a proper bevvy, although it was just a bottle of lager and then a stop at Mick's Chippy on the way home.

One of the first big nights we had out in town, when we thought we were right Jack the lads, was when we decided to get into this place called the High Street on New Year's Eve when I was seventeen. One of the lads knew a bouncer, and he said it was a posh do so get dressed up. We were dead excited, because it was our first real night out on the lash in a proper club, and everyone got togged up in their dress gear, the best kecks and shirts and all that. When we got there, they wouldn't let us in because we were too young, so we sneaked in round the back because we knew one of the kitchen staff, and were so chuffed when we walked in ... only to stand out like a bunch of pricks because we all had the dress gear on, and everyone else in the whole bloody place were scallies, dressed in their trackies and all that. So we were soon escorted out.

One night I did manage to hit the pop properly was when we decided we had to go out and have a proper session in a pub. So we went to another place in town with forty quid each in our pockets, and decided to get drunk on as many different drinks as we could. God, it was carnage. I think the place was called Fridays, and it had this DJ box up some steps, and Calvey says he found me halfway up the steps, throwing up and crawling around in me own sick. Nice. The thing is, most of the lads I knew were pretty heavy on the pop by that age, but we didn't really give it a good go because there was too much at stake.

I look back now, and they were innocent days, and we were bloody naive really, the things we did. But it was around that time that I got my first taste of how things change for you, once you get even the smallest bit of success in football. I was eighteen, I think, and we were still together as a group, most of the gang who hung around down by Mick's Chippy, even though by then I'd got into the first team at Liverpool. Up until that point it was just a dream for me, football was what I did with my mates and I just wanted to do it for a living, become a professional footballer. I worked hard and sacrificed a lot, and it was all directed towards this dream of making it. Making me mum and dad proud. No one tells you though that as soon as you do make it, then your whole life changes, because people look at you different, even some of the people you grew up with. It's not just football, see, it's money for a start and fame too. Pop star levels of fame. I scored a few goals, got my name in the papers, and suddenly people were asking all these questions about me, where I came from and what was I like?

What was I like? I was this kid who hadn't done anything much other than play football since he was ten years old. When we hung out, there would be some girls who would be around too, and I ended up going out with Gary Brown's cousin Lisa Brown for a bit. Nothing too spectacular, just a teenage thing. Anyway, she told her story to the paper! We'd kissed a bit and gone out for a bit, and then she was revealing 'her story' to the papers, the *Sunday Mirror*, I think it was. The gist of it was that I'd apparently gone out with her, but dumped her as soon as I made it big. And I used to sit on the steps outside her house, explaining the offside rule to her as well. Interesting stuff like that. I'm not sure if even I was that boring . . . although I was obsessed with football so it's probably true! Apparently they paid for that, and to cap it all somebody sold pictures to the papers as well, to illustrate the story. I heard they paid twenty or forty quid, something massive like that!

We used to go up to Wavertree to a bloke called Stuart's house, and took pictures of us larking around up there, stuff like a few of us sticking our heads out of a tent, one on top of each other like the Monkees. And they were the pictures in the papers. I wasn't bothered in the slightest, didn't give a monkey's and I have a laugh about it with all the lads. Still mates. But it shows you, doesn't it? There I was, a few months into the game, and a couple of me mates were apparently selling crappy, boring stuff to the papers. How do you deal with that? I've never been bothered about any of that stuff at all, personally, even though over the years some of it has got pretty outrageous, and not much of it has been entirely accurate. It's fair game really, I've come to learn that. I had to, didn't I? Comes with the territory. Bit of a shock though, when you're still a kid, and don't know anything. Even more of a shock to me mum, and that's the real problem with all the shit you get thrown in when you follow your dream of becoming a footballer. What will your mum think when you get splashed all over the papers? As I've said, you don't even think about that when you're playing all those games as a kid, hoping and praying that you'll get somewhere.

It wouldn't be so bad if you were prepared for it, got training in how to deal with it. But I was a little lad who played football every night, pissed around with his mates, and overnight, literally overnight, came fame. Nothing had changed in my routine, except that when I went down the chippy and got me special fried rice, it would be wrapped in a newspaper that had my picture all over it. It's no wonder I struggled to come to terms with it all.

Somehow, that first incident summed it all up for me. It was a warning of what was to come, if I'd been smart enough then to realize. I've been called all sorts in my career, accused of not being a proper role model, and not appreciating the life I've been blessed with. The thing is, you go from one life where you don't have to answer to anyone but your mum and dad, where no one gives a fuck about you, to another, where they'll buy pictures of you sticking your head out of a tent off your mates for forty quid. No wonder it's taken me so long to work it out.

FOOTBALL, FOOTBALL, FOOTBALL (2)

I'd like to say that I had a rich and varied life as a kid, that my enquiring mind gave me many hobbies and interests, which I pursued enthusiastically. I can't though, can I? In the words of me mum, my life was football, football, football.

From the moment I woke up to the moment I went to bed, I was thinking about it, talking about it or playing it. There were those games in the street and on the all-weather, and even by the time I was six, I was serious enough for me dad to take me down there and practise every night. By the time I was eight, he reckons he'd got me kicking properly with both feet, and heading the ball like I was a centre half, even though I was tiny in those days. I was quick as well, and good at athletics at school, but I never bothered with any other sport. I was only interested in football.

These days, by the age of six, you can be signed up at the academies of all the clubs around the country. I've seen them, these tiny little lads, and they go through from six being coached, so by the time they're ten or eleven, they already know what it is all about, and the coaches at the professional clubs have influenced them greatly. I know that places like Crewe are unbelievable, with the manager getting personally involved down there in the selection and direction of the youngsters, even coaching them himself when they're under eight, so that he's getting these incredibly technically gifted kids coming off the conveyor belt, offering exactly what he is looking for.

It wasn't the same with me. I didn't play any organized football at all until I was eight or nine, and the only coaching I got was from me dad and me uncles. It's amazing to see how things have progressed even in the short time since I was a kid, and it's all because clubs have now realized how important it is to bring through their own talent. Look at me or, say, David Beckham or Michael Owen. We came along, gave our clubs years of decent service at the highest level, and then they could still cash in on us, and make bloody millions in the transfer market. Between us, we gave our clubs a combined service at the very highest level of about twenty-seven years or so . . . and they sold us for nearly £50 million. God bless us. If the clubs manage that even occasionally, they're in heaven.

There's this huge financial incentive for the clubs to produce youngsters, and yet it seems bizarre that only in the last five years or so have they realized it fully. Now, the academies are as professional as the rest of the football set-ups, if not more so, given the way they can get these kids from the age of five or six and are so scientific in their approach with them. But not too long ago, the approach was far less professional.

Steve McManaman desperately wanted to go to Everton because he supported them and so did his dad, but he was still a small kid at sixteen, and pretty weak. So his dad went up to Goodison and said he needed three years as a trainee, because he might not be strong enough in the first year, and get left by the wayside. It made perfect sense, and nowadays, the academies would insist on it, because they could see the logic. But back then, Everton's attitude to him and to countless other kids, including me, was, 'We'll give you a year, son, to sink or swim, because there's plenty more where you come from.'

Liverpool were a bit more sensible with him, and gave him the three years he wanted, and I think that someone at Everton should be getting kicked up the backside to this day. It has changed so much now because the clubs are terrified of missing a Beckham or a Fowler, and now they have a scatter-gun approach, where they offer these professional contracts for years to just about all their kids, so they don't miss out. They also scour the whole country and right across the world for any talent, and you look at some of the youth teams, at the likes of Arsenal and Manchester United, and the names are amazing. It is so professional now, that I just know I wouldn't have been allowed to develop in the way I did, or have been left alone for as long as I was.

My life as a footballer began at St Patrick's primary school, the place where me dad had gone when he was a kid, and the team that he played for as well. I think I was nine years old when selected, and already I was noticed as being a talent beyond my years so I was put into the under-11 side. We didn't play many games, maybe the odd friendly match, but I do remember scoring plenty of goals, even back then. I was so small, and I was playing against these kids two or three years older than me, but I never had a problem physically on the pitch. My pace helped, and from the age of eight or nine, I always had this sense of where to stand, where to move on the pitch, and how to find space beyond even the biggest of defenders. If the school team was hardly the greatest test for me, it did almost immediately take me onto the path that would eventually lead to a professional career.

Every year, the best kids in the primary schools would be sent to the pitches on Penny Lane, at the very far end of Toxteth, so not all that far from where I lived. Another bus journey, in fact. It's the same Penny Lane the Beatles sang about, but for me, it's just this long road that runs down towards the very south-east end of Toxteth from the posher areas the other side of Sefton Park, which is this fantastic country park. Penny Lane starts in Mossley Hill, where me mum now lives. Both John Lennon and Paul McCartney lived just down the road, in Allerton and Woolton, and they used to come down to Penny Lane when they were kids, because not only is it a road, but it is also the area of shops around the junction where it joins with Smithdown Road. Out of interest, Lennon also lived in Toxteth when he was a student, in a house over the road from where me mum lived when she was little. Anyway, Penny Lane's not very glamorous, I must say, it's not this fabulous place where all these trendy, interesting people hang out, all Bohemian and exotic. It's just a pretty drab road, with the usual shops and traffic and grey buildings. They must have been on some pretty powerful stuff by the time they got round to writing that song, but it is still the place where dreams were formed. For the Beatles, and for me.

I remember getting the letter from Liverpool Schools Football Association, asking me to trials at Penny Lane. It was like winning the pools. I held it in my hand for ages, and then pelted around to show me dad, after shouting to Mum that I'd got the trials. The system back then was that all the talented primary kids were invited for a series of trials lasting quite a few weeks, and from there, they'd select a squad to play competitive matches for the Liverpool Schoolboys under-11 team. My school wasn't generally one of the stronger ones, although way back when me dad was a kid, Ian Callaghan was a couple of years above him and he went from Toxteth to play for Liverpool and England. It was quite a moment to get selected for the trials, and made my boasts when I was a tiny little lad that I was going to be a footballer seem more realistic. Me mum says now that even when I was five, I was always saying I'd play footie when I was older, that I was definitely going to make it.

Well, you've got to have confidence, haven't you? Mind you, when I arrived on the night of my first trial, I wasn't confident at all. We got there, and there were all these other lads around, big lads, all with the right kit and what seemed like a swagger, and I said to me dad that I wasn't getting changed, I wasn't going into the dressing room with the rest of them. He couldn't work out why, and kept asking me what the hell was wrong, until I eventually had to admit that I felt stupid because I had a scabby pair of boots. All the other kids had these fancy ones, with the proper studs and all that, and the proper make, all flash and new, while mine were Gola or Winfield or something, and dead old. I didn't get changed with the rest that first week, just sneaked around the side and put my kit on and went out there.

It was something that really bothered me, and maybe

reminded me that there was a different life out there. It's funny, because me mum and dad were really bothered by it too, and even though they didn't have any money at all, and sometimes struggled like mad to make ends meet, they went out and bought me a top pair of boots, Nike ones, dead expensive. I remember the next week being at school, and me dad came down to the gates and called me over. I was there thinking, Oh no, what have I done now? And he gets out this amazing pair of boots, and shows me them through the bars of the gate. What a moment. I couldn't wait to get home and try them on. Size three they were, and it was just one of those memories that you keep for ever. The next week I strode into that dressing room and sat right in the middle, and started jabbering to everyone and showing off me boots. They did the trick as well, because I did well in the trials over those weeks, and got into the Schoolboys squad.

Mr Dodd and Mr Milne were the teachers that ran the squad, and we had a hell of a good side. Tony Grant, who is still a big mate of mine and played for Everton and City before he went to Burnley, travelled down from the north end of Liverpool, up by Sparrow Hall, for the trials, and he got into the squad as well. There was also Paul Flaherty, a striker who was every bit as good as me, and Peter Gick who we called Rambo because he was so strong and brave in midfield. There were a couple of other lads who were eventually picked up by Tranmere. We beat everyone, and as the centre forward in this incredible team, I obviously scored a lot of goals. Tony Grant says he can picture me to this day, a little lad who never stopped talking, always laughing and joking and pulling pranks . . . and scoring goals. He says he doesn't even have to look back to see who got our goals in the various finals we played in. In all the time I was there, we got to every final we could have done for Liverpool Boys – with the exception of one.

But it was the first final that sticks out most in my mind. We won every game we played that season at under-11 and, eventually, we got into the final of the area cup, which was to be played at Goodison Park. Jesus, what a moment. There was me, Everton daft, going that season when they won the double to every game I could as a wide-eyed ten-year-old, watching Sharpie and Andy Gray batter everyone. And then, at the end of all that, this team of primary school kids played on the turf that all those heroic deeds were performed on, the same pitch that Everton blew away Bayern Munich on one of the greatest nights of my life.

We played Wirral Boys in the final, and won 5–0. You know what I can remember about that match, more than anything else, was how big the pitch was. They didn't bring it in because we were eleven, we played on the same pitch as all those heroes. It was a huge pitch to cover with my little legs, but I did okay, because I scored two goals, both tap-ins I think, but to me, they were exactly the same as the goals that Everton scored the year before against Bayern. Even though I was about three yards out, I didn't just roll the ball into the net, but smashed it, like you do as a kid. You can imagine what it's like playing in a game like that when you're eleven. That's where your dreams come from, because you think, if I can score two here at Goodison, then I can't be bad.

I never really knew how good I was though, partly because I hadn't played any organized football until then, and partly because you just don't know when you're a kid, do you? I was always saying I would be a footballer, but then every kid I knew said the same. I remember playing for a local Sunday league side that won everything, called Thorvald, and me dad came to me after one game, and said that the manager, a bloke called Dave Roberts, had been speaking to him during the game with a group of the other dads. Apparently, he'd pointed over towards me, and said: 'See that lad, he'll play for England one day, believe me.' The thing was, I was so tiny, and all the dads, even mine, burst out laughing, but he was adamant and got really annoyed when the others were laughing. Even I thought he'd been on the bevvy, although it was still great to hear.

Back in my Thorvald days we had this kid in the team a year younger than us, called Francis Tierney. He was brilliant, incredible at that age, and he seemed far better than me. I used to look at him and think, I'm nowhere near as good as him, and he did seem to be above the level of the rest of us. Franny went on to play for Crewe and, ironically, he was all set to join Liverpool from there – the fee had been agreed and the deal done when he went off on holiday in the summer of 1995. But when he went away, he got a bit bevvied, got into a bit of trouble and Liverpool pulled the plug on the deal, or so I heard. He stayed at Crewe, got a bad injury, and then eventually moved on to Notts County, so it just shows you.

Even though I knew I could score goals there were kids around who were better than me. I learnt that when I went off to Nottingham for this big training camp, when I was twelve years old. My memory is a bit sketchy now, probably because it was a bad experience so I've put it out of my mind, but me and Tony Grant, and one or two others, had progressed from the under-11 schools side into the Merseyside area team, and then we were selected for this massive trial in Nottingham, for what I recall was the North of England FA trials. Granty remembers it differently. He says it wasn't that important, but in my mind, it was a trial for North of England that led eventually to the Lilleshall selection process.

So we were excited, and scared. We were put on a train, and for me, it was just about the first time I had ever been away from home, certainly on my own. I was confident and loud in my own circle, but when we got down there, I was out of my depth, and so I went in my shell, like I tend to do in those situations.

The training was spread over a week, and it was good fun, a holiday camp playing football. Even so, some of the kids there were far better than me, I can honestly say that. That was a crushing blow. We had to take the train journey back to Liverpool knowing that we hadn't made it, dealing with that rejection for the first time in our lives, and it was hard at that age. I felt empty, partly because I hadn't made it, partly because I suppose I didn't do myself justice, but also because in my mind, all these kids were better than me, and suddenly, I'm starting to wonder whether I have what it takes to make it. It was my dream, to play football and buy me mum a big house, and me dad too, and here I was on this long train journey snaking across the country over the Pennines in Yorkshire, on a miserable day, just sitting there and thinking, What if I'm not good enough?

I had trials for England Schools, and Granty says we got down to the final twenty-five for the squad, but I'm not so sure. Anyway, again they rejected me. They said that it was because of concerns over the physical demands placed upon me, which was a fancy way of saying I was too small. I could always grow though, couldn't I? I began growing when I was fourteen or fifteen, and up until then, me mum feared I would never sprout up, that I was going to be a tot for the rest of my life. But I knew I'd begun growing inside, even before that. After sailing through my early life and getting into the Liverpool Schoolboys team when I'd hardly played a competitive match, those setbacks were enough to spur me on, to give me even more determination that I would improve and show I could do it.

It was around that time that I had the good fortune to come under the influence of one of the people who has been most important in the development of my career after me dad. When you left the under-11 schoolboys, there was a gap for a couple of years with Liverpool Schoolboys, so I went away to play for Sunday League teams, and the South Merseyside representative sides. It was only at under-14 level that the Liverpool Schoolboys started again, so it was off to Penny Lane for more trials. It was there that I met Mr Lynch for the first time. Bob Lynch is retired now, but he was a schoolteacher from Whiston who ran the schoolboys teams at under-14 and under-15 level. To this day, I call him Mr Lynch, and so do me mum and dad, because we have all always held so much respect for him and appreciated what he did for me. He is still my greatest supporter.

We went down there for trials, and I met up with the likes of Granty again, but there were a whole lot of different lads now, as people grew or developed. Mr Lynch says that there was no way I was ever going to be overlooked, because he had taken one of his sides down to Woolton to play against a representative team made up of players a year younger, including me, and he says I destroyed his side that day. The first game I played for him, he remembers, I scored my first goal with a bicycle kick from about twenty yards out, which is the way I used to do things then, try audacious things from anywhere.

I loved my time with Liverpool Schoolboys and Mr Lynch. He would look after me, and instil in me the discipline I was to need when I was trying to become a professional later on. He says to this day that he had no doubts I would become a professional, and that even then, he didn't try to coach me because it was all instinctive. Instead, he used to try to gently show me how I should behave, and give me some guidance in growing up. He had his rules, and we all learnt to respect them. You had to turn up in your uniform, and if you didn't, you couldn't play. The same if you'd been off school for any reason, with no exception, not even a big match. I never really misbehaved. I was always cheeky, but never disrespectful. There were times when my exuberance got the better of me, and times when my practical jokes drove everyone mad. There was one time, when we went to Switzerland for a tournament and all us teenage lads were away together for the first time, and the second morning, we all woke up and our eyebrows had been shaved off. We'd all had it done in the night when we were asleep and nobody could work out who had done it.

It was only years later that I admitted to Mr Lynch that it was me . . . and I'd shaved me own off, to make sure I didn't get caught. Another time, I had my first introduction to Manchester United when we played at their Cliff training ground, and I did a full-length dive into the foot bath outside the showers, which was about three inches deep, which would have been some way to get an injury. Mr Lynch guided me in the right direction, and I think for all the stick I have taken and the image people have of me, I'm not all bad. I know how to behave, I know how to show respect when it's due, and I understand what is required of footballers. It's just that sometimes I forget! It was Mr Lynch who helped me to understand all that.

He knows exactly what I'm like, exactly what makes me tick. When I was getting some stick in the local paper recently because I tapped me head at Goodison after scoring with it, he wrote in to complain and point out that I was a decent fella really. He has always looked out for me, and he has watched me all the way through my career. He was there when I made my Liverpool debut, and came to all the games at Anfield. He was there at Maine Road, with me dad, when I made my debut for Manchester City. I spotted them in the crowd during the warm-up, so I trotted along and had a chat with them while the rest of the team were sprinting around.

I can remember once when I was down at Penny Lane one freezing night, and I wasn't feeling too good. I had to get the bus home, but he said he'd take me on the back of his motorbike. It was one of those old things, with a big oval windscreen at the front, and as he was backing it out, a car crashed into us and we both fell off the bike. The windscreen was smashed all over the floor, but he picked it up, said get on, and drove me off home. I've never been so scared in my life. I'd never been on a bike before, and I was clinging on the back, shitting meself all the way home. It was freezing as well, but it shows what he would do for me.

Under Mr Lynch, we had another cracking team, with me up front alongside Dele Adebola, who was a big brave striker who played for Crewe and Birmingham. Granty was in midfield. I remember his old fella was a character as well, and his dad, Tony, and mine used to pal up together. We went all over playing in tournaments, and they would come with us, a great family atmosphere where everyone would get on. There were a few other lads who made the grade, Eddie McCullough, Carl Conroy and Kevin Fitzpatrick who all went on to sign pro forms. And we never got beat except once, when it really mattered. It was in the English Schools trophy when we were in the final year, and we had a great run that got us to the semi final, where we played Sheffield. As a kid, you never think about these things at the time, but that was a massive game for us.

We went through all the schools process, building to that

one game. In my whole schoolboy career, that was the biggest game because it was all that we worked towards. Not that we got there. We played at Bramall Lane, under floodlights, and it was a tense match. I remember I wasn't fit. I'd hurt my shoulder and me dad went up to London Road to get this horrible, gunky tar stuff that I had to spread all over it for a week, to try and get the bruising out. It didn't work, but at least it sorted out the pot-holes on my back. I wasn't really right, but played anyway, and scored a couple of decent goals. The game was 2–2, and late on, I ran through and had a shot that beat the keeper, hit the inside of the post, rolled right across the line, and hit the other post before coming back out again. If it had gone in, we'd have been in the final, but instead, it was back over to Anfield for the replay, which we lost 2–1, after another very close game.

Three things I remember about that game. I just wasn't fit, and if I had been it might have been different, not that I'm being cocky or anything. Also, we played it in the day, which was unusual, because we played all our Schoolboys matches in the evening, and somehow, we thought that had contributed to our defeat. And third, playing at Anfield. As a kid, the thought of it would have left me cold, and I wouldn't have been able to show me face down the Bankhouse with me dad and me uncles. But going out there was an exhilarating feeling – even though I couldn't admit it because I was still an Everton fan, and lads like Granty were massive on them and would never have let me live it down. By then I'd decided I wanted to sign for Liverpool, and this was the first taste of the experience that I'd set my heart on. Playing for Liverpool, walking down the short corridor, down a small flight of steps, touching the 'This is Anfield' sign as you walk under it, and then running out onto the pitch to the roar of the crowd.

There was quite a big crowd that day, and I was thinking as I walked out, I can get used to this. I don't think I touched the sign because all the other lads were watching, but I sat there in the dressing room, this huge space with wood panelling all round and our kit on the pegs set out around the room, the massage table in the middle, the baths to the side all dead smart, thinking, This could be me one day, sitting here alongside Ian Rush and John Barnes, playing as a professional footballer.

There was this lad who played for Liverpool Schoolboys three years before me, and I sort of knew him because we had been up at Liverpool at the same time training in the evenings, although not together because we were different age groups, and he was like me because he was an Everton fan, but decided to play for the other lot. And he'd just got a game for the first team. The Liverpool first team, for Christ's sake. Just a kid like me, training like me, from an inner-city council estate like me. And he was a professional footballer. Had a funny name, like it was being said by a deaf person. It was Steven McManaman, of course, and he was this little kid who suddenly grew when he was about sixteen – like me – and ran like a new-born foal, all awkward like. And he was playing for Liverpool.

I sat there thinking, It is possible, I really can get into the first team at Liverpool, I really can be a footballer like I always dreamt of when I was little. Some players I've spoken to, they say that they always knew they would make it, right from when they could first remember. Fuck knows how. I went through my whole time, scoring goals for Liverpool School-boys, breaking the Merseyside Schools scoring records, winning finals like the Gillette Under-15s Cup and the national Counties Cup and scoring in every round along the way, and I never knew that I was going to make it. Like I said, I always saw kids around me that were better, and when we went to Nottingham, I thought there were about 500 better than me.

There were at least twenty-five better than me when we went for the English Schools trials, probably more because I don't remember it at all like Tony Grant, and never once did I think I was guaranteed the chance of becoming a footballer for a top club. I fucking hoped and prayed every night like, but I didn't know what it took to make it, so I didn't know if I had it. And I was a little fart, so that was always in the back of my mind as well. That day though, I sat there thinking, It really can happen, I can do this. And then we went out and got beat.

That was the only big game I lost as a kid. I played for

Merseyside Boys in the county competition, again with Tony Grant, who was captain of just about all the teams I played in. That was the fourteen and fifteen age group, and again, we had to go for trials up at Savio High School in Bootle. We won the national final at fifteen against Durham, in a game at Spennymoor, I think, and I'm sure I scored a couple that day, although I can't even remember the score now, just that we won quite comfortably. I also managed to play quite a bit of Sunday soccer too, even though I was also training with Liverpool as well as playing for Liverpool and Merseyside Schoolboys. No wonder me mum says I only ever 'did' football. I loved it as well, got up every morning thinking, Where am I playing today? Get school out of the way so I can go off and play footie.

We played a lot of big games, at Anfield and Goodison, over at Tranmere, and mostly at South Liverpool's ground, down by Garston somewhere. I played Sunday football for a team called Singleton first, in the South Merseyside league, and I also played in the representative side. Our big rivals were Dovedale, but we won everything for two years. Then I played for Thorvald for two years, and when we finished playing for Merseyside at fifteen, quite a few of us from that team went to a team up in north Liverpool in the West Derby league called Wylco for a year. I think we must have won about four cups and the league and a couple of other competitions, and I ended up as the top scorer in the league . . . and I still haven't had my medals yet! I still want them as well, although Granty thinks that they may have given them to him, to pass on, and he forgot.

I broke loads of records apparently, at most levels, although the God's honest truth is that I haven't got a clue about any of them, about how many goals I scored or which famous footballer's schools scoring records I broke, because it's not exactly important, is it? What is important is that it was a wonderful time, the time of my life really, and all the serious business of my football career was developing. It was progressing, in fact, on a journey on the number 26 bus to the Belmont Pub in Anfield.

3) ANFIELD ROAD

Liverpool first tried to sign me when I was ten years old. I'd played about three serious games in my life, and me dad was approached by this bloke who had stood there on the sidelines at a Liverpool Schoolboys under-11 match, watching and not speaking to anyone. It turned out it was a fella called Jim Aspinall, who was to have a big influence on my career. Jim was a smashing bloke, and everyone in the city knew him through his love of Liverpool, and the kids that he kept turning up for the academy.

He died at the age of seventy-two in 2004. The sad thing is that I went to visit him in hospital the day he died, but I got there just a few minutes too late, so I never got to speak to him. It would have been nice to thank him for all he did for me and tell him how much he meant to me. Jim was always interested in the club he worked for, always talking about it and thinking about the future, and always showing a great interest in the young lads he found and sent up to the academy. It didn't matter to him whether it was one of the kids who went on to become big stars, like me and Macca, or one that didn't make it. He was passionate about all of us and, most of all, passionate about his job. When I got to the hospital ward his son was there and pointed out that Jim's bed overlooked Fazakerley playing fields, so right to the end he was still watching the kids play.

I remember vividly, years later when Phil Thompson was assistant manager under Gerard Houllier. The pair of them had just bombed Paul Ince out of the club and it was very acrimonious, with a lot of bad feeling all round. Not long after, Jim turned up at Anfield with a kid he reckoned would be a star for the future, a lad that could be a big signing for the club. It was Paul Ince's son, Thomas. Thompson went off on one at Jim, shouting at him, 'What the fuck have you brought that kid here for?' He was saying all that sort of stuff about a kid who was barely out of primary school, and wouldn't say boo to a goose. Jim fixed him with his stare, waited until he'd finished his ranting, and then said, 'Because the kid's got talent, and that's all I'm interested in – bringing in kids who are the future of the club.' He wasn't bothered by anyone's personal opinion, he was only interested in doing what was best for Liverpool Football Club, and in his mind, Thomas Ince was an outstanding prospect who could be one of those kids who went on to make it. So what if his dad had criticized the manager, the future of the club was all that mattered. Jim would never be bullied by someone like Thompson, and that incident summed up why people in the city of Liverpool hold so much respect for him.

The interesting thing is that when Jim died, Thomas was still at Liverpool, and looking like he could be something of a player. You never know in football, but if the young lad could make it through, then I think that more than anything would be the perfect tribute to Jim's memory. That first day we met Jim, he gave me dad a card and said he'd like to talk to us about joining Liverpool. That was it. No bullshit, no promises, simply that they were interested and there was no pressure. At the time, Dad thought I was far too young to consider committing to any club, too young to even think about a career in football. At that stage he wanted me to enjoy my football and learn about the game, and if I was considered good enough when I was older, then we would talk to the clubs that were still interested. It was something that we stuck to, but Christ, it was difficult given the number of scouts who used to beat a path to our door.

Jim Aspinall was there virtually every week. From the age of ten through to when I was nearly sixteen, he was there so often he was almost a member of the family. Me mum swears she used to look at the clock and get the kettle on because she knew it was time for one of Jim's visits. The thing was, they knew I was a mad Everton fan, and me dad went around the country watching them all over, so they knew they had a job on their hands keeping me out of the hands of the enemy. The lads in the Liverpool Schoolboys team like Tony Grant, they were all mad Evertonians, and already hooked up with them, so I think everyone assumed I would join the Blues. Granty was convinced I'd join them when I agreed to go down to the FA Cup final in 1989 with all the Everton trainees. They had a coach trip, and got tickets for the game, and I was there still supporting Everton for the final against Liverpool.

Secretly though, I'd just begun to harbour dreams about emulating Ian Rush, who scored two that day, and was eventually to have a big influence on my career, and a big impact on me as a young forward learning the game. Granty said it was the moment he thought I'd choose Everton, after doubting it for so long, but really, I think I just fancied going to the final with me mates, and getting a free trip into the bargain. I was still gutted when Everton lost. If I'm honest, from the age of ten it was always a contest between the two clubs who would get my signature, but it was Liverpool who always seemed to show the most interest.

Some players I know, especially the ones who went to Lilleshall, had offers from just about every top-flight club, and went around every single one, getting the sarnies, meeting all the stars and snaffling free stuff. I don't see the point, because a visit to a match and meeting the manager of a club when you're a fourteen-year-old kid who can barely open his mouth, that's hardly going to give you enough information to make the biggest decision of your life. These days, it seems there is a different agenda. The top youngsters can command some pretty heavy incentives to join a club, and they probably travel around to see what's on offer.

I heard of one kid being induced to go to a club with the

offer of a house for his parents, so that when they moved to the area, they had a brand spanking new home to live in. Unreal. Other kids, their parents get big-money offers – and we're talking hundreds of thousands of pounds here – just for the signature. It is big, big business. Me, I got a red training top when I signed for Liverpool as a schoolboy, and that was that.

Me dad didn't get any money, he didn't get a house or any other inducement, and that's the way Liverpool have always behaved. In recent years, they have lost out on more and more kids, and they realize now that they have to compete with some of the other big clubs. It's a tough old business, but you can understand exactly why clubs are prepared to invest so much money in the best kids, because the potential returns are unbelievable these days. It's worth a punt of a couple of hundred grand on a top kid, when you think of how much he might be worth in a few years.

Anyway, I didn't do the smoked salmon circuit, even though me dad was approached by Manchester United, Chelsea, Wolves and a couple of others. All these blokes turned up at the house, asking us to go down and meet the manager because I was their number-one target, which was a load of old bull, obviously, but pretty good to hear when you're a kid. Me dad kept saying no, apart from Liverpool and Everton, and I did go along and have a look around both clubs, and funnily enough, I think I also went for a trial at Preston, for some reason. They offered me a place on the spot, but again, me dad said no.

With Everton, I can remember going to a game and going into the dressing room beforehand, and Stuart McCall was there. He came over and made a real fuss of me, had a chat and then presented me with a ball, and he also gave me a pair of his shorts. Tight get, he might have at least given me his bloody shirt! But it was a big moment for a young lad, to meet these players that you idolize from the terraces, and to hear them say that they've been told all about you, how good you are and how many goals you've scored, and how you could be in this dressing room one day. It builds you up, it does. I know now, of course, that it's standard form; they try to get any decent kid in the dressing room and get one of the lads to say a few words to make them feel good, and it's obviously a good philosophy. I don't know what these professionals thought of me, this tiny little lad strolling in there, about two foot tall and everyone saying I was supposed to be the next big thing. I bet they thought, Oh aye, we've heard that one before.

What me dad decided was that I would take trials with both Liverpool and Everton, but not commit myself to either. I was never going to argue with me dad, and when I look back, I think he was dead right, because what's the point of committing yourself when you are eleven years old? I went up to Liverpool, and had a few trial nights with them, and enjoyed the experience. There were lots of kids there, some already signed up to the academy – not that it was called that back then, it was the Centre of Excellence – and a few trialists, and they put us through our paces, and it was no bother to me, no different to the stuff that we did with Liverpool Schoolboys down at Penny Lane.

After a few nights, they asked me again to sign, but me dad said no. Then I went for a trial at Everton, and after one night, they wanted me to sign there and then. But me dad simply thanked them, and said we'll wait. We talked about it, and he spoke to Jim Aspinall, and what we decided was that I would go and train with Liverpool, get coached by their academy staff but not sign anything. I went back to Everton a few times, had a few sessions with them, but for the most part, it was twice a week on Tuesday and Thursday nights up at Melwood, which is Liverpool's training ground, unless it was really cold, and then we went inside at the Vernon Sangster gym just behind Anfield.

Some of the kids I knew couldn't hack it, especially when they discovered birds and booze. It sounds glamorous enough, training with Liverpool, but you had to be there, twice every week no matter what the weather, through blizzards and rain, howling winds. No hanging out with your mates on those nights, no evenings off when you didn't feel like it. And we didn't have a car to get me there, so it was a number 27 bus from Toxteth up to Shiel Road, and change at the Belmont pub for the number 12 to Melwood Drive, and the short walk into the training ground. Then it was the 12 back to the Belmont, and then the number 26 back home. It was hours, and you'd get home knackered, crawl into bed thinking that you'd have to miss school the next day, although me mum never let me. A lot of kids, they couldn't be bothered doing all that, but me, I loved it, I couldn't wait to get on the 27 and start that journey up to Anfield, to train with all me mates, with good blokes like Frank Skelly, Dave Shannon and later Hughie McAuley coaching us. I don't think I was ever late and I don't think there was one night I didn't want to go.

I never used to play any games for the Liverpool kids' teams, just train with them and play representative football with Liverpool and Merseyside Schoolboys. But one day, when I was about eleven or twelve, we had this practice match against a Scottish side that the manager then, Kenny Dalglish, had brought down. I played very well that day, and later Jim Aspinall came down to see me dad again. He said that Dalglish had seen me, and thought I was outstanding, and he'd told Jim to get that little Robbie Ryder at all costs. Jim said that Dalglish had laid it on the line, and said: 'We want him right away, Jim, go and do your work.' Again me dad said no, and so a few weeks later Jim came down to ours with a message: 'Mr Dalglish wants to see you.'

So we got the bus up there again, this time to see the manager of Liverpool Football Club. I'll say this now, Kenny Dalglish was always a real gent with me, treated me properly right the way through, and always had faith in me, even when I was this snotty-nosed, cheeky-faced Scouse kid who didn't know his arse from his elbow. If I genuinely didn't have a clue whether I could make it, and thought there were plenty better than me, Kenny never seemed to doubt me. He got me and me dad in his office up at Anfield, and he came straight out and said he'd give us anything we want so that we'd sign.

Now, I'm not saying he was offering us money, because I don't think that was ever on the agenda with Liverpool, certainly not back in my day. But what he meant was that they'd give me a contract when the time came and guarantee me a professional deal when I reached seventeen. Again, me dad said thanks, but that he didn't want to dive in. Kenny was devastated, but we cheered him up a bit when me dad said that I loved training up there with Liverpool, and would definitely carry on. From that day, Kenny was always inviting us up to Anfield or Melwood, just for a chat to see how I was getting on, how I was feeling, had I changed my mind, that sort of thing. Steve Heighway was also very good to me and me dad and we always got on very, very well with him. Kenny brought him back to Anfield to replace Mal Cook and run the Centre of Excellence, and he was brilliant for all the lads.

I always had a great deal of respect for Steve Heighway, because he treated the lads properly, always did the right thing and always had the welfare of the kids at heart, which is more than one or two of the coaches at Anfield when I was coming through the ranks. It made me laugh, years later, when I heard stories of Gerard Houllier saying they'd not had any decent kids through, and that they spent millions on the academy for no benefit. In the next breath, Houllier would suggest that he found Steven Gerrard, and brought him into the first team. I saw him say that on the telly more than once, that he found Stevie. Where did he find him? In the Liverpool reserves, and captaining the England under-19 side, that's where! I think he might even have played for the under-21s by then, as well. I'll tell you what, if you claim that as finding someone, then we could all be scouts.

Stevie, like me, was brought through the ranks by the patience and professionalism of Steve Heighway and his staff, who tried to teach the kids not just about football, but about how to behave properly, and become decent people. He's a kid like me from a council estate in Liverpool, and he's a star, not just on the pitch, but off it too. He's a decent, smart bloke, and he got a lot of that from Steve Heighway and the academy staff at Liverpool. There was a picture taken when the academy opened properly of me, Macca, Dominic Matteo, Stevie G, Michael Owen, Jamie Carragher and David Thompson, all kids that had been nurtured by Steve Heighway and his staff, and a line-up that would cost a fair few million on the market. And there was Houllier moaning that he didn't have any kids coming through. The saddest thing of all is that after Houllier went through Anfield, there were only two of those kids left at the club.

I remember Steve Heighway took me and me dad up to Melwood once, to have a cup of tea and meet all the players and coaching staff. Kenny was there, of course, because he'd probably set it up, and we met everyone. We came away, the pair of us, thinking this was a homely club, with no airs and graces, and a good place for a kid to be brought up, which was probably the idea, I suppose. Kenny was pretty clever.

One of my best memories from that time was the day when Kenny Dalglish drove me home, and parked right outside our house on Windsor Street. Kenny Dalglish in Toxteth in this big white sports car, a Mercedes I think it was. We'd been playing up at Anfield and I got changed and went outside to find me dad. As we were standing at the bus stop waiting to get home, this car pulls up and Kenny shouts out, 'Where are ye going?' Me dad said Toxteth, but I think he misheard us and thought he said Croxteth, which is in the other direction, and on the road out to where Kenny lived in Southport. He said he was going right by there, and to jump in, but when he found out where we really lived he still insisted on taking us home.

We drove down Upper Parliament Street and swung into Windsor Street, and I even wound the windows down, so that everyone could see us. I took an eternity to get out of the car, with Kenny Dalglish hanging out the window saying goodbye, but you know what, not one of my mates walked by, and not one of the neighbours stuck their heads out their windows, even though they were all nosey buggers. So me greatest moment, me getting dropped off by Kenny Dalglish, and there was no one there to see it. The next day, for the first time in my life, I was first kid in at school, ready to tell the whole world. Of course, not one of them believed me, thought I was just ragging them. I should have taken a picture.

When I was up at Melwood, I was there with Phil Charnock who started at eleven at the same time, and went right through to the first team with me. Later there was also Ashley Neal, Phil Neal's son, and a kid who played for England Schoolboys, Lee Bryden, and John Scott, who was captain of the Scotland Schoolboys. Surprisingly, none of them came through, and I was the only one who made it from my age group, though Dominic Matteo was a year older and progressed into the team around the same time as me. That's why I say I didn't know if I would ever make it, even though people like Dalglish had so much confidence in me, because there were some fantastic kids who never made the grade.

I saw so many wonderful players at all the levels I played at. You see some and you think, They'll definitely make it. And when they don't, it knocks you sideways, because then you're thinking, What the fuck are they looking for? All the schoolboys trained together, and so we'd be mates with kids a year older or a year younger, especially when you made it through to YTS. I didn't really know Macca, because he was three years above me, and had gone full time by the the time I'd got YTS, although I'd first come across him when I was eleven and playing for the Liverpool Schoolboys, and he was in the under-14 team at the same time. You're hardly mates then though, with such a big age gap. I was mates with Dominic Matteo, who again I knew from about the age of eleven, and who had been recommended to Liverpool by Kenny Dalglish's greengrocer.

There was one lad who was a mate from the year below me at Melwood called Ian Frodsham who was from Kirkby. He played in central midfield, and right the way through you could tell he was going to make it, that he was just a fantastic footballer. He seemed to have that bit of extra quality, something that made him stand out head and shoulders above the rest of us. He went right through with me, and was on the verge of getting into the first team not long after I had been given my first start by Graeme Souness. And then suddenly, he died.

He had gone with the youth team to America, and when he flew home, his back had stiffened up and was sore. When the club got it checked out, he was diagnosed with cancer, and he died not too long after. It was so tragic, and to this day I still think about Ian, and what would have happened if he had not been struck down. I know he would have played for the first team, and he had it in him to become a big star, a big player for the club. And at the age of nineteen, with his whole life and a glorious future in front of him, he was taken. For months afterwards, I was affected badly by it, because it tends to put into a stark perspective everything you passionately believe in. We were kids together, with exactly the same dream, me from Toxteth and him from Kirkby, both of us interested in one thing – to become professional footballers.

That is all you ever thought about then as a kid: could it be you? Would you be the one out of thirty or forty lads, out of hundreds of thousands of lads, if you think about it, who would make the grade? And just as he was about to fulfil his dream, Ian died of cancer. I went to the funeral with all the rest of the Liverpool first team, and sat in that church with tears in my eyes, thinking that the ambition we shared was a load of bollocks compared to the loss of his life. What did it all matter when he could be taken away at the age of nineteen? It was a surreal feeling, a haunting one. We played in the Coca-Cola Cup final not too long after, and I dedicated my medal to him, but that seemed like a hollow gesture really. You wonder why a person with so much talent could be denied everything that was there waiting for him, the life that he had worked so hard to enjoy. When Liverpool built their academy a few years later, they named the indoor sports arena after him, and so his name lives on around the club. He has not passed into legend like he might have done, but at least down the years they will still be speaking his name around Anfield, God bless him.

I somehow managed to resist signing for anyone until I was nearly sixteen. It was quite a strange thing to do, not to sign for Everton when I was such a massive fan, and had so much feeling for the club. They also had much better facilities at Bellefield at the time. Liverpool's training ground had not been developed, there was no state-of-the-art academy, and I don't think the hierarchy had quite cottoned on to how important cultivating your own kids can be. And yet I was always leaning towards Liverpool, even if they thought I would probably end up at Goodison. I had been up to Everton again at fifteen, and again they had asked me to sign straight away, but I always felt more at home at Liverpool, just felt a certain loyalty to them because they had looked after me since I was eleven, had instilled certain ideas and values into me. I knew everyone around the place and instinctively felt more comfortable about it.

When I was a kid and hadn't even signed schoolboy forms, I used to go up there for the whole school summer holidays and train with the YTS lads, help them do all the jobs around the place and stuff like that. Steve Heighway let me, even though he wasn't supposed to. It was a wonderful feeling, a schoolkid training like he was a professional, and even doing the boot cleaning and the brushing up felt as though it was the best job in the world. It was those little things that eventually persuaded me that Liverpool was the club I should sign for.

I remember I was down at Penny Lane just before I was sixteen, playing for the Schoolboys, and there was an Everton scout called Sid Benson who was chatting to me dad, and he said he really wanted us to sign. Jim Aspinall was standing over the other side, looking worried as usual, and I called me dad over saying I wanted to tell him something. When he came over, I blurted out: 'I want to sign for Liverpool.' Why? Because it was what I knew. I was happy there, had a lot of friends and it felt right. They did things in the right way too. Dad went straight over to Jim Aspinall and told him, and you should have seen the look on the fella's face. He said, 'Right, we'll do it right now,' and before we could say anything else he had us in his car on the way up to Anfield.

There was a school match going on up there, and quite a few of the Anfield officials were around, including Tom Saunders, who was a director and was also the liaison between the board and the coaching staff, because he had done some management when he was younger. Jim went and whispered in his ear, and then he went out into the stand to find Steve Heighway, who was watching the match. Jim and Steve dashed downstairs and drew up a YTS contract on the spot. They called Tom Saunders down to witness everything, spoke with me dad and then got me to sign it.

They did what Kenny had promised all those years before, and offered me a year's YTS with a guarantee of a three-year professional contract to follow. After all that time playing football at Penny Lane, at Bootle, at Melwood and Anfield and all around Merseyside and eventually over most of the country, after all those dreams and fears, all those scrapes and laughs, what had been on my brain since I was six years old had finally become a reality – I was going to be a footballer. Not just a kid who was kicking a ball around doing the commentary inside his own head, but a real, honest-to-God footballer, and I was going to be paid for it. It was £29.50 a week to be precise, and they also gave me mum about £300 a month for looking after me ... although I think it should have been about ten times that, given everything she used to do for me (still does for me, in fact). It was the greatest moment of my life.

What I didn't realize was that getting the YTS wasn't the end of all those years of hard work, and all those countless hours dreaming, but the very start of it. And I got a fairly harsh introduction into the new world I was entering from a source I was to become familiar with over the years ... Mr Phil Thompson. He was the reserve team coach when I first arrived at Anfield on a YTS, and I quickly found out why all the other kids used to warn you to keep out of his way, and muttered about him constantly under their breath. He was so loud around the place, always bawling people out and having a go. I didn't mind that particularly, but what I did find not so good was the way that he seemed to knock people and test their confidence at such a young age. Maybe this was just his way of getting the best out of everyone, and doing the best for the club. It was probably just his coaching style, even though it wasn't to everyone's taste.

There was one moment in particular, not long after I had signed my forms, that I learnt all about his methods. I was in the dressing room before a reserve team match, cleaning up and setting out the kit. I was putting the shirts on the pegs in number order around the room, as you do, and when I got to number nine, I held it up and looked at it all starry-eyed. I was a kid, full of beans, who had just been given his dream, and as I held it in front of me, I said to the other lads something like: 'This shirt should be mine,' or something to that effect. What I didn't realize was that Thompson had come into the dressing room and was standing in the corner watching me.

I turned around and he seemed furious, you could see the anger in his face. And he completely took off at me. He didn't hold back at all as he gave me all the guff about not being fit to lace the number nine's boots, how I'd never be a footballer, all that sort of thing. And all because I said I wanted that shirt – the reserve team shirt. It wasn't Ian Rush's shirt, it was just the next step up for me, after I had already played for the A and B teams. I realized that was his first test for me. Thompson didn't last long, because Graeme Souness, who was the manager by then, was getting reports back on what he was like.

Souness told me years later that he just didn't like the way Tommo dealt with the kids that were coming through to the reserve team, didn't think it was the right introduction to Liverpool for them, and when he had the chance, he got rid of him. I heard stories from some of the other young lads back then, that Steve Heighway had laid into Thompson, really slaughtered him in front of the manager, and believe me, that is something because Steve Heighway is a gentleman and not the sort of bloke to go around laying into people. I know one or two of the lads had gone to Steve and complained at the treatment they were getting when they moved up from the Centre of Excellence to the reserves, because some of them were my mates. According to Souness, the final straw came for Thompson when he was supposed to have made some comments to the Manchester United coaching staff about Souey, when the gaffer was in hospital after his heart operation, and he got sacked.

He might have tested the confidence of a few of the lads, but he never got to me and, to be fair, he left me alone after that. Then again, I had plenty of newfound confidence to spare now that I was signed, and I wasn't frightened of showing it. God, the things I did. All the stuff that happened later in my career, well I rehearsed for those moments when I was a sixteen-year-old kid, playing in the Lancashire Combination. When I signed for Liverpool, I could finally play proper games for them, and I went straight into the B team, which was where all the sixteen- and seventeen-year-olds were first blooded.

I was scoring goals right from the off, and I was very sure of my ability now that I had been given the promise that I would become a professional. I had begun to grow at fifteen, and so I wasn't quite the little fart any more (just a bigger one!), and I think that gave me some confidence too. I remember one game when we played away at Bury against their A team, which was basically their reserve side. Their manager was John King, who had been around a long time, and was a tough old pro who played in midfield and used to kick people up in the air. I think Souey once broke his leg in a game. He was giving it loads, and his side were kicking lumps off me. I'd scored one goal and they responded by giving me a fearsome kicking. It was fucking brutal. They were these old lower-league pros, and they were pissed off because I was giving them the runaround.

So what did I do? I only went and got the ball, ran around the defence and the keeper, stopped the ball on the line, got down on my hands and knees and headed it into the net. Fuck me, it went absolutely crazy on the touchline, from both sides. John King was bawling at his side to kill me, and Sammy Lee, who was looking after us that day, was going equally fucking mad at me for doing it. Christ, I was lucky to get off that pitch alive, but it was funny though, even if Sammy made me write a letter to Bury afterwards to apologize for what I did. I wonder if they've still got that letter in their dusty old files somewhere. I'll have to ask Gary Neville to ask his old fella.

When I signed, it was the B team and then the As for a year, all the time doing my apprenticeship where I had to clean out the bath, do the boots, the changing rooms, hang the kit out and all that stuff, and then I was into the reserves. I loved it. I never minded doing the shitty jobs, and I loved being around all the top men like Rushie and John Barnes and Macca, who had just got into the first team around that time.

He was a great lad, still one of us really, the YTS kids who stuck together like a little silent Mafia around the place.

Calvey used to come up and watch me with me dad, used to get the bus up from Toxteth but end up walking, just like I used to do all those years ago. He says I scored just about every match I played in, but I'm fucked if I can remember. What I do remember is that Souey always had great faith in me, just like Kenny did, and he was always good to me. One moment sticks out in my mind, just after I got into the first team. I got injured at Bristol City in a Cup tie when I had a hairline fracture in my ankle. The gaffer was under intense pressure then – and he actually resigned about a week later, when we lost at home to City in the replay. But in between, he took the trouble to come and speak to me.

We had signed a young striker called Lee Jones from Wrexham, and he was lightning quick and a good finisher. For a young lad like me who had played only about twenty-five games for the first team, it was really worrying. You've got a broken ankle, and you're thinking, Shit, they've already got someone in there who can replace me. But Souey came to see me, and told me not to worry, because the club had great faith in me and everyone there was convinced I would be a big star. Those are the sort of noises you need to hear from your manager, especially when you're dealing with the first major injury of your career. So much is going through your mind anyway, wondering how long you'll be out for, and whether you'll be the same player when you come back, that it's easy to get carried away with all the worry.

I guess by then, deep down, I already knew that Souness would always back me, even if he did jack it about a week later. A lot has been said about him in his time as manager at Liverpool, but I can honestly say that I've got nothing but admiration for him. It's obvious that he fell out with a lot of the senior guys around the club, the players that had been there for years, and he was trying to shake things up. But the funny thing is, when you're a kid and you're on a hundred quid a week or whatever, and you're desperately trying to force your way into the side, nothing else matters. You don't even notice the politics, never mind get involved with them. All I was interested in was getting my debut for Liverpool, pulling on the red shirt and fulfilling my dream.

God, I wanted it so much, and as soon as you get around the fringes of the first team, you're just dying every time they pin up a team sheet, wishing and hoping and praying that your name will somehow miraculously be on it. I don't care how good you are, how much you know you're gonna make it, or how often people tell you not to worry because you'll be in the first team in no time, that wait when you get in the reserves and begin pushing for the senior side, that is the most agonizing wait of all. And believe me, I did have to wait.

I'd played hardly any reserve team games when I got my first sniff of things at Anfield. We had just won the FA Cup in May 1992, Macca had produced a blinder at Wembley and Rushie and Michael Thomas scored in the final against Sunderland. Then, on the following Tuesday, we had a testimonial match at Wrexham for Joey Jones, who had won the European Cup with Liverpool back in 1977, and was always a fans' favourite at Anfield, so there was a pretty big crowd. We might have taken the FA Cup down there too, which was another attraction. And of course, there was me on the team sheet, which must have added, oh, eight or ten to the gate.

The gaffer called me in, and he said that I was down to travel with the squad, that he wanted to give me a chance, because he thought I had a big future at the club. I had turned seventeen a month before, and here was the manager calling me in to say that I would be part of the team that had just won the FA Cup. For once in my life I was speechless. It was an incredible feeling, being told that you were going to make your debut for the Liverpool first team, even if it was only in a testimonial game, and it didn't really count. I think I made it home from Melwood faster that day than I have ever done. I could barely speak to me dad, I was so excited. Me dad came down to watch, along with me uncles, Calvey and some of my mates and I can say that it ranks up there with some of the greatest moments of my career, just because it was the first. I don't think I got a kick, although I do remember that we drew

2–2, and that quite a lot of the cup final side were in the team, including Rushie, who scored the equalizer after I came on the pitch as a fifty-ninth-minute substitute for David Burrows, and there's a like-for-like substitute if ever there was one, by the way. So I'm claiming the influential contribution, even if I was standing out on the touchline minding my own business.

The Wrexham keeper got injured in the first half and they didn't have another, so David James had to go in goal for them, because he had travelled down to be on our bench. And he saved a penalty, I think it was by Mark Walters, and I can remember the stick both of them got in the dressing room afterwards. I don't know who got it worse, but it was a right laugh. And I was part of it. Fucking magic.

So I'd broken through, made the first team, and was told by the manager I had a big future. I went away that summer with Calvey and Dom Matteo thinking I was about eight feet tall, which was approximately twice my size, even then at seventeen. I was doing all the calculations during the summer. If I could get into the first team on the first day of the season on 8 August, I'd be exactly seventeen years and four months, which would mean that I would be six days younger than Maxwell Thompson, who was the youngest ever player to represent Liverpool when he made his debut back in the seventies at seventeen years and 128 days. Well, you've got to dream, haven't you?

As it happened, I was in the reserves at the start of the 1992–93 season, and didn't even make the squad for the pre-season friendlies when the first team went away to Paris for a tournament. Not that I seriously considered I had any chance of getting into the squad. We had Dean Saunders as well as Rushie, two top-class forwards, and there were Ronny Rosenthal and Paul Stewart, both internationals who could play up front as well. The gaffer had used Mark Walters and John Barnes as strikers, so I wasn't seeing the biggest of opportunities for me around that time. At the end of that season he also bought Nigel Clough for a lot of money, so I wasn't exactly holding my breath.

When I finally did get into the side over a year later, the

gaffer told me that he had wanted to put me in much earlier, but the rest of his coaching staff had persuaded him against it, because they all thought that I was too slight still, that I wouldn't be up to the physical demands of the game at that level. I had grown, but I hadn't filled out much, and I suppose they were right. If I'd have gone in at that age, then I might have struggled with the physical stuff, and that could have affected my development. So it was back to the reserves for that lost season that seems to have erased itself from my memory – probably because we had a new reserve team coach in Sammy Lee who didn't shout as much, and so didn't wake me from my dreams about making my proper debut for Liverpool Football Club. Twice that season I was convinced my big moment was about to come, as all my family trooped up to Anfield when the gaffer said I was on the bench. The first came on 13 January 1993, when Rushie was injured, and Dean Saunders had been sold by then. We had a bit of a makeshift strike force, and nobody in reserve, so I got the call against Bolton in an FA Cup replay at Anfield. It was a weird game too. It was the first year of the Premiership and they were in the second division, miles and miles below us, but they gave us a torrid time and got at our centre halves, who I seem to remember were Torben Piechnik and Stig Bjornebye on the day. Mark Wright was dropped for some reason.

Anyway, there I was sitting on the bench, itching to get on, but at the same time dreading the call because we were getting whacked. I was running up and down the touchline warming up for most of the second half, partly to remind the manager that I was there if he needed a goal, and partly to get away from him, just in case he was thinking about actually throwing me on. We lost 2–0, and I was pretty relieved in the end not to get on the pitch, because the lads got mullered after that defeat, and Souey went ballistic afterwards about the lack of pride in the team. I didn't get another sniff then until the final day of that season, when we played Spurs at Anfield after a lousy couple of defeats against Norwich and Oldham. By that time, Phil Charnock had already made his debut with an appearance as a sub and then a game in a cup tie against Chesterfield, and

I was thinking it was about time I got my chance – as you do, when you're eighteen and still a daft lad.

I can remember the game vividly, because we had been pretty shit for much of that season, but we ruined them at our place, and went 3–0 up just after half time. I was warming up proper style then, looking over at the gaffer thinking, Christ, he's got to put me on now, because we're battering them. But I think things went against me because they scored twice, meaning that it got quite tight at exactly the time he would have been thinking about giving me a go. So I had to sit down, and then in the last five minutes we scored three times for what was our best result of the season, but I still didn't get my bloody chance even though we won 6–2, for Christ's sake, and you'd have thought it was the perfect chance to blood a young kid.

It's incredible really, what goes through your mind when you're trying to get into the side as a young professional. You sit there, knowing that you're not gonna get your chance unless either someone gets injured or fucks up, and you can't help but start thinking, I hope somebody gets a slight injury, or we just go on a little bit of a run where we lose a few matches, but it doesn't do too much damage. It's a cruel sport in that sense, because a lot of the time the people on the fringes can only really profit when something goes wrong.

I went away that summer a bit depressed because I hadn't made the breakthrough when I really thought it would happen for me. And yet in the back of my mind, I was thinking that it hadn't been much of a season for Liverpool and the strikers hadn't done too much apart from Rushie, who still managed to score over twenty goals despite being in a side that struggled at times. Ronny Rosenthal had played a lot of games and hardly scored any goals, Mark Walters had scored a few but he was really a winger, and Dean Saunders had been bombed out by Souey. So I was thinking that maybe as an out-and-out striker who the manager kept saying he liked, I had a chance the next season. Being on the bench for the final game helped, but there were still those nagging doubts. I had scored goals at every level I played, but could I do it at the very top? Did the manager really believe that I could, if he still hadn't put me in?

I hide it pretty well, but I've always been a bit of a worrier, and during that season there were nagging doubts in my mind. By then though, there was already something else that was nagging away at me, even though I knew it was bollocks and I should put it from my mind. As it happens, it is something that has never gone away, no matter how hard I have tried to tell myself that it doesn't matter, and tried not to think about it. As a seventeen-year-old, I tried to laugh it off as being ridiculous and just not worth the energy of even thinking about it. And yet here I am more than a decade later, still haunted by the same stuff that bothered me as a kid and put my family through hell.

4 CHARLIE

Since I was seventeen, I have been tormented by a nasty, vindictive whispering campaign that has repeated the same thing over and over and over again: that I am a smackhead, that I'm on the charlie, that I do drugs. Even now, I find it absolutely insane that anyone can possibly believe it. And yet plenty of people seem to. It's fucking crazy. If people only knew how much I hate drugs and what they do to wreck lives. If people only knew the reason why I hate drugs so much, maybe they'd be a little slower to throw this mud at me. I have lost two family members through the devastating impact drugs can have, so to me they are nothing but evil.

It all began when I was a boy, still training with the reserves up at Melwood and just starting to make a name for myself. I was living with me mum and hanging out with the lads down by the chippy, I still hadn't even had a proper bevvy, never mind been out to the night clubs, and yet there were these stories going round about me. The first time I heard it was back in 1992, when I was earning £29.50 a week. And as I reflect on it thirteen years later, think about how stupid it all is, I still hear the stories now. Let me repeat that – thirteen years it's been going on, and each story gets more elaborate.

The latest one, in 2005, is that I'm supposed to have checked into the Priory to sort my drug problems out when I wasn't in the Manchester City team for a few weeks. Out of the squad, so it must be drugs. It couldn't possibly have been something simple like a barney with the manager. A mate who's a City fan and works in the media even rang me to say that some fella was trying to sell the 'story' to the papers. It never appeared, of course, mostly because it wasn't fucking true, but it doesn't stop people trying to make money out of these lies anyway. Sometimes, when I hear the stories, I can't believe that people continue to peddle them, or are still falling for them. Is it even remotely possible that a sportsman at the very highest level of the most professional game in the world could possibly have survived at that level for that time with a drug habit? Is it bollocks.

Let me say now, once and for all, that the stories are not true. Not now, not then, not ever. It is an insult to me, and an insult to me mum and dad. And that is the painful thing. For all the fact that I have learnt to live with the whispers, even learnt to laugh at some of the more ridiculous ones, me mum and dad have been hurt so much by it. When I was first considering the idea of telling my story, we talked about the crap flying round about me, and I thought I shouldn't bother dignifying such nonsense by even mentioning it. But when you see the effect it has on me mum and dad, then I think it's only right that I at least try to put the record straight, even if I know that there are some people out there who aren't interested in the truth. Me dad is so angry about it, so disgusted by the sickness of some people, that it churns him up inside, it really kills him, even now. He is convinced that all the rumours stem from Evertonians who hate me because I have always scored against them. And do you know what? After supporting the Blues for all those years, after following them all around the country and bringing me up as an Everton fan, he wants nothing to do with them. He says he's ashamed to be connected with them in any way, and doesn't want his name mentioned in the same breath. Me? I stopped being an Everton fan when they started chucking pies at me.

Sometimes, people look at you as a so-called celebrity, and I don't think they can realize that you are a normal person, with real feelings, a family who read the same stuff as everyone else, and hear all the same rumours. It's a laugh having a go at someone in the public eye, and it doesn't matter if they get some stick because they earn enough money ... and they wanted all that attention in the first place, didn't they? D'ya know what? I probably agree.

When you come from Toxteth, you don't start moaning about 'the price of fame', you just cling on to the ride for fucking dear life. But what about my family? My wife Kerrie is the nicest person on earth, and together we have brought our three girls up properly, to respect people and have decent values. How does Kerrie feel when she hears the rumours that, let's face it, reflect equally on her? What will my three children feel when they get to understand what 'smackhead' means, and that their dad has been called it all his professional life? Look, I'm no fucking saint, I've pulled plenty of stunts in my time, and I've not always behaved in the right way.

One of the main things I'm trying to say in this book is that it doesn't make sense to almost demand that footballers come from a certain area and have a certain mentality, and then expect them to immediately forget everything that got them there, forget their background, and behave like something they're not. But at the same time, just because I'm from Toxteth doesn't mean I have to be a druggie. In my mind, that's what it boils down to. You're from a certain place that has problems with drugs in certain small areas, so you have to behave in a certain way. That's why the rumours started about me, I'm sure. Never mind that the majority of families in Toxteth are decent, hard-working people, who have the same sort of values as everyone else. And never mind that your mum and dad, the people who pride themselves on bringing you up right, get a kick in the teeth every time some smart-arse has a cheap dig at your expense.

Liverpool. It's the biggest village on earth, and the gossip is vicious. Being a footballer, you're a target for everything. If you go out it's not for a quiet drink, but for a wild night on the lash. If you have a bet, then you're addicted to gambling. It's funny, but I know Michael Owen had to address all the rumours over him having a so-called betting addiction in his book, because they had got to such ridiculous levels. While he likes a bet, he's hardly in J. P. McManus's league. A quiet, sensible lad like Michael, and even he has to defend himself over this sort of horse-shit. I love the city of Liverpool, and when I moved away I got homesick, even though I was only living in Leeds. But it's tough being someone who's well known around the city, because you're fair game for everyone in it.

I got to the stage where I could hardly go out when I was playing for Liverpool, because I was such a target. Even after being a professional for twelve years, I get up every day and have to pinch myself that it was me who came through the system to become a footballer. But that doesn't make it any easier to deal with all the other stuff that comes along with it.

To be branded a drug addict for the whole of my career, can you imagine how difficult that is? To have your mum and dad being told all these things by people who swear that they're true. One time, all over the back of me mum's house was painted with the word smackhead. Daubed in white paint, in letters about ten foot high. She was really, really upset, and not just because it took ages to get it all off. It's frustrating because she knows that it's not true, but there is nothing she can do to stop it or convince people. And even after all these years, it refuses to go away.

You've got this thing in Liverpool where rumours go around, and they spread and spread, until after a while they become fact. I sometimes wonder how the hell they all started, because I was never one of the Liverpool lads who went down to London at the weekends and hung out in the trendy clubs there. I never really went out with any of the big-time celebrities who started hanging around the football club, and that's the obvious source of rumours. I never did much apart from go to the same couple of bars in Liverpool and the same couple of clubs, and they were the ones all the footballers from Liverpool and Everton went to.

So it comes back to the Toxteth thing. I suppose it doesn't help when the city is so divided because one team's supporters are always going to be looking to stir things up. It's difficult to describe the Everton–Liverpool divide. When I said it was strange I chose Liverpool ahead of the Blues, I mean purely because once you support one of the clubs you never change, and your loyalty is total. If you're from the city and you support one of the clubs, then people just assume you will join them if you're good enough.

Macca was desperate to join Everton, but they fucked him about so much that he was almost forced to go to Liverpool, and I know for a fact that at Anfield they were surprised to get him. I think it was the same with me. There is this line drawn, and there's no crossing it. As a fan it is passionate, and the heroes of the other side are the enemy, it is as simple as that. In fact, it's worse than that, they are the embodiment of evil. I had crossed the line, and I suppose that made it even worse. It didn't help that when I first came into the Liverpool team I made a bit of an impact.

It's always hard to talk about your own deeds because you look like a big-headed bastard. But what Wayne Rooney's doing now, I did that back at about the same age. Except that I scored a shed load of goals, and people were saying I was the most natural goal scorer since Jimmy Greaves. In fact, he wrote an article in a newspaper saying I was better than him, which was an incredible thing to say. I don't want to do the old 'it was better in my day' thing, because I fucking hate that, but I think sometimes time diminishes achievements, and some people may have forgotten the impact I had when I first arrived in the Premiership. I scored thirty goals a season in each of my first three full seasons, and, as I said, I always scored against Everton. In many ways, the phenomenon that surrounded me was even bigger than the stuff Wayne Rooney gets now . . . and the Everton fans really fucking despised that. So if there was something they could seize on, some tiny little rumour that just wasn't true, then what the fuck, they would do it anyway, and let's face it, that's what football is all about, isn't it? That mad, passionate, blind support of the fans. If you took that away then you wouldn't have a sport, even if it can be damaging at times, as my family know all too well.

My mate Stephen Calvey laughs about the number of times

people tell him that they've seen me out on the town taking drugs, when it was impossible for me to have been where they said I was. There was one time that sums up what I have had to deal with perfectly. I was playing for England abroad, and he got a cab over to another mate's house to watch the game. I didn't know whether I would be in the starting line-up or not, so he didn't know what the team was when he was on the way over there. So he goes to the cab driver, who's got the radio on, 'What's the news on England, mate? Have you heard whether Robbie Fowler's playing?'

Straight away, the reply comes back: 'That Fowler, he won't be playing, he's a smackhead. They won't pick him, because they know what he's up to. Everyone does, it's common knowledge in Liverpool.'

So Calvey doesn't say anything, and just asks, all polite like, how he knows, and the taxi driver turns round to him and says, dead confident: 'I know cos I've seen him last week. I had a drop-off up on Granby Street, and I saw him in a Mini Metro, waiting there until a fella pulled up alongside him and did the deal, and I saw him hand over some coke.'

Then Calvey laughs out loud and says he's my best mate, and not only do I not own a Mini Metro, or ever go down to Granby Street – which is the road in Toxteth we were always warned off when we were kids – but he's known me for most of my life and he knows that I wouldn't be seen dead touching the stuff. And anyway, I was out of the country when this was supposed to have happened. So the taxi driver pulls a big grin, all sheepish like, and says: 'Fucking rumours, hey, you know how they get started. It's terrible innit?' Just like that. He knew it was bollocks, but he was happy enough to spread the rumour just because he'd heard it himself. The same happened with a friend of Macca's who was at a rugby club over on the Wirral, and this bloke from off the telly was in there saying the same thing, that he knew me and he'd seen me taking some coke. Again, when the bloke was challenged he admitted that he hadn't seen me in person, but that someone else had told him that they'd seen me, so it must be true.

But when you get people like that saying it, someone who's quite well known, then I suppose people will always start to believe it.

The rumours started before I did. By that I mean that I hadn't even got into the Liverpool first team before people were saying that they had seen me out in Liverpool taking drugs. It's weird, it really is, because you do wonder who the hell first came up with it. The first time, Calvey was round at me nan's and he got a phone call from his dad who was all worried. He said that one of Calvey's uncles had been told by a bloke at work that we'd been seen out in town snorting some stuff. I don't think I'd even been out in town at that age, being so small for my age even at seventeen. His dad Lennie realized it wasn't true, because he knew us well enough, but it was understandable that he was worried and wanted to say something to us. It didn't stop the rumours though.

Some time afterwards I was at me dad's house and he was following me round, so I knew something was on his mind. When I went over to me mum's he followed me over there, and when I went into the back room he came in and closed the door behind him. He looked at me, cleared his throat, and then he said that he was sorry he had to ask me this but he kept hearing all the rumours about me taking drugs, and he had to know if there was anything in all these stories.

Someone in the pub had come over to him and said he had better watch out for me. I couldn't believe what I was hearing. I looked at him and said don't be so stupid, and I was hurt he even had to ask the question. Me dad knew straight away there was nothing to worry about, and he apologized immediately. Since that day, he's never asked me again, and he knows there's nothing in it. He's never raised it in my company again, even though I know he's outraged about what our family have had to go through, and he's still seething inside about all the things we've had to put up with. In fact, he says he still feels guilty that he ever had to ask me in the first place.

The funny thing is, I was quite naive about all that sort of stuff for a long time. Calvey remembers a time when we were out, and we were standing on the edge of a group of people who were talking to some of our mates. One of them, this girl, eventually sidles over to me and sort of whispers, 'Do you fancy a bit of our charlie?' Straight away, I blurts out that I'm not interested because I've already got a girlfriend. I thought she was talking about her sister or something, I really did, and it was fucking embarrassing actually. Calvey pissed himself when I told him, and he still does now when he reminds me about that story only about every other week. But that shows how naive I was when I was younger.

It does happen in football, just like it happens everywhere else. There are players who have admitted to taking it, like Paul Merson and Gazza, and there have been quite a few who have been caught like Adrian Mutu. I think they catch about twenty or thirty a year, taking some drug or other. That's because they test us all, and that includes me. I've been tested loads of times, probably more than most, in fact, no doubt because of all the rumours. I've got no problem with that. I reckon I've been tested every year since I came into the game, and I have got absolutely nothing to hide. Me dad is always saying to people that he'll have a bet with anyone who'll take it, and I will be tested every week for the next four years if people like. That's how chewed up he is about it.

We got to the point where George, my financial advisor, went to Liverpool and said enough was enough, it was hurting me mum and dad too much, and we had to do something about it. You're in a terrible situation with stuff like that, because if you say nothing people assume it must be true, but if you come out and say something about it, then people automatically think that there's no smoke without fire. You can't win and I know that some people will say that I'm protesting too much about it all now. But sometimes you have to set the record straight, even if it is just to get the whole thing off your chest. In early 1998, Liverpool actually went to the lengths of putting out a statement confirming that I had been tested countless times and had proven beyond all doubt that the rumours were untrue. They also explained that the club had a policy of testing their own players regularly, and that I was subject to those tests just like every other player. It read:

'Our players undergo regular and strict drug testing in conjunction with the FA and Sports Council and nothing has ever shown up.' Fat lot of good that did in dispelling the rumours, mind.

I know that people will point the finger at me and say I have hardly helped myself, and there are two incidents in particular that they use against me. For starters, people say that I have only got myself to blame because I made matters a million times worse with my now infamous goal celebration against Everton back in 1999. Fuck me, they've got a point! We played them at Anfield on the first Saturday in April, and during the week before Calvey and me had come up with a cunning stunt. We didn't tell anyone else about it, but we both thought that if I scored against them then it would be hilarious to have a go back at the Everton fans for all the stick they had given me over the years.

I must admit I was sick of all the abuse they had thrown at me along with the pies, and all the chants they always came up with about me being a smackhead. It really did my head in, and I'd had enough. So we decided that if I scored at the Everton end, then I would take the piss in proper style by getting down on my knees and sniffing the line in front of them. My idea was simple. As a message, it was: 'Take that, you cunts.' Not subtle, I know, but I wasn't auditioning for the Cambridge Footlights. In my mind all I was doing was having a go at the Everton fans for giving me so much stick over the years. I'd show them who was a smackhead, by scoring a goal against them and – if you'll forgive the crap pun – rubbing their noses in it.

In fact, I scored two that day, but nobody remembers the second because it all kicked off after my celebration. I was at the right end, the Anfield Road end, and then ran the few yards to the little away section and got down on my knees and started with my big hooter on the line. I was pissing myself, I really was. Macca was already on his way over to celebrate with me, but by the time he got there, I was down on my knees. You should have seen his face. He was dragging me up, trying to get me out of there because he could hear how fucking crazy the Everton fans were going, and I think he realized straight away the reaction it would get.

I think he was smiling, but it was one of those fixed grins, and he was whispering through his teeth, 'Get up, you daft wanker.' But I wasn't finished, so as he pulled me up, I just jumped down again and carried on. He looked at me, and you could tell he was thinking, Ah shite, what do I do now? He kind of shrugged and just left me to it, fucked off right out of there. It was hilarious. I was down there sniffing the line until Incey came over and dragged me up to celebrate, and then I gave a big fist up to the Everton fans and got off sharpish. Mental.

Even now, I can't understand some of the reaction to it. Okay, it wasn't the smartest move, and I realize that I shouldn't have been so obvious in taunting the Everton fans, even if I still think they fucking deserved it. But I couldn't believe some of the stick I got over the next few weeks. I remember putting on the telly one night and there was this bunch of journalists on this programme talking about me and what I did. One fella, some posh twat from a broadsheet, I think, was going on about the example I set to the poor kids, how I was condoning drug taking, encouraging it amongst impressionable youngsters, and basically saying what a disgrace I was because it sent out the message I was on drugs. Did it bollocks.

This fella was trying to make out he was so smart, and yet he couldn't even see the bleeding obvious, that I was sending out exactly the opposite message. I didn't take drugs, I wasn't a smackhead and I was sick of being called it, especially by the Everton fans who hated me so much. The message I was sending out there, which was completely clear in my mind, was that if I was supposed to be a smackhead, how the fuck could I score goals against Everton and rub their faces in the dirt? How could I be a top sportsman and do everything I have done if I was taking all that shit? It was a way of telling them that if they carried on with all that abuse, then I was going to stuff it up them even more. It was an attempt to get them to think about what they were doing, and even make them stop. And it was supposed to be funny. Hmmmmn. It didn't exactly work. Even now, I can't see how what I was trying to do could ever be taken as a sign that I was on drugs.

The stuff from the journo was typical of all the things said and written about me in the next few weeks, and by the end of it the idea of me being a druggie was reinforced rather than removed. Since that day, what was a local rumour chanted by Everton fans has almost been accepted as common currency, and so I don't suppose I helped myself there even if I thought I did at the time. Just before he left City, Kevin Keegan told me that he did a press conference, and some journalist had referred to my 'drug problems' in it. As if it were fucking true. Keegan put him straight of course, and the fella did apologize, but it just shows you how these things can get so out of hand. I am sure there are plenty of people out there who believe it all, even though there is not a shred of evidence, and even though if they stopped to think about it for just a few seconds, logic would tell them that it couldn't be true. It is the nature of some people, isn't it, to make stuff up and repeat it so often that they believe it's true. Mind you, that press conference was just after I had scored at Goodison with a fantastic header and I had run around the ground tapping my head to remind them of my aerial ability . . .

The second major incident which people somehow believe shows I am involved in drugs, is the night when I was assaulted in a Liverpool hotel by two men who I didn't know from Adam. In Liverpool, you always get people wanting to have a pop at you, it comes with the territory. It's usually opposition fans who want to tell you how shit you are, or people who want to tell you it's a disgrace that you can possibly earn so much money. Then there are pissed-up people who just want to have a chat but don't realize how aggressive they are coming across. It's no problem, you learn to live with it even if it comes as a massive surprise when you first make the grade. But this was different, it was far more sinister.

The case eventually went to court, and every single detail came out before one of the men was sent to prison for unlawful and malicious wounding. Yet people still believe that there was some drug element to the whole incident, and that I was involved with the two blokes in taking drugs. What really pisses me off is that nothing could be further from the truth, and thankfully the truth did come out in court so it was there for everybody to hear. It was in April 1999 again, just a few weeks after the Everton game and following a match at Anfield against Villa. It was my last game of the season because after that I was suspended for the remainder of the campaign, partly because of the 'sniffing the line' business.

So I went out, and there was absolutely nothing wrong with that on a Saturday night when your next game is four months away. What we used to do at Liverpool when we did go out was end up back at the Moat House Hotel, which was the place where the team always went for an afternoon kip and a team meeting before home matches, so we knew everyone there and it was a pretty safe environment, or so I thought. We would go back there because it is hard getting a taxi in Liverpool after a night out, and it was easiest to call one from the hotel. I was with Macca and Calvey and a couple of others, and we went back because they were getting a cab home, and I was getting picked up by Kerrie from the hotel. They jumped in their two taxis and headed off into the night, while I sat in the lobby waiting for Kerrie to arrive.

I needed a slash, so I went to the toilets before being picked up. The Moat House has toilets on a corridor next to the lobby, and then behind that there is a bar where the residents can get a late-night drink. When I went into the toilets there were two blokes in there, and as I finished they began to follow me out. One of them shouts up behind me, 'Hey, Robbie lad, do you want any charlie?' I just turned round and looked at him, and told him to fuck right off because I wasn't into anything like that. That was it. I was on my way out and I kept on walking, but apparently that gave the fella a bit of a cob on and he ran up behind me and sparked me on the back of the head. Then the other fella joined in and smacked me in the face a few times. I had a face like a welder's bench with a broken nose and plenty of cuts and bruises.

The two blokes tried to run off, and as I staggered into the lobby there was this Liverpool fan who had come over from

Ireland and was staying at the hotel who'd seen what happened. He ran after the blokes and tried to stop them escaping, and they turned on him and one of them bit him. His name was Anton, and one of the good things that came out of that nightmare was that Anton and me have kept in touch ever since, and become firm friends. I see him from time to time and he's a decent bloke. He always says he can't believe what those animals did to me, but it was something and nothing really.

It wasn't very pleasant, but that was all that happened, two fellas got a cob on because I told them to fuck off when they offered me some coke. The bloke who was sent down didn't even contest the charge or contradict my version of what happened, and as I say it was all revealed in court. And yet people prefer a different story. It is just unbelievable. I've heard that I was supposed to be in a toilet cubicle with a known drug dealer, and that I was obviously in there up to no good. The fact that I got smacked because I told someone offering me drugs to fuck off seems to have escaped the attention of everyone who wants to peddle all the shite still.

Sometimes it still makes me angry, especially when me mum or dad are upset by it. Not long ago, City went to Portsmouth and when we got to the ground, there was this bloke there from Liverpool who was working down there apparently. He just comes up to me and says all casual like as though he knew me, 'All right, Robbie lad, you still on the stuff then?' Me dad went ballistic when he heard that, because he can't believe his own people – my own people – could say things like that. As I've said, I'm no saint, and I don't want to be one because that would be pretty boring. But I've always taken my profession seriously, even if that's not always the impression people have got.

When I was a kid, there was the usual stuff, you go away on holiday and have a good laugh with your mates, drink too much and that sort of stuff. I know that I've had a few too many drinks on occasions, got bladdered when I shouldn't have, and there have been a few times when that was out of order. But not that many. I don't go out before a match, only immediately after a game. Three days before, I don't go out, and I never have. Even when I was a little kid training at the Centre of Excellence, I wouldn't leave the house on Friday nights. My mates would come round to ours and stand on the doorstep, so I didn't have to leave the house.

Okay, a lot of people now say you shouldn't drink at all, and as I get older I can see the wisdom of that where I probably would have thought it was bollocks at the start of my career. As I've got older I've finally begun to understand the importance of diet to an athlete, where again when I was a kid I thought I could eat anything and get away with it. The thing is, I didn't know any different, and there was nobody at Liverpool back then who would make an issue of it, who would point out the merits of a proper diet or abstaining from the booze. I don't think anyone else really understood it back then. But as far as drugs are concerned, I've always known different. I've been brought up to understand the rights and wrongs of that, and I would never have dreamt of jeopardizing my career by snorting some shit up my nose.

D'ya know what? When I do go out for a drink I always have bottles of lager, and if I ever have to put an unfinished one down for any reason, I won't pick it up again. I'll just leave it and get a fresh one, because I'm concerned that someone could have tampered with it. No matter where I am I do that, because I know that there are some sick people out there who would happily put something dangerous in your drink, and I don't want to risk it.

Look, of course there are the temptations you get as a young footballer. What has happened over the past decade, since I first came on the scene, is that Sky's money and exposure have turned footballers into teen-idol celebrities and that has changed everything. Yeah, players like George Best always had that, but they were one-offs. Now, everyone who kicks a ball is a star and can be on the front pages as easily as the back. It wouldn't surprise me if there were some of the young kids now falling for the temptation of drugs, because – let's face it – society has moved on and it's far more a part of popular culture these days.

If half the kids in the country try recreational drugs, then there's a fair chance a few young footballers get caught up in it. I've heard the stories like everyone else, but I just wouldn't make the mistake of believing any second-hand shit like that. I've read the papers about parties and roasting and dogging – whatever the fuck that is – and again, you know that with the celebrity of some of the young lads these days, they are bound to be surrounded by women all wanting a piece of them. If they're single, then what's the problem with that, so long as it doesn't get in the way of the football?

I've had one or two things written about me in the papers, especially when I was younger, but the gist of most of it was that I was a single young man – very young – and I went out with a few girls, and then they sold their stories to the paper. I can't imagine why anyone would find that interesting, and it's certainly not a scandal. As a teenager, I think people would find it more alarming if you didn't have a few girlfriends. More and more these days, though, you get these women who sleep with footballers, get a bit of cash for their stories, and then get some fame on the back of them. They end up on the telly as C-list celebrities themselves. That's a bit of a worry because it doesn't take a genius to realize it can be open to exploitation. And believe me, some of them are not geniuses.

There seem to be some people around who will go to any lengths to earn a few soiled notes. Of course you must get footballers who have been bad lads, done some wrong things, because you get that in all walks of life. At the same time, I know that some of the stuff you read in the papers is not true, or exaggerated beyond all recognition. There was a real frenzy not so long back when there were rape allegations against some Newcastle players. No charges were even made, and you would imagine that the people involved would get the benefit of the doubt, because that's supposed to be the way the system works – innocent until proven guilty. Not a prayer. It was the same with the Leicester City players involved in the allegations in La Manga. Again, no charges were ever pressed, and there was plenty of evidence that there was a financial incentive behind the false allegations against the players involved. And yet by the coverage of the whole affair, you would assume they had been locked up and the key thrown away. You get these little media frenzies. There's one story that sparks it, and then they're all on the lookout for any other story involving a footballer that will reinforce that idea. That's when all the parasites come crawling out, ready to distort anything to make it fit for a few quid.

There was one time I remember well, when the media were in the middle of one of their 'players drinking' outrages, during qualifying for the 2002 World Cup. This time it was under Sven Goran Eriksson, and there really wasn't much they could get into, because the squad under Sven was like a litter of kittens. I can't even remember what sparked it, but I think there was a bit of shit flying around about Stevie G going for a bevvy in his local when he was on a day off in between matches, and they were on the hunt for something else.

One morning we picked up the papers, and there, in the *Express* I think it was, was a story about me and Macca breaking a curfew to go drinking in a Liverpool bar. It was on the Tuesday before a game the next Saturday – the final qualifying game against Greece at Old Trafford, if I remember rightly – and we were all given the night off. The two of us plus a couple of others went into a restaurant – not a bar – had something to eat and left at around 9.30 p.m. Hardly hell-raising, and certainly no curfew broken. But they didn't let that get in the way of a good story.

The owner of the restaurant even produced the till receipt to show what we had eaten and what time we had left, and the fact that there were two beers on the whole bill (the rest was orange juice). But the damage was done because there was a story in the papers saying we had been out boozing. Macca and me went to the FA and said we should do something about it, but they didn't want to ruffle any feathers in the media in such an important week, and so they quietly let it drop. It was bollocks, pure and simple, but again it was a false impression of me, and no doubt added to my legend. I've had a few of those, believe me, and at the bottom of most of them is always the desire of someone to make a few quid, even if it's dirty money.

We had a bit of a problem with that sort of crap in our family a few years back. Me sister Lisa went through a very short stage where she rebelled, like most kids, and she tried a few things. It was nothing, and it's her own private thing anyway, which has got nothing to do with anyone. But then she gets these people turning up trying to blackmail her, saying that they would go to the newspapers and say she was involved in drugs and drag my name into it unless she paid them some money. We went to the police right away, and they were pretty good about it. They got Lisa to organize a meeting with the blackmailers, and then she was wired up just like in the movies. It was pretty exciting actually.

So then she went along with all this electronic stuff on her, and with the police tailing her and listening in, and we were all holding our breath wondering what would happen. But the fuckers never turned up! That was years and years ago, and it was never a problem for her or for me. But you can see how these things get out of hand, how people exploit the tiniest little thing, or think they can screw money out of anyone who is in the public eye for whatever reason. And if they can't get to you, then they try your family. Sick really, and no wonder me dad gets so heated about it all.

If people only knew the real story, then I don't think they would ever say such awful things about me. The truth is, we have endured harrowing pain in our family because of the awful damage that can be done by drugs. It's a private grief really, and I don't think that anyone in my family will thank me for dragging it all up again, because the hurt is still there. It is still very raw.

My cousin Vincent was a lovely lad, a real gem and everyone in the family loved him. We're quite a close family, me mum's brothers and sisters have always been around at our house and we've always helped one another. Vincent was my mate. I used to play with my cousins a lot when I was little. But as he got older, Vincent got in with a bad crowd, which is easy to do for any kid, and he got mixed up in drugs and stuff like that. He had his problems, but fair play to him, he tried his best to get clean and he sorted himself out.

Vincent showed a lot of character to get on his feet and put it all behind him, and everyone was proud of what he did. But he just fell back in one time, just a small slip, and I think his heart gave out. I don't really know to this day how he died, but I don't think his body could take it after he cleaned himself up. I'll never forget him, and even now, every day, it breaks my heart and that of everyone in our family to think what happened. His mum, me Auntie Pat, obviously finds it so hard even now when I talk about it, and I don't want to make it any worse for her. But she also lost her daughter Tracy, who got involved with a bloke who was on drugs, and he killed her. He was sent down for manslaughter, but of course it was a terrible, horrible ordeal for Auntie Pat, God bless her.

If people could see what a devastating effect it has all had on her, how she has to live with it every day of her life, then I don't think they would be making jokes about drugs, and about me taking them. I can see first hand what sort of effect even messing around and dabbling a little bit can have. I have seen how it can destroy lives, not just of the people involved, but also their families and the people close to them. If people could feel the pain that me Auntie Pat has suffered, if they could feel what I feel when I think of Vincent, then they wouldn't be so quick to make all these unthinking, flippant allegations.

Maybe now it's a little easier to understand why I get so angry when I get taunted by opposition fans; why I sometimes react when it's probably wiser to ignore everything; why me dad is so upset by it all, and hates the Everton fans so much, even though he was a passionate supporter himself. I know me Auntie Pat will be upset if she reads this, I know the hurt she will feel all over again, and I know that hurt will never go away for her. I just hope people can look a little into their own hearts and try to understand some of what she has to go through, even if it doesn't ever stop them having a go at me. Why would I ever even think of taking drugs after all that?

I'm not trying to be the martyr, and there's no way I expect me saying a few things about my own family will change anyone's mind. But I think it might just help some people to understand me a little bit more, and to see that I am a person too, with real feelings and a real family that hurts like everyone else. I don't expect sympathy, and really, I've come to terms with most of the crap that is thrown my way. If I'm really honest, I laugh about the majority of it now.

What I have learnt over the years – even if it took me a bit long – is that the less you go out, then the less chance there is of people making trouble for you. It's stupid really, that the same old stories still exist about me that were doing the rounds when I was a teenager. I'm married now with three children, for Christ's sake. Do people really think that I've got the sort of wild lifestyle that can justify all those rumours? It's crazy, and yet people still look on me as some kind of incredible party animal – and I know that there are plenty out there who still believe the drugs stories.

The extent of it is that I still have the odd session on the bevvy, which I know isn't probably always the best thing to do, especially now that I'm getting into my thirties. I bumped into Tony Grant a few weeks back and we went for it big style as we talked about the old times. It's not a particularly common thing though – like all the other players these days I understand now the importance of looking after myself, of refuelling properly and getting the right lifestyle. It's second nature now to almost everyone in the game because football has changed, and footballers have changed. Only one thing hasn't changed, in fact, since I got my big chance in the professional game as an eighteen-year-old kid . . . those fucking rumours, of course.

MAKE AND BREAK (5)

When the summer of 1993 came, I was wondering what I had done wrong. To this day, I don't know why Souey didn't put me on during the Spurs game on the last day of the season, when we were cruising and the sun was shining. It couldn't have been the win bonus because mine was about five quid. I did find out eventually, though, why I didn't get on during the Cup tie against Bolton back in January, when we were garbage and got stuffed by a team who were then in the second division. One of the lads told me some time later about an exchange that had occurred in the dugout, when I had been sent up the touchline to warm up during the second half. There was a punter standing behind the Liverpool bench, getting angrier and angrier at what was happening. So he starts screaming at Souness to 'get the kid on, he can't be any fucking worse than the shower you've got out there'. And apparently Souey turned round and just said to the bloke that he didn't want to ruin me by putting me in with that load of crap. Somehow, even then a year before he quit Anfield, I think Souey knew that the writing was on the wall for him. He never won around the senior pros at the club, and he knew he wouldn't have enough time to fashion an entirely new team – didn't have enough time to wait for the likes of Macca, Dom Matteo, me and Jamie Carragher to come through and help him.

He could have thrown me on against Bolton, if only to deflect a little bit of the flak from himself, because crowds are always a tiny bit more indulgent when there is a young kid getting a chance. He didn't do it though, because he didn't think it was best for me, and I think that is a mark of the man. If I'd known that when I went away for the summer break I'd have slept a lot easier. As it was, I still had an irrational worry inside that I wouldn't be given my chance, that they felt I was too small, that I couldn't quite cut it at the top level, or I had messed up somehow. You can't help it.

There was one moment during that year when I did fuck up, and I thought I may have blown my chance. Even though they thought a lot of me, I was still training with the reserves, still getting changed in the away dressing room with the YTS lads when all the senior players were in the home dressing room. It was a strange system back then because we got changed at Anfield and then got the bus over to Melwood, about three miles away. Souness sensibly changed all that – even though he inevitably got some stick for it – and eventually we used to report to Melwood and work exclusively from there. It was only then that I got to move up to the senior dressing room, and that was a long time after I had actually made my first team debut in such spectacular style.

Anyway, still with the reserves and still pissing about, we used to have a right laugh on Fridays when we had to bundle the kit. It was only washed once a week in those days, just dried after every session, and by the end of the week it was stinking. When it was finally washed we used to have to put a full kit together for each player, which meant you put shorts, socks and a training top on top of a towel, and then bundled the whole lot with a shirt, which was tied around it to hold it in place. Every Friday we'd have a massive big scrap with the bundles, throwing them at each other's heads.

One week we were having this big barney, and Ashley Neal put his head around the door at just the wrong moment, because I launched a bundle right at him. It smacked him full pelt, and he had to have four stitches in his eye. I was in deep shit and got sent to see Souey, who gave me a formal warning.

He told me I was one more warning away from getting bombed out, and I calmed it down a bit for a while, because there was no way even a joker like me was going to throw away everything he had worked for.

It probably wouldn't have come to that anyway, because everything pointed to the fact that they thought I had a chance, and I now had confidence in my own ability. Problem was you had to get an opportunity to prove you were up to it, and I still hadn't had that chance. It was well over a year since I had played in that testimonial, and the closest I'd come to a game was twice shining the bench with my arse, even though in both matches the conditions were right to put me on. Phil Charnock had got a game, and Ian Frodsham seemed to be on the verge of it, and sometimes I wondered if I would be left behind. You have to be tough mentally to get through what is basically a ruthless world. That's why I think most players come from the working-class areas, because you have to be so single-minded and can't have any room in your life for anything else. You have to be able to put up with so much shit because you want it so badly.

It really is a funny thing why there are so few middle-class kids making it at the top level, and I suppose it's partly because they have so many other things to distract them. I'd be interested to find out why it has happened like that for so long, even these days, when football touches more people than ever before. It probably doesn't help to think too deeply. Too many questions, and you've got no chance. It's a bit like joining the army and doing your basic training.

There is still a pretty old-fashioned mentality in football where they try to break the young kids to see whether they have the mental strength to cope with what can be an incredible amount of pressure at the very highest levels. Phil Thompson was a coach who would push youngsters to see how tough they were, and a lot of the young lads coming through fucking despised him for it. I'm amazed he never got properly sparked out there. One time I thought it was really going to kick off in the dressing room when he was reserves boss, when he started having a right go at a young striker called Wayne Harrison, who Liverpool had bought from Oldham and had high hopes for. Wayne answered him back, and so Tommo starts on with that ole shite about putting your medals on the table. So Wayne snapped straight back at him, 'No fuck it, let's put our fucking toes on the table.' Tommo has only got four toes on one foot, so you can imagine how ballistic he went.

Everyone else in the dressing room was pissing themselves and trying to push their fists in their mouths to muffle the noise, because obviously he wasn't the sort of coach you wanted to do that with. But there are an awful lot more around like him, maybe just a little less obvious. Even if you get past those, then you still have to fit into a team environment, and it's one with a lot of vicious hierarchies and political infighting.

You hear plenty of stories of senior professionals twatting the young lads, in fact I've seen it happen a few times. Nicolas Anelka caused outrage at City when he turned on one of the kids for no reason one day, but a lot of the time it goes unnoticed. I escaped most of that at Liverpool. Dean Saunders and Steve McMahon roughed me up a few times for being a cheeky little git when I was a YTS, but that was pretty harmless. I escaped the worst of it because I was small, and they didn't want to pick on a little kid. Also because I was cheeky and made a few of them laugh, but just about knew where to draw the line, I usually got away with it. It is essential that you can deal with that, because these fellas will be your teammates eventually, and you have to prove to them that you can fit in, be part of the team and they can trust you. If you don't, then you won't make it, no matter what talent you have. I had all these fears swirling around in my head, all these worries about getting my chance and actually taking it when it finally did arrive. I was trying to work out all the little signs, the nuances of a club, to see if it would be me next to be hauled into the first team squad, just like Macca a year or two before. What happened that summer of 1993 though, made me feel an awful lot better. After being told I wasn't big enough, I wasn't good enough, I finally got my England call-up ... and I think I maybe proved a few people in blazers wrong.

It hadn't mattered to me that I missed out on playing for

England Schoolboys, because when I got to the trials I thought I was out of my depth. Mr Lynch felt differently though. He was gutted that I wasn't selected, and to this day he thinks I was kept out of it unfairly. He thinks it's rubbish they said I was too small, and the moment I finally did get an England cap I know was a very proud moment for him, as much as for me. The call came in November of 1992, when I was given an under-18 cap against Switzerland in a match at Port Vale.

It was a quiet night for me, I only got about three touches . . . and scored a hat-trick. We won 7–2 and me dad and Mr Lynch were really jubilant afterwards because I think it proved their faith in me. Mind you, it didn't seem to impress the selectors, because the next game in February of 1993 I was only on the bench, and when the squad came through for the UEFA under-18 Championships to be played in England during that summer, it was clear I was only a reserve. Story of my life, I thought.

I was behind a kid from Leeds called Jamie Forrester, and Julian Joachim was also ahead of me. Both of them were very quick, which seemed to echo my England experience a few years later. It was a good time though, and we had a fantastic team with a great atmosphere. The manager was a bloke called Ted Powell who was your typical schoolteacher type, very strict and a real disciplinarian, but he also had a great way of getting his ideas across and he could coach you brilliantly on the finer points of the game. His assistant was a coach called Alec Gibson who was a great lad, and interestingly now works with the Manchester City academy, so I still see him and catch up on things. Our physio for the tournament was Dave Galley, who went on to do the same job at Liverpool under Gerard Houllier, and is still there now. He is a great mate and we keep in touch all the time.

Every time I see him, I remind him of the time he took the running with the under-18s, and had us following behind him in twos as we did laps of the pitch. As we reached the goal-mouth, he turned around to see we were all doing it properly . . . and ran smack into the side-netting of the goal. It was just unlucky for Dave that so many of that eighteen-man squad went on to such heights in the game, because we all still bring that up, when he was stuck in the net like Spiderman's victim. Dave is a big, fit, impressive hulk of a guy . . . with the smallest calves in the world. We always wondered how he ever got across a cattle grid.

We were in a group with France, Holland and Spain, so an easy passage to the final then. It didn't half look like a group of death in the first game when we played France at Stoke in the middle of July, long after everyone else had gone off on holiday. We were outplayed for quite long periods of that game, and as it got towards the end, we were drawing 0–0. So there I was sitting on the bench – again – thinking that surely I would get my chance this time. It came when the coach put me and Kevin Gallen, a kid from QPR who was a year younger than me, on for the last fifteen minutes or so. It turned the game, he scored with seven minutes to go, I scored with five left, and we won 2–0.

From that moment, we were in the team together and it was a partnership that was to give me my first real taste of success at the top level of football. It's hard to describe how much that tournament meant to me. I was part of the squad at Euro '96, and that was a mind-blowing experience for a twenty-one-year-old, but to get your first honours for your country, and to be part of a triumphant squad on home territory, was something special. God, I was thrilled with that goal, and not just because it got me my place in the team. Everyone who had given me support in my career so far was there, Mr Lynch, me dad, Steve Heighway, the Liverpool coaches. And I had come through for them, and for my country, and it made me proud.

Next game up was Holland, with a fantastic team that included Patrick Kluivert. We stuffed them. I scored after ten minutes, Kevin Gallen and Julian Joachim both got one before half time, and we were home and dry, 4–1 at the final whistle. Already Kevin and me had formed a great partnership as well as a great friendship. Mind you, I blame him for getting me in trouble with the police. The next year he was still playing for the under-18s, and it was at Port Vale so me and Calvey went over to see him in my new motor, which I think was a Passat.

We got to Congleton and bloody broke down. There were some traffic police there who took one look at these two scallies in a decent car and assumed it must be nicked. They had to contact Liverpool so that we could prove we were who we said we were. We used to get stopped all the time when I was a kid, three or four of us in a decent car when I was still a teenager driving around Toxteth. Bit fucking predictable really.

Kev was a great lad though, and I think it was only injuries that stopped him having a career at the very top. He played in the Premiership with QPR and did very well, and I've always thought he had the genuine talent to make it at the highest level. Both of us that summer were at the same level, and we both had big futures ahead of us. It just shows you how thin that line can be, how arbitrary success and fame are. I got injuries later in my career, and they affected me, but not as much as Kevin. I was lucky, he wasn't. He was the record goal scorer for England under-18s for a while, and I always felt he should have been with a top club.

Kevin proved that in the run we had to the final in 1993. We played Spain in what was effectively a semi final because we were both unbeaten and whoever won was through. It was incredibly tense. Mark Tinkler, another Leeds player, scored for us early in the first half, but they equalized (even though they were down to ten men by then) and with twenty minutes to go we were hanging on. That was my moment. It was everything Mr Lynch had been working towards, everything me mum and dad had prayed for when I was little. Everything I had dreamt about. I was wearing an England shirt, in a proper match at a professional ground in front of a big crowd.

It's funny now, but the telly coverage had Don Howe talking about the game, and whether this bunch of kids could handle the big crowd and the pressure-cooker atmosphere. At Walsall. A team that included Gary Neville, Sol Campbell, Nicky Butt, Paul Scholes, me and Kevin Gallen, Julian Joachim, Darren Caskey and Chris Casper, who also played for United. I think they wouldn't mind having that side at Walsall now. But then, in the summer of 1993, it was a big deal for us, and an ordeal when Spain started playing some good football and really came back at us. It was a test of character for a bunch of kids who didn't know yet whether they had any. And I scored a hat-trick in sixteen minutes. I've still got a video of that game, and you should see me celebrate. My first goal came a few minutes after they scored the equalizer, and the whole place erupted. Julian beat a man on the left and laid it inside for me, and I lashed it into the back of the net. I ran over to the corner and celebrated like it was the winner in the FA Cup final with the whole crowd going mad. I scored a free kick soon after, left foot over the wall, and sent their keeper the wrong way, and with five minutes left I got the hat-trick when I volleyed a right-foot shot into the corner from the edge of the box.

I did a TV interview straight after the game when they gave me the Man of the Match award and the first thing I said to the interviewer, Nick Collins, was that I was two-footed. It had pissed me off in the build-up to the game that they were saying I was all left sided, even though I'd scored a volley against France with my right foot from about thirty yards. It's a funny interview, because I was pretty relaxed, and not bad at it even though it was my first proper one. I kept saying like, like, but apart from that I was comfortable enough. And yet a few months later the press fell for it when Souey told them I couldn't do interviews because I wasn't ready for it. In some ways, I think that gave a false impression of me for a long time, because a lot of the media assumed I was too thick to meet them, and that I had to go away to get speech coaching before I could talk in public. But the reality was that Souey was chucking them a line to keep the hype away from me.

So, through to the final against Turkey at the end of July, and we were playing in front of nearly 25,000 at Nottingham. It was obviously the biggest game of my career so far, and I even had a few nerves. Anyone who has ever played in the same team as me, they'll tell you I never get nervous. Never. Maybe that is what made me a decent goal scorer, because I've never really felt pressure and I've always been able to stay calm. That Sunday night I wasn't completely calm, because I knew how much winning the final would mean, not just to my career, but more importantly to the people around me. They were all there, watching and hoping that I would deliver. I didn't, but I won a penalty, which Darren Caskey converted with twelve minutes to go, and we won. In my career that is up there with my best memories.

I finished top scorer in the tournament, and it changed things for me. After that I knew I was ready. I had never got into any of the England Schoolboy teams, never been a chosen one. The kids that had gone to Lilleshall were in the England sides from about the age of five, being told they were the best from as soon as they could kick a ball. They knew that they would make it, while I just had the words of Phil Thompson ringing in my ears, telling me that I'd never be fit to wear the number-nine shirt of Liverpool. Now though, I knew I could eventually wear that number-nine shirt and score goals as well.

There had always been the nagging doubt thing about me being so slight. Again, it probably sounds daft now, but there was a real question mark over me back then, of whether I would be too small to really make the grade. Now I went back to Merseyside knowing that I had the ability if I got my chance. I went back the day after everyone else as it happened, because Mr Lynch had said he'd drive down with me dad on the Monday to Lilleshall to pick me up, and when I realized that the rest of the lads were going home the night before, I didn't think it was fair to put him out, so I was there on me own with just my dreams to keep me company.

By the time I got back to Melwood, they'd all fucked off on the pre-season tour, which I wasn't considered for because of the tournament. Souey had been out and spent millions on Nigel Clough who was a damn good player, but if I'm honest I never saw him as an out-and-out striker, more a drifting midfielder or a third striker behind a front two. Ronny Rosenthal was on a week-to-week contract, so basically bombed, and when I looked at the rest of the squad I couldn't see another striker in it. I probably had a part in that as well, and not just because they fancied me as a forward by that time.

As a YTS you were allocated one of the senior pros to look after, to clean their boots and whatever. I got Dean Saunders, who used to mess around and give me a hard time, but then he was bombed by Souey so I got Steve Staunton. Bombed. Steve McMahon. Bombed. Rosenthal. Bombed. I was a fucking jinx, and by the time I was promoted to the reserves, there wasn't one of the senior players who'd let me near their boots. My plan was working though. In the pre-season, Cloughie got flu and so they played Paul Stewart up front, even though it was obvious Souey didn't fancy him by that time. Mark Walters filled in up front as well, but everyone knew beyond the front-line two there was no one, and one of the strikers was really a midfielder.

So when the 1993 season kicked off against Sheffield Wednesday, I was feeling that maybe my time would come. The gaffer had spoken with me when he got back from the pre-season, said he was impressed with what I'd done in the summer Championships, and if I kept working hard and kept my head down, then I'd get my chance. I was made captain of the reserves for a tournament in Scarborough. I felt nine feet tall at the start of that season . . . a feeling that lasted precisely thirty-nine minutes. Cloughie scored two against Wednesday, either side of half time, and formed what looked like a fantastic partnership with Ian Rush. Bollocks. Still, I'd scored in the first two reserve games that season, and Souness was talking about putting me up to the senior squad. I didn't have to wait long.

What happened to me in the autumn of 1993 was absolutely insane. I was caught up in this whirlwind that seemed uncontrollable and unstoppable. It is hard to describe the effect getting into the first team of a major club has on your life. There is the obvious money aspect these days. When I was a kid, you used to pick up the Sunday papers all the time and read about this famous old pro who had hit hard times, was living in a bin or something like that. Nowadays you don't hear those stories, and it's all because of the effect Sky's money has had on our game. That's not the half of it though. Even after I won the European Championship with England under-18s, I used to go out with me mates down the chippy and just hang around, not being bothered by anyone.

As a reserve, you'd go to the training ground and walk in and out and not one of the fans hanging around outside would give you a second glance. I'd drive by in me Escort, or in me Uncle Alan's Maestro, which I used to borrow because I thought it was so souped up and powerful, and nobody would even bother looking in the windows. They'd be standing there waiting for the proper cars to turn up, the Beemers or Mercs driven by the likes of Barnsie, or Rushie, or even the Porsches that Julian Dicks and Razor Ruddock would be in. The only autographs I ever signed were for little kids around Toxteth, who'd heard of me being 'the footballer'.

Then, suddenly, one day it went ballistic. I was the archetypal 'overnight sensation'. I remember soon after I got into the first team me and Calvey went for a drink in a bar in town, and there were a group of Irish lads in there. They spotted me and grabbed me, put me on their shoulders and they were away, dancing down the street, singing at the tops of their voices with me perched up high above this group of massive blokes, laughing and shitting meself at the same time. Things like that happened all the time, and it took some getting used to. Little things always brought home the influence being a footballer had on people. One time, at the end of that first season, me, Calvey, Dom Matteo and a couple of his mates just booked a flight to Falaraki without finding any accommodation.

We got there early in the morning and went into the first bar we got to. In there, we met a few lads who said we could kip down at their place, and took us back to meet their mum and dad. The mum was so thrilled that she got out of bed to give us a place to lie down, and then cooked us breakfast. A bit later, she asked if I would go in and wake her little lad up. I crept in and shook him and said it was time to wake up. As he came round, he looked at me, then put his head back on his pillow. Then he turned again, and started rubbing his eyes. Then he just jumped up and ran out of the room at about 700 miles per hour. Seconds later, he was back, decked out in a full Liverpool kit, with even his boots on. All without saying a word!

Liverpool had started the season with three wins, and Cloughie started his Anfield career with four goals in four games, but then things went tits up pretty sharpish. Three defeats on the bounce culminated in a bit of a pasting at Goodison, and we lost 2–0. The knives were out for Souey then, and he knew he had to do something. He'd already bought Neil Ruddock and Cloughie, and then went out and splashed another big fee on Julian Dicks after the start of the season, but still things weren't happening for him.

Most of the press were right into him by then after he sold his story to the *Sun* when he had the heart bypass operation, and he admitted years later that he thought the Liverpool job had come too soon for him because he had tried to change things too quickly to make his mark on the club. He said when he left that he felt the senior players in the dressing room were out to get him, and there was obvious tension with him and some of them. People slagged him off so much that season, and I heard plenty of the talk in the dressing room about him from some of the players – mostly the ones who had fallen out with him – but how can I say a word against him? He gave me my chance in football for a start, and for all his hard-man approach – and he was hard, believe me – he cared about Liverpool, and he cared about those players who put it in for him.

Sometimes, I think most of his problems came with those players he felt didn't care as much as him. I was a kid who was enjoying life and concentrating on getting into the first team – getting my life off the ground – so I didn't have a clue about what was going on in the dressing room, the personalities and politics. Remember, I was always in the reserve changing room at training, even when I had actually broken through with the seniors, so I didn't hear the day-to-day squabbles and plots, even though I was told there were one or two people around who were saying it might be better if we weren't winning because Souey could get sacked.

People might think that sounds shocking, but believe me, in a football dressing room you do get that, course you do. Some characters, if they're not playing, if they don't like the manager, if they don't like the look of the future, they don't try. There were players like that in Souey's day, players like that when I got to Leeds, even one or two . . . well, one actually

... like that at Manchester City. You often hear of players getting managers the sack, and you can see how it happens. If the manager is in a strong position it doesn't happen, because he can just fuck them off. If he has a weakness in any way, then it goes on, because some players just don't give a monkey's. It's rotten, but it happens, and looking back, it must have happened to Souey, although I can't pretend I know too much about it.

Souness made some bad buys, and he admits that he came in too strong and alienated some of the players he inherited when he should have got them onside. He was fucking ferocious in the dressing room if he lost his temper, and I'll admit I was scared of him. He was not the type of manager you wanted to make angry. He was a bit of a thrower when he got mad, and you didn't want to be around for that. There were times when he lost it, one time he smashed this tray of tea and it went all over the players in their suits. Not one of them dared say a word. But he was always fair, especially to the younger players, who he always promoted and wanted to give a chance. He has always said that he made mistakes, like selling Stan – Steve Staunton – and letting some of the senior players leave before he had lined up replacements, or had time to bring the kids through properly. But I still believe that he wasn't given a fair chance at Anfield because of the mistakes he made early on.

He's a smart guy, so still to this day I can't understand why he sold his story to the *Sun* when he had his heart operation. I know it sounds cynical, but that operation should have worked for him like it worked for Houllier years later, but instead it was a fucking nightmare. In the end I think he gave the money – fifty grand – to Alder Hey Children's Hospital, but by then the damage was done. The *Sun* is hated on Merseyside after what they wrote in the days after Hillsborough, even now, even by people who don't remember much about that terrible tragedy. By Everton fans as much as Liverpool.

Living in Toxteth, I knew all about that. Everyone in Liverpool did. Does. Now, getting into the second decade after it happened, the players at Anfield still won't sit down and talk exclusively to that newspaper because they know the effect it would have on some of the club's fans. I know the paper is supposed to have apologized, and I remember hearing something recently when, in their paper, they were telling the people of Liverpool that it is time to move on. But with all due respect I think it's up to the families of the people who died, and the people of the city in general, to decide individually when it is time to move on. Souness, back in 1992, should have understood that.

To be fair to him, he wasn't a well man and his judgement must have been slightly clouded, but he had people around him who should have made it clear to him that it was professional insanity. I was just a kid when Hillsborough happened, just turned fourteen and even though I was training with Liverpool a couple of times a week, I wasn't part of the club then. But I could sense the pain around the place, and around the city, and I could feel the despair. It is hard to explain to someone who's not from Liverpool how much those terrible events hurt our city, and not just because of the tragic loss of life. There is still a lingering sense of injustice because of the way the people of Liverpool were somehow blamed for that tragedy, and no one was ever made to answer for the criminal neglect that killed so many innocent people. Yet all Scousers seem to get is that insulting shit about us being Self-pity City. It does seem almost incomprehensible that Souey didn't realize what he was bringing on himself.

It was pretty grim, because all the other papers were out for him after that, and the fans didn't understand it either. They questioned his judgement, and when the supporters start asking questions then everything is put under the microscope. There is a simple philosophy everyone connected to football understands: you'll be forgiven for virtually anything when you're winning. Lose, and you get away with nothing. Souey didn't win enough, for many different reasons, and that basically was behind all the other crap he had to deal with. But it is too easy to go along with the rewriting of history to assume that he did fuck all right at Anfield.

He was – is – a bloody good manager, and I still believe he

would have got things right eventually, when he had settled down properly with his own squad. He is an amazingly charismatic character, a man you can just sense has walked into a room even if you don't spot him, because he has this incredible presence about him. How much would fans at a lot of the clubs these days give for a manager like him who placed so much emphasis on young, talented British players? We've got to the stage where entire match squads are made up of foreign players, and who in their right mind can argue that that is good for English football?

When Souness was in trouble, he understood that the fans really want to see local talent coming through. He also knew that he had far more of a chance of getting a response from kids who had something to prove. The gaffer was clearly trying to push some younger lads into the team, and the likes of Macca, Rob Jones, Mike Marsh, Don Hutchison, Jamie Redknapp, Steve Harkness, David James, Phil Charnock, Dominic Matteo and – eventually – me, were all given a chance by him. All young British players that he brought through the ranks, or bought cheaply. Under pressure, he still managed to do the right thing for the club, and he left a decent legacy when Roy Evans took over. Five regular England internationals and two Scottish with eventually about 150 caps between them. Now that is a basis on which to build a team. Maybe he'd served a purpose too, because when you think about it, Liverpool Football Club could not have remained anchored in the past for ever, even if the template Bill Shankly set out worked so well for such a long time. Football changed dramatically in the early 1990s, and Liverpool had to adapt along with everyone else. Souey helped that process, even if he, the messenger, got shot.

His message to me on the Wednesday afternoon of 22 September 1993 was quite simple: 'Do it for me.' We were at the Royal Lancaster Hotel in London, and I was part of the travelling squad for the Coca-Cola Cup tie at Fulham. We'd just lost to Everton and the papers were full of the idea that changes had to be made to the team, so I was hopeful. I'd travelled with the squad before, Oldham and Norwich are two of the places I can recall, but I'd felt a million miles away from the first team. This time I thought I had an outside chance, although I wasn't really imagining that I would play.

Me dad had travelled down to London to stay with some of his cousins, just in case. He rang the night before to find out, but I'd been told nothing. Then, before we had tea around about five in the afternoon, Souey pulled me to one side and said I was in. Jesus, my heart nearly jumped out of my chest. It felt like I had one of those Aliens in there, trying to get out and eat the manager's face. I've already said I never get nervous, but make that one exception. I stood there watching the manager's lips move, but not really listening to what he was saying. I think he told me that I was playing for a reason which was obvious: I was good enough, so I had to go out there, be my normal self and I would score. But he could have been going on about *Coronation Street* not being the same since Albert Tatlock died, for all I was listening.

I was trying not to get nervous, and at the same time getting excited, wondering how I was going to tell me dad, and what it would be like. I can't really tell you what it was like, because I was almost in a trance, it all just flashed by me. I remember seeing me dad climbing the fence in the Liverpool end before kick-off, and putting his fist in the air to tell me to go out and do it. Then the game itself. I was standing there as we were about to kick off, looking around and thinking that it just couldn't be real, me lining up alongside some of these players. Ian Rush was in the side that night, and he is probably the greatest Liverpool striker of all time. Me and Ian Rush, up front together. Get out of here. It was unreal, and it was something that took a lot of getting used to in my early days at Anfield. Some of those guys who were my teammates – MY teammates – were unbelievable players, players that wrote chapters in the club's history. Men like John Barnes, Jan Molby, Steve Nicol, Ronnie Whelan and Bruce Grobbelaar, they were great, great players. They may not have got on with Souey, but you can't argue with what they did at Liverpool. Coming into a side like that was like the first time I ever got dragged into a lap dancing club (kicking and screaming obviously) . . . my eyes were popping out of my head!

Rushie scored early on, Nigel Clough got a second just before half time, and I had a hand in both of those goals. I came off at half time and the manager said that I had done well, been unselfish, and to keep it up. That was it. No going overboard, just calm advice. Rushie was talking to me throughout the game, telling me where to run, what to look for. They scored to make it 2–1 after the break, and it was a bit tense as we got into the final twenty minutes. I remember seeing Macca warming up on the touchline, and entering the final quarter of the game I assumed he must be getting ready to replace me.

When the ref stopped play, I almost trotted to the touchline, but the signal went out to Jamie Redknapp to come off, and I was still out there. That was another incredible thrill, playing well enough as a teenager that the manager didn't automatically substitute me. We got to the last ten minutes, and it was still close, and then, with seven minutes left, the moment arrived that will live with me for the rest of my life. My first goal for Liverpool. Don Hutchison was way out on the right, and sent in a deep cross. It was one of those balls that keepers hate that drift into the area between them and the strikers. The Fulham keeper stayed on his line, I ran in and met it perfectly on the half volley from the left-hand edge of the six-yard box, as good a strike as I could have prayed for on my debut. I knew it was in as soon as I hit it, and I didn't even know what to do. The Liverpool fans were in that corner, so I turned to them first, and then turned back to my teammates with a stupid big grin on my face. I think Rushie came up and grabbed me, and was laughing his head off. Macca must have been there before him, because every goal I ever scored, I swear he was always first to come and celebrate with me. God, what a moment, my head was a bag of clouds.

In the dressing room they were all congratulating me, telling me how well I'd done, but Ronnie Moran, he was brilliant. I always liked him. He could be quite tough and put you through it in training. But he had the right idea did Ronnie. This was a fella who had played for Liverpool in the fifties, then been brought in as a coach under Shanks. He had been part of just about every great Liverpool team there ever was, and he had coached the greatest players in the history of the club. So when Ronnie spoke, you listened. He had your respect even before he opened his mouth.

Some players who came in later, like Stan Collymore, I don't think they showed him the respect he deserved. He's probably forgotten more than Stan ever knew. He had this uncanny ability of keeping your feet on the ground, because he had seen it all, seen plenty of strikers come in and score goals on their debuts . . . and then disappear off the face of the earth. I came into the dressing room buzzing and barely able to take in what had happened, and he was really pleased, said I had done very, very well, but he said the job was to ensure it didn't go to my head.

He has a deep, gruff voice, Ronnie, and he doesn't speak loudly – so he was almost whispering when he talked to me – said that a good player would build on that start, would take it into the next game and show he could do it again. The trick was to be doing that in six months, and then six years. It wasn't negative because he was thrilled for me, just like the gaffer, but he wanted it to be the start. And I listened. I know people have a view of me that I'm some sort of cocky loudmouth, but that isn't me. I've always been one of the jokers in the dressing room, messing about and having a laugh, and why not, because hey, I'm playing football for a living. But people like Ronnie, Graeme Souness, Roy Evans who know the business, they have always had my total respect.

Ronnie Moran was a big influence on my career, because he helped me get a perspective on what happened to me in the early days, and helped me understand what I had to do to be a success, and more importantly, to stay there. I'm not saying that we always saw eye to eye, because he could be a hard man and he often chewed you out. There were times when we had different views, and times when he could be a right pain, but the thing with him was that he didn't bother about reputations. If you did something wrong, he told you, and you listened, because you knew he had been there before with the great players of the past. Ronnie always said getting there was the easy part compared to what came next. The hard bit was to stay there, and I understood exactly what he meant from that very first night at Fulham.

It was a hurricane. It was a force of nature that I had absolutely no control over. It was fucking mental. It is an incredible thing to become an 'overnight sensation' in the pop star era of professional football. I don't think even Sky realized what they were doing when they came up with their master-plan to sex up the sport. Everyone is used to it now, David and Victoria Beckham are the King and Queen of the tabloids and every half-decent footballer is a star and a pin-up, even if he's got a face like a bag of spanners. Score a few goals, shed a few tears, shag a few pop princesses, you're an A-list celeb.

There has been such a shift in football and popular culture over the past ten years, that now, from a distance of a decade away, it's probably hard to get a real grasp of what happened around that time when I first came onto the scene. In 1993, it was there for the first time, massive exposure because the Premier League was trying to get off the ground, and Sky was trying to flog its dishes on the back of football. They wanted to make big, big stars out of players, they wanted them to be soap stars, pop stars, film stars even. Attractive, controversial figures that would sell. And the rest of the media was happy to follow because they were smart enough to see where it was going.

I suppose I was perfect for all that, even if I'm not claiming to be an oil painting. A kid from Toxteth who had made the big time and didn't care. Or so it went. Ryan Giggs and Lee Sharpe had already got the treatment at Manchester United, Macca was starting to get it, and I was next up – one of the first, and I didn't have a clue what was going on. One minute, I was a kid cleaning the baths and throwing the bundles, going home to me mum's little terrace where me nan and grandad also lived. The next I was all over the papers and across the telly, the Toxteth Terror . . . which kind of said it all. I'm not saying I was a bigger star than anyone else, because Rushie, Kenny Dalglish, they will always be bigger football idols for the Liverpool fans. But it wasn't that kind of stardom, it was the sort of stuff where they wanted to know about your private life, where even an eighteen-year-old kid's first girlfriend or night out with an MP's daughter made the newspapers, and it was all so different that I don't think anyone understood it. Ronnie Moran certainly couldn't, or Souey for that matter, and definitely not me.

I've never been comfortable with the being recognized part of a footballer's life. I know that sounds daft, because with the exposure we all get it's inevitable. I'm not complaining, far from it, but like, I still don't enjoy going out shopping, because even now I don't deal with people looking at me. I can't do it sometimes, I can't go out. I don't know how to react when people stare, it's a very difficult experience for me. It's not that I'm precious or anything, it's purely that I don't know what to do, except look a bit stupid back. I hate it sometimes, and I've had it for twelve years. You get people talking to you that you've never met before in your life, and again, that can be quite hard because I'm not exactly a master in small talk – the finishing school in Toxteth wasn't all it was supposed to be.

I've had it all since I was eighteen, the obsessive interest in every aspect of my life, not just the footy, and it is the maddest thing ever. By now I'm more or less used to it, and I can handle most of it, although I still get a bit pissed off at times, especially when you get dragged into stuff in the papers that makes everything seem twenty times worse than it really is. Even recently that happened to me, with a couple of stories and snatched pictures of me having a beer taken on someone's mobile that basically made something out of nothing just because they were chasing footballers again after the accusations against the Newcastle players. It ain't even worth going into, and the thing is, not only can I handle it now, but me family are also a bit more used to it, so they know most of the stuff is bollocks. When you're a kid who knows nothing though, and everyone around you doesn't fully understand what is happening either, then you make mistakes . . . and those stick with you. I know there is an image of me that has stuck for most of my career, and it isn't flattering. I know plenty of people think I'm some thick, ignorant scally who doesn't give a fuck about anything. And I can understand why, as well, which ain't bad for a thick scally.

The media, especially the tabloids, don't deal in shades of grey. It's black or white, good or bad, and nothing in between. Early on with me, a couple of things happened and it was easy to portray me as the kid from the wrong side of the tracks, blahdy fucking blah. What's funny is that most people these days realize that the papers can distort things, and don't always give an accurate picture because it's their business to make everything sound as sensational as possible. And yet the public still take their view of 'celebrities' exclusively from the way they are portrayed in the media, even though they know it can't be accurate.

It's always the early impressions that stick, and I came across as a bit cocky early on, which was easy to put across as being arrogant. There was one thing in particular that I think fucked me up badly, and never really allowed me to escape that early image. It was an interview I did in a lad's magazine with Macca, which was probably a mistake in itself but, again, in the mid nineties, those sort of mags were new as well, and we didn't know the way that they would eventually come across.

Anyway, this bloke was interviewing the pair of us, and he said he needed to go to the bog. He'd done this questionnaire for us, and left it with us to have a look at while he went off. So the two of us, we were reading out the questions, and giving some joke answers, you know the sort of stuff that a couple of young lads will amuse themselves with in private. Likes: birds with big tits. Dislikes: Gary fucking Neville. That sort of stuff. Juvenile, but only messing about between ourselves. The fella came back, asked us the questions, and we gave him the proper answers, the sensible stuff. Only problem was, the fucker had left a tape running, which we didn't know about, and when we left he played it all back and then printed it. Not the proper answers, but us pissing about in private.

Of course, there was a major fucking stink, with people saying we were a disgrace, and it showed the total lack of respect for our positions we had, and how ill-educated we were, how arrogant, how rude, how typical. One bloke even wrote that we should be sacked. I got hammered over that, with the gaffer pulling me in and giving me a major bollocking. That was one of the first major interviews I gave, and I was pictured as some crude, boorish thug, because of course the journalist never admitted in the piece that he had done us over.

And I don't think I ever recovered from that, especially when all those rumours about the drugs started to fly around. Now, I wouldn't make that mistake, because like everyone else I've seen how it's all developed. Players now have publicists, media experts, super-agents, gofers, all that sort of stuff. The kids that come into the game, they have grown up with it, and they know what to expect, because it's been out there for ten years now. When it's new though, it's a different story. I admit, I couldn't get my head around it.

God, the exposure I got was frightening. I remember before the FA Cup final in 1996, after only my second full season, we were playing Manchester United, and they had players like Giggs, Sharpe and Cantona in their side, as well as some of the kids like Beckham and Scholes coming through. But I was the one who seemed to get all the attention.

It sounds crazy now, but the *Daily Mirror* in the week of the final ran three days of news features on my life and times. Not on the sports pages, you understand, but in the front of the paper, like I was a member of Take That. There was hardly anything to say, of course, because as far as I was concerned, I hadn't done anything yet. I was still twenty-one and living at home, and I'd been on holiday three times in my life ... once in a caravan in a field in Wales. Yet there it was, stuff about the two girls I think I'd kissed by then, and stuff about me mum and dad splitting up, which was a bit painful. We were staying at a hotel in London, and the press who covered Liverpool were staying there as well.

The guy from the *Mirror* who reported on the football on Merseyside at that time was a decent bloke called Richard Tanner, who I knew quite well, and who was quite honest about the whole business he was involved in. He always used to joke that he had a tin hat in his car for when he came to Melwood, and had to talk his way out of the latest crap his paper had dropped him into. I grabbed him in the lobby of the hotel towards the end of the week, and took him into this little room at the side of reception. Basically, I asked him what the fuck was going on, and why his paper was doing all this stuff about me. I was honestly puzzled why they were so interested in my private life, and pretty angry about it because I couldn't understand why they were doing it.

His reply sticks in my mind to this day. 'Robbie, I won't lie to you, there's nothing I can do about it. It's the price on the ticket, mate,' he said. We had a chat for a while, and he said he could make a few excuses and pretend to try and get his paper to back off, but there was no chance because footballers had made the crossover into pop stars, and they wanted everything they could get on me. At that time, from what he told me, I was regarded as the biggest story in football. Bigger than Beckham, who didn't make his name until the next season when he scored from the halfway line against Wimbledon; bigger than Giggsy or Gazza, who'd had their turn in the tumbler. Even then, I didn't get my head around it. How could I be a bigger story than Eric Cantona, when I was just a kid who lived with his mum and went down the benches with his mates?

Funny thing is, Tanner moved from the *Mirror* and Merseyside and now covers Manchester for the *Express*, so I see him around a lot these days. I bumped into him just after Wayne Rooney went back to Everton with Manchester United for the first time, and we were laughing about the coverage on the telly. The commentator was going on about how the reception he got must be the worst ever, how intimidating it was and how awful it must be for the poor lad. Fuck me, that was schoolboy names compared to what I used to get from the Everton fans. There were some wicked barbs about drugs and stuff that I'll bet even David Beckham – or his missis – hasn't heard.

Tanner was saying that it was funny because Rooney was experiencing what I used to get all the time. As he remembered it there was actually even more hype around me when I first got into the Liverpool team. It's odd how time changes everything, but for a while it really did go crazy around me. Maybe people – especially the younger fans – will look at the stage in my career when I guess you get called a veteran, and find it hard to believe that I was the subject of all that hype and interest. He couldn't have been bigger than Rooney, could he? But it happened and I don't suppose I was equipped to deal with it.

What I was equipped to do was score goals. From the very start I found it easy, and I'm not being big-headed about it. I'd always scored goals since I first kicked a ball, apart from when I had a couple of games on the left wing in my early teens. When I first started training with the big boys at Melwood, I had a bit of a panic that I wouldn't be able to do it at the top level because it all seemed so frighteningly quick, but as soon as I got into the first team that went away, because right from that very first game at Fulham I scored, and made a proper contribution.

We stayed down in London after that game, because we had a game at Chelsea at the weekend, and I was on the team sheet again, for my first Premiership start and against one of the big clubs. A proper game. I was excited but the gaffer told me I had already shown I could do it, and there was no need to think I had to prove myself so just go out and play like I always had been doing. We lost 1–0, but I did okay, and I had a shot cleared off the line. Next up was Arsenal, and again I did okay, we got a draw and there was suddenly a lot of interest in me because it was my debut at Anfield for the first team. It was such a great moment for me, because my whole family was there, me dad, me uncles, Mr Lynch, me mates, and I don't even know how I got my hands on all the tickets I had needed. I think I must have polished up my scrounging routine from the Bankhouse pub all those years ago. I hadn't scored, but I'd done well against two of the biggest clubs in the league, and it looked like I was on my way. I was eighteen years and five months, and I had acquitted myself well, without setting the world alight. What happened next, though, got those fires raging.

Tuesday 5 October 1993 was the night I made a little bit of Liverpool history. It was the return leg of the Coca-Cola Cup tie with Fulham and, by now, I was confident enough to believe that my name would be on the team sheet. Souey played just about his strongest team as it happened, and we gave them a right stuffing. And I scored five. It was one of the greatest nights of my life, and the sort of thing you can't even dream of. It was my fourth game for Liverpool, and I almost scored a double hat-trick in front of the Kop.

In fact, I should have done, because I had a chance at the end which the keeper saved. It was only the fourth time in history that anyone had scored five goals for Liverpool, the last being Rushie ten years earlier. I didn't do anything spectacular, just got in the box and got a couple of tap-ins after the keeper parried shots, got on the end of a couple of crosses and ran on to a through ball from Cloughie for the fifth. There was only a small crowd at Anfield that night, but for me they were singing my name so loudly I thought it would make my ears burst.

All the way through the game Rushie was urging me on, telling me how well I was doing and that I could get more. He was talking me through everything again, and he was showing where I should make the runs, even though I was probably taking up his space all the time. At the end he was the first to congratulate me, and he was really proud of what I'd done. The boss was the same, and even Ronnie Moran was thrilled ... but he still managed to point out that I should have had a sixth, because the chance I'd missed at the end was an easy one that I should have taken with my eyes shut! That was Ronnie all over. He knew it was an important moment for me and for the club, and he knew that the first job was to get me back down to earth quickly, because we had another game in four days' time. But he was thrilled all the same.

My life changed that night, but not immediately. People have asked me since how I celebrated such an incredible achievement. With champagne? With a night out in a swanky Liverpool night club? Actually, I went straight home to me mum's and then went down the chippy for my usual order of special fried rice with barbecue sauce, and a can of Irn Bru. Then I was back home, watching the highlights on the telly, talking me mum through it all, and I think Calvey called round with some chips and gravy of his own. If I had any feelings about that night, then most of all I was happy for me mum, because without her I would have been lost in the early days.

She was always there doing absolutely everything for me, the only thing she didn't do was get me dressed in the morning. She even used to pack for me when I went off with the team for an away game. I knew she was proud of me, and so were the rest of the family, even if they were still all Everton fans, and that meant a lot to me when I got into the first team. I remember me Uncle Alan, who sadly died of cancer, being so thrilled that I had scored those goals, but so gutted that Liverpool had won. It was like that for all of them. Even now, the whole family – all my cousins and nephews and nieces – are Everton fans. The only ones who aren't are Lisa, Anthony and Scott, for obvious reasons. And me dad of course. You can imagine what it's like though, coming from a massive Toxteth family, and having one of you playing for Liverpool and making an impact like that. It was a great feeling, I can tell you.

Next game up was Oldham, and I scored again, a bit of a miss-hit actually, but I must be the only person on earth who will remember that now. After that, I didn't look back. I scored a hat-trick against Southampton in only my fifth Premiership game, I scored a good goal against Villa which was live on BSkyB and got me noticed even more, I scored two against Spurs at White Hart Lane, and I was part of the team that was 3–0 down to Manchester United at Anfield, but somehow fought back to draw 3–3, with two goals from Cloughie and an equalizer from Neil Ruddock. That was some night too, an incredible game to play in when you're an eighteen-year-old kid.

The fans were baying for blood because it was United, and as each goal went in it got louder and louder, until the hairs were standing up on the back of my neck, never mind theirs. When Razor scored at the end, the roof came off. Seagulls died. It was a quite incredible time. Souey had asked the press not to bother me, but I think I was getting about 100 requests a week to do things, and I was being mobbed everywhere I went. Before, when I went in and out of Melwood, the only people who bothered me were the gate-men, who were still checking who I was. Now, I couldn't get out of the fucking place. I was stuck there signing autographs all afternoon. Not that I minded – I loved it. The autographs I gave then I spelt out my name properly so you could see exactly who it was, and it took ages! It was a weird time though, because all this incredible stuff was happening to me, while the manager was still getting crucified.

What strikes me when I look back on those few months when I broke into the team was that we hardly lost. I made my debut in the middle of September and Souness decided that he'd had enough at the end of January. In those four and a half months, we only lost four matches, and one of those was on penalties to Wimbledon in the Coca-Cola Cup. Another was an away trip to St James's Park, and losing there is never a disgrace, no matter who you are.

The Chelsea defeat in my first Premiership match was hardly a nightmare either, because we lost by a single goal, and we did enough to win it. So that only left what was probably a bad defeat at Sheffield Wednesday where the finger could be pointed at Souness, because he'd dropped Rushie and I think that backfired on him badly. But he also played young lads like me, Harky, Rob Jones and Dom Matteo in that game, with Jamie Redknapp and Macca also regulars at that time, so it was a pretty young, promising team. We beat City at Anfield towards the end of January to go fifth in the table, and we weren't a million miles off the top, despite the nightmare at the start of the season, when we'd lost five out of six league matches. But we'd drawn at Bristol City in the FA Cup in the midweek before the City game, and that proved to be a disastrous match all round.

The knives were really being sharpened for Souey then, and I think he was beginning to believe there was no way out. Whatever he did, the media were having none of it. What made matters worse, I think, was that I broke me leg in the game at Bristol City. We had played there two weeks earlier, but their floodlights failed towards the end of the match, so we had to replay it, and that was to prove pretty bad luck for me . . . and may even have had a far-reaching effect on my career. Rushie had given us a lead, and with about twenty minutes to go I went into a challenge with a defender, and got a bit of a kick on me ankle. I didn't think it was anything, but as I tried to carry on the pain got worse and worse, and in the end I had to come off.

They scored almost as soon as I left the pitch, probably because of the disruption of the injury. I was strapped up, but the next day I couldn't walk and I went off to hospital for some X-rays. They showed that I had broken the bottom of my leg, just above the ankle, and that was me done for nearly two months. In the long run, I have had so many problems with ankle injuries, and I do wonder if they can be related in any way to that break back when I was eighteen, because the doctors said that it severely weakened the joint around the ankle. I was gutted because I was in the form of my life. I had scored fifteen goals in my first twenty-two matches for Liverpool and I felt that every single time I went out onto the pitch I would score. Calvey always says that in the early days, if he wasn't at the match he would flick up the Ceefax, not to see if I had scored, but to see how many I had scored. It was the first major injury of my career, and it couldn't have come at a worse time.

That draw in Bristol told Souey a lot about the problems that he had been battling against with the team. He reckoned he hadn't got the backing of the senior players he inherited, and I think he also believed that he didn't even have the backing of some of the players he brought in. Most of all, I think he was just sick of everything, of the massive stick he was getting and the pressure he was under. Because of my broken leg, I wasn't available for the replay at Anfield a week later, but we lost 1–0, and watching from the stands it wasn't the best effort from the lads.

Souness said later that he happened to have a room in the hotel next to the suite where the Bristol City side held their team meeting before going up to Anfield for the match. That was lucky, and a coincidence, obviously, that he could hear every word of what was being said. Apparently, their manager said we were a sack of shite, and if they got stuck into us we'd wave the white flag, which is basically what happened. That sickened the gaffer, and two days later he went to see the chairman and resigned, even though they tried to persuade him to stay on. He said later that experience of hearing a second-division side laugh about his players was enough to make his mind up to go, but I've always felt it went much deeper than that. The politics around Liverpool were bad at that time, and I've heard a few stories that he wanted to sign players and had them vetoed by the board.

One thing you have to know about Souness is that if anyone tried to stop him doing things his way then he wouldn't stand for it. There definitely seemed a bit of that in his decision to leave, and I know that Roy Evans suffered similar problems later on, so it wouldn't surprise me. It really did surprise me that he threw the towel in though, because he is no quitter. When I heard, I was gutted. Truly gutted.

It was like the bottom falling out of my world. I was eighteen, I'd played just over twenty games and now the man who had placed all that faith in me was off. And to cap it all, I'd broke me fucking leg! In those circumstances, you're thinking, If only. If only I hadn't got the injury, then I might have been able to change things against Bristol City. If only that cup tie hadn't been abandoned, we probably would have won it there and then.

For the first time in my career I experienced real despair because I was thinking that I'd have to start all over again. A new man would mean he was bound to sign a new striker, because even if he was going to give me a chance, I was injured and he'd need cover . . . so what would happen to me? It lasted about five minutes of course, because Roy Evans was promoted to the position of manager, and everyone breathed a sigh of relief. It's funny, because losing a manager is a momentous thing, it changes everyone's life, but most people at a club give it about thirty seconds' thought, and then start talking about the racing again. When Kenny Dalglish resigned I was still fifteen, barely turned a trainee, and I hardly knew what it meant, even though it was a sad day because he was such a great fella.

It was weird for a few days, and then everyone acted as if nothing had happened. It was the same with Souey. He was a great bloke and I had a lot of respect for him, so I was upset. But then life goes on, you're in the next day and everyone has forgotten all about him, apart from the ones who are celebrating! It probably helped that it was Roy who replaced Souness. I don't think there was one dissenting voice in the dressing room, because everyone recognized that he knew his football, he was a decent bloke and he had the right sort of ideas. Like Ronnie Moran, I'd always held a lot of respect for Roy Evans, always looked up to him, and listened when he spoke because he'd managed half of the greats that had been through Anfield and played in the same team as the rest. It's a surprise to me that Roy was out of football for so long after he finally left Liverpool, because what he doesn't know about the game isn't worth bothering about. He was the perfect choice by the board, and it was the start of a new era. For Liverpool, for Roy Evans, and for me.

GOD (6)

When I got established in the Liverpool team, the players there called me God. Then the fans did. How mental is that? I know this sounds crazy, but not so long ago I was interviewed by a television programme that was examining the role of religion in football. They asked me, was I God?! Not any more, mate, that's for certain. But back then, during my first incredible four years at Anfield, there were times when things got so out of hand it seemed like some of the supporters really did think I was their God. Or their saviour, anyway. When Roy Evans came in, he had a bit of a nightmare to start with. I was out for seven games and we won only two of them, got stuffed out of sight at Southampton and Blackburn as well. The gaffer – which is what Roy was instantly called – had said that he wouldn't have put me in when Souey did because he thought it was too early.

Six months on, I returned from injury, the doc looked at me, I trained for a couple of days, scored in a reserve match ... and straight away I was playing against Everton at Anfield. So much for easing me in gently. To be fair to him, Roy admitted he was wrong to have questioned Souey's judgement, and I think he only ever left me out three times in his whole time as manager. All that stuff later about the Spice Boys, I remember vividly that Roy was asked whether I'd let him down ever. He said he only wished that he could have had eleven Robbie Fowlers in his team, because then he would never have lost.

I made my comeback on 13 March 1994, my twenty-fifth appearance for Liverpool in my first season. And I scored one of the most memorable goals of my career. The defeat at Goodison in September had prompted Souness to put me in the side, and the return against them persuaded Roy to put me back in. It was live on BSkyB and the ground was full, which was not always the case that season, as surprising as that may sound now. Funnily enough, one of the things I remember most about the game against Fulham at Anfield when I scored the five goals, was that there were only about 12,000 spectators in the ground. Imagine that at Anfield, it was virtually empty ... I'd played in matches there for the Schoolboys team that had more people watching. This was Everton though, and it was full, and we owed them one after the embarrassing defeat early in the season.

The manager had initially struggled and was desperate for a win over them to get something out of the season. I was equally desperate for obvious reasons – it was my first ever derby. The only disappointment was that Granty wasn't playing. He'd made the bench that season for them, but didn't break through for another year. But they still had some great players – Dave Watson and Neville Southall in particular, who I'd watched when I was a kid and idolized them. Big Nev was one of the greatest keepers I'd ever seen ... and I scored against him. We had gone one up when Rushie scored, but Watson equalized immediately and it became one of those ferocious derbies with tackles flying everywhere. Then, just before half time, John Barnes flashed a pass in behind their defence and I outpaced Big Dave to the left-hand edge of the box. As Southall came out, I clipped the ball across him into the far corner and it hit the inside of the post and went in. Fucking hell. Again, I didn't know how to celebrate. I was gonna have to work on that. I sort of had this two-fisted thing, just looking around with a big stupid grin on me face. It was the winner in that match, and I think that cemented my place in the hearts of the Liverpool fans.

It was an incredible moment for me, because my whole family was there watching and I'd scored against Everton. I'd scored against Everton! God, half of them have never forgiven me. I know the Everton fans haven't, because from then on I seemed to make a habit of scoring against them. It all started that day, real worship from the Liverpool fans and hatred from the opposition. It wasn't just the Everton punters who despised me either. Manchester United fans have always, always hated me, and I used to wind them up along the way. Still do really. But then, I suppose anyone who has played for Liverpool, Leeds and Manchester City would.

It's a funny thing, the hatred you get from the terraces. There are thousands and thousands of people screaming abuse at you till they're scarlet in the face, getting so mad they can barely get their words out. They're shouting they're gonna fucking kill you, they're gonna rip your head off and shit in the hole, they're gonna string you up from the roof of the stand. Thousands of them do it at exactly the same time, frothing at the mouth they're that wound up. And they're three feet away behind a knee-high wooden hoarding. You need a sense of humour sometimes, believe me.

You need proper advice, too. I count myself incredibly lucky that I had such good people around me to show me the way to become a proper footballer. Roy Evans once said that there was nothing the staff could teach me, because it was all instinctive. But there was plenty he taught me, and Ronnie Moran, and Dougie Livermore, and Steve Heighway and Sammy Lee. And Graeme Souness of course. They kept my feet on the ground and told me every single day in my first few years that it wasn't just about me, it was about working for the team, putting the success of the team above all else. Some of the kids these days, they could do with Ronnie Moran around to help them understand that. Ronnie once said something that stuck with me. He reckoned that the kids coming through the academies these days, they're coached from so young all the ball skills, the juggling skills and that, they have all the attributes, especially pace, but they're not taught how to play football.

We did five-a-side all the time, and the staff would be saying we had to pass and move, pass the ball around, play as a unit. Think as a team. Every one of the coaching staff had that creed, which had been laid down by Bill Shankly, and it's never changed in football, no matter what else is different in the modern era. Look at the top teams, Arsenal, Chelsea, Manchester United. They're full of stars, but they have to fit in with the team – there's no space for the cocky, selfish individual. It's all about the team, and passing swiftly to the man in the best position. Ronnie Moran taught me that. And Ian Rush.

Of all the good fortune I've had over my life, I was probably luckiest to have come under Rushie's wing when I first arrived at Anfield. He was so good to me, and I'll always be grateful for that. He didn't need to be. He is a legend, probably the greatest striker Liverpool have ever had, and for me, he's right up there with Alan Shearer as the best I've ever seen. I've captained my club, my country, scored in Cup finals, lifted trophies and I've now become the third-highest scorer in Premiership history. I've made plenty of mistakes too, but it could have been a lot worse. If it wasn't for the help and advice in those early years at Anfield, I could never have dreamt of having that sort of career.

Ian Rush, or Tosh as he's known, is a good friend now, and he said he simply took a shine to me. When you're an old pro, who's done everything in the game and earned the status of a legend, which is what Rushie was, then you don't have to go out of your way to educate a snotty-nosed kid like I was when I first started at Melwood. But he always had time for me, and when he spoke to me it was always worth listening to. I'd like to say he divulged the great secrets of the striking arts, like a magician passing on his tricks to an apprentice, but – even if this is going to disappoint a lot of people – there are no real mysteries.

I remember Macca came up to me one day at training, and he asked me exactly how I managed to hit the ball so cleanly, strike it so well. He used to be out there for hours, and then I'd come along and smash it into the corner of the net with no back-lift. It did his head in. Anyway, he asked me, and he was waiting expectantly, looking for some secret, and I paused, waited, then whispered . . . 'I dunno.' When I hit a ball, I don't think about how I do it. When I find the very corner of the net, I don't know how I do it. I just do it. I'm always being asked how I score goals, and I honestly don't know the answer.

What Rushie did was help me with the little things, about bending the run to stay onside, about hitting across the keeper from the angle, so even if he gets a hand on it he'll push it back out. Even those things, though, aren't hard-and-fast rules, as Peter Schmeichel will tell you when he went for the one across him in the Cantona comeback game, and I smashed it in at his near post. Tosh talked about timing the runs, about saving energy and about working for the team. The strikers had to work hard to close down, and he was the master of that. He told me some of the defenders' tricks and how to handle them, and he talked to me occasionally about the responsibilities I had as a Liverpool player.

It was always a big Anfield tradition that the senior players would look out for the young lads, and instil the values of the club in them. They were winners, and the kids learnt from them how to be winners themselves. That's what happened with Rushie. He showed me by example, because not only was he one of the greatest goal scorers ever, but he was also a very good professional. What I did, from the first day I started training with Liverpool, was watch him. I never took my eyes off him. A lot of the things I do even now, they're pure Rushie, because watching him was a lesson. Playing alongside him, getting encouragement from him and benefiting from his advice was the best education I could ever have had.

We played together quite a few times during that 1993–94 season, about thirty games in total, and we got thirty-seven goals between us. I got eighteen goals in my first season, from thirty-three games. He beat me by one, but between us it was a hell of a record. People suggested that maybe we were a bit similar, that we couldn't play together, that we made the same runs and got in each other's way, but those thoughts didn't last too long. By the end of my first season, even though I didn't score that many goals after I came back from the injury, we had formed a deadly partnership.

I had just turned nineteen, I was earning £500 a week after being given a pay rise soon after I got into the first team, and I had formed one of the highest scoring partnerships in the Premiership with one of the legends of the game. What made it even better was that I had arrived in a fantastic dressing room with so many players that I could learn from. Tosh was the obvious one, but there was also John Barnes, who was such a talented footballer, and a dedicated one too. Barnsie liked a bit of a moan, and sometimes he used to dwell too much on the tactics and the strengths of the opposition when he should have left that to the coaches, but what a player. I know he didn't get on with Souness, and I know that when Souey arrived at Anfield as manager he felt Barnsie was past his peak, but I don't think so. I don't think I've ever seen a more talented player in training. There were things he could do that you used to stand and applaud. Sometimes, his presence alone would win matches for Liverpool, because he could dominate the opposition. He never gave the ball away, and in training he could do absolutely anything.

When I was a kid first going up to Melwood, I'd sometimes hang around watching the first team doing their stuff, playing the five-a-sides, and I was transfixed by him. Later on, just before he left, he maybe went a bit far in training sometimes, questioning what the coaches were doing, but he wasn't the problem that some have made out. I've read some things with people claiming that he used to run training under Roy Evans, and if he didn't like it he'd just walk off, but that's simply not true. As he got older he obviously got stronger opinions and he wasn't afraid to air them, but that's what had always happened at Liverpool – the senior players were given responsibility, and their opinions mattered. It was expected that they showed leadership, out on the pitch and also to the young lads on the training ground in the week. When I came through, that's what happened, and I'm grateful for that. There were others like Steve Nicol, Ronnie Whelan, Jan Molby, and later, Steve Staunton when he came back to Anfield under Roy, and they were all an influence on me. All characters, all winners.

Steve Nicol was a scream, and I must admit I always got the impression he didn't like me. Never said anything to me, but didn't like me. There were legendary stories of him being tricked by the old Liverpool players because he was supposed to be a bit slow, and he was a right character. When I got into the side, I used to take the piss out of him like everyone else, and I don't think he took too kindly to that, some bit of a kid ripping him when he had played all those games and won all those things for the club. He was an easy target though. I remember when we went on a tour of South Africa after the end of my first season in 1994, we played against Aston Villa, then a team from Cape Town, and finally the Kaizer Chiefs, who are probably a better band than they were a football team. It was a bit of a money-maker and a blow-out for the lads before they went off for the summer, because none of us were involved in the World Cup that year.

You can imagine, end of season, summer off, in South Africa, everyone had a bit of a blast. The lads used to go out and get bladdered at night, but the kids in the squad – me, Dom Matteo, Phil Charnock and Lee Jones – we didn't bother because we were so young. I had only just turned nineteen, and used to watch from the sidelines while they went for it. Anyway, the gaffer said we could all have a drink after one game, but then we had to get serious with training the next day, so no booze. The next morning, Roy Evans came down to breakfast, and saw Steve Nicol there with about eight massive beers all around his table as he tucked into his bacon and eggs. The boss went ballistic, and started shouting that he'd told everyone they could have a drink the night before, but in the morning the serious stuff had to start. So Steve turns round, fairly cabbaged, looks the boss in the eye, and says, 'But gaffer, this is still from the night before.' Even Roy saw the funny side.

There was another night, we were staying in these lodges in the countryside, and when it got dark it was pitch black. Me and Dom were out for a stroll, and suddenly we saw one of the lights come on in the distance. We sneaked up, and there was Steve Nicol, wandering around his room bladdered, playing human pinball. He hadn't realized his curtains were still open and he had a massive floor-to-ceiling window and so everyone could see what he was doing. He shoved his hand in his pocket, grabbed all his money out and then spent about ten minutes looking for a place to hide it. Eventually, he stuffed it under the mattress and crashed out. Under his mattress! We were pissing ourselves and egging each other on to break into his room and nick the money, but eventually bottled it.

Bruce Grobbelaar was on that tour to South Africa, and you can imagine how much he was in his element. He was always telling us all these stories of the fellas he shot in the bush, and he was surrounded by all these shady characters who were wandering around the hotel. He could be pretty fearsome, and don't forget he'd had that bust-up with Macca on the pitch in the Charity Shield, but he was another one who was an incredible character, and he was great with me. I got on well with him and enjoyed being around him so much.

People keep asking me now about those games that he was supposed to have thrown, because I played in a couple of them. One was at Newcastle in November 1993. It was the *Sun* again who did him, and they taped him saying that he had thrown a couple of goals in during that match, which we lost 3–0. It's true he was shit in that game, but then we all were, one of the worst performances of the season as I remember, and I honestly don't think that he let any goals in deliberately that day. The same happened against Manchester United a couple of months later at Anfield. We drew 3–3, and they went 3–0 up early on, but if he was supposed to have chucked the game, why did he make a great save late on to stop them from snatching it after we had drawn level?

There was one other match he was supposed to have fixed, at Norwich, but I was injured for that and didn't travel, so I don't know. What I do remember is that the senior lads used to play cards on the coach travelling to matches, and sometimes they could get up to reasonable stakes. If they lost a big one, then it was usually a cheque written out to the winner, but if

Brucie settled his debts he would sometimes pull out an envelope shoved full of these crisp, brand-new notes. To a kid like me on £500 a week, that was a massive eye-opener. But we knew that was him being a bit flash.

The fact remains though that Bruce was a winner, he competed for everything and it just doesn't fit in with his character to do anything like that. He said that he took the money as a sting to prove that the bloke giving it to him was corrupt, and if you think of it logically that seems to fit in more with his performances in the matches he was supposed to have thrown when he actually played a blinder. The gaffer knew him well because he'd had Bruce in the reserves way back in the early eighties, and had worked with him for about twelve years, and he swears blind that he wasn't the sort of bloke who could chuck a match.

That trip to South Africa was memorable for one other reason. I met Nelson Mandela. He came to the match at Ellis Park against the Cape Town Spurs and we all lined up to speak with him. He even wore a Liverpool shirt, bless him. There I was, a nineteen-year-old on his first big tour with a top English club, just off the streets of Toxteth and meeting Nelson Mandela, who hadn't been out of prison long. I know that everyone seems to have met him, and he must be bloody sick of lining up having his picture taken with every two-bit celebrity from just about every country around the world, but God it was a real thrill for me. Even me dad was impressed. The thing I remember too was how cool he seemed, he didn't have any bitterness or anger or regret, even though it must have been incredibly raw for him. He came across to have a word with me, and it was then I discovered that he is a bit mutton – he had these great big hearing aids in his ears, and they were whistling so loud they were playing a tune. It wasn't exactly a sparkling exchange either.

When I was at Liverpool, Macca took the piss out of me once by calling me Lester Piggott because I talk fairly quiet and mumble a bit . . . and also because I've always had problems with my sinuses, so I'm a bit nasal. With Nelson Mandela being a little deaf, he mumbled a fair bit too, so we had this conversation where neither of us knew what the other was saying, just nodding heads and exchanging these massive big grins. But what a fella. He came onto the pitch before the game and had his picture taken with the lads with a huge South African flag, which has pride of place in the trophy room. I swear, I was a teenager from Toxteth who knew fuck all about politics, but I could see what an incredibly impressive person he was, and it was his humility more than anything else that came across. Mind you, I did joke with him that Robben Island was a picnic compared to chucking-out time in Toxteth.

When I look back at what happened in my first four years at Anfield, it's hard even for me to take in what I achieved, and how incredible it all was. I don't think any kid has ever had quite that start to Premiership, not Wayne Rooney or Michael Owen. Even Alan Shearer didn't make that much of an impact as a youngster. In my first four seasons, or three and a half really because of the injuries, I scored 120 goals. In those four years, I went from being a quiet kid who knew nothing to being a football idol who seemed to be known around the world. I also went from being skint to being, well, a millionaire I suppose, at least on paper. And it kept getting better and better. If my first season was pretty good for a teenager, then my second one was fucking incredible. You don't think about it at the time, you get on the rollercoaster and ride. There were all these legends around me, and for them it was just another day's work, so I was hardly going to strut around and blast off to everyone about how great I was and how monumental it all was.

Yet when I look back now, I can see that it was virtually unprecedented. In my first season, the highlights after the five against Fulham were the goal against Everton and a hat-trick against Southampton when the Kop was chanting my name for the whole of the second half. But I'd had a quiet second half of the season when I came back from the injury, and Liverpool finished in their lowest position in the league for thirty years, way down in eighth place. I was away in the clouds because I was playing for Liverpool in the Premiership, but when I think back we were shit really. Souey had got rid of all the senior players who had won so much, and he bought indifferently to replace them. Bought some brilliant players too, but a lot of rubbish that shouldn't have been playing for Liverpool Football Club. Which made it pretty tough for Roy. We had a fucking rotten pre-season as well, getting stuffed at Bolton and hardly winning a match. I didn't score in any of them either, until the final one just before the 1994–95 season got under way, and we played in Berlin against Hertha. I scored a hat-trick, one of them a peach of a goal, and suddenly we were all lifted for the season, thinking it would be much better than we had dared hope when we were beaten out of sight by Bolton.

We began by beating Crystal Palace 6–1 at their place. I was up front with Rushie, and both Nigel Clough and Lee Jones were completely out of the picture, so I knew I would be getting a game. In fact, I got fifty-seven that season, a 100 per cent record that only Jamo (David James) matched. And I scored against Palace, which helped my confidence. Then we met Arsenal. It's funny, there are some sides in your career who you always enjoy playing against, and Arsenal were mine, along with Aston Villa. I always scored against both of them, and always played very well. I don't know why, because Arsenal were a great team with probably the best defence in the country, but I always fancied my chances against them. I always seemed to be up against Martin Keown, who took everything so seriously and got himself massively psyched up against me. Then I would take the piss and put one through his legs or something, just to make him a little bit more angry. They came to Anfield on the second Sunday of the season, in front of the Sky cameras. By then, I'd got a reputation, and a lot of the focus was on my partnership with Rushie. They did this montage on my goals before the kick-off, and said Arsenal had to watch me carefully. Clearly, they couldn't have been taking notice.

You go into some games knowing that you'll score goals, knowing that everything is right and your head is spot on. That's the feeling a striker needs, and I seemed to get it nearly every week in the early days. I don't know what it was, just a sense of things being right. It was a tense, tight game against one of the title favourites, then on twenty-six minutes Jamie Redknapp floated one into the box, Tosh got above Martin Keown – funny, because he was doing his nut about being beaten in the air by Rushie – and when it fell, I lashed it into the corner of the net. Three minutes later, Macca rolled one across to me, I beat Keown – again! – and put it right into the far corner through Lee Dixon's legs. Even I was impressed with that one. The whole place was in uproar. To score two goals against the best defence in the league so quickly. But barely two minutes later, Barnsie sent me through and after the obligatory beating of Martin, the shot was saved by David Seaman, but I was the only one left standing and I put it into the empty net from a tight angle. A hat-trick in four minutes and thirty-three seconds, the fastest in Liverpool history, in Premiership history, and the quickest since the war. All that against the legendary Arsenal back four. When we had kicked off the game, I'd had a bit of a laugh with Ian Wright, who had had some new tattoos done. Every time I scored, we went back to the centre circle, and I asked to have a look. After the third goal, we were at the kick-off again, and he came up to me and said that he was gonna get a bandage and cover them up because they were inspiring me too much.

That was a cause for celebration, so it was off down the chippy again that night, with some ribs thrown in as well as the special fried rice, and back to me mum's with the lads. The thing was, with Sky there and them still trying to pump their coverage for all it was worth to get more viewers, my perform-ance was a gift to them. What they wanted were images to hang their coverage on, and idols to sell dishes. I was a goal scorer and I was young, and that season I was hot. So I got the full treatment. I was everywhere, the goals shown over and over again, the papers full of pictures of me, everyone wanting to know about me, and I guess that hat-trick cemented me in the public eye.

It was then that the God nickname began to stick. My life had already changed, but it gathered pace after that. It's not something you think about too much, but everyone wanted a piece of me. One morning, I came down to breakfast and my face was on the back of the cornflakes box. Weird. Villa were up soon after the Arsenal game, and so there were more goals guaranteed – two more, left-foot shots from the edge of the box that flew in – goals against Southampton, Burnley, Blackburn, Wimbledon, Ipswich – two in three minutes – Spurs and Chelsea – two in a minute! All by the end of November.

Over Christmas, we won all four of our matches in six days, and I got a goal in each one of them to take us into third in the table. We beat Arsenal again, this time in the quarter final of the Coca-Cola Cup, and we beat them at Highbury too, where I scored the only goal in the last minute of the game. We also stuffed Manchester United at Anfield and got through to the quarter final of the FA Cup. After all the trouble during Souey's reign, everyone was getting excited again about Liverpool. Roy Evans was from the boot-room, and a decent, media-friendly guy. More importantly, he had assembled a young team that was scoring goals galore, and was really exciting to watch. It was the year when Rob Jones, Macca, John Scales, and Neil Ruddock were all called up for the England squad, followed a year later by Jamie Redknapp and me, to go with the established internationals we already had. Everyone was saying that this was the return of the real Liverpool, and it was all being led by my goals. You can imagine how the TV lapped all that up, and wound up this incredible hype.

In the semi final of the Coca-Cola Cup, we played Palace again. After mullering them at their place in the league, we were pretty confident, but the first leg at Anfield turned into one of those games. They had wised up after struggling early in the season, and were much stronger at the back. It was an awful game, we had a few chances but couldn't get the goal, and as we went into injury time at the end of the match it was still goal-less. The crowd were restless, and everyone was resigned to a tough match at their place in the return. Even as the referee was about to blow his whistle for the end of the game, John Scales sent the ball out to Rob Jones, who fed it along the right touchline to Macca. In the time I played in the same team as him, Steve must have done this 2,000 times, I swear, and he did it again, beat his man and swept the cross in to the far post. Rushie lunged for it, the ball was blocked and spun out towards the edge of the area. I was waiting there, on a different run from the maestro, and on my right side I sneaked in front of Richard Shaw and had to hit the shot instantly on the half volley with my right foot. It went into the very far corner of the net, into the side net again in fact, and as far as goals are concerned that's one of the tough ones, hitting off your wrong foot instantly, with only a tiny target to aim at.

What I would say is that unlike most strikers, even some of the very best ones, I've always been pretty comfortable with both feet and I've scored some pretty big goals with my right foot, despite the fact that when I first came onto the scene everyone always said I was completely left sided. Anfield erupted again. The game was on ITV with Brian Moore commentating, he went ballistic and I was all over the telly and the papers once more. We didn't play the second leg for three weeks, because their pitch was waterlogged, but we beat them 1–0 in that one too, and I scored again, a left-foot shot this time from a pretty acute angle, in the side of the net to boot.

Y'know what? A few years later I read a newspaper column by Robert Lee, who played for Newcastle. He wrote some pretty nice things about me, and one of the things he said was that when I hit a shot, it always went into the side netting. Not outside the goal, obviously, but inside when I scored. And I'm pretty proud of that. I've always scored goals throughout my career – even if people think I haven't managed any since I left Liverpool – and one of the reasons is that I can always find the angles, and the corners of the net. Dunno how exactly, except that I always have had an image of where the goal is exactly in my head when I'm in the penalty area. And I do know that helps.

So we were in the final, my first final in my first full season. On April Fool's Day. Against Bolton. Our bogey team. Fucking hell. We pissed it actually. Macca was brilliant, tore them apart and scored two fantastic goals. I didn't score, but I thought I played pretty well, and I found the whole experience incredible. This is what it's all about. Walking out at Wembley with the noise of the crowd and the anticipation on the air. No matter how many times that's happened to me, I've never got used to it, the hairs always stand up on the back of my neck, and I always get that incredible buzz from the sense of what is about to happen. You know when you hear players banging on about winning trophies being all that matters, and you're thinking, Yeah, right, but the fifty grand a week fucking helps, mate. Well, that's what they mean. Of course the money is important – show me anyone who ever turns it down – but there is nothing better than that moment when you walk out on the turf and you see all that colour around the ground, fans so intense and hyped up and screaming at the tops of their voices. You get a taste of it, and Christ, you want more.

For my first time, it didn't matter that we were playing a first-division side, and it was only the Coca-Cola Cup. It was a final, my first one, and I was standing there on the pitch looking around at Ian Rush and John Barnes, and thinking, Yeah, I'll have a bit of this. We'd travelled down two days before, stayed in a big London hotel, and I don't think I slept more than about three minutes because I was so hyped up. There is always so much build-up around any Cup final, the press days and the television interviews and the expectation of the fans, and I loved it all. And then we were on the bus on the way to Wembley, the fans already there with their flags and scarves, cheering us as we nudged by. That first time, I was knocked out by the flags with my name on them. You see a picture of yourself, and see the word God underneath, and that's mind-blowing when you are still nineteen. I spoke to Rushie the night before about the game, and he talked me through it, said that the trick was to see it as another game of football, just like the one I'd scored a hat-trick in. He'd played in European Cup finals, he was there at Heysel and played a game that night after all the carnage, all those terrible deaths. No idea how he managed that. He knew what it was all about, and he helped me through it brilliantly. But I wasn't nervous, I loved it all.

I had a laugh out on the pitch, with all the noise and everyone screaming, wandering around with Macca waving at the crowd. And it was amazing, because with all those people in the ground, I picked out me dad straight away, there with some of me mates and Mr Lynch. This was a long way from Penny Lane, even if it was a short space of time. I went over for a quick chat, told me dad I'd come and give him the winner's medal later, and that's exactly what happened. We went up the steps, I got me medal, celebrated on the pitch and then went over to me dad again and I handed it over, complete with the little presentation box, velvet inlay an' all that. He gave me a hug, and there were tears in his eyes, he was saying, 'I just can't believe it, all those games down the all-weather, practising with the little ball . . . it paid off, son.'

Then it was off to the Royal Lancaster for the party afterwards, and a quick call to me dad to see if everything was all right. He goes, 'Yeah, everything's all right, had a bit of a problem with the medal, but it's all sorted now.' Apparently, he had gone back to the car park after the match, and before he got into the car he'd pulled the medal out to have one last look at it. But as he flipped open the case, the medal skipped out and rolled off down the road, like in the cartoons. Then it spun around and around, right around the outside of a grid, balancing on the edge of it, before tipping over . . . on the other side. Dad had shut his eyes by that point, thinking that he'd gone and thrown my first proper medal down a grid in the middle of north London.

We had a real celebration that night and I joined in, probably for the first time. Before that, I was a teenager, on the edge, and when they went out on the piss, I didn't tag along. It was like when we were in South Africa, they'd go out for a bevvy, but leave me and Dom and a couple of the other young lads behind because we weren't part of it yet, and probably also because the gaffer told them to leave us out of it. That was the day I graduated though, to become part of the team proper, and move up from the reserve dressing room to the big boys'.

I think it was also the day that my friendship with Macca stepped up a level. I had known of him since I was ten years old, because he had been the big star of the Liverpool Schoolboys team when I was a kid and he was the player we all wanted to be. But he was four years older than me, so we were hardly mates because that's a massive gap at that age. He was training at Melwood too, and the time when Steve Heighway let me go up there for the summer to train and help the groundstaff I got to know him a bit, but largely the age groups were kept apart so we never did much more than walk by each other. When I became a trainee he was already on the fringe of the first team and he was big mates with Mike Marsh. He used to look out for me because we were both Scousers in the squad, but we weren't the inseparable pair then that everyone made out.

Even when I got into the side I was still with the younger lads, and he was more mates with Don Hutchison and Jamie Redknapp, but of course we got to know each other better. It just clicked really. I think we were pretty similar because we were from the same background, had the same development, both thought we would play for Everton but ended up at Liverpool under Kenny Dalglish, and both got into the side at a pretty young age because Graeme Souness had faith in us. We had a similar sense of humour and mischief. I was livelier, a bit less restrained shall we say. Macca's reputation as a 'scally' was the same as mine, but really I don't think he was ever a bad lad – like me! I don't think I ever saw him proper drunk, and he was always the one in our squad who would try to calm situations down, and keep everyone under control. He was a great foil to me, and also a massive influence on my career. I was shown some stats the other day that examined where my first 100 goals for Liverpool came from ... and Macca created almost a quarter of them. That was twice as many as anyone else, and it's an amazing statistic when you think about it. From the whole team, Steve McManaman created twice as many goals as all the other players, and he still managed to score plenty for himself as well.

When we were teammates, there wasn't a better player in the Premiership. He was stunning, the way he could control matches and make everything look so effortless. A lot has been said about him, and there are a lot of people who have tried to taint his reputation at Anfield, because it suits their agenda to make out that Liverpool were inconsistent until Houllier arrived, so it must have been Macca's fault. The fact is, he was the best player for about five years on the bounce, and nobody did more for the club under Roy Evans. Look what he did when he went to Real Madrid. He was superb at fitting into the team and making things work, and when he left the Bernabeu they said that they would struggle because there's no one like him to link the defence and the attack. He did that brilliantly with us, and I'm not the only one who rates him as one of the best players they have ever seen at Liverpool.

Michael Owen has always said that Macca was the best player he ever played with . . . apart from me, of course! Sometimes he was incredible to watch, and I'd be standing there admiring his work rather than getting on the end of it. I can remember vividly one game against Leicester when they had a defender marking him. Lots of sides used to do that – which is unusual in English football – because they were so scared of what he could do. This time it was Colin Hill, the Northern Ireland international. He was following Steve everywhere, and Macca suggested they go off to the bog together. I was standing alongside them, and Macca was going: 'Fuck me, Colin, you must be some shit player if all you can do is track someone else around and kick them.' And fair play to Hilly, he grinned and replied back: 'You're not wrong! I'm crap. Do us a favour and don't make me look too stupid!' A lot of players were made to look crap by Macca, and I was so grateful to be playing on the same team as him, as I know Michael Owen was. When you're a striker and you rely on service you need someone like him behind you, and every striker in the Premiership was jealous of us because he was so unselfish. At his peak, there was no one better, and I'd even include David Beckham in that, and certainly all the rest that Sven Goran Eriksson used to pick ahead of my mate.

Macca's got this look of someone who doesn't really give a monkey's, but believe me, he does. He always has. He's a great professional, never late, never let anyone down, intelligent enough to understand what was being asked of him in any situation, and an incredible athlete. He used to piss all of us off in training because he could run all day, and it came so easy to him. And he used to piss us off when we went out, because he could drink as much as anyone else and still appear completely sober. Looking tuned in is always important to him. When you come from a council estate in Liverpool, how you come across is important. You don't want to be seen as a biff: some busy bollocks like Gary Neville, or someone who has sold their soul like Beckham. The mates we've got, if either of us gives it the big bollocks, then they'd destroy us. He's like me, he's got mates from when he was a kid who knew him when he was two foot nothing and had holes in his kecks. He'd be mortified if they thought he was getting above himself, or playing the big star, and I feel exactly the same way. Sometimes, I think that's why we both come across as if we don't give a fuck, and I think that's why a few managers – England managers in particular – haven't understood the pair of us.

But he cares, and I do too. I really care. Maybe that's one of the things about my parents splitting up, you get that insecurity where you worry about how people see you. So you put on an act where you make sure nobody can accuse you of selling out or whatever, when really you're churning up about what they might think of you. And all that is played out in front of an audience of millions, because every spit and cough is written about in the papers and shown on the telly. Macca and me became closer and closer as my first full season went on in 1994–95, and in some ways – but not all ways – we were a bit like brothers. It's just that we are so comfortable in each other's company, kind of knew what each other was going to say and bounced off each other.

He was the big brother, obviously. He looked out for me, kept me out of the worst scrapes and apologized when I went over the top. People have always said we were inseparable, but it wasn't like that. When he went to Madrid, the first time I ever got to see him was his last game for Real. Four years after he went there. And he didn't even fucking play. We were mates, close mates, used to room together for Liverpool, stick together on England duty, go out after matches for a bevvy. His dad, Davie, is mates with my dad, and I know his auld fella really well – still speak to him to this day. We have even got the same friends really. I know all his mates, he knows mine, and a few of them are mates of both of us. He's got this friend called Gordon who has stuck around him for years, and he has been my mate too since I met him through Macca. And like Calvey, he's been there through it all.

Stevie and me – or Shaggy as he has always been known, because of his fucking awful haircut – we were two lads from the inner city, him from Kirkdale, me from Toxteth, who came together at the same time when this incredible thing happened in football and we rode it together. We're not the same though. He's a much more private person than me and far more self-contained. You never really know what he's thinking, and he always has this screen for the outside world. He can speak to anyone, but he won't let his guard down to hardly anybody. And he'll think a lot more about things than me. I've always been a bit headstrong and impulsive. If I think something, then I'll say it. If I think I'm being mistreated, then I'll blow me top, have a go and fuck the consequences.

Macca will always say to calm down, try to diffuse the situation. He's one of the lads, but he can be apart from that too because he can see where things are headed and cut it off before it gets there. There was a now notorious Christmas party at Liverpool when Houllier first took over back in 1998. There was a tradition that the senior players would organize things, get the lads and a few of their mates together and have a bit of a blow-out. There'd be the odd stripper, plenty of bevvy, and a right laugh, just like plenty of other Christmas parties across the country. Harmless really, especially because we would always schedule them away from matches so everyone had plenty of time to recover.

There was a tradition – for decades – that we would all go in fancy dress, and the new lads would go up on stage and sing a song, and when everyone had had enough then they'd chuck beer all over you. That year though, the atmosphere seemed different, and it was Macca who'd spotted it. Everyone else had just got pissed and had a good time, but he was fretting because he could sense something wasn't right. Eventu-

Oh, baby — me aged one.

A famous look on a famous hooter.
I should have got it sponsored.

Top. Me and Mum relaxing together.

Above. The boys: Calvey, Gordon and young Scott, all lads together.

Right. Calvey and me preparing for a players' party.

Above. Our wedding day, Kerrie looking as beautiful as ever.

Above right. Kerrie and me on holiday.

Right. Kerrie, me, Mum and Lisa on Lisa's wedding day.

A goal against Arsenal, just for a change.

The joy of goalscoring, better than a cup of tea any day!

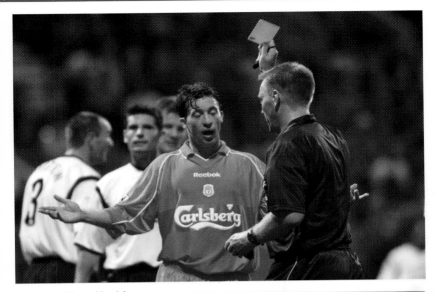

A rare disciplinary blemish.

Oh, it's getting hot in here.

Dad enjoying
a tender moment
with Madison.

Oh, brother:
Anthony playing
the caring uncle.

Great Scott:
George and me
with Madison.

The girls in my life: Jaya, Mackenzie and Madison in Fowler team strip.

Tiger Tiger: not fancy dress, just a bored afternoon in the house!

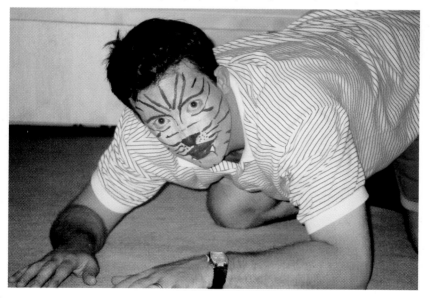

Calm down: ready for another Christmas party.

Another bored afternoon, this time recovering from injury.

We've come a long, long way together: Macca and me in Majorca.

ally, he spoke with security at the venue and they nabbed one of the strippers with a camera who had taken pictures. Unfortunately, they must have had two cameras and the pictures turned up in the *News of the World*. Again, they were pretty harmless, Jamie Carragher and a few of the young lads up on stage having a bit of a sing because it was their first year. But a big deal was made of it and Macca had been astute enough to recognize that. He was astute enough to recognize that all the players who wrote for that paper got off lightly too . . . Shaggy was the one who, even in the middle of a massive Christmas piss-up, could step back and see what was happening and try to sort it out before it got out of hand.

It's funny after all the scrapes I've been in to say that Shaggy has been a restraining influence on my career, but that's the way I look at it. I've read some snidey stuff saying that Macca used to make the bullets and then get me to fire them, but that's rubbish. Stan Collymore even went so far as to single Shaggy out as being a sneak who used to wind people up and come across all innocent himself. As an example, he cites the time in March 1997 when I was fined by UEFA for lifting my shirt at Anfield during a Cup Winners' Cup tie against Brann Bergen, to reveal a slogan supporting the dock-workers who had been sacked in Liverpool. Collymore tried to make out that it was Macca's idea, and he had said whoever scored first would lift their shirt, knowing full well that it would be me who was far more likely to score, and far more likely to get done.

The truth is that Macca was the one who tried to keep me out of trouble. It was his uncle who gave him the T-shirts, which had a Calvin Klein logo on them, but the CK formed the middle letters of the word doCKers, and underneath was a message supporting them. We both decided to wear them, but Shaggy kept saying to me not to lift my Liverpool shirt if I scored, wait until the end when we swap shirts, and then we'll be able to show off the T-shirts underneath without causing a real fuss, and without getting into trouble. It would be a gesture of support without going over the top and getting everyone into a lather, without creating more hassle than we already got – which more or less summed up Macca's way of thinking. But not mine.

I agreed with him 100 per cent, reassured him a thousand times that I would definitely wait until the end of the match and would take my shirt off when we went to wave to the fans, when no one was really looking ... and then went completely mental when I scored, took the shirt off and pulled down the T-shirt and ran over to all the photographers to have me picture taken! I got a stern warning from UEFA and fined about a grand, which was a disgrace when you think how justified the cause was. Macca stuck to the script and showed his T-shirt at the end without any of the photographers even noticing. He also sent the dockers a lot of money to help them: we both did in fact but of course that was not publicized, partly because we'd have died if anyone thought we were trying to get a bit of publicity from sending some cash to support such a good cause.

When I first got into the Liverpool team, my usual routine would be to get my work done on a Saturday afternoon and then go out with a few mates into town to some bar or other, pretty quiet really. As things developed, I would go out a bit more with the rest of the players, Macca in particular, and with some of my friends and his mates. There were times when we had a bit of a blow-out, but mostly it was just the evening after a game – we would go out, have a few beers and make a late night of it.

Our usual routine would be to go to a hotel in town that we used, go on to a bar run by someone we knew, and then maybe into a club. We would always end up back at the hotel where we would get a cab home. In the early days, before my wife Kerrie came on the scene, there would be women around wanting to talk and all that. But really, it wasn't that wild, wasn't that out of the ordinary. You can look at it now and say oh, you shouldn't be out late, even when there's not another game for a week. But a decade ago, that is the way it was. Nobody took the piss, but all the lads went out for a few beers because that's what they'd always done . . . and it had worked pretty well under Shankly, Paisley, Fagan and Dalglish.

Rushie still did it when I first arrived, so did the likes of Steve Nicol and Ronnie Whelan, and nobody thought much of it. The point is, football has changed over the past decade so much, and so behaviour has had to change with it. People have accused me of all sorts of indiscipline, all sorts of crazy behaviour, but it is only in the light of how players are expected to behave now. I honestly think that I didn't do too much different from any other player back then. The United lads would like a blow-out, and they won fucking everything. I had some nights with Nicky Butt and Paul Scholes on under-21 duty around that time, and they said that plenty of players at their club knew how to party. Times change, and things come to be different. These days, we are all aware that drinking is no good for an athlete at all, and if you can stop drinking altogether then that's the most sensible thing.

In my first full season I thought that a bevvy wouldn't hurt you, so long as you could run it off the next day, and still have a few days to prepare. So did, for example, Roy Keane. I also thought I could eat what the fuck I liked, because I was training every day and I would burn off the calories. I was a kid from a sprawling estate right in the centre of Liverpool. What did I know about diet and the mechanics of all that? Nothing. Now I'm aware of what can help, what is bad for you, what is the best diet for a sportsman, when to eat, what not to eat, blah, blah, blah. Times change, and mistakes look a lot worse when you judge them by a different set of rules.

It's the same as the fame that I found in that first full season. It took a hell of a long time to understand what was happening. Between us, me and Rushie scored fifty goals. A half century of goals from two strikers – it was completely unheard of. I only turned twenty in the April at the end of that season, and I got thirty-one goals in all competitions – twenty-five in the Premiership, which was only bettered by Alan Shearer, the sod. I also won the PFA Young Player of the Year. Sometimes, as I talk about my career and list the things I've achieved, I think people are gonna call me a big-headed git for droning on about what I've done. But even now when I look back, I can't quite believe what happened to me, and it's frightening sometimes to think about what I achieved in those early years. I didn't realize I was that good!

I went into the Anfield club shop one week in my second season and saw a lifesize image of me that was a coat-hanger for keeping the creases in your clothes. Who the fuck would buy that?! Except me, of course. I've got two. Then at the end of that season, they gave me the PFA award. I don't want to drone on about it, but it's a vote of all the professionals in the country of who they thought was the best player that season, and I won the junior award, alongside Shearer . . . again. That was more nerve-racking than anything I'd done on the football pitch.

The gaffer told me that I'd been short-listed for the award, which had been won by the likes of Andy Cole and Ryan Giggs the previous two years, and then they announced that I'd won it and I had to go down with him to some swanky hotel in London to pick it up. I had the full waiter's outfit on, with dickie bow and all that, for the first time in my life, and I sat at the table waiting for them to give me this award, swigging lager like it had gone out of fashion. I swear I was half pissed when I got up there, mumbled a few words about being proud and sat down again. But it was an incredible moment. You know you've arrived when you win an award that's voted for by your fellow professionals. To be there alongside Shearer, who to me has always been the best, this incredible goal scorer who I have always looked up to, in front of a room of players from all the different clubs, it was quite emotional for me. I was thinking that I had done me mum and dad proud, that I'd have a trophy on the mantelpiece that would show that I wasn't half bad.

All that happened, and never once did I stop to think about it. These days, players have got agents who are part of big companies from America, with branches all around the world. They have PR people, media analysts, stylists, assistants, the whole pit crew. And they know exactly what they have to do to make themselves more famous, to become a hero. There are a few players who are very calculating, their agents have told them they have to do well for England, score an important goal in an important game, and then they can cash in. They do it, as well. I've been in games where players have refused to pass, and take every opportunity for a shot on goal, because they know if only they can score then the whole world will be praising them. It's all very planned, almost regimented, and they control it, milk it for all it's worth. Me, I didn't even realize it was happening, and never once did I even stop to think about it. By the end of that 1994–95 season, I knew I was famous because Nelson Mandela and Robbie Williams had asked for me autograph. I knew it because I would get stopped in the street all the time, and I would even have people hanging round outside me mum's house. There would be girls in clubs standing there staring, trying to talk to my mates to get a chat with me ... and I knew it wasn't because of my dashing good looks! I got asked for about 2,000 tickets for every big game, from people that I hadn't heard from for years, or never even heard of at all.

I got into trouble all the time too. At Christmas in that second season, I got a great present from the FA – a fine of a grand because I showed me arse to the Leicester fans at Filbert Street. I don't know what it is about that place, but I was always getting into trouble there.

This time, they were giving me a bit of stick, even though it was Christmas, saying I was a thieving Scouse bastard and questioning me parentage, so I just pulled me shorts right up to show the cheeks of me arse and then I wiggled it at them. It was a laugh but a few of the snappers took pictures of it, so I was down at Lancaster Gate trying to explain that one ... a sign of things to come. I think I got off so lightly because I was earning peanuts at the time.

The fine wasn't the problem, actually. A few days afterwards I was interviewed by the police because they'd had some complaints. Imagine, there were about 2,000 people screaming stuff that made even me blush, but as soon as I had a little go back, just hoisted my shorts up a bit, they were running to the police saying how offended they were! Funny thing was, all the letters sent to the cops – and there were dozens of them – had exactly the same wording, so obviously someone at Leicester was trying to orchestrate something against me. In the end, the police told me they wouldn't do anything because of that, but it was a bit worrying for a nineteen-year-old kid to have a charge hanging over his head for a while. I soon got used to that, though.

One of the hard things to learn when you come into the game is how to deal with the fans. Playing for the ressies, there are eight blokes and a dog most of the time. They shout at you, but it's the odd comment and sometimes it can be hilarious. When you first get into the senior side though, the abuse you get from the crowd is incredible. After I played my first game at Fulham, we had a match at Chelsea and I saw some of it there. Christ, my eyes were popping out of my head because I'd never heard anything like it. All those people, and God do they hate you. And the noise too. Deafening. After a while, you just blank it out and realize that the easiest way to shut them up is to score a goal. That really pisses them off. But early on in your career, places like the old Southampton ground and Portsmouth are murder, and obviously going to Goodison or Old Trafford is never easy. It's always the tight grounds where the fans are close to the pitch that are bad.

I've got to be honest, when you're a young kid just coming into the game and someone is screaming abuse at you, saying things about your family and what they're going to do to you, your first instinct is to wade in there and smash them one. You wouldn't take it off some wrong 'un at school, so why would it be any different with some loudmouth knob-head in the crowd? It makes me chuckle when you see the fans on the terraces, handing out dog's abuse. They stand there, screaming stuff that if they did it to someone in the street, they'd be arrested . . . or get flattened.

When Cantona went into the crowd to sort that fella out who was giving it to him, I reckon most of the professionals were thinking, Good on you, Eric. He was banned for about twenty years for that, but I remember a Rugby League game a few years before when this winger got the same sort of abuse every time he got the ball. In the end he chucked the ball down, climbed into the crowd, and gave his tormentor a right crack. The ref came along, blowing his whistle like fury to drag him back ... and then gave a scrum down for a knock-on and got straight on with it! Mind you, there are some places you're probably as well staying as far away from the touchline as possible.

There was another incident that year, when I got sent off playing for the England under-21s against Austria. I got wound up by the centre half marking me and kicking me all game. In the end, I lost it, and turned round and lashed out at him. The ref came over to give me a card, and I lost it with him as well, told him what a wanker he was because he had missed everything else that had gone on. Problem was, his English was perfect and he sent me off for foul and abusive language. I got a mullering from the press for that. I was described as this explosive hot-head, who shouted his mouth off and didn't think about what he was doing. Which was about right. So there I was, public enemy number one for a while. I got a ludicrous four-game ban from the Under-21 Championships, and eventually came back for the crucial game in the group against a Portugal side that had Figo, Carvalho and Rui Costa in it. I did all the interviews with the press who were out there, saying that I had learnt my lesson and that I wouldn't make the same mistake twice.

I was quoted in the *Mirror* before the game as saying, 'What I did that night was stupid, and it will never happen again.' Well, that bit was true. Only problem was, there were plenty of other stupid things I had not explored yet! After the game we had a bit of a blow-out. There were quite a few of the lads there who had been in the under-18 side two years earlier, like Kevin Gallen and Nicky Butt. There were a few wild moments, which resulted in me, Kev and Trevor Sinclair ending up back in the room deciding to rearrange some of the furniture. Predictably enough, we made a bit of a mess and all hell broke loose. Nothing really happened, we damaged a lamp and there was some pen ink that got spilled on the bed. But the hotel had a moan, the management got on to us and the press got to hear about it.

Of course, then it was blown up out of all proportion, it was a major scandal in the press and we were reported to the FA in disgrace – for breaking a fucking lamp. That's the worst thing about the FA, they're spineless. Whenever the press make a bit of a fuss, try to create a story by revving things up – which is their job I suppose – they just cave in and go along with it, even when they know it's all bollocks. They're so scared of the media it's laughable. So, I was back down there to explain that one, and I don't think my excuse that a herd of elephants happened to pass through that night with the local circus went down too well. I was fined again and warned that any more and I would never play for England again. For breaking a lamp. I know it sounds a bit weak now, but it was all harmless fun. We were three lads still in our teens, and we were bored so we started messing about.

I've never tried to make excuses for the things that have happened in my career. There's stuff I did and I know I shouldn't have. Sometimes I knew straight away, like the line sniffing, or a few of the things that happened later with Houllier. Looking back now, I think you could say I was a bit excitable. Some of those things that happened, if they were going on now I'd just sit back and let the young lads get on with it. I was a kid though, and I was always in the middle of it. Just messing about mostly. I have always loved a laugh, and at football clubs there is always someone who is prepared to play the practical jokes. I can't tell you the number of times I've had the handles cut off my bag and carefully placed back, so when I pick it up I've just got handles in my hand. Had me shoes cut up, had someone piss in my drink.

I got my own back on Razor Ruddock once, by giving him a pint of lager at the Christmas party that I'd had a piss in. When he drank it I told him and he didn't bat an eyelid. I think he was used to it by then. I was pretty bad at Liverpool, but I wasn't the worst. Steve Harkness, one of the best lads they have ever had at the club, was a real joker and he always kept everyone entertained. Nothing outrageous most of the time, just dumping people in puddles when it's raining on the training ground, or moving all your furniture out of the hotel room, that sort of thing.

Most of it happens to relieve the boredom, because when you get a group of twenty young lads together from similar backgrounds, and with nothing much to do because you can't go out on the lash, then there's bound to be a bit of pissing about. When people ask me about some of the incidents I've been involved in, and whether I regret them, I always say the same thing. Never. Look at what happened to me. In my first two years, I came from nowhere to becoming one of the most recognizable faces in the country. I went from being flat broke to being a paper millionaire. And I didn't have a clue what was happening to me. I was a bit of a pioneer if you like.

I've read recently that I was the first of the 'Sky' generation, and I reckon that's true. Football was turned on its head at the start of the nineties. Suddenly there was so much money and so much fame on offer to anyone who could score a goal, and no help in trying to deal with it. All that just dumped on kids who had no education in dealing with it, no fucking idea. And I had it all. I didn't deal with it always in the most sensible of ways, as you can already see. But what do you expect from a kid who didn't even realize what was going on at the time? I winged it. I played football, scored goals, and saw my face on the telly every five minutes. I got hounded by the media, by the fans and by people who didn't have a clue about football, but thought they knew me. Every game I played, something seemed to happen that made me a little bit more famous, or a little more notorious. I never analysed it, never thought about where I was heading or how I should react. I just reacted how I always reacted, instinctively, cheekily, sometimes stupidly. And I had the time of my life.

7) MONEY-GO-ROUND

One of the funniest songs I ever heard about me came from the Manchester City fans when we played at Charlton soon after the *Sunday Times* put me at the top of their 2005 sporting rich list. To the tune of 'Yellow Submarine', they sang, 'We all live in a Robbie Fowler house.' I was killing meself when I heard that, and it at least took my mind off the game. Funny. Even funnier when they followed it up by chanting, 'Robbie is our landlord.' What they were getting at was the fact that the newspaper said I was worth about £30 million because of the money I'd invested in property. Apparently, that made me the richest sportsman under the age of thirty in the country. Complete bollocks, I'm sure about that, because the figures are all guesswork and the guesses are from half-baked stories about players' riches from the tabloids ... which is not always the most accurate source, given that they think of a figure and double it most of the time.

But what is true is that I do have a lot of properties. At the last count, it was almost 100, although I'm sure it's pretty obvious if you've got this far into the book that I don't count them very often. Since 1998, the investments made for me have gradually built up a portfolio of properties and office space, which are let out. Mostly, they are in the Glasgow and Greater Manchester areas, some on Merseyside and a few in the Home Counties around London. I mention all this for two reasons.

One, because I've never once for a second felt let down. Quite the opposite, I feel incredibly, ludicrously lucky. Lottery-lucky.

When I've been going on about the lack of advice and direction that was available when I came into the game, that's because me and some of the others who started at that time in the early nineties were almost breaking new ground, so no one knew how to deal with it. Loads of us suddenly got the sort of fame and adulation that had previously been reserved for incredible icons like George Best, and we got far more money than even he ever got. What we didn't get was the support that young players get now, but that's not because we were let down, but because football has had a decade to get used to it, to understand it, and put that support in place. As they say, mistakes were made.

Mostly by me, it has to be said. But not when it came to the money. I don't think there are any fears I'm going to end up as one of those classic cases of players who enjoy the high life but eventually suffer the same fate as an old banger at the roadside. Piston broke. Probably not going to be a Sunday-newspaper sob story. Which brings me on to the second point. For all the fact that I was a naive kid who was taken from one world and thrown into another very different one, for all the fact that I was a paper millionaire at the age of nineteen when I'd never had a pot to piss in before – and I will cheerfully admit that I didn't have a clue what to do with it when I got it – I did get help from Liverpool in that one crucial area. I have Graeme Souness to thank for that, but mostly I have the man he put me in touch with, George Scott.

No one at Liverpool could have predicted what was going to happen in football as the nineties unfolded, but Souey realized straight away that I was going to need looking after. When he was in Glasgow with Rangers, he had worked with George on some investments, and had used him to help some of the players up there. Ally McCoist was one, and George is still helping him to this day. Me dad had done everything for me when I was a kid, he was the one who talked to Liverpool when they wanted to sign me, decided when the time was right, and talked about what kind of contract they would give me when I turned professional after the YTS period. Yet he was the first to admit that he didn't know anything about negotiating or investments, apart from those you made down the bookie on a Saturday afternoon.

Nowadays, agents pick up kids when they are trainees still at school. By the time they get anywhere near the first team, everything is sorted for them. I didn't have a clue about agents or anything else. The only advice our family knew we could trust was from Mr Lynch, and he was a schoolteacher. So Souey knew I desperately needed help, and he knew he had a man who could help me. I have much to thank Graeme Souness for and, above all else, I am grateful for the fact that he recognized the potential of my talent, and he recognized my interests by ensuring I had the best possible advice when it was time to negotiate a proper contract, even if Liverpool could have capitalized in the short term if I didn't.

George is a financial advisor to me. He's also a close and trusted friend. And in a way, he's almost like a second father to me. I'm not here to bull him up, because that would do his shed in, but he's played a massive role in my development. Basically, he figures massively in my story. And the funny thing is, I'd never have had such an incredible, important person in my life if Souey hadn't resigned the manager's job at Liverpool, which was above and beyond his call of duty to me.

We weren't happy with the club when I got my first professional contract. In fact me dad was fucking livid. To this day he reckons Liverpool tricked us. When he took me up to Anfield that day back in 1990 to sign, he shook hands on a deal, and he reckons they didn't stick to it. He never asked for anything, no money, no back-handers or anything like that. He just wanted an assurance that I would be guaranteed a proper professional contract, and they gave it. Liverpool said I would be a YTS for a year, and then I would join the professionals on proper money. Me dad was delighted, because he thought that meant I would have a real chance. There was no way they would agree to put me on professional money if they weren't serious about giving me a proper future. Yet when it came to it, I didn't get the professional deal for almost two years, and when I finally did I was on £220 a week, which eventually went up to £500 a week. That was a lot better than the £29.50 a week I got as a trainee, but if it was professional money, then the rest of the lads in the squad were being taken for a massive ride.

I remember I got home with my first ever professional pay packet, ripped it open in front of me dad, and his face just dropped. Not because it wasn't much money as such – because he knew I would get that if I did the job – it was more because he thought they had conned us, had spun us a line about getting a professional contract just to make me sign the YTS. He realized then that they probably do that to all the kids, give them a crock just to get them on the books. Dad was just saying over and over, 'They conned us, son, conned us.' And he was worried because it meant that I was back there with all the rest of the trainees, no further up the ladder, and definitely not guaranteed a future. Just another number, a low-risk pay-out of a few measly quid. The only comeback we had was for me to score goals to make them pay up the real money, the money that we thought we had been promised . . . so Liverpool were winners all ways up. I suppose that's how it works.

I was on that money until I got into the team. In fact, I was on peanuts until I scored the five goals against Fulham, and then they couldn't get me in quick enough to sign another deal. I was rewarded for equalling Liverpool's goal-scoring record in one match with a pay rise to £500 a week. Not bad, but hardly cigar time. It was funny though, because I scored those goals at Anfield, was splashed across all the papers as the next great English striker, and within three days I was in the office, being told how highly they valued me, and asked politely to sign on the dotted line. That was a laugh. They talked with me dad on that contract, and of course I signed it. I was hardly going to walk away after I'd just scored five goals for the club in only my fourth game.

A few days later Souey called me into the office and said that I needed someone to look after me, sort out the finances. He pointed out what we knew already, that me dad couldn't do it. He said that I should be looking for a bigger contract, and if I wanted he could introduce me to someone who could help when I got one. I went home to discuss it with me mum and dad, and they said maybe we should get Mr Lynch to come along to meet the bloke Souey had recommended – George Scott. So we had a meeting at the Royal St George Hotel in the centre of town, and in walked this well-dressed, silver-haired gent. He talked about savings plans and invest-ments and all that sort of stuff, and if I'm honest my eyes glazed over after only a few minutes. But I could see he knew what he was on about, and Mr Lynch was pretty impressed too.

We shook hands, and George was on board. Later on, he told me that Graeme had rung him, said that he had a kid who was going to be a superstar, one who would be at the very top of the game, and desperately needed someone to look out for him, to help him avoid all the usual pitfalls. Then when he got to the meeting, he walked in and saw me, a spotty-faced little kid who didn't look like a special footballer, who didn't look much like a footballer at all. In fact, he wondered if he had got the right place. Thank God he had.

At that stage though, it was just a question of doing some financial things on my behalf – basic stuff on savings because I hardly had a whack to invest. Then Souey, to his credit, called me in again and admitted that the time was right for me to start looking for a lot more money, it wasn't fair that I was on such a small contract when I was one of the few players in the side doing it for him at that point. It was good news, but I still didn't have an agent to do the negotiating, so me dad rang George and asked if he could help. George had worked for me on an hourly basis, charging the minimum for his services. So it seemed a natural progression for him to help on the contract. Problem was, Graeme was also a client of his and it was an obvious conflict of interests, so he couldn't really act for me. It was a real predicament, and George eventually said that the best thing he could do was recommend a decent agent who could do the negotiations. That was in the middle of January 1994, and me dad was a bit gutted because he thought we had got some trust going with George. But then the problem was solved overnight, because Souey quit on 28 January. As I said, it was decent of him, but he didn't need to go to those lengths! There was one drawback though, it was Souey who had said that my contract was shit and I deserved much more, and now he had cleared off without us agreeing a thing. So I had someone to negotiate for me, but no one to negotiate with.

That's where George proved his worth. I had signed a five-year deal at £500 a week, and even though I was still a teenager that didn't seem like a very good contract as the goals started to go in. He is a hard-headed businessman from Glasgow, a tough negotiator but a fair and honest man, and he went in to see Roy Evans and explained what Souey had been proposing, and also explained that Liverpool could hardly expect me to be happy if I was going to stay on wages that were about a tenth of the top earners at the club. Roy is another gentleman, and he said he would speak to Peter Robinson, who did all the financial stuff at the club. And that's how we ended up, in the November of that year, walking into that meeting at Melwood with Mr Robinson, the gaffer and Tom Saunders, to sign what they said was an historic deal for both the club and for football.

Initially, the contract was worth £3,000 a week, but it was designed to rise very quickly, as well as including pretty good appearance money and bonuses. It was another five-year contract, and over the course of it I worked out that it was worth quite a bit more than a million quid. And it was guaranteed. That was a strange experience. I can honestly say that I have never been too bothered about the money side of football. When I came into the game, that was the last thing on my mind. Okay, I realized that if I did well then it would pay more than working down the docks, but money never inspired me one bit. Getting a few girls might have done when I was that spotty teenager who met George, but the truth is I was obsessed with football, and with scoring goals, and that was just about the only thing on my mind.

I probably had the right approach . . . and the right advisor in a tight Scotsman (his words, not mine!). You see all these young players now, and it is amazing how mad they can be when they've been in the game for only five minutes. You can see the dangers too. If you won the lottery, then you'd want to splash out on something special, wouldn't you? Most footballers come from nothing, their families are from council estates and don't have any money. There are no classes in how to look after your millions, and you need proper advice, otherwise it is so easy to blow it all. There are plenty of ways to lose your money.

There has always been something of a culture of gambling around football, and it's not difficult to see why. Apart from anything else, it is something to occupy the mind that doesn't involve going out doing anything that might affect your performance ... although losing hundreds of thousands like Keith Gillespie did – and plenty of other players have, by the way – could affect you pretty badly I suppose. I like a bet, and that has inspired a few other passions for me, but I've never gone mad, and I didn't bother at all back then. Cars are another passion for many footballers. It's a thing I eventually got into, but when I first got into the team at Anfield, I was fearful that everyone would think I was a flash git if I suddenly splashed out on a massive new car, so I kept the old banger for quite a while. It was the same with everything else. I was terrified of people thinking I was some sort of big-headed idiot who forgot his roots as soon as he got a few bob in his pockets, and I went around for ages like a doley. It was probably more the background I came from than any real awareness of how to look after money that reined me in during those early days.

Eventually though, I got to thinking that I should pay back me mum and dad for everything they had sacrificed in helping me to get where I was. I had always said that if I made it, I would buy me mum a house. We have lived with me nana and grandad, and I thought it would mean so much to her to get a place of her own. She has never asked for anything, and never moaned about anything, even though she's had some terrible problems to deal with. I didn't think me mum would want to move far from Toxteth where her family and friends all still lived, so I started having a look around the local area, but in the posh bits. Mossely Hill, at the top of Penny Lane, has always been quiet and a nice place to live, so I took to driving up there, lurking around, worrying that the locals would call the cops because some scally from Toxteth was casing the joint. There was a place on a quiet road that seemed to fit the bill, big enough for me mum and me and the rest of the family, but not too fancy or *Footballers' Wives*.

Most important to me was that it was still in Liverpool, because I didn't want to turn my back on where I had come from, even though we'd been getting trouble occasionally with my car getting scratched and things like that. So I rang George, and I said that I'd kind of seen a house that I'd like to buy, that had the shops and bus routes for me mum, and schools for Anthony and Scott, and was quite nice but not too posh, and anyway, err, I was wondering, err, if well, err, I could possibly afford it. George laughed and said I could probably afford about ten of them. I think it cost around £250,000 at the time, but to me, it seemed like millions. It was such a lot of money to be spending on a house, and I could hardly get my head round it. George said he'd come down and have a look at it with me, and if we liked it, then he'd put an offer in.

So we made an appointment, turned up on the hour, knocked on the door, and this stunning woman answered the door. She took a look at us and said, 'Which one of you is the footballer?' I was gutted, especially when she casually mentioned a few minutes later that she was a page-three model, and she was selling up to go to London to continue her career. As we were looking around, another woman came in who also lived there, and she was an even more stunning page-three girl. I was nineteen years old, and my eyes were popping out of my head! I don't think I looked at the house for even a minute, despite dragging the visit out to about an hour!

Eventually, George had to wrestle me out of the house, with me saying how much I liked it and what good taste they had an' all that. As they waved goodbye and closed the door, he was smiling a polite smile, offering all the pleasantries, and then he grabbed me by the lapels, swung me round up against the wall by the door and said in a stage whisper: 'I don't want you ringing the estate agent with some excuse about how you've got to come back on your own to measure up!' Point taken. But we did buy the house, and me mum loved it. She still does, even though some wanker spray-painted the back wall. After that, I thought it was only right that I bought me dad a house too, although he never asked for one. We found one close by to me mum's, and he moved in there with me Nana Louie, and me cousin, Mark. They are still close, me mum and dad, and they still see each other quite a lot, and it's good they live close by.

I bought a flat on the Albert Dock in Liverpool city centre a couple of years later as I got a bit of independence, although when I say independence I still used to take me washing around to me mum's every week to be done. I got into cars a bit more as well. I've had the lot, Porsche, Mercedes, Range Rover. I'm not in the David Beckham class, and I'd never get one of those Pimp My Ride tank things, but as I've got older I've found some ways of spending money on motors.

The first proper one was a BMW three series, and I was really excited about that. It was better than the first bike I got for Christmas, one of those BMX bike things that I was so in love with that I used to sneak it up to my bedroom. I'd seen the Beemers around the training ground, and I knew I'd get one eventually, but I didn't want to go mad ... I didn't want anyone pointing the finger at me. In the end, George took me to Glasgow to buy the car of my dreams, and it was such a big thing that I had my picture taken for the trade magazine, with me grabbing hold of the keys as though I'd fight anyone who tried to take them away. It was a step up from the club VW Golf that I inherited from Bruce Grobbelaar, meaning it was basically fucked.

I liked that car though. The day I got it must have been around Bonfire Night, and I drove over to where we used to live to show it off. I saw me brother Anthony, who was about fourteen at the time, sitting by a fire in the middle of the waste ground round the corner, smoking a crafty fag. So I drove by, and shouted, 'Oi, come here, you.' He didn't recognize the car or the person inside so he got all cocky and started going, 'Who the fuck's that?' Then I wound the window down, and you should have seen his face as he realized how much trouble he was in.

I know things wouldn't have worked out the same for me if I hadn't had George as the rock behind me. Less than two years after Liverpool had given me what I thought at the time was a decent deal, what I thought was more money than I could even dream about, he was back in there pointing out that Sky's money meant clubs were paying players a damn sight more than they had ever got before, and given that I was regarded as the best goal scorer in the Premiership alongside Alan Shearer by then, I should be up there alongside the highest-paid players in the club. Stan Collymore had come in by that time, and he was on massive money, as were Rushie and John Barnes. George eventually got them to double my money, and then to raise it quickly to ten grand a week with a promise that when football knew where it was after the next TV deal, my contract would be reviewed again.

By then, Liverpool had got an idea of how he could play hardball with them in negotiations, because he had threatened to take them to court over my image rights. It's a common thing now that players get a certain percentage of money from their clubs for the sale of any items with their name or image on. In the early '90s though, it was unheard of, but I became something of a trailblazer in that area – and probably set a precedent for everyone else – because George had told Liverpool they were trying to fleece me and they would have to cough up hard cash.

It was an incredible situation, and thank God the papers didn't get hold of the story at the time because they would have created merry fucking hell about it. Imagine: one of the highest-profile footballers in the Premiership suing his own club. I can't imagine what the court case would have been like, it doesn't bear thinking about. It all started when a guy in Scotland approached George to do a video about my life story, which obviously wasn't exactly run into a major series at that point. Liverpool had a relationship with Granada Television at the time, who produced all their videos and publications for them. So we set up a meeting with Mike Turner, the commercial manager at Anfield, and Peter Docherty from Granada, plus the man who wanted to make my video, John Williams.

It was a problem getting footage because Liverpool held the rights, and they were kicking up about us doing it, because Docherty dropped the bombshell at the meeting that they were going to produce a video of their own about my first 100 goals for the club. All hell broke loose, and George took great exception to what they were trying to do. But Docherty was adamant he was going to make his own video, and there was nothing we could do about it. I wasn't that involved, but even though I'm normally pretty laid back about these things, even I could see it was a right load of bollocks. How could Liverpool make a video about me without my permission, and without coughing up a penny, while they refused us the right to have footage of our own? It stunk, but they went ahead with it anyway, so George got heavy with them. We issued solicitor's letters, had meetings, threatened them, and said we were going all the way to court. It got to the stage where I thought I might even have to think about leaving the club, because they didn't seem interested in my feelings or in treating me properly.

It was a ridiculous situation, but it became incredibly serious. In the end, though, they fucked up and we got 'em by the balls. In the interviews on their video, they alluded to the fact that it was an official Robbie Fowler product. My name is a registered trademark, and they couldn't just use it like that. They got legal advice, and in the end they agreed to pay me £2 for every video. I think they sold about twelve, so it wasn't exactly a fortune but it was the principle of the matter. One of the reasons I think they paid up was to stop the story of us suing them getting out, because it would have embarrassed the club massively, and also because it might have opened the floodgates. After that, players started to investigate their rights more at clubs, and it is not uncommon now for some of the top players like Rooney to earn serious money from their share of the profits their image generates. Maybe they should thank me.

George also sorted out my endorsement contracts. I've had a couple in my time, from the cornflakes thing, where I was the prize in the box, to a big boot deal with Nike, but I've never really been that bothered about them. Again, there are players who will put their name to anything . . . we used to take the piss out of Jason McAteer rotten for the shampoo advert he did when he shook his hair like some supermodel. Fantastic lad Jason, he did a brilliant thing organizing a sell-out charity match at Anfield to raise funds for the Tsunami relief fund, which I played in and enjoyed immensely. At one point, there was a forward line of Kenny Dalglish, Rushie, me and John Aldridge in that match, which was a bit mouth-watering.

Anyway, Jase wasn't necessarily the brightest. He was called Dave, because we already had a Trigger at Anfield, Rob Jones, named after the less than intellectual character from *Only Fools and Horses*. So we had to think of another one for Jason, and someone came up with Dave, which is the name that Trigger always called Rodney by. Hardly comic genius, I know, but we found it funny, especially when he went and did something as stupid as make a shampoo advert. He thought it was only going to be broadcast in Ireland, but it got a showing over here too, and the next day at work, Jesus, he got hammered. Me, though, I never thought any of that was worth it. I got offered a jet-ski once for endorsing something, but where was I going to ride that, on the Mersey? The money from most of these things was good, but when you're on big wages what does it mean? Is it enough to sell your soul for, to make yourself look greedy, or stupid, or both? I think it is hypocritical to be involved in endorsing hundreds of things, getting your picture in the papers and on the TV all the time . . . and then complaining about the invasion of your privacy. I was criticized before the World Cup finals in 2002 for being one of the few members of the England squad who didn't attend that glitzy bash David Beckham threw for charity. I know it was for a great cause, but diamonds and white tails? That's not really me, is it? If I'd paraded in there in front of all the press with the missis, how could I have then told them to fuck off when they wanted to snap me on the beach? It's a difficult balance.

The boot deal I signed with Nike was one of the biggest they had ever agreed with a footballer. My first contract, though, was with Puma for just two years when I first arrived in the team, and me dad took the cheque because it wasn't that much. But when it came to my first proper contract, we were talking to Nike and to Adidas, and George did the negotiating while I sat at the back of the room looking in the boxes of gear they had to see if there was anything I could snaffle. It was hilarious because we got a written offer from Adidas, and George got his Tipp-Ex out and changed the figures on it . . . and then took the letter to Nike and said if they matched that offer then they had an agreement. They thought about it for a while, said they couldn't believe Adidas were offering so much, but in the end they didn't want to lose me to one of their biggest rivals.

We couldn't believe it worked, but it did, and we were pissing ourselves. I was with them for six years at about £350,000 a year, plus massive bonuses. Which was a bit of a result. Now though, I haven't got a boot contract. I was offered a new deal by Nike, even though I had done my knee ligaments and was out for a year with ankle problems, but I pissed them off when I turned up at the meeting wearing Adidas trainers, so the offer they came up with was a lot less than I had been getting. George thought he might as well go back to Adidas as I was fond of wearing their stuff, but they said at that time I didn't present the right image. Can't think what they meant. In the end I got a few offers, but none of them were worth bothering with. I didn't want to wear crap boots for the sake of a few grand. That's not being flash, it's just that I don't want to be seen to be chasing around for a few quid, when the money we are being paid is obviously fantastic.

My big contract hike came just before my twenty-fourth birthday, not long after Houllier took over at Liverpool. I only had a year left on the deal I'd signed in 1996, and Arsenal and Manchester United were both sniffing around, sensing they could get me out for peanuts because they could exploit the Bosman Ruling. That made Liverpool nervous, because Steve McManaman was about to go to Real Madrid for nothing, and the fans had kicked up one hell of a fuss over the stupidity of losing out like that.

There was a story behind that. Everyone thinks that he turned his back on Liverpool, did the dirty on them and walked out on the club that produced him for nothing, because he could get a massive contract if he went for free. But the truth is, Liverpool really were that stupid. His mum had been ill for a while, and he wanted to stay at the club, even though he had got into the final year of his deal. The year before he had almost gone to Barcelona when the club tried to sell him behind his back, but really his heart was genuinely at Anfield and he wanted to be close to his family, even though there was interest from Real Madrid, Juventus, Inter Milan, Lazio and Bayern Munich. They negotiated for a while, and eventually around September 1998, the Chief Executive made an offer that Stevie thought was good enough, and he accepted it. But then he was told that the offer would have to be ratified by the board first, and he was asked to wait for a couple of weeks. When it finally came back to him, the board had said they couldn't sanction such a deal, and offered less than had already been agreed.

Obviously, he said how the fuck could he agree a deal that was considerably less than one that he'd already shook hands on with the club only a couple of weeks before? It was madness, just crass stupidity, because Macca only had one course of action left open to him after that – to leave. When the finger's being pointed about that episode, even now, it's always Stevie who is made out to be the greedy one. But Christ, Liverpool fucked up. They knew he was worth maybe twelve, fifteen million, they knew he had six months left on his contract, and they knew he'd sign because he had shaken hands on it. So what did they do? Ensure that he left for nothing! He went on to be Man of the Match in the Champions' League final a year later, so maybe that was an error. You wonder who was behind that decision. But whoever decided they should withdraw that offer, they cost Liverpool a lot of money.

It was against this backdrop that my negotiations were taking place. I had about a year and a half left on my contract, so it wasn't quite as urgent and I had been told by George that it was better if we took our time. The thing was, the Sky money had kicked in and wages were going mental by that stage. I know plenty of people will call me a greedy bastard, but I always ask this question: if the money's there in the sport, who do the fans want to get it? With all that investment from Sky, clubs had plenty of money and there were an awful lot of people taking it out. Owners of clubs were making millions and millions, and agents were taking their share too. Would fans prefer it to go to them, or to the players and coaches that actually create the game? I suppose they'd actually like to get in for a reasonable ticket price instead of the incredible amount that clubs charge these days, but that isn't going to happen. For me, it was sensible to hold out, because of the way things were going. If other players were being paid huge amounts of money, then it was only natural for me to want the same.

I don't think Houllier or the board wanted to be seen to be making the same mistake as they did with Macca, and there was a determination to sort things out. We actually talked from the previous summer, but things didn't get very far. In the end, it became annoying because Liverpool seemed to be trying to put pressure on me to sign, and the way they thought they could get through to me was emotional blackmail from the fans. It seemed to me that they started to drop the idea quietly into the media that I was holding out for a huge figure. That's a fair enough tactic I suppose, if it was true, but it wasn't. I was asking for far less than they had offered Macca, far less than other players at the biggest clubs were on, and far less than a lot of players at Anfield subsequently received.

Yet all the papers and the radio phone-ins were full of this greedy little scally asking for fifty grand a week to play football, when he should be honoured to be wearing the red shirt of Liverpool. I remember one incident where the *Daily Mirror* went out to get me. They seemed outraged that a kid from Toxteth could dare to ask for so much money – even if they had got that figure totally wrong. So they sent poor old Richard Tanner out to where I came from to ask the people what they thought about it. Basically, he was told to get lots of reaction from dockers and brickies and bin-men asking who the fuck did I think I was, how dare I ask for so much money? He went down my old street in Toxteth, and after a while he knocked on my old front door, the very house I had grown up in. This lady came out, and he told her the story about this greedy footballer with this incredible wealth when nurses were paid peanuts and what did she think about that outrageous situation? Don't you think it's immoral for a footballer to be holding a club to ransom like that? The woman said she thought I was bloody marvellous and I deserved as much as I could get. In fact, she thought I was so good I should actually ask for more. She thought I was the best footballer in the country, and a really nice lad as well! He couldn't believe it, so he thanked her and turned away. Then she said, matter of fact, just as he was walking up the path: 'Oh, by the way, love, if you want to know my name, it's Mrs Fowler ... I'm Robbie's auntie!' Tanner told me that story himself, and he also said that he changed tack after that and went down the docks instead, to see if anyone there would have a go at me. He spoke to about twenty people, and every single one of them said exactly the same: 'Good luck to the lad. If he can get it, fair play to him, I'd do exactly the same.' He went back to his paper and told them his story on Fowler's contract was that the people of Liverpool backed him to the hilt. Strangely enough, they never ran that angle.

The radio phone-ins were far worse. One of them, I swear they whipped up such an incredible feeling against me that after a while people were ringing in asking, 'Who the fuck does that scally Fowler think he is?' In the end, me dad got so annoyed about what was happening that he rang the radio station himself, and he went ballistic with them. Strangely enough, the programme was immediately pulled off air. Again, the figures they were throwing about as fact were totally incorrect. But it didn't seem to matter because it was open season.

It's amazing how wound up the media gets about players' wages ... as though they would turn down the money themselves if they were offered it. It was a difficult time for me because of that, and I was worried sick that people would believe it all, and think that I was some greedy flash bastard who didn't give a toss about the football. Of course I was concerned about the money, who wouldn't be? But I left all that to George, he did all the negotiating and I never even bothered going to the meetings.

The fact is that the football always mattered far more. When we had the meetings, I was always much more interested in what they were saying about the new manager, and who he would buy, what direction the club was going in. They told me he was going to be given massive money to bring in top players, that the team would be built around me and Michael, which is why they wanted the pair of us to sign new contracts, and they said that the aim was to put Liverpool back at the summit of the Premiership, and of Europe too. It sounded pretty convincing, this guy who had been involved with the French World Cup winning team getting more money to spend than Manchester United or Arsenal or any of the other big clubs, so in the end I said that I didn't want to go anywhere else, I wanted to sign a new deal for Liverpool, and if they made me a decent enough offer then I'd be happy to commit myself to the club for life. And I meant that, I really did. On 24 January 1999 I put my name on a new four-year contract that was worth about £30,000 a week, which was almost half what the papers said I was getting, although it did rise through the course of the deal to closer to forty grand a week. Not at all bad, though. I was going to have to find some better ways to spend it.

My biggest indulgence has to be the horses that I own in partnership with Macca. Believe me, you can spend some money in that game. Actually, we've done all right, maybe even breaking even, which is some result considering some of the fees you have to pay. Racing is a real passion of mine, and Macca is fairly addicted too. So is Michael Owen, and when I was at Liverpool, Didi Hamann was also a real enthusiast, which is a surprise, given that he'd never even seen a race-track until he came to England. I know plenty of people think footballers and horse racing is a cliché, but it's different to the seedy image of a wrong 'un in a mac with a woodbine in the bookies. For me it's a release, an escape.

A day out at the races is a wonderful experience, something

that is hard to put into words. There's the sporting element, and when you are an owner you've got all the excitement and adrenalin of top-class sport, but it doesn't knacker you out. Even these days, managers don't mind too much if their players go racing, so long as they don't hit the pop too hard, because it is a way of relaxing that doesn't interfere with the full-time job of being a professional athlete. As I've said, I've never won too much backing horses, because I've never had a proper massive bet on my runners. If the trainer says he fancies it, then I'll have an each-way wager, but mostly our horses are entered into decent races, so the prize money is worth winning and the odds and form are pretty easy to read. It's not often you can make a killing. I did have a chance with my first ever runner, which went off at 33–1 and won at a canter, but typical of my luck, I was away on under-21 duty at the time in Portugal, and didn't get the info in time for me to get some money on. The rest of the lads cleaned up, and I swear I have never lived it down.

That horse was some horse. Some Horse, in fact. Not some horse as in some brilliant horse, you understand, but Some Horse as in when the punters are standing in the betting shops listening to the feed from the racetrack, the commentator will be describing the race and then he'll say, '. . . and some horse is coming up on the outside . . .', and everyone in the bookies will go: 'Which fucking horse?' Needless to say, that was the idea of a twenty-year-old wisecracking smart arse. Me. There were eight of us, all with an interest in racing, and we decided that if we were going to have a day off and go to the local courses, then it might be more interesting to have a runner. Nobody wanted to do their money, so we all put a grand in each; me, Macca, Neil Ruddock, Dominic Matteo, Jamie Redknapp, Phil Babb, Rob Jones and John Scales.

We had eight grand to buy a horse, so our chances of winning the Derby were not high. Our chances of getting anything better than a milk-float nag weren't too high either. But we knew a fella who knew a fella, who put us in touch with a trainer called Michael Meagher, who trained out of Ormskirk, a town north of Liverpool that is not exactly a hotbed of racing, is not exactly a hotbed of anything, in fact. I heard that they declared a national holiday and put the bunting out when Barry Cowan, their most famous resident, won a match at Wimbledon. Their second most famous resident is the burglar who unwisely broke into Duncan Ferguson's house when he was still at home. But Michael was a great bloke who knew his racing inside out, and he indulged us. He's the racing manager now for Trevor Hemmings, and quite a big name in the racing world . . . a step above the days when he had to put up with a group of lairy footballers looking for another Shergar for the price of one of Big Dunc's pigeons.

He got in touch and said he'd found us something that actually had a leg at each corner, and did we want to find a name for it? We all got together to think of something clever and tried the usual jokes, Betty Swollocks, Mary Hinge, that sort of thing, but we couldn't get away with it. It was me who eventually came up with Some Horse, mostly because I was a daft kid and the rest of the lads liked my sense of humour. And in the end, he turned out to be some horse in the best sense of the phrase because he won two of his seven races before he got injured, and sadly had to retire. He ended up in a field, being looked after by one of the stable girls, living the life of Riley, so it worked out okay for him.

Some Horse gave us the bug though, and so the heavyweight syndicate upped the ante to about twelve hundred quid each, so we could really splash out, and we got another horse with Michael. Time for the gathering of geniuses for another barnstorming session, and after a cultured debate that taxed us for hours, we came up with the inspired name of . . . Another Horse. Again, we were hoping for that perfect betting shop scenario of the commentator shouting out: 'Some Horse is leading inside the final furlong, but wait, here comes Another Horse closing on the outside . . .' It didn't happen though, because Another Horse wasn't quick enough to get up on the outside of anything very much, not even me after a particularly heavy night on the tiles.

You need something as a professional athlete to take your mind off what can be a mind-numbing routine of training, resting and playing. Those two horses gave me the perfect diversion. I was hooked, and so was Macca. It was fascinating getting the calls off the trainer, giving us the news of how our horses were doing, what they were aiming for, how they were training, what all the gossip in the racing world was. And we both wanted to step it up a bit, get a little more involved, it's just that we didn't know how. As it turned out, it was a chance event that gave us both what has turned out to be a tremendous relationship with some wonderful people and with a thrilling sport.

It was the Grand National that was delayed for three days because of the bomb threat, back in 1997. Because the race was cancelled and they had to stay around all over the weekend, all the jockeys went back to the Moat House Hotel and had a big piss-up, and we came in right in the middle of it. Going in the door, it was like a scene from *Phoenix Nights*; y'know, with the dwarves, where they squint and say: 'How far away are they?' I'd met the champion jump jockey Tony McCoy once before, and we got talking to him and Graham Bradley, who was his big mate and had just packed in riding after working for Martin Pipe, who McCoy rode for. From there we became firm friends, even though Tony is an Arsenal fan, and Brad follows Leeds, of all clubs.

Tony is an incredible guy. I don't think I've ever seen a more dedicated sportsman, or a more talented one. He is a genius in the saddle, the best jump jockey there has ever been – and one of the nicest men you will ever meet. If you didn't know just how much of a legend he is, then you'd never find out from him because he is so modest and genuine. He is not interested in celebrity of any sort in the slightest. Yet when he is doing his job, there is nobody more single-minded. Graham's the same, an incredible guy. He made the news a while ago because he was caught up in the race-fixing investigation because they connected him with a couple of shady characters – even though there was never a claim he did anything wrong – and was warned off racing by the jockey club, which means he couldn't work in the industry for a while. But I can honestly say that I have never met a straighter, more honest man to deal with, and if you knew him you'd say there was absolutely no way that he can have been involved in anything serious. What has happened to him is a travesty. He is an absolute diamond, and an incredible character. There is not a funnier guy around, or better company, and few people who know as much about the game as him.

As Macca and me got friends with him, we discovered that he was setting up as a bloodstock agent, buying horses for clients and advising them. Until then, we had been involved in a small way with flat racing, and the jump game was uncharted territory because of the fear of one of your horses getting hurt. But Tony and Brad made us realize the excitement involved, and the fun you can have with National Hunt racing. So we commissioned Brad to buy us a couple of horses, and what a decision that proved. He went to Germany and found a big grey horse called Authaler, which is a common German surname, and is well known over there for the work of some famous philosopher or something like that. We didn't pay much for him, but he proved an instant success, winning some decent races and setting us up nicely. He was a fantastic horse, but McCoy reckoned he was gay because he was never gelded, and one day Tony was milling around on board him at the start of a race, and didn't realize that he had got next to a mare in season.

Normally when that happens, all hell breaks loose with the horse going mad and trying to get it on. But Authaler just stood there not blinking an eye or taking any notice at all . . . which raised a few more suspicions about him. We put the horse with Martin Pipe, because Tony and Brad recommended him, and me dad, who is also a keen racing man, made a few enquiries and everyone said he was the best. They were right. He's another true genius at the game, a brilliant trainer who can always get the best out of his horses. And he has always been fantastic with me and Macca, treating us like family when we go down to Devon to see the horses, and according the same welcome to me dad and Davey, Stevie's old fella, who are both mad keen on the nags. Not that I can actually see the horses, because it turns out that I am allergic to them. I suppose that's something you don't discover growing up in Toxteth, because the closest I came to a horse was when they charged down our street with policemen on their backs during the riots. It was only when I eventually got to a racecourse that I found out I had a problem.

Another of the horses that Brad found for us, Bernardon, was running at Cheltenham, and Martin Pipe's other jockey Richard Guest was on board. Before the race we went into the parade ring, and I was making a fuss of the horse, patting him on the nose and telling him to win for us. The next thing, blotches started appearing all over my face, and then I started to get short of breath. It was as though my throat was closing and I felt faint, and a bit panicky. I was rushed to the medical room where the doctor turned pale when he looked at me. I was given an emergency antihistamine injection, and they made me lie down on the bed, with cold compresses on my head. Groggy and still wheezing, I looked over as the door opened, and there was Richard Guest limping into the room. It took a while to sink in that it was him, and then I shouted over: 'What the fuck are you doing here? I thought you were supposed to be riding our horse.' He looked back at me, and as he flopped on the bed next to me, he whispered through a painful grimace: 'I was . . . until I fell off at the first.'

We struck gold with Authaler. He was so good that six months after he started running in our colours – classic white silks – Macca and me were offered two hundred grand from someone who wanted to buy him. Maybe we should have taken it, because soon after he damaged the tendon in his leg, and was unable to race any more. One of Martin Pipe's stable girls bought him off us for quite a bit less than that original offer, about two hundred grand less, in fact, and he too is enjoying his retirement in a field, lazing around all day. His success got us going, and after Authaler we went up a level with another German horse called Seebald, who cost quite a bit more but turned out to be an incredible buy. He is almost top class, a decent stayer who has been up against the very best horses in the business and given them a run for their money.

It looked as though he would become one of the top chasers,

but he never quite made it. Seebald finished second to the Gold Cup winner Best Mate, and also second to another top-class horse, Azertyuiop, in a £50,000 race at Sandown. Early in his career he won some big races, and we have always had some thrilling rides out of him. A couple of years back, he was leading coming to the last in a big race at the Cheltenham Festival, only to fall when it looked like he was the stitched-on winner. He has more than paid his way, which is probably a bloody good job, because after Seebald we haven't had much luck, even though we have bought some pretty good horses. Samon was injured badly and tragically had to be destroyed. The same happened to a very good horse of ours called Major Lando. In only his third race he came in a brilliant second, but as he crossed the finishing line he tripped in a pot-hole and broke his leg. That is the terrible side of the game. You get so attached to your horses, but you know there is always a danger they could be injured. It is heart-breaking, but it is the price of the game. Bernardon has now had to retire as well, but at least he is still healthy. We sent him to train with Richard Guest, but he couldn't get him fit so there was no choice but to let him out into the field. After all that, the Macca and Growler partnership had just two horses, Seebald and Simoun, and with all our football commitments at City and the lack of chances to see them, we decided to keep it at that. But the plan was always to get a few more horses when we both retire and see if we can win one of the top races at Cheltenham, or even better, Aintree, which is still the best racecourse in the world, naturally.

Because of the brilliance of Martin Pipe and Tony McCoy, and the knowledge of Graham Bradley, we've managed not to lose any of our money on the racing game. Thanks to George, I've managed to invest it wisely. Since 1998, we decided that the best place to invest was property. In partnership with a great friend of both George and mine from Glasgow called Big Sandy, we started buying up properties to let with the idea that it would provide me with a decent income when I eventually have to retire from the game. I've got pension plans, but that seems like a much better idea. George is a financial advisor, and he originally kept the money in various basic investments, but as I started to earn more, it made sense to think about the future and make the money work harder.

Sandy knows the market particularly well, and we picked exactly the right time to get involved, which is probably why I came top of the rich list. The fact is though, the property investments are not worth as much as they said in the list. For a start, I'm in partnership, and also they have overestimated the value of the portfolio. As I said, it's guesswork, based on the stuff in the papers. And the only reason anything was in the papers about me and property was because I bought a couple of houses in Hertfordshire to use as corporate lets to diplomats and that sort of person. It was a good idea to branch out, but the *Mirror* got wind of it, and at that time there were rumours spreading like wildfire that I was a target for Arsenal. They had expressed an interest in me soon after I bought the London houses, around 1998, they had even made an enquiry about me. The house purchases were part of a much bigger plan, but of course the paper put two and two together and made a back page out of it. George explained the real situation to their reporter, and then he printed that story instead! Since then everyone has picked up on it, and they've regularly updated it to say I've got even more money and even more properties.

Even Gazza has bought into it. In his book he revealed that he's more or less broke because of some bad investments and his divorce. Then he mentioned me as an example of someone who's done the right thing and invested his money wisely and is rolling in it! Thanks, Gazza. Of course I'm doing all right, and it's good sometimes to think that I'm in this position because I reckon there are plenty of people out there who think it's only a matter of time before the kid from Toxteth falls on his arse. A lot of it is hype though. That rich list, it makes me laugh because with me at the top, they've taken into account all the investments, and the property portfolio, and then come up with a vague figure that's not even accurate. But all the rest of the footballers on the list, their figures are based purely on their earnings from their clubs, as if they just put their money under the bed like Steve Nicol after a night out. These days, footballers get the best advice to go along with their huge salaries, and I reckon many of the top players have pretty smart investments.

Macca and me, we've got plans beyond the racehorses. There's one idea that has yet to come to fruition, but if it does then it will fulfil another ambition of mine. We've been in talks to buy a golf course in Wales that has a small hotel on it. We've been talking about it, that's all, but if we can pull it off then we hope to build a new hotel and develop the course to make a top-class facility. It's not far from Celtic Manor where the Ryder Cup is going to be held, and I reckon that would help it become a real success. I love golf. I play with Macca and Steve Harkness a lot, and some of the City lads. So imagine that. The Macca and Growler partnership moving into golf courses. We'll be rivalling Jack Nicklaus soon. Maybe we'll get him to design the course.

Actually, the idea is to pursue it as an investment, like all the other properties and business premises. But it would be something to own a golf course even if it's probably only a dream. It would save on green fees for a start. Maybe, it would also show that I've come a long way from those days when we used to sit on the benches, dreaming about a football career. And maybe it would finally put to rest that Spice Boy tag that I have to admit did my head in when I enjoyed my best years at Liverpool under Roy Evans. I'm not claiming to be some sort of property expert, I've just been lucky enough to be involved with some friends who are. But if people are prepared to ditch that Spice Boy tag – even if it means they follow Gazza's lead and call me Mr Moneybags – then I'll settle for that. Apart from the drug taunts, that one innocent phrase has caused me more grief than just about anything else in my career.

SPICE WORLD (8)

What is a Spice Boy? I'm fucked if I know. Honestly, I don't have a clue. What I do know for absolute certain is that whatever it is, I'm not one of them. It was the *Daily Mail* that came up with the name as an insulting term to the lads at Liverpool who used to go out clubbing down in London after a game (when they had got the rest of the weekend off). Plenty of the Manchester United lads do that these days without any problems, but it seemed to be an issue for Liverpool back in the nineties.

The thing is, I reckon I only went down there once or twice for a night out in all the time I was at Anfield, and yet I was lumped in with the rest of the crew. I suppose it's my own fault, though, because I didn't give a toss about how people looked at me in those days, and it never crossed my mind to point out the truth, or distance myself from what I realize now was an incredibly negative and damaging phrase. Two little words that's all, and yet what were incredible times at Anfield – successful, exciting, breathless seasons when I played probably the best football of my life – are dismissed with contempt by those two tiny words.

Don't get me wrong, things happened and they shouldn't have. I look back now and I can see how close we were to becoming a truly great side. The fact that it didn't happen is a real regret. I look at it and I know that I could have behaved differently, I could have been more professional, followed a better diet, drunk less, stayed out of trouble. But would that have made me a better player? I scored more than thirty goals in each of my first three full seasons. I won awards, caps, finished top of the scoring lists, all that stuff that when you trot it out makes you sound like a big-headed get. I know I was a bit cocky, but I honestly don't believe I really let the manager down during that time.

The fact is, if more of the players had reached the level I was at for those seasons, then we would have won more. Again, that's not being big-headed, just realistic. Roy Evans was always great to me, and has always been loyal. But then I did it for him. He took over in January 1994 and was boss until the summer of 1998, when the club made the senseless decision to bring in Houllier as his joint manager. In four and a half years I scored 115 goals for him ... and I was injured for six months or so of that. So don't give me the Spice Boy bollocks – I scored thirty goals every year for Roy Evans, and only Rushie and Roger Hunt had ever done that for Liverpool.

What annoys me most, though, is this enduring idea that I was always swanning around, going to opening nights, fashion shows, swanky restaurants and clubs. Don't make me laugh. Yeah, I went out on the piss, but it was with me mates and we went out in Liverpool to the bars and clubs that we had always gone to. And we only ever did it after a match, so it was hardly big time. No champagne, can't stand the stuff. No VIP sections. No modelling assignments – I was too bloody ugly.

I went down to London a couple of times to do the TV show *Soccer AM*, with the very friendly Tim Lovejoy and the even friendlier Helen Chamberlain, and I went with Calvey and Gordon who got themselves on the telly by pretending to be Norwegians when they were accused of being my scally sidekicks. The only other time I went was for the Brit Awards, when the Spice Girls were performing and that Ginger one wore the really short Union Jack dress with her backside hanging out. It was there that I met Emma Bunton, and because of the papers constantly linking me with her it was easy for them to come up with the connection between the Spice Girls and the Spice Boys of Liverpool.

The reality though is very different. The only reason I was there was because Macca had a business involvement with Simon Fuller. He was managing the Spice Girls at the time, and Macca got to know him through his own financial advisor, who also worked for Fuller's company, 19 Management. Because of that, we got an invite to the Brit Awards and the after-show party. It was a blast, and we had been given the day after off, so it was no problem with the manager or the club.

At the party Simon Fuller introduced us to his clients, who included Cathy Dennis, and I think Annie Lennox was another. Then we met the Spicies. They were massive then, honest. Emma was a nice girl, very friendly, and we got talking. She said she'd never been to a football match and would love to go, so being the chivalrous gent that I am I said I'd sort it out no problem. That was it. There was no relationship and we didn't go out. In fact, we have never even clapped eyes on each other again.

I have spoken to her a couple of times, and it was interesting for both of us to hear what each other had to put up with. But she never did get to a football match because she was mad busy travelling around the world milking their moment of fame for all it was worth. I was busy playing for Liverpool and England, and hardly got a spare moment either. It makes me laugh how that brief meeting was built into epic tales of a relationship – crazy! We were friends of friends, and yet somehow the talk of the tabloids for a while.

I do know she is an incredibly nice person who is kind and friendly, and we had a lot in common. I remember when I did my knee ligaments and was in a hospital in the Midlands, which was a miserable time in my life. I was cheered up no end by some flowers and fruit that Emma and Mel Chisholm sent to me. A great gesture from two great girls, who took the time to think about someone they knew, despite their hectic lifestyles. That was that though, the full extent of it. Yet every day for about a year I would pick up the papers and the gossip columns were full of this romance between the Spice Girl and the Spice Boy, and from then on the phrase was cemented in the minds of the nation. Cheers.

The funny thing is, soon after, David Beckham met up with Victoria Adams and they obviously had a proper relationship. Given that he also became something of a fashion clothes horse, by rights it should have been the United players who were the Spice Boys, but by then the name had stuck with us, and there was no getting off the hook.

There's been so much crap said about Liverpool in the nineties that it is hard to know what is true and what is myth. When you look closely at where all that Spice Boys criticism comes from, then to me it's obvious that it's just a bit of piss-taking because we didn't win anything. There has been loads of talk about wild parties, excess drinking, half the players modelling and doing adverts instead of training, travelling to London all the time, a lack of discipline on the training ground and celebrity girlfriends. All of it is true to a certain extent, but each one is an isolated incident that doesn't add up to the big picture that has always been painted. Maybe the celebrity girlfriend thing did most damage, because the impression it gives off is the jet-set lifestyle, flitting from one opening night to the next.

As well as me being friends with Emma, Jamie Redknapp went out with the singer Louise Nurding and eventually married her. Who would say that was a problem? They are a fantastic couple and she's so down to earth that there was never any chance of Jamie getting caught up in the celebrity world. There was the odd page-three girl linked to Phil Babb, John Scales and Jason McAteer, but again, that's not exactly unusual in the football world, is it? Stan Collymore was a bit of a sucker for a celebrity girlfriend, but I don't think Stan counts, does he? The modelling idea is just rubbish. It only happened once, when David James did a shoot for Armani, modelling their boxer shorts, and he didn't even get paid for it (except in Y-fronts). That was it, and it took him about half an hour. Yet I swear, even now you read all this stuff about the lot of us modelling instead of playing.

There were no big telly adverts either, none of that came along until Michael Owen scored that goal in the 1998 World Cup. Barnsie did a Lucozade advert – I-so-ton-ic, he's not got any better on Channel Five! – and Jason McAteer did the shampoo ad, but that was in Ireland, and no one in the squad would dare do another one after the merciless kicking he got for that. There was the odd wild party, because the Christmas do always got a bit out of hand, but what's the problem in that? I remember one year, must have been 1996, the party went on as usual, with all the familiar things that had happened for the last thirty years. A few strippers, the new lads having to get up on stage to sing a song before they were drowned in beer, and then drinking to the early hours. Paddy Berger was there for the first time after signing the previous summer, and beforehand he was saying that he wouldn't join in, because he didn't drink and he wanted to go home early to his family, that sort of thing. At the end of the night as I was leaving the club, I walked out to see him with a large brandy in one hand, and a cigar in the other, with him going: 'I love your Ingleesh parteees!'

All harmless fun of course, but later, when everyone went back to the Moat House, a few people got into the bar for a nightcap. It kicked off in there, but only amongst a few friends of the players and some gate-crashers. No players were around by that time – about four in the morning – but the police were called, and there were sirens blasting off outside, flashing lights and the whole Merseybeat experience. The big problem was, the local radio station's offices are right opposite the hotel, and the bloke on their night shift looked out of the window to see a scene from a TV programme unfolding in front of him. One quick check saw it was the Liverpool players' party, and by the morning there were about twenty TV crews and photographers outside. Of course, none of the players knew what the hell was going on. They walked out blinking, looking hung over, still in the fancy dress they had worn the night before. The snappers had a field day, and it was all over the papers as another example of the Spice Boys' wild party lifestyle . . . and we were stuffed again.

There was a group of lads who did travel down to London on their time off, largely because they were from there. Jamie Redknapp, Razor Ruddock, Phil Babb, John Scales, Jamo, occasionally Michael Thomas, they all used to go down to London to meet up with their friends and family, and they'd go out to a couple of the trendy clubs like Browns, or whatever the cool places were around that time. Stan would go all the time too, along with Jason McAteer and Mark Kennedy, who had signed from a football club in London. They were all mates, and hung out together and I don't think they did any harm. Maybe in hindsight it wasn't such a great idea to travel so far, but it was hardly every weekend, and anyway, no one made a fuss about it when Beckham did it, or Rio Ferdinand and a few other of the United boys. I guess it's different if you win.

There were other things that shouldn't have happened, and caused us unnecessary problems. I'll be the first to admit that looking back now, there was a drinking culture around the place, even if it was common at the time. Most definitely, the gaffer should have put his foot down and stopped the lads from going to London quite as often as they did. We had a tight-knit group that used to socialize a lot together and it built team spirit massively, but there were times when we overdid it, and even though Macca and me and the likes of Dom and Harkey never went down to London, we probably still showed our faces around town a bit too much. I know now that my diet wasn't right either – too many Chinese takeaways and McDonald's! – and I wish I had been steered in the right direction earlier. Maybe the gaffer should also have put his foot down a bit more over the celebrity connections with the club, not because it was a problem as such, but if only to protect himself against all the accusations that followed. Rob Jones was a great one for socializing. He knew all the celebrities, and often went out with them.

One morning, he was late into training because he had fallen asleep at some traffic lights. He was mates with Robbie Williams, and also claimed to be best buddies with Noel Gallagher, although we weren't too sure about that one. We asked him to prove it once, and he came in with this signed photo ... which said: 'To Rob Jones from Noel Gallagher'. Sounds like best mates to me! Stan was also mates with the likes of Jay Kay from Jamiroquai, and quite a few TV celebs like Danni Behr, Jo Guest and Donna Air used to hang around at matches, along with plenty of pop stars and actors. That just heightened the image of playboys, and it came to a head when we played at Aston Villa at the end of one season. We'd already qualified for Europe so the game wasn't that important as we couldn't get any higher in the league, so Phil Babb persuaded the gaffer to let his mate Robbie Williams come on the team bus with us to the ground. He even walked out on the pitch when we got there to take in the atmosphere, and that was wrong, because it was saved up and used against us and the boss as an example of how we were running the show.

It shouldn't have happened. We should never have put the manager in that position. He has got so much stick for that, but it was the fault of the players pure and simple. I have my own story of Robbie Williams at that time that makes me laugh to this day. We went for a night out in Liverpool with him, and we ended up at a bar called Plummers. While we were in there, we realized there was a karaoke going on, so everyone was egging each other to enter. Robbie Williams had a go, and sang 'Mac the Knife'. I have to say he was pretty good. Then me and Calvey got up and did 'All My Loving'. After that we got off, but the next day, someone came up to me dad on the railways, and said: 'Hey, tell your Robbie that he has to pick up his prize for winning the karaoke last night.' So me and Calvey beat Robbie Williams in a singing contest. Maybe I had the wrong career.

There were plenty of other things that happened, that maybe made things look worse than they were. One of the most famous incidents that I regret was when Neil Ruddock and me came to blows on the tarmac at Speke Airport. Or rather, he came to blows and I took the blows! It was after a European game early in the 1995–96 season, in some godforsaken Eastern European shit-hole. Vladikavkaz it was, and it was so bad you couldn't even sleep in the beds in the hotel, they were so full of fleas. You had to have the lights on too, so the cockroaches didn't come out. The only food we had was the stuff brought in by our own chefs. And even though we won out there we had trailed for a while, and it was a terrible game. So when we got on the plane to come home, the lads were in a frisky mood. I took me shoes off to be more comfortable for the flight, and when I came to put them on later, they had been cut into pieces. It was a typical prank and I wasn't bothered, because I had a pair of trainers in my bag in the overhead locker. When I swung it out though, the handles came with me and the bag stayed where it was, because they had been cut off too. When I got into the bag, I found that me trainers had been cut into pieces too.

By then, I realized revenge was required, and I narrowed down the culprits to John Barnes, Steve Harkness and Razor Ruddock. I was going mad by that stage, because I'd gone all that way to be on the bench, and I was pretty pissed off. I decided I was going to get all three of the fuckers back, no matter who did it. Problem was, I chose Razor first. He was going through a bit of a marriage crisis at the time, and he was trying to patch things up with his missis. She'd made a gesture by buying him these really nice, dead expensive Italian leather shoes that he was fond of showing off . . . so I cut them into tiny little pieces. He had a proper cob on. He was really aggressive and was going on about me having to buy him a new pair, because they meant so much to him. 'Fuck off,' I said, 'I've had me whole fucking wardrobe cut up.'

We got on the tarmac, and he was even more aggressive, and he told me again I'd have to pay. I just laughed at him, and I think that did it. Bam. He turned round and twatted me in the mouth. I had a cut nose and lip, and blood was pouring off me. There was a trail going from the tarmac right into the baggage reclaim. I didn't go down though, contrary to some of the stories that were told afterwards. Maybe I should repeat that: I didn't go down!

Mind you, I might have, if what I planned to do next hadn't been intercepted by David James. I stood there for a while in shock, thinking that he'd just smacked me in the gob. Then I thought I wasn't going to let him get away with that. Fortunately, Jamo stepped in and grabbed me in that bear hug of his, and told me not to be so fucking stupid. The press were getting off the plane behind us, and they would see everything. God knows what would have happened if he hadn't stopped me from getting to Razor, I'd probably have been in hospital for a week. For a few weeks after that, things were a bit tense, but we shook hands and got over it, and we're still best mates. You know after Kieron Dyer got smacked by Lee Bowyer and loads of players came out to say that sort of thing happens all the time in football? Well it does. Maybe once a week in training. You get these incredible competitors, all taking the piss and taking each other on, and it's bound to spill over at times. The funny thing was, that incident didn't make the press until quite a few days later when it leaked out to the Sunday tabloids, even though the reporters on the flight had followed my blood from the plane to the terminal like it was a red directional line. In the end, though, that was used as yet another stone to throw at Roy Evans, which was a big regret for all of us.

It's the myths that have grown up around that time that have caused the damage, and again for me they seem convenient. When Roy Evans left Liverpool, it was easy to do him down, suggest that it was a holiday camp under him and the club had no discipline, because that made the job of his successor so much simpler. If you portray the previous regime as a disaster that will take years to sort out, then it buys you time and makes you look an awful lot better. It didn't help when a few players came out and hyped it all up, because they were trying to generate publicity for themselves. Razor seemed to do that. He said we had a motto, which we all said after matches, no matter what we did: 'Win or lose, first on the booze.' That sounds like we really didn't give a fuck, but the truth is, it was a joke. I hated losing, so did more or less everyone else in the squad. When you have a group of lads together largely from the same working-class background and with everyone desperate not to be ridiculed, then you piss about, act cool, joke around. We might have said it, but it wasn't a true philosophy.

This isn't to say there weren't any problems at Liverpool at the time. There were a few players who didn't act professionally enough, and quite a few mistakes were made. If there was a fault with our mentality, though, it was that we always wanted to win in style, always looked to play exciting, attacking football. When it came off, believe me, we were the best team in the Premiership by a mile. Too often it didn't though, because it is hard to be cavalier every week in such a tough, physical league. As for the lifestyle, well, yeah, sometimes it was wrong. By now, you must be able to tell my attitude towards it all. We made mistakes because it was a learning process. Suddenly, there was more money and more celebrity around than anyone in football had ever known. To a bunch of young lads who became millionaires overnight, it was easy to indulge a little too much.

I'll say this, though, the Arsenal side that won titles when I first arrived in football, and the United side that began to dominate as I made a name for myself, both of those teams were much wilder than us, and I know that from some of the stories that I've heard on England duty. They got away with it because they won. You look back now and you think, Christ, we did some crazy things, but that's judging by today's standards. It's like when they lived on pie and chips in the seventies. You wouldn't do it now. As football developed in the nineties, as more and more foreign players came into the game, you couldn't get away with so many things. But when the drinking culture was pretty dominant, when United were the biggest party animals of all, then you were on the same level.

Stan Collymore tells a story of agreeing to join Liverpool and going down to meet up for a night out with some of the lads he was friendly with. Apparently, he arrived at the hotel in the centre of the city and went up to one of the players' rooms. The door, surprisingly, was open so he waltzed straight in, and just happened to be confronted with the sight of a famous footballer lying back with his arms behind his head, being noshed off by two girls either side of him. Hmmmm. Seems a bit strange that you would be in a large, busy hotel with two girls, and not even bother closing the door. But it's that sort of story that was associated with Liverpool under Roy Evans, and sadly for him it has stuck. The biggest myth of all is that Roy was soft, and put up with anything from the players, which made us a completely lawless group. He wasn't. In fact, if anything, Roy could be fucking ruthless, but he did it with a smile on his face and rarely an angry word. It all has to be put into context, that's all.

When Roy took over, he was given the job because Souey had been too brutal, had upset too many people, had shipped too many players out too early, and had caused so much friction in the squad that there was little or no team spirit. So when he took over, the board made it clear to the gaffer that he had to rebuild morale, smooth things over and make it a happy, harmonious place to be again, just like it was in the glory years. And that's what he did. He made training fun, he made the lads feel like they belonged, he made us feel that we could talk to him and were part of something. He knew he had big changes to make still, because for all the young lads Souness had introduced that were quality players there were also a lot of players there who the gaffer thought weren't up to Liverpool standards. And he wasn't shy of making decisions, either. Look at what Roy Evans did in his first six months in the job. He got rid of Mark Walters, Julian Dicks, Paul Stewart, Torben Piechnik, and Ronnie Rosenthal. There was no sentiment either, because he quietly ended the Anfield careers of such servants as Bruce Grobbelaar, Steve Nicol, Ronnie Whelan and Jan Molby. He got rid of Nigel Clough as well, and then eventually phased out even John Barnes and Ian Rush. That's not soft.

Don Hutch was a perfect example. He was a fantastic player, a real talent when his head was right and a decent lad. But he was a bit mad. Macca told me a story of when he went up to Newcastle for a night out with Hutch, which is where he came from. They had a bit of a blow-out, and it ended with Macca having to knock on Mrs Hutchison's door in the early hours of the morning to get in . . . tell her that her son had been arrested and could she go down and bail him out. At the end of the gaffer's first season in charge, Hutch was at it again. He went out on the lash to a bar called Labinsky's, and hooked up with some students. But he overstepped the mark, and got himself pictured dropping his kecks and slapping the label of a Budweiser bottle over his knob. That was the final straw, and Roy booted him out. He got us together at the start of the season and said he wouldn't tolerate indiscipline, wouldn't have that sort of behaviour. Even though Don was one of the best players at the club, he was no good to anyone behaving like that so he had to go.

The same happened with Francis Tierney, the kid who had played in the same local Sunday league side as me. Liverpool agreed to sign him in the June of 1995, for a fee of around £1.5 million. But before he arrived for pre-season training he got involved in a couple of incidents while he was on holiday, no doubt celebrating his big transfer. So the gaffer called the whole deal off, even though the kid's career was ruined. He took some incredibly tough decisions too. When we played Manchester United in the FA Cup final in 1996, he had to choose between Mark Wright and Neil Ruddock, who was one of the popular players at the time, and everyone thought he would get the nod.

But the boss reckoned Razor hadn't been doing it for him, hadn't shown the right attitude in training, so he was bumped out of the team. All hell broke loose, but the gaffer had the bottle to front him up and explain why he had done it. He had Razor in a few times, and Julian Dicks and Jan Molby, and slaughtered them in front of everyone for being over-weight, said he wouldn't tolerate it, and they would be out of the club if they didn't get it off. Again, that was designed to make the point about standards and discipline. The same happened when we had a pre-season friendly at Bolton in his first summer, and Dicks and Mark Wright were rubbish. After-wards he laid into them, and they responded by saying it didn't matter because it was just a friendly. So the gaffer said in that case the rest of the pre-season tour to Norway didn't matter either, so they might as well not bother going on it. That was the end of Dicks, and Wrighty was bombed for ages too, and every player realized Roy meant business.

The gaffer wanted to get the spirit back into the squad and he achieved that. I don't think I've ever been involved with such an incredible group of players, with so much character, except maybe the 1996 England squad. There was so much fun, so much togetherness in that bunch of Liverpool lads, and it was a squad that was fantastic to be around. There were so many jokers in there, Harky, Jamo, err, me! The usual juvenile stuff to keep everyone on their toes, and just keep people laughing. No day was the same, and hardly ever was any day a drudge. It all sounds like some big excuse when you say that now, because we hardly won anything in those four years, and you can't escape from that fact. Yet when I look back, I remember an incredible team ethic and togetherness. Under Roy Evans, Liverpool came fourth, third, fourth and third in the Premiership, won the Carling Cup, got to the FA Cup final and the Cup Winners' Cup semi final, as well as various other semis. We also played some of the best football in the club's history at times, even though we were rubbish at other times. It was a blast, and it worked for me, because I scored thirty-one goals in 1994–95, thirty-six in '95–96, thirty-one in '96–'97 and then unlucky thirteen when I got injured in the gaffer's final season. We finished third that season, and if I hadn't been out for so long and had been able to get near my previous years' tallies, then who knows where we would have ended up?

As it was, third place was judged as not good enough, and they brought Houllier in to act as the 'tough guy', obviously forgetting what had happened under Souness. For me, the problem wasn't discipline or the manager not being tough enough, it was simply that the board didn't back Roy Evans as strongly as they should have done. They gave Houllier about £140 million to spend and had they given Roy a fraction of that, I'm sure he would have taken the final step. He had a good young side, a potentially great young side, in fact. As well as me and the likes of Macca, Rob Jones, Jamie Redknapp, Dominic Matteo, Collymore, Berger, Jason McAteer and Jamo – all young players who had become regular full internationals – he was grooming another batch of brilliant youngsters to come through and join us, like Michael Owen, Jamie Carragher, David Thompson, Danny Murphy, Stephen Wright and Steven Gerrard. All of them top-class players and top-class characters. Jamie Carragher, for instance, developed into a world-class centre half. I have always admired him – a funny, generous, decent person, who would always be the first man you'd want on your side, because he's such a fantastic spirit.

They have all achieved in the game, and that side could easily be playing together now, and would give anyone a game. But the problem was we lacked experience in vital areas. We had John Barnes, Rushie and Michael Thomas, but when they were getting to the end, the manager was denied the funds to go out and bring in the players he really wanted – the experienced players that could have taken us to the next level. In particular, I can remember vividly he came to me and asked about two strikers he was trying to buy that he thought would complement me perfectly when it became clear that Stan Collymore wasn't going to be the answer. Teddy Sheringham was one when he was looking to leave Spurs, but the board said they couldn't spend money on such an old player, who was maybe twenty-eight at the time. Manchester United weren't so short-sighted, and look what he did for them. He won them the European Cup for a start.

I've got to be honest, I would have killed to have had Teddy providing service for me. In my career, it's amazing, but I've never really had a partner who has been there alongside me to create things, apart from maybe Mark Viduka and Harry Kewell at Leeds. When I got into the Liverpool side Rushie was there, but he was a predator even though I think we played brilliantly together. Stan was a great player, but there were problems that we will come to later. Then Michael Owen came along, and quite clearly he was a young striker who needed service, and wasn't going to provide much of it. Even when I got to Manchester City, I found myself alongside Nicolas Anelka ... and he passed about as often as a *Mastermind* champion. Jesus.

Teddy would have been ideal. So would Jari Litmanen, but again the board didn't back the manager properly, so that even though he was a Liverpool fan and was desperate to come to Anfield, he got a better offer from Barcelona and decided he couldn't afford to turn it down. The same happened with Marcel Desailly when he had to choose between Liverpool and Chelsea. And Lilian Thuram. They wouldn't let Roy buy Dion Dublin or Matt Elliott as centre halves either, or Jaap Stam. Even Emile Heskey had to wait for Houllier to arrive before the money was put up for his move, which had been agreed when Evans was manager. I can also remember that Roy approached Juninho through a mate of mine who was a journalist, and he even met the Brazilian's dad, who was also his agent. But there wasn't the money around to make it happen. If the gaffer had been able to get even a couple of those more experienced players, then we would have been a very different proposition, and converted some of those top-four placings into Premiership triumphs.

Roy did bring in some players, and not all of them were a success. Some weren't good enough, or were overawed by being at Liverpool. Sean Dundee was probably the worst, and players like Oyvind Leonhardsen and maybe even Karlheinz Riedle didn't seem to hack it being at such a big club. Interestingly, they were all foreign players he brought in, the ones who were supposed to have the right attitude and the professional approach that we apparently lacked. He brought in Paul Ince, and he was heavily criticized for that move, but I reckon Incey was a clever buy for Liverpool, and a success. Incey's a strange one. He's a decent guy, and brilliant at helping build team spirit, but he can be a pain in the arse as well. He was superb with the lads, always the first to get the drinks going at a function, but also great with the younger lads, helping them fit in without putting too much pressure on. He was exactly what Roy was looking for, because off the pitch he was great socially, a leader who kept the spirit going brilliantly.

I know Michael Owen looked up to him, and so did Jamie Carragher. But out on the pitch he was horrible, a real nark who was never afraid to say exactly what he felt about our performances and how people were doing, just like Roy Keane at Manchester United in fact. That was what Liverpool needed at the time. He was always going on at you on the pitch. One of the funniest was when we played for England together in a game in Malta. When we arrived it was about 42 degrees, and the doctor told us twenty minutes in the sun, maximum. Me being from Toxteth though, I thought I could manage longer than that and fell asleep out there. When I woke up, my chest was redder than the Liverpool shirt. We played the next night, and as the ball came to me for an easy chest down, I tried to control it with my shoulder. Incey went spare, called me all the names under the sun and asked me what the fuck I was doing. 'I've got terrible sunburn, Incey, don't make me chest it,' I whimpered. Even he had to laugh about that.

We had a great young squad with some fantastic players, but we were all a bit quiet. Incey wasn't. He was an aggressive bastard who gave the team the real discipline it needed. In his first season – 1997–98 – even though Incey was the only really experienced pro because we lost John Barnes, Michael Thomas and Rushie, Mark Wright was injured for the whole campaign and Razor was completely bombed out when he was sent out on loan to QPR, we still finished third. And I missed nearly half of the season, when I had been on the best scoring run of any striker in recent history. A couple more experienced players added to that squad and we were there, we really were. Especially because Michael had taken off at that time, and there was apparently a lot of money to spend. But for me, the board panicked and brought in Houllier, when they needed to be patient as the side matured and the kids came through.

Maybe the season before – 1996–97 – had soured things, and turned the board against the gaffer so that they couldn't see he was actually rebuilding and coming up with a fantastic young side. We'd had a good campaign that year against some difficult odds, started off with a 3–3 draw at Middlesbrough, and then gone ten games without defeat, with seven wins on the bounce. In fact, we only lost three games until the turn of the year, and one of those – at Manchester United – was daylight robbery when we battered them but they were given a dodgy winner. But we didn't have a big squad, not much cover for Barnsie and Tommo in midfield even though they were veterans by then, and nothing up front beyond me and Stan. It sounds crazy now, but the only other striker in the entire squad was Lee Jones, who had never started a game. Razor was out a lot that season too, as his lifestyle caught up on him, and the gaffer wouldn't tolerate it.

We were still a good side though, until we started getting injuries in the second half of the season. We reached the quarter final of the Coca-Cola Cup, the semi final of the Cup Winners' Cup and were still in the title race when we entertained Manchester United at Anfield at the end of April. But Michael Thomas got crocked, and missed most of the second half of the campaign. And Barnsie got knackered really. We had lost at Chelsea in the FA Cup when we were 2–0 up and Macca had missed a sitter just on half time to make it three. Even then, the knives were out for us. But we battled on, and by April had two massive games, against Paris St Germain in the semi of the Cup Winners' Cup and United in the league, within a week of each other. The trip to Paris came first, and we were woeful. Stan was a disgrace and was substituted at half time, and I recall as we trooped off for the interval two down, a Scouser standing right by the dugout bellowed: 'Taxi for Collymore.' He got fucking mullered in the dressing room, and if there was any doubt that he would be leaving the club, then it disappeared that night. We lost 3–0 and there were no excuses, because we were a much better side than they were, and we should have stuffed them.

Of all the games under Roy Evans, that was the one we should have been ashamed of, because no one played that night and we came away embarrassed by our performance. In the second leg we battered them, and could have scored five or six, but only managed two and were out. In between, we played United in a game that had we won, we would have cut the gap at the top to one point with three matches remaining. Again, we were woeful. Barnsie scored, but we didn't have the legs in midfield, we lost 3–1 and afterwards he and the gaffer had a big row in the dressing room. Stan Collymore has made a big deal since he left the club of the fact that Barnsie made the decisions and ran the show, not Roy, but that day he knew exactly where he stood. By the exit door. It was his last start for Liverpool.

The title race was over. Worse, it was my last match of the season because I had got involved in a scrap with David Unsworth at Goodison against Everton the previous game. The fucker had been winding me up, kicking me all over the pitch, and doing the shitty things that defenders get up to. He caught me late, I remember, and stood on me. I got up and had a go, and the referee was over with his red card. It was nothing really, merely derby passion in a game that we had to win, and they were desperate to stop us. But it meant I was suspended for three matches. In those final three games, the gaffer had to blood Michael Owen, even though he was only seventeen and about two foot six, because there really was no cover. For a lot of the season we had played with me up front alone, because Stan was pissing around and Roy had had enough of him.

The thing was, we needed one more win from our final two matches to finish second, guaranteeing a place in the Champions' League, which would have at least made up for the disappointment of a title that we probably should have won, if only we'd had a tiny bit more depth to our squad. But with me suspended we had a rookie up front, and a waster who already knew that he was being sold to Aston Villa. We lost at Wimbledon – always Liverpool's bogey side, and so we had to go to Sheffield Wednesday for the win we required. To this day, a lot of the lads think that Stan Collymore didn't try a tap-in that game because he knew he was off. His agent had pulled him a whole month before the end of the season, and told him a transfer to Villa had been sorted, which probably explains why he was so woeful in Paris and so disinterested against Wednesday. He probably thought he wasn't going to help the fuckers he was leaving behind get into the Champions' League, and again he was dragged off at half time to a chorus of boos and jeers.

I know it sounds a bit big-time of me, but if I'd played in that match we definitely would have won. They lost their keeper through injury, and then the sub keeper was sent off! So for the last fifteen minutes or so we played against a side down to ten men with a full back in goal. I remember he made an incredible save from Macca from about two yards, stopped about another four, and we missed about five sitters. Michael Owen hit the post in the last minute, but even though we laid siege to their goal we couldn't get through. So David Unsworth not only cost me a £60,000 fine, he also cost Liverpool a place in the Champions' League. I'll bet he's fucking thrilled about that to this day, the Bluenose get!

The shame was, it probably cost Roy his job. If we had got in the Champions' League, then we would have had more money to spend on the players he tried to attract to the club, and we would have had the glamour of top European competition too. Surely the board would have backed him more as well, instead of starving him of funds, despite selling Stan for £7 million. With the side Roy was already building after adding Incey, and the way that we performed the following season in finishing a solid third, I think we would have done well, especially if Roy had been able to add a little more experience. Ifs and buts, though, don't win trophies.

If that sounds like a robust defence of Roy, then it reflects the fact that he was a far better manager than he has since been given credit for. He has suffered because the man who took over from him slaughtered the previous regime, and played on the idea that discipline was too lax, that the club was crumbling. It was naughty to destroy a man you had worked with for six months, but then I suppose that's the way the game always has been ... although I don't remember Roy Evans doing that when it was in his interests to demean what had happened under Souey. Maybe if he'd kept saying a five-year plan was required to rebuild a shattered club he'd have got more time. But the thing is, mistakes were made that helped hammer a few nails into Roy's coffin, and I think he'd be the first to admit that.

They are mostly little things that, had we won more trophies, would not have mattered. One of those things was the cream suits at Wembley, when we played Manchester United in the cup final in '96. Because Jamo had done that photo shoot for the Y-fronts at Armani, he said he had a contact who could get us some smart cup final suits, which is always a tradition. When they turned up, they were a very light cream, and a lot of the players asked what the fuck was going on because they were a bit naff. But it was only a suit, and it wasn't as if we had all got together to say that we had to wear something outrageous to show what a bunch of glamorous celebrities we were.

Apparently the designer had been told that it was often a sunny day at Wembley for the final, and he thought the colour would be appropriate. It was a scorching day, and so in that respect he was right. Except that when we lost, the sirens went off as if World War Three had broken out. We were slaughtered. It was easy to use the suits as a metaphor for the way we had under-achieved on the day, and the way that the image of us as playboys had now stuck. People had expected a classic final because that season we'd had two brilliant games with United, when I'd really come good.

The first, at Old Trafford, was the most memorable for me . . . although the two goals I scored that day don't seem to have been remembered by anyone else! It was the Cantona comeback game after he'd been banned for eight months for his brilliant kung-fu kick on that fella at Crystal Palace, you know the charming bloke who'd only said, 'Off you go, old chap, it's an early bath for you.' Anyway, he happened to make his return against us in the most explosive game of the season. Nicky Butt scored early on, but then I had the game of me life. I smashed one in from an acute angle on the left of the six-yard box, which was a Goal of the Season contender and did Schmeichel all ends up for sheer pace on his near post, which without doubt pleased me just about as much as any goal I've ever scored. Then I knocked Gary Neville off the ball – always satisfying – and chipped Schmeichel to the sound of tumbleweed at a gutted Old Trafford. Only problem was, Cantona then converted a predictably dodgy penalty, and I was erased from history. In the return at Anfield we stuffed them 2–0, which rubbed it in nicely, and I scored both with goals just before half time and full time, one a belting free kick that again embarrassed Smikes.

So we were all set up for the final, irrespective of what we were wearing beforehand. We still had a Liverpool kit on out on the pitch, and that's all that really mattered. United were wounded by the way we'd given them such a hard time in the previous two games that season, and were determined not to let us play. We went down there with a game plan to try and get at them, try to open them up, and although they talked a good game it soon became apparent that they were not inter-ested in playing at all, just in stopping us at all costs. It was a horrible game, so negative it was painful to play in – and that was down to United's approach on the day. And the thing was, it was like that because they were so scared of us.

They had Roy Keane man-marking Macca to the exclu-sion of everything else, which when you think about it is an amazing thing for a player of that quality. They also sat on Jamie Redknapp and Barnsie to stop the supply getting to me, because of what I had done to them. Then they double-teamed me, because Stan had a shocker and could have been marked by the linesman that day. Their tactics were to stop us playing, presumably looking for penalties because they had no ambition whatsoever, and because even though they were Champions that season they knew we had the beating of them. They had a lot more experienced players than we did, the likes of Cantona, Steve Bruce, Gary Pallister, Keane, Schmeichel, Denis Irwin, and as a young side we couldn't come to terms with their limited game plan. Looking back, there's no shame in that against such a quality, experienced side, but we were taken apart anyway, because of those white suits, and because we had been part of such a crap game. Funny how no one remembers how bad United were, though, and that's because they won.

I think on balance there were a few other things Roy should have done, which is easier to say now of course. Maybe he should have been firmer with the board, and demanded that he got the players he wanted like Teddy Sheringham. He could be a tough guy, Roy, even with the directors at the club, and it surprised me that he didn't push it with them. Not many people know this, but the year before they brought Houllier in, the board had the idea of bringing Kenny Dalglish back to act as the Director of Football, to give Roy a hand and stave off the criticism that there wasn't enough discipline or general seriousness around the place. Personally, I thought it was a great idea because Kenny was an absolute star as far as I was concerned, the man who had driven me down our street when I was a kid in his massive car.

But Roy quite rightly thought differently. He did meet Kenny and talked it through, and could see the sense in the idea, but the gaffer wasn't too happy about it. He thought that if the side started winning then Kenny would get all the credit, but if we lost a couple of games then the fans would be chanting Kenny's name and there would be a massive amount of pressure for him to get back into the manager's chair. Just as happened at Celtic, in fact, when he was Director of Football with John Barnes as manager. So Roy resisted, and he gave it to them in no uncertain terms. They didn't pursue it in the end, and he also saw off the idea of John Toshack doing the role. He should have done the same with his transfer fees, but I think he got himself into a bad position because he had put himself out on a limb to make the biggest transfer in Liverpool history up to that point, the signing of Stan Collymore. And if it's ever possible that one single decision brought Roy's Anfield career to a premature end, then perhaps that was it.

After the 1994–95 season, it was clear that we needed some reinforcements in midfield and up front. The gaffer had bought John Scales and Phil Babb so we were strong at the back, but we had lost quite a few players as he went about the job of getting rid of those he thought weren't up to it. That season, Rushie and me had played exactly fifty matches together, and scored fifty goals. But he was well into his thirties by then – he'd made his 600th appearance for Liverpool in the November – and it was a bit much asking him to play so many games. Nigel Clough was on the way out, and would be sold early into the new season. So the gaffer had to buy someone.

Stan had done the business for Nottingham Forest that season, with the goals that had taken them into third in the Premiership, and he was hot. United had tried to buy him, but got Andy Cole instead, and he was a Liverpool fan. Jamie Redknapp had approached him when they had met for an England get-together, and got on really well with him. There had been stories coming out of Forest that Stan wasn't well liked by the rest of the players, one time they had even refused to celebrate with him when he scored a goal. But Jamie and a couple of the other lads who used to go down to London said he was all right, that he would fit in okay at Anfield. Roy was keen, and in the summer of 1995 he paid a club record £8.5 million for him.

Everyone was thrilled because they thought we would complement each other, and that it would give us the goals to challenge for the title, with the strength we apparently had in defence. For me, it was difficult, because I obviously regarded Rushie as a great partner. We had scored so many goals together, and he was an Anfield legend. I didn't think he should be dropped, and naturally as a young lad (still only twenty) I was worried that he would take my place. I don't think I helped myself by coming back off my holidays in Falaraki with dyed blond hair and a lairy attitude. The gaffer and Ronnie stepped on me straight away, and I was dropped from the side for the first time in my career. It was a shock to the system, but they were right. I had got a bit cocky, had gone a bit wild on holiday, and maybe I didn't have totally the right frame of mind when I came back. That blond hair was a year before Gazza made it popular, and it obviously made me look fucking stupid. Took me ages to grow out as well. I was left out for two matches despite being the second top scorer in the Premiership the previous season, and it gave me the kick up the backside I needed. Rushie got injured, though, and in my first start I scored against Spurs. From then on, I missed just one game – the one in Vladikavkaz that I was so grumpy about – and Stan and me forged a fantastic partnership.

It started slowly, as we got used to each other, and we didn't do particularly well in the league, but after our obligatory defeat at Wimbledon in September we didn't lose for two months, and then it was only a fluke that a crap Brondby team knocked us out of the UEFA Cup. I started scoring and couldn't stop. I got four against Bolton in my 100th appearance for Liverpool, the two at Old Trafford in Cantona's comeback, two against Manchester City, two more against United at home, a hat-trick against my rabbits at Arsenal, two each against Forest, Leeds and Villa, where we were three up after six minutes. They were exciting times, because we were also on that great run in the FA Cup, beating Rochdale, Shrewsbury, Charlton and Leeds to reach the semi finals, and I had scored in every round. By the start of April, we had clawed our way to third in the Premiership, just a few points behind the leaders, Newcastle, who we had to face next. And we had a semi at Old Trafford against Villa three days before. Exciting times indeed.

It was as much as my little brain could cope with. It was just before my twenty-first birthday and, incredibly, just four days before the semi final, I had made my England debut. Imagine, within the space of a week, I was getting my first cap for my country, playing in the FA Cup semi final and then in a Premiership game against the long-time leaders that could put us right in the title race. Fucking amazing. I really had arrived. By then, before the beginning of April, I'd already scored thirty-one goals in what was a mind-blowing season for me. And somehow, it was about to get even better. The semi final against Aston Villa is still one of my greatest memories. The second goal I scored that day will go down as one of my best ever. I had put us one ahead early on with a header, but it was tense for much of the game as they came back at us. With four minutes to go, we had a corner, it was half cleared to me on the edge of the box, and I smashed a left-foot volley into the top corner. Martin Tyler, doing the commentary for Sky, said simply: 'You are looking at a goal-scoring genius.' Boy, was I on a high. I don't think I have ever had such an emotionally intense period as that in my life. I was plastered all over the papers, and as I've pointed out earlier, I was given the full pop star treatment, including the exposés on my private life, even though I'd hardly done anything. It was mental, surreal, and slightly bewildering, even though I was obviously loving it as well.

We got another against Villa to win 3–0, and then it was

on to Newcastle at Anfield, and the task of getting right into the title race. They needed to win to go back to the top, after Manchester United had caught them, so it was a real game, and with the extra hype that Sky were getting good at. It was built up as the heavyweight contest, winner takes all. It turned out to be one of the great nights in football history. It has been voted as the game of the decade, the best ever game in the Premiership, Sky's best sporting moment. Andy Gray said it was a privilege to be there. Kevin Keegan was very emotional afterwards, saying that he would carry on playing that way even if it got him the sack. Ronnie Moran was just shaking his head, asking what the fuck had gone on.

I don't think I have ever seen a better atmosphere at Anfield than that night, not even for the European Games in 2001. It was absolute bedlam, insane. And it was a privilege to be part of it. When you look back on your career, there is no doubt that the medals are the things that give you satisfaction. The winning is everything to a professional, because to get to the top in the first place you need a frightening amount of compet-itive spirit. But being part of games like that, which are regarded as classics, that gives you the buzz too. Less than two minutes into the game, Stan did what he was best at and escaped down the left, crossed, and I put it in with me nose. I knew that big hooter would come in handy for something. But it was one of those nights where there was madness in the air, and they were ahead by half time when Les Ferdinand and David Ginola showed how vulnerable our defence was. Back we came, though, and when Macca did their full back and pulled it back from the right, I met the ball so sweetly and curled it with the outside of me foot past Pavel Srnicek.

The occasion had got to me then, because I slid on my chest and followed the ball into the net to give it a header as it nestled in there. Even then they weren't finished and Faustino Asprilla, who produced a trick that night that I've never seen bettered, put them ahead again and we looked fucked. Our fans went mental though, picked us up and dragged us back towards their goal, and when Stan tapped one in on sixty-seven minutes we all knew we were set for something incredible. He had the game of his life that night, and he scored again two minutes into injury time when he smashed one past Srnicek at the near post to take the roof off. I think we stayed on the pitch for about ten minutes afterwards, just to take in the atmosphere. Keegan was suicidal, because he knew they were out of the title race. We were right in it. And yet three days later we went to Coventry and got beat, and that was it for us too. We've been slaughtered for that defeat, people using it as another example of the fact that we were big-time Charlies who couldn't hack it in the bread-and-butter matches.

But I prefer a simpler explanation. We were fucked. That Coventry game was my forty-seventh of the season, and at the end of a week when I had played for England, in a Cup semi and in one of the most intense matches in the history of football. There was no rotation then, and most of the other lads had played the same number of games. We were just burnt out, and found it hard to lift ourselves after such a demanding week. I hit the post twice at Coventry, and had we won maybe we could have just pipped United to the title, but really I think we were such a young, inexperienced side that we weren't quite ready at that stage. A week later we lifted ourselves to snatch a draw at Goodison when I scored my thirty-sixth goal of the season to equalize two minutes from time, but really we were shot by then and we won only two of our last seven games that season.

The rot had started in with Stan by that time. Well before the Cup final there were already murmurings, and at the rather subdued end-of-season party after we lost to United I can remember Jamie Redknapp speaking to some of the lads, apologizing for helping bring him to the club. The gaffer, in an unguarded moment late in the evening at that London hotel, admitted what plenty were already thinking: he would have to get rid of him because he was so bad for morale. He said Stan would be gone by the start of the next season. Nobody argued. And yet Stan Collymore was one of the most talented, charismatic footballers I have ever seen. Sometimes, especially in the early days, I'd watch him in training and think he could be anything, with his natural ability and incredible athleticism.

But Stan was never going to be a true great, because he was lacking a fundamental quality that gets you to the top. Mental strength. Stan had the body for football, but not the mind. I've heard Roy speak about him many times since, and he always says the same thing: 'He did the best he could with the limitations he had.' The gaffer used to argue that Stan over-achieved, because most people with that flaw never get through what is a pretty ruthless selection process at clubs. Believe me, they push you mentally more than they do in any other area to see if you can survive. If football had a more caring, more tolerant environment, then I think he would have been much more of a success at Anfield than he was.

Stan has said since that I didn't talk to him for the two years that he was at the club, that we were like Teddy Sheringham and Andy Cole at Manchester United, who apparently hated each other's guts. I can honestly swear that I haven't got a clue what he is talking about. I reckon that I spoke to him every day – when he actually turned up – during his time at Liverpool, and I never had a big problem with him. I didn't understand him, I admit that, and by the end I realized that his attitude was doing terrible damage to the team. He needed to go. But I've never really had any problems in any of the squads I've ever been in. I'd like to think that my teammates would say I was popular, and one of the lads. Stan was never that, and that was his problem. He couldn't connect with the other players, and because of that he found himself at the edge of things. When that happened, he began to disconnect, stopped wanting to be part of the team, and started to undermine it instead.

It's only now, years later, that I have any grasp of what was going on in Stan's head back then. Like most of us, he's probably far more insecure than his cocky, confident image portrays. He wanted to prove himself and he wanted to be admired at Liverpool, and from day one, he gave the impression that he needed to be the big star at the centre of things. You look at his career, and he had success where that was the case, at Southend where he had come down a division, and at Forest where he scored all the goals, even if the other fellas hated him. Everywhere else he ever played, they always recognized his talent but decided that he didn't have the head to be a footballer.

The first game he played for Liverpool, he scored the winner and the Kop chanted his name. Straight after, he gave an interview to the press lads, essentially saying that Liverpool needed to learn quickly to adapt to him, because he wasn't getting enough of the ball. In his first game, he was telling everyone they had to change to make sure he was the main man. But it wasn't done that way at Liverpool. Not long after that, still in his first month or so, he did a magazine article saying that Liverpool had paid so much money for him, but were then asking him to do things their way. If he cost the club that much, why didn't they see him as their biggest asset? From that moment, all the lads were going, 'Aye, aye, who the fuck does he think he is?' He got a lot of the lads' backs up with that, and there was suspicion of him from then on. The manager hauled him in and gave him a major bollocking because he could see the effect it had on team morale. It wasn't helped when he went to stay with Jamo when he first arrived at the club, but then went back to Cannock and started slagging the big man off. Jamo was very popular in the squad, and it was a stupid thing to do. He was a bit mad, Jamo, but a wonderful, generous, infectious bloke who was the heart and soul of the team. He was incredibly popular because he was such a character, even if no one would room with him.

There was the time when Bjorn Tore Kvarme arrived at the club, and he drew the short straw of rooming with him. Jamo is a sleepwalker, and he used to trash his room in his sleep. Really trash it – smash things up. One night, we were away at a hotel all in our own rooms for a change, and suddenly we heard this screaming. It was Bjorn. He was shouting, 'Get him off me, get him off me . . . he's trying to kill me.' There was a connecting door between their rooms, and Jamo had smashed it down in his sleep. Then he had grabbed Bjorn by the throat, and was throttling the life out of him. Without waking up! So it was maybe fair enough Stan not wanting to stay at Jamo's house too long, but to take the hospitality of him and his family and then start slagging the fella off was all wrong.

Again, it turned people against him. Stan was always saying how good he was and the truth is he could have been as good as anyone. We went to Amsterdam for the opening of the new Ajax stadium. By then, Stan was on the skids and not getting a game. One night at the bar, though, he was going on about Patrick Kluivert, who was probably the best striker in the world at that time, and saying: 'I know I'm better than him. He couldn't lace my boots.' It is easier to understand why he was like that now – he has revealed he is a depressive with deep-rooted problems. But at the time most of the lads thought he was arrogant and above the rest of us. He never joined in anything. He didn't even turn up for the first Christmas party after he signed, and he spent most of the second one when he finally deigned to join in holed up in the bogs with the strippers.

Most of all though, it was his attitude to the gaffer that caused so much friction. Stan has moaned plenty since he left that Roy Evans was too soft, that the manager wasn't a strong enough character to control the team. That's such a laugh, because the one person who caused problems that needed controlling was Stan. And Roy only indulged him because he'd spent £8.5 million to make him Liverpool's most expensive player, so he had to stand by his judgement and try and do what he could to make him fit in. It was fucking obvious to everyone that the hard-line approach wouldn't work with him. Whenever Roy tried that, Stan switched off completely. So the manager cajoled him, and turned a blind eye to a lot of things, hoping to tease the best out of him. It worked at first, but gradually Stan started to take more and more liberties, which began to generate more and more friction. He refused to move up to Liverpool after his brief fling with Chez Jamo, even though he was ordered to.

All that travelling up the M6 clearly pissed him off, because soon he didn't bother. He'd ring up in the morning, and say he had a bug or toothache or the dog ate his homework. Most of the time he rang to say his mum was in hospital. It got to the stage where we thought she clearly must be a nurse, she was there that often. It wasn't on, and it started to cause resentment. Again, the players got the impression he felt he could play by different rules to everyone else. When you see someone blatantly taking the piss while everyone else is trying to pull in the same direction there is always a problem. It was made worse by the fact that Stan was such a complex character he found it hard to mix with the lads. He had no problem chatting with the birds, revelled in that, but when it came to the essential art of mixing with your teammates, he was fucking hopeless.

It sounds like an insult to him, but it's not. He was a great talent, but fragile mentally. And if you are going to make it in football, then you've got to be able to take all the jokes and banter that go on in a world where most people are aggressive, competitive working-class lads with little or no education. Stan couldn't hack that, because everything to him was a slight. Stupid things, like the time when we were sitting round a table, chatting away, and Stan got up to get something. Tony Warner, our reserve keeper and another man well respected in the group, sat in the free chair. When Stan came back he demanded his chair back. Tony told him not to be stupid, and do what anyone else would do, pull up another chair. But Stan wouldn't have it, and launched himself across the room. A massive fight broke out, and when the gaffer tried to break it up he got a whack across the mouth for his troubles. Not a wise move.

Another time, he saw his arse with Steve Harkness in an incident that may explain why Stan turned against him with those accusations of racist comments all those years later when he had moved to Villa. Harky was the joker in the team. He got up to some terrible tricks, and everyone was a target . . . everyone. One of his favourite tricks was to leave a little piece of shit in your toilet bag. He'd done it to me, done it to everyone, and you just bided your time and got him back. Stan took offence massively though, which was fair enough, because let's face it, it's pretty disgusting. But in the context of the team and what went on, there was no way Stan was being picked on, it was a practical joke that went on all the time. But he was incapable of seeing things that simply, and all bets were off with Harky after that, because he insisted he was being singled out. Every team needs someone at the heart of it, who makes things tick, and Harky was probably that with us. Sometimes he overstepped the mark, but it was all harmless stuff. Stan couldn't fit in with that, though, and didn't have any idea how to handle it, which just made the gap between him and the team wider. In the end it got to the stage where Stan hardly talked to anyone.

On the days when he bothered to come in, he didn't speak, did the minimum and cleared off sharpish. In the first year, most of the lads grumbled but put up with it, until his performances started to slip off. By the Cup final, there was a fairly strong opinion that he was far more trouble than he was worth. We scored fifty-five goals between us that season, and there were moments when Stan's brain clicked in that I thought we were the ideal partnership, because he had a massive talent and the ability to create as well as score goals. But I always sensed that he resented my success, and gradually he stopped passing to me. I know that sounds impossible with a professional footballer, but I swear it was the truth. If he thought I could score, he wouldn't pass. For what it's worth my opinion is that Stan never got his head around the fact that he was just another cog in the Liverpool team, never understood that at Liverpool they bought players to fit in with the team, no matter who they were. When he couldn't do that, his days were numbered. The only surprise was that he got another season. I think Roy desperately wanted him out after the first year, but it was a hell of a decision to sell so quickly a man you had spent so much money on, so he fudged it.

In hindsight that was a mistake, and his signing was a mistake that proved massively costly for us all. We were on the verge of something, but his character disrupted things and slowly but surely began to undermine the whole squad. When he got away with ridiculous excuses, other players tried it. When he took the piss, others did too. And things did break down. In the 1996–97 season Stan was dropped on no fewer than twenty occasions, and he was also taken off at half time four times, which is a damning statistic. That's virtually half a season that he missed, and half a season when I played up front on my own, because Rushie had been sold to Leeds at the start of that campaign. Yet we still could have won the title. Had Stan played anything like he did in his first season, I think we would have done. I scored thirty-one goals that season, which wasn't a bad effort considering I had to work as a lone striker for much of it. It was hard to score goals, even harder when you didn't get a pass. I had a very slow start, just two in eleven games at the start of the season, but when Stan was bombed things picked up, and I scored at Sion in Switzerland when Stan was first axed to go on a run of seventeen goals in fifteen games, which even by my standards back then was a bit special.

The highlight, apart from my usual goals against Arsenal, was the game against Middlesbrough on 14 December 1996. I was twenty-one years old, and that brought up my 100th goal for Liverpool, in 165 matches – one game earlier than Ian Rush had managed it. There had been a lot of talk about that record, and it had begun to bug me a little. I scored after twenty-three seconds in that match, and looked at a pretend watch on my wrist, which really pissed the Boro players off. I heard a story that when we played them next, Emerson had a T-shirt on under his strip which read 'Fuck off Fowler'. He never scored though, so I never got to see it. I scored three more times against Boro that day, the second one on twenty-eight minutes bringing up the century. It was a relief, and I had a T-shirt of my own which nicked a catch phrase off a Sunday TV programme that starred Bez from the Happy Mondays. He was always saying, 'Job's a Good 'Un', and that's the message I showed when I lifted my shirt for the crowd. When you think how Rushie scored goals for Liverpool, and the teams he played in, to beat that record of his was so satisfying, possibly my greatest achievement at Anfield. But one thing I want to put straight, I didn't write 'God's Job's a Good 'Un' on that T-shirt. We all had our nicknames written on the T-shirts to identify them, Macca's was Shaggy, mine was God. Underneath that I wrote Bez's message, but it was never supposed to read as though I had identified myself as God.

There were other notable moments in that season. The goal against Sion was my first in Europe, and I scored against Everton again at Anfield. We won seven out of seven in September, and by the turn of the year, after my little scoring run, we were top of the Premiership by five points. I also scored one of the finest goals of my career in Bergen against Brann, when I took the ball with my back to goal, flicked it over my head and turned in one movement to lash it in at the near post. It was a dream goal, matched only by a similar one at Villa when I did the same thing to my mate Steve Staunton. The very next game after Bergen, we played Newcastle at Anfield again, and again we won 4–3. This time, we were 3–0 up, but they came back to 3–3 after we defended sloppily, only for me to head the winner deep into stoppage time after a brilliant cross from Stig Inge Bjornebye. It wasn't as good a game as the previous year but it was still pretty thrilling, even if the gaffer was doing his nut about us show-boating when we were three up.

Then, on 24 March, came the game that changed a lot of people's perception of me. Until then I had been seen as a cheating scally, basically. An hour into that game against Arsenal, I was sent running into the penalty area by Mark Wright. As their keeper David Seaman came out to meet me, I tried to go around to his left side. I tripped, but he had made no contact. It wasn't a dive, I simply lost my balance as I changed direction sharply, but the ref thought I must have been fouled and he pointed straight to the spot. Instinctively, I turned to the referee, Gerald Ashby, and said, 'No, no, no, Ref, it wasn't a pen,' as I waved my hand at him.

It was a bit fucking dippy to be honest, and I could hear a couple of the lads shouting at me to shut the fuck up. The referee couldn't change his mind, so I turned back to Dave Seaman, and just said sorry to him. I don't really know why I did it. I was a young lad and it wasn't a penalty, so I said it, that's all. I suppose I was being truthful, and maybe I didn't want Dave to be sent off (or for him to clobber me!), because he was a mate of mine ... and a damn sight bigger than me. I don't really know what was going through my head, although I have never been a cheat, never thrown myself to the floor at any time, and I have never agreed with this idea in the game now that if you can commit a defender and get him to touch you, then you go down. I've always had a different idea, that if you can commit a defender, then shoot, even if it is a little old-fashioned. I got a letter off Sepp Blatter after that, which was a bit flattering. 'Dear Robbie,' it said. 'I want to congratulate you for the act of sportsmanship which you demonstrated in the match between Liverpool and Arsenal. It is the kind of gesture which helps maintain the integrity of the game.' The President of FIFA was writing to me, telling me what a role model I was! It's just a pity that letter arrived a day before the £900 fine from UEFA landed on the doormat for showing that T-shirt backing the sacked dockers – nothing was ever simple with me.

It was a strange season, and a frustrating one, because for much of it we were close to achieving something, but we were being undermined by the problems that ate away at the morale of the squad. There were plenty of highs for me, especially the record for the fastest to 100 goals in Liverpool history, but at the end of it all my own personal achievements didn't make up for the feeling that we should have won the Premiership that year. A lot of the players pointed the finger at Stan, put all the blame on him, but I don't, not now. He was just not suited to a club like Liverpool. I don't think Stan had the right sort of mind to be a success at a big club, with a lot of top stars. He was more suited to being a big fish in a small pond. That wasn't his fault, it was just the way he was, and I'm sure if he could have changed his character he would have liked to have done.

Lots of players have weaknesses that stop them getting to the top, it's just that Stan's were in his head. It seems that he is still battling those weaknesses even now. The regret I suppose is that when Liverpool had big money to spend on the top class they needed to help a great young squad achieve their potential, they signed Stan Collymore. Not that the gaffer could ever have known what he would turn out like. But it is a real shame things turned out like that, because there is no doubt he did undermine morale at Liverpool, and in the second season in particular when stories started coming out, it backfired on the manager and eventually undermined his position.

There was one occasion, after Stan was dropped against Sion, that he was selected for a reserve game at Tranmere and he refused to play. The stink that caused wounded the gaffer badly, and I don't think the board ever forgot. Stan had to go, there was no doubt about that, and he was sold to Villa at the end of the 1996–97 season for £7 million. But they were two wasted years when a group of talented, young international footballers had lost their direction and lost time. In reality there were probably lots of reasons for that. But managers are defined by their signings, and when you spend a club record, then it is judgement time. The judgement on Stan, whichever way you look at it, was damning, and that – perhaps unfairly – hastened the end of the Roy Evans era.

The gaffer was given one more season to turn it around after Collymore was sold, but he wasn't given the money to spend on new players, and most of the campaign saw him fire-fighting and trying to patch things up. We got Incey for the 1997–98 season, but lost experienced players like John Barnes, Michael Thomas, Neil Ruddock and Mark Wright. Jamie Red-knapp missed a lot of that campaign too, but there were some brilliant young players coming through, along with a clever buy in Danny Murphy. What we didn't have was a centre half, and they wouldn't let him buy one, which was fucking stupid. My view is that he was on the way to building a brilliant young side that had a real English emphasis, and he might have got there with the right backing. Earlier in this chapter, I've named fifteen players who were in the squad at that time who were under the age of twenty-five, and were either estab-lished internationals or were to become so. But Roy's fate was sealed unless he won the league. We lost to Boro in the semi final of the Coca-Cola Cup, lost a stupid match to Strasbourg in the UEFA Cup, and got done badly in the FA Cup at Coventry. Under the circumstances, though, third wasn't a bad

finish. It could have been better, could have been worse ...
apart from for me. Personally, it was a fucking disaster. The
year 1998 was my Annus Horribilis. I suffered an injury that
blighted my career, and Gerard Houllier arrived at Anfield.

ENGLAND'S DREAMING (9)

The 1997–98 season had started out pretty badly, and maybe that was a sign of things to come. On our pre-season we played in Oslo against a Norwegian select eleven, and I was on fire. I scored twice. Michael Owen, playing his first game alongside me, scored another, and we were cruising. Late in the game just as the gaffer was preparing to take me off, I turned sharply and twisted my knee. It was agony and I knew immediately that it was a bad one. I'd strained the ligaments and that meant I missed the important final weeks of pre-season and the first seven games of the new campaign. That was two months, and it ruined my season. I was always chasing it after that, and even though I scored a few goals, I was never as sharp as I had been in the previous few years. I scored after fifty seconds against Bolton, but then got sent off, which meant another absence, and it was like someone was teasing me before they delivered the knock-out blow. That came on a Monday night in a televised game against Everton, on 23 February 1998. And it was the worst moment of my career.

My left knee exploded in that game. The medial ligament was snapped, the cruciate ligament ruptured and the cartilage was torn. To borrow the official medical term used by the doctor at the time: my knee was fucked. It was late in the game and we were chasing the win after Incey had put us level. There was a high cross slung into the box and I jumped with the Everton keeper Thomas Myhre. I've watched the video of the game since and he seemed to jump into me to take me out. I'm not blaming him because most of the damage happened as I landed, but he caught me that night. I actually tried to get up and carry on, but my leg collapsed under me. I knew it was bad when I saw the look on the face of our physio, Mark Leather, or Judas as he has always been known. He went white. I crawled off straight into an ambulance and was ferried immediately down to a clinic in the Midlands where Jamie Redknapp had got his knee done the previous summer. The doctors told me it was so bad that they couldn't guarantee anything, not even that I would play again. If I did, they said it was the sort of injury that usually kept players out for a year or more, so I had to get my mind tuned to that. But all I could get my mind tuned to was the fact that I was out of the World Cup, and my England career was down the pan.

I never had any luck with my England career. Even when I'd had enough of being on the bench and decided to retire, nobody noticed because I got bombed out before I could tell anyone. Nineteen ninety-eight, though, was the lowest point for me, and the year that stopped me having the sort of career for my country that I probably should have had. I have won twenty-six caps for England, and scored eight goals, which ain't too bad considering that I started only eleven games. My best days for England, though, came before that injury in 1998. If you were being unkind, you'd say my best days full stop. It all began for me with the under-18 team, remember, and then I was called up for the under-21 side by Lawrie McMenemy, who was the assistant manager within the England set-up at that time. I made my debut in San Marino. Nice place. (Not sure where it is, mind.) We played in a town called Serravalle with a seething, packed emotional crowd of . . . 100 people. We used to get more watching us at Thorvald. It was one of the few times me dad never watched me, and he was gutted because I scored on me debut. After four minutes in fact. We had been on the pitch beforehand and Lawrie had pointed to the goal, and asked me if I fancied myself scoring in it. Of course I said yeah, and he said, 'Good lad, cos you're playing.'

That game came two months after I made my Liverpool debut, and over the next two years I played another seven times for the under-21s. Would have been a lot more, I suppose, but I was a bad boy getting sent off against Austria, and then daring to get a bit of pen on me bed-sheet in Portugal. That cost me, because Terry Venables had got word to me via the rest of the lads in the England squad that he wanted to bring me into the fold, but it seems there were a few people within the FA who were worried about my reputation and put a block on it. I sat there back at Anfield, with the clock ticking down on Euro '96 – which was going to be England's biggest tournament for thirty years – and I was like one of those contestants on *Pop Idol*: pick me, Terry, pick me! As a kid, I used to be Graeme Sharp in the streets, scoring for Everton. And I used to be Gary Lineker occasionally too, scoring for England.

I was a young lad, coming up to my twenty-first birthday in 1996, and, like every English player in the Premiership that season, I was desperate to somehow be involved in the squad Venners was putting together to try and win the European Championships on home soil. I was scoring goals, but everyone at Liverpool was getting the international call while I had to sit on my arse at Melwood, like Billy No Mates. First it was Rob Jones, then Macca in 1995 along with Razor Ruddock and John Scales. Jamie Redknapp got a call-up early in 1996, and I was expecting the kit man to beat me to the next squad. Even Stan Collymore had been called into the squad the season before the Championships, and I had outscored him two to one. There was a get-together at the end of '95, and I was called into that, which had me dad bouncing off the ceiling. But I wasn't in the next squad. It did me head in to be honest, not because I thought I should be playing particularly, but because by then you could smell Euro '96, and what it would mean to the country. And I would have killed to have been part of that.

The call came at the end of March 1996, my miracle month. Not only did I score twice in the Cup semi and against Newcastle in the game of the decade, I won the PFA Young Player of the Year award for the second time. And I won my first England cap. The PFA award was extra special, because at the ceremony the gong was presented by Ian Rush. It was his final season at Anfield after his incredible service and he was handing over the number-nine shirt to me. He got up at the top table to announce the winner of the Young Player prize and smiled as he said: '. . . and the award goes to . . . my son Robbie Fowler!' What an image. The greatest striker Liverpool has ever had, handing over the baton to me and showing just how close we were with those touching words.

It made me proud. As proud, in fact, as when I got a tap on the shoulder from the gaffer at the training ground on a typically blustery March morning. 'You'd better chuck out those carrier bags and buy yourself a decent suitcase, Robbie son,' he said. 'Terry Venables has called to say you're in the England squad.' I dropped me bacon sarnie. Fucking hell, I had a chance. Me mind was racing as I was calculating what prospect I had of actually getting a start in the game against Bulgaria, and who else might be pushing for a place in the final twenty-two for the European Championships in June. Stan was still on the verge of the squad, and of course there was the main man Alan Shearer who was always going to be first choice. Teddy Sheringham was favoured, and he had worked with Venners. Les Ferdinand was playing brilliantly at that time, Nicky Barmby was another favourite of Venables, and Peter Beardsley was still on the scene, while Ian Wright was tearing things up at Arsenal and Andy Cole had moved to Manchester United to create a clamour for his inclusion. That was seven strikers I had to get past to get into the England team, every one top class. I knew my chances of making the final twenty-two were pretty slim, but I'd met every challenge I'd had so far in my career, so why not this one? Actually, if I am being honest about my twenty-year-old thoughts around that time, then they were more like: England? Wembley? Euro '96? Bring it on!

England wasn't a problem for me, because Venables had so many Liverpool players in his squad. Going for the get-together at Bisham Abbey it was just like being away with Liverpool. I went down with Stan, as it happened, although he didn't get another call-up until Glenn Hoddle became manager. I liked Venables, thought he was a brilliant coach and – just as importantly – a great man-manager. He worked people out, always knew how to get the best out of them, no matter how difficult and complicated they were.

When I first joined the England squad, I was twenty years old, a lively Scouse kid who was full of himself, but shy when outside my own environment. From the first moment I walked into Burnham Beeches, though, I was made to feel part of the squad, or the 'family' as Terry always called it. I was very much on the edge of a group with some big characters and big leaders in it, men like Tony Adams, Alan Shearer, Stuart Pearce and Gazza, but somehow the manager made it feel as though I was the most important person there. For Venables, if you were selected then you belonged. Later, Glenn Hoddle had this knack of making a division right down the squad between those who were in the starting eleven and those that weren't. If you were with the stiffs, then he made you feel worthless, that you were somehow a second-class citizen. Venables had this incredible ability to make everyone feel included, as though they were part of one big extended party.

I was called up to play against Bulgaria (who had finished third in the 1994 World Cup) on 27 March 1996 and we met up at Burnham Beeches on the Sunday before the game. I was like a little kid on the way down, chatting excitedly about everything I would experience with Macca and Jamie, asking loads of questions about what it was like, what some of the other players were like, how was Venables. They were taking the piss saying that you had to be in bed by nine, and the manager came around with a torch to check all the lights were out – that sort of thing. But when I got there, the atmosphere was fantastic. The England manager had a ritual with every squad where everyone, all the players and the staff, would meet up at the hotel at a certain time, not in some function room or stuffy office, but in the bar. As it was some days before the game, everyone would have a bevvy, relax, sit down and chat. Any new guys would be welcomed, everyone would chat to them and all the staff would introduce themselves. You could have a pint, talk things around and find out what was expected of you. Stay up late if you wanted. Venables was very clever because that way, he got everyone together, and made it seem as though it was all a laugh, a relaxed enjoyable affair. But at the same time, there was always the subtle message that in representing England it was a big deal, like you were doing something important because you were the best. He made you feel as though you wanted to do it because it was such a big honour and responsibility . . . and yet it would be a real scream.

There hasn't been a better group of England lads than that squad back in 1996. Straight away I felt as though I'd always belonged. It helped that Macca had been there for a year or so, and he was right in the middle of it by the time I arrived. Alan Shearer was one of the leaders, and I looked up to him. To be catapulted from the training on a Tuesday night with a bunch of Scouse kids, to getting into the England squad less than four years later, you can't help but believe some of your publicity, especially after finding it all so easy. But I never thought I should be in the side ahead of Shearer. He was on another planet, one of the best strikers I've ever seen, and I can say quite happily that I watched him every time I trained with England, to see what I could learn from him. He was so strong, so determined, and worked so hard for the team. As I've said, along with Rushie, Shearer is the best I've ever seen.

Then there was Psycho. Fuck me, Stuart Pearce was scary. When he tackled in training you knew about it, even though you were on the same team. But his image is all wrong, because he's quite an intelligent guy, always wanted to go out and visit the museums and sights whenever we were on international duty. He always had an instinct to lead when I was involved in England. I remember at the end of the game against Spain when we had drawn 0–0 after extra time, everyone had slumped to the ground, drained by the experience, and he was the one going round, screaming at people saying that the job wasn't done yet, so get the fuck up. Tony Adams was the same. By that time he was a born-again . . . but I'm not quite sure what! He frightened me, did Tony, because he seemed to talk a different language – I could never understand a word he said because he used all these strange words and even stranger silences. But he was our leader, this big man who stood up and roared, and never have I seen a more impressive character. Dave Seaman was another huge character, a genial character who was so assured. There was some talent in the squad, too: Macca, Shearer, Les Ferdinand, Teddy Sheringham, Darren Anderton, Incey.

Gazza. What can you say about him? Insane. Great fun, impossible fun. But completely mad. I loved him of course. I was twenty years old and he was thirty, going on twelve. So we hit it off immediately. He was like a hyperactive kid too, always having to do something, be entertained, be contained! During Euro '96, I don't know how he performed as well as he did, because I swear he never slept. Not for about a month. We were staying at Burnham Beeches and had the place to ourselves. He'd be up at 5 a.m., and straight into the gym for a couple of hours of weights. Then he'd just be kicking around all anxious till the rest of us got up. He hated that me and Macca never used to get up till late, so he'd be at our rooms, knocking us out of bed. Then it would start.

Me, Macca and Jamie Redknapp had to take it in shifts to baby-sit him. It was an hourly rota, with the other two getting a couple of hours off. It would be badminton, tennis, snooker, out for a walk, videos, golf – anything to keep him occupied. By the end of the day, we were all cabbaged, except Gazza, of course, who would still be going strong. We always stayed up late, but he stayed up later, then he would have a glass of wine to get off to sleep, and a couple of hours later it would start all over again. Everyone loved him, though, because there's not a bad bone in his body. His jokes could get out of hand at times, because they were so stupid that even footballers tired of them. But most of the time, you were just killing yourself laughing at him because he didn't care. He told us about this joke he played on Gordon Durie at Rangers, and it summed him up. Durie got a brand-new Merc, and he was dead proud of it. Gazza got the keys, and hid a kipper under the glove compartment. Eventually, the smell got so bad Durie knew that he'd been 'Gazzered', and hunted around till he found it. Fair enough – typical Gazza prank. So he had the car cleaned, and had the windows down every day on the way to work to clear the smell, which was lingering. Trouble was, it didn't go away. After two months, it was there even stronger than ever. Eventually he had to send it back to the manufacturers to have it investigated . . . and they found a second kipper, which Gazza had hidden under the back seat. Unbolted it, taken it out, replaced it. Now that is pure genius. It was that sort of mentality that kept everyone entertained, and forget Bulldog Big Bollocks, or whatever his name was, Gazza was the England mascot in Euro '96.

I had to get there though, which meant I had to do well on my debut. It was a Wednesday night at the end of March, a wet Wembley night, and I was on the bench. Me dad was there with his mate and George, and Mr Lynch was there too – with twenty-five kids from St Margaret's School, all of them praying I would get on. I reckon I warmed up about eighty times that night, just to remind Venables I was still there. I started warming up a second and a half after kick-off. It worked eventually too, because as I was running down the touchline for my fifteenth mile of the evening, the coach Ted Buxton shouted down to me to come back and strip off. Funny thing was, I wasn't nervous in the slightest. This was everything every kid who's kicked a ball dreams of, a sell-out Wembley crowd, and your England debut, under the floodlights. I was so excited and so expectant and I couldn't wait to get on. I've been accused of lacking pace, but I didn't that night as I charged on to replace Les Ferdinand with about ten minutes to go. I was like the fucking road-runner. Except that I barely had the chance to go beep beep and the referee was blowing his whistle to signal the game was over. Still, I'd made my debut, hadn't fallen on my arse and Venables spoke to me afterwards, said he was really pleased with my attitude, and was desperate to get me involved. It's just that he didn't know who to leave out, because his strikers had done nothing wrong.

So I went away feeling good . . . but still worried about getting into the squad for the big one. Next month, we were back at Wembley again, against Croatia, and this time I was on from the start so I must have done something right. Again,

I felt comfortable, not nervous or worried, and I think Terry's approach along with his coaches Bryan Robson and Ted Buxton went a long way to helping me with that. At the end of the season, after the disappointment of the Cup final, the England squad for our notorious jaunt to Hong Kong and China was announced, and I was in it. Again though, there was a catch. We were taking more strikers than places, and the manager was going to have to bomb one of us. Imagine that, getting all the way out to the Far East, and then missing out at the final hurdle. Peter Beardsley was the unlucky one – everyone really felt for him – and somehow I had become part of the squad for Euro '96. I don't know about football coming home, but I was going nuts.

That trip to China and Hong Kong was nuts too, thanks to Gazza. Again, the manager was really clever with that, because he took us completely away from the whole build-up to the tournament, away from the pressure and let us have a blow-out. Mind you, I don't suppose even he thought it would turn out the way it did. The tone was set on the flight out, when Gazza got involved in a row with one of the stewards on the plane, and ended up having a bit of a scrap. The pilot saw his arse and said that he was going to stop the plane in Russia and boot us all off! Now that would have been some story. But we created a few anyway. We played the games, did the business, I got another cap against China and then the tour was finished, so Venables gave us the night off to have a blast. It was me and Gazza who started it. God, he can be annoying at times. He's got this thing where he makes something up, and he repeats it, and then he really believes it's true. We were at the bar and he started shouting to the rest of the lads, 'Hey, Growler's just chatted a bird up by asking her if she comes here often!' He believes it now, he really does. He kept saying it, so I grabbed him, and we had a bit of a wrestle. Nothing serious, but I ripped his shirt a bit, so he tried to pour a pint over me. Then he did it to Teddy, and Macca, so they ripped his shirt off. When Bryan Robson arrived, everyone was daring Gazza to do it to him, because obviously he was mad enough to do any-thing. And he did, the mad bastard, ripped Robbo's shirt clean off, the assistant manager, and someone with a reputation that no one would mess with!

He went away and hid for a while after that, but the party went on. The lads were boxing by then, and eventually one of the players said it was time to go in the dentist's chair. The bar had this massive chair that you had to lie back in while they pour shorts down your neck. We all got in, all had a laugh, drank a few beers, sang a few songs and went home. No problem, not even that pissed. But some punter in there had a camera, and fuck knows how he did it, he got the pictures back to all the papers in England to cash in. We woke up the next day and all hell broke loose, because there was Gazza in the chair, with me and Macca standing right beside him, roaring him on, our shirts ripped to shreds and hair matted with beer that had run down our clothes. Even now when I see those pictures I think, Ah Jesus. They look terrible. Just horrible. It was a laugh and it wasn't that bad, but it was as if World War Three had broken out. The media went crazy because we had dared to have a beer and relax, a month before the tournament got started. There was another great story too on that trip that never got out. One of the lads pulled a bird and she ended up back in his room. The next morning he woke up after she left, and got a call from reception saying there was a gift for him. Intrigued, he had it sent up and there was a parcel, nicely wrapped. When he opened it, there were his own boots. Puzzled and still bleary-eyed, he looked around his room for the first time to see that it had been stripped of everything: kit, money, cards, even the toiletries from the bathroom. At least she had a pang of conscience, and sent his boots back!

On the way back, Gazza had another brain-storm that had more serious repercussions. He was bladdered and had already had a bit of a set-to with one of the FA bods. Then he tried to get some sleep, which is always a bad idea on a flight full of footballers. Especially a group like that. Inevitably someone gave him a slap. Alan Shearer, I think it was, and it was hard enough to knock his head off. Gazza went ballistic, because he finds it hard to sleep at the best of times, so after being woken up he went over the edge. He was walking up and down the aisles smashing everyone, trying to find out who did it. He came down to the seats where me and Macca were sitting and he whacked the TV screen in front of us, which spluttered a few times and then went out. I think he did the same to Les Ferdinand's screen. In the end, one of the FA bigwigs had to come up to the top deck where we were, and plead with him to quiet down. The airline, Cathay Pacific, didn't see the funny side, and they gave us a bill of about five grand, which was a bit steep for a couple of mini tellies. We all had to pay £500 each, making it an expensive slap.

We got back and thought nothing more of it, until the day we were supposed to go down to London to join up with the squad for the start of the tournament. All over the front pages of the Sunday papers was the story that me and Macca had wrecked the plane. Combined with those pictures of the dentist's chair it made me out to be a real yob, a scally from Toxteth who had come on the England scene and was dragging it all down. I was the wild boy, twenty-one and completely out of control. Or so they said. Actually, I was a kid who had a laugh pulling some of the stunts I used to do with me mates in the street. And of course I had another kid in Gazza to goad me on.

First impressions do stick though, and those weeks tarred me for ever in the minds of a lot of people. It's hard to change people's first image of you, especially when they are as graphic as those dentist chair pictures and the headlines in the *News of the World*. We knew we had to do something about it, so we sued the newspaper. We'd had a meeting and a statement was issued claiming collective responsibility, but that was hardly enough, and so we broke ranks to say it wasn't us. Hand on heart, we had nothing to do with it, and that was made absolutely clear to the newspaper. They decided to fight it though, and so Euro '96 came and went, and everyone forgot about it all. We were preparing to go to court, and I told Gazza that if we did, then we were going to name him, which we had skilfully managed to avoid until that point. He said it was fine, so long as we told him beforehand so he could get out of the country. Eventually, about four or five years later they settled, but there was no chance of it helping our reputations by then.

At the Championships themselves, Big Al and Teddy showed why Terry Venables had so much faith in them, with some brilliant performances. I was never going to get past them into the side, but I had a fantastic time as the baby of the squad, and even though nobody seems to remember this, I did manage to play in two matches, the first against Holland when we stuffed them 4–1. That was some experience for me, my first competitive tournament game, and I got on to help destroy a side that contained the likes of Seedorf, Kluivert, Davids, Bergkamp, Overmars, Cocu and De Boer. I got on against Spain too. In that game, it was 0–0 and we went to penalties and it was a tense affair in the centre circle as we waited, with Stuart Pearce doing his job to psych everyone up, even though he must have been bricking it himself, because he was one of the nominated penalty takers.

We had our five for the shoot-out, in an order already worked out: Shearer, Pearce, Platt, Gazza and Sheringham. But hang on, Teddy was subbed, so who would take it? Bryan Robson came up to me and whispered, 'Are you up for the fifth?' Course I was. I didn't have to think about it for a second, because I had taken penalties for Liverpool, and I was hungry to score any sort of goal for my country. But Christ, it was some responsibility for a kid, taking the fifth penalty in the quarter final, all your dreams and nightmares rolled into one question. Hierro missed the first, our four scored, and Nadal stepped up. If he scored, I had the fifth penalty to put us through, everything would be on me. I was torn between praying he'd miss and praying he'd score, because I fancied meself to get the winner. It's funny, but that one moment might have changed my England career. I'd have been the hero if I'd scored, the kid from Toxteth who took on the world, the brave young lad with nerves of steel . . . as all these thoughts were still swimming through my head Nadal stepped up, Dave Seaman swooped down, and we were through. No need for heroics from me, The Keeper had done it for us. I still wonder now what might have happened, though. I was pretty confident I'd have buried it, obviously, but who knows? Poor Gareth Southgate got asked the same question by Robbo at the end of extra time in the semi final with Germany because Venners never made any substitutions so I wasn't on the pitch, and look what happened to him . . . he made a good few grand out of a pizza advert!

I didn't know it at the time, but Euro '96 was probably the peak of my England career. I was just a kid, the wide-eyed boy who had stayed up late and crashed the party and I was hungry to get more of it, but it never quite happened for me. Those few weeks in June 1996 were some of the most exciting of my life. Being locked away with that bunch of lads in Burnham Beeches for over a month, having such a scream and feeling the tension gradually growing as the nation got behind us, that was heaven. Terry Venables had done his job perfectly because he had got the blend in the squad exactly right, with players from so many different clubs, and no dominant clique, no imbalance between young or old or quiet and loud characters. I don't think I have ever got anywhere near the atmosphere in that squad on international duty since that time and, to me, it's no surprise that England has never come close to repeating the success that Venables had, even if he couldn't quite lift the trophy because of that bloody penalty shoot-out.

All the lads loved him. Gazza, of course, worshipped him, but so too did the thoughtful players like Gareth Southgate, Tony Adams and Macca, who still rate him as the best tactical coach they have worked with. The experience will never fade, the passion of the nation. We could see it every time we went to Wembley, the people on the streets cheering us and waving about a million flags. Normally, when you are locked away from the public, you don't know what is going on, what the feeling is like amongst the fans, but that year we felt everything, we joined in with all the emotion, and it was fantastic. We used to sing 'Three Lions', the Skinner and Baddiel song, for a laugh on the team coach. Gazza, the wrong 'un, had it blaring out of his room at all hours of the day and night, with tears coming down his face as he sang along. He wouldn't even get off the coach as we arrived at the stadium whenever it was playing, because he wanted to finish singing along. It was that sort of atmosphere though, and it was a shame to be going home. When we lost to Germany we went back to Burnham and had a massive piss-up to drown our sorrows. Gareth Southgate was inconsolable, and we all tried to cheer him up a bit. Gazza and I had one more schoolboy trick up our sleeves, a food fight with those squeezy bottles of tomato sauce, which was a laugh ... until the mad bastard sneaked into the kitchens and found a massive catering tin of the stuff as big as a drum, which he tried to pour on my head. The next day, I woke up with the world's worst hangover, but a great feeling because of what I had been part of, and what was to come. For me, Euro '96 was just the beginning. How wrong I was.

Glenn Hoddle took over as England manager after that summer, because the FA thought that Terry Venables was a bit dodgy in business. Sometimes, you look at the decisions that the faceless people behind the scenes take, and it makes you cry. How can they have done that? We had just enjoyed the most incredible tournament that had inspired the whole nation, made the whole country feel proud again and have faith in the international side, and what do they do? Effectively sack the manager who had created it all and proved himself the best in the world, and bring in someone to replace him who didn't last the course. I know hindsight is a wonderful thing, but here we are a decade later, and we are still paying the price of that senseless decision. With that group Venables had put together, and the youngsters that were coming through at that time, there is little doubt in my mind that Terry would have taken the next step forward.

After three months of Glenn Hoddle, I was pretty sure we would do fuck all. People always ask me whether Glenn Hoddle really was mad. Of course he wasn't, but he was strange. Very strange. To a young kid like me from inner-city Liverpool, some of the stuff he did I couldn't understand at all, couldn't relate to it in any way. To me it was just mumbo jumbo. In fact, to my inexperienced twenty-one-year-old head at that time, it was fucking barmy. I realize that people could turn that on me and say it was me who was too thick to understand his 'revolutionary methods', but it wasn't only me, it was almost every other member of the squad. Even the ones who could get their heads around all the faith-healer stuff, even the ones who were supposed to be mates with him like Darren Anderton and Incey, they thought he was unapproachable, odd even. It's all very well the England manager taking a different approach and trying new methods, but you have to know what you are dealing with in football, and as I keep suggesting, young men from the inner cities are not always the most open-minded of groups.

Surely the best coaches size up their players and take them all along with them. I've always been suspicious of coaches that can't handle different personalities, because that way you exclude so much talent. Of course, some players will never fit in, fair enough, but most do if they are handled sympathetic-ally. Isn't that the aim of coaching, to get the very best out of disparate groups? Venables did, Sir Alex Ferguson does, Arsene Wenger does. Glenn Hoddle didn't. With him, everyone had to conform to his rigid thinking, or they were gone. Early on, we heard stories, and players were thinking, This can't be right. Ray Parlour was bombed after he went to see Eileen Drewery and when she stood behind him and placed her hands on his shoulders he said, 'Short back and sides please.' David May supposedly lost any chance of ever being involved because he laughed during training on his first get-together. I don't know if they are the sole reason for Hoddle's decision about them, but you can believe it.

For me, the worst thing was the situation with Eileen. She was a lovely woman, don't get me wrong, and her husband Phil was a real decent fella, a down-to-earth diamond bloke. Some of the lads swore by her – people like Gareth Southgate reckoned she helped an awful lot. They used to run a pub in Essex, apparently, and when I went to her house to see her, I spent most of the time in the back room in a bar that Phil had made in there, having a couple of beers and a chat. I got the impression he couldn't get his head around it either. I honestly don't have any problems with what she did, because who am I to say whether a faith healer could help people or not? In fact, I heard stories about some amazing things that happened, that were supposed to have cured injuries and helped people get fit again. Mind you, Darren Anderton went to see her quite a lot, and I'm not sure that's the best advert for her healing powers!

Anyway, it wasn't the fact that she was available, I think that was fair enough, maybe even a good idea for the psychological effect it could have. It was more the fact that Glenn used to put players under incredible pressure to go and see her. It was made clear in no uncertain terms that if you wanted to be involved in his squads then you had to go and see her. It was ridiculous really, because everyone felt obliged to go, and not everyone could play! It was just a little bit sinister too, because I remember that even Michael Owen felt he had to go along, and he was just a tiny kid at the time, who had done nothing, not had an injury or even a drink, and there he was getting all his demons checked out. He was in there for half an hour or more, which didn't seem right.

It was Incey who came to me and said that Glenn thought it would be in my best interests to go down and see her. 'Fuck that,' I said, 'me mum would kill me if the priest at St Patrick's ever found out.' But he was insistent. He said that he really thought it was important that I went, because it sent the right message to Hoddle, it was what he was looking for to put me in the team. Macca was the same, he went through the same process and even though he kept saying no, he cracked. I went down there with him, Incey, Les Ferdinand and Ian Wright. They were in there for ages, so I had a couple of beers with Phil, and a bit of a laugh. Not bad this spiritualism thing, I thought. Eventually, after what seemed like hours of us sitting there having a few beers, it was my turn. I went in, and she put her hands on me, kind of warm they were, and it was a funny sensation. She asked me a few questions, I mumbled a few responses, and then she pulled away after about three minutes, said she couldn't do anything for me because I had three demons in there, swirling around and fucking me up. I got out, and I swear I was pissing myself.

Three demons, wait until the lads heard that. I was pretty

proud of those demons actually, and so when we met up next time I walked in and announced it to everyone. Then Gazza piped up, 'That's nothing, she told me I've got five.' Typical Gazza, he has to outdo everyone at everything! I was gutted. I think that when Eileen became part of the official England staff things got more serious, when she was in the hotel with the players, giving treatment. That was when the press started to get on to it. In the end, they made a big deal of it, and it was portrayed as Hoddle's downfall, but the reality was that one or two of the senior players in the squad around that time had made it clear to some of the FA officials that the manager had lost the players, there was no respect for him, and there was a real chance we wouldn't qualify for the European Championships of 2000. That set the alarm bells going, and when they found an excuse to ditch him, they moved faster than David Beckham does to join in the celebration when an England striker scores a goal.

Hoddle couldn't relate to the players. He talked to us like we were kids. He had the cream of the nation's footballers, and he used to make us sit down in front of him while he told us how to do things. Top, top players would be training and he'd stop everything, and in front of everyone tell them that they didn't know what they were doing. Then he would show them how it ought to be done. When the strikers did practise for their finishing, it wasn't the wide players who crossed the ball in for us to get on the end of. Some of the best wingers in the country – in the world – would be sitting there watching as Glenn put in all the crosses to us, so we had the right delivery. He might as well have played himself. I don't think he ever spoke to any of the players, he left that to John Gorman (his assistant) while he took a massive step back, distant and detached.

Around the hotel under his reign, it was so boring and dull. You used to be desperate to get back to your club, to join the normal world again. These were basically the same group of lads and yet when we arrived, it was straight up to the room, lock yourself in and only come out for training. That was one thing, but then there were the rules. Suddenly, there were millions of them. You couldn't go out to the town around Burnham any more – we were not allowed a night off to go anywhere, even if it was five days before a game. We asked to go and see a fight once, and he turned us down flat, even though it was almost a week before the game. You couldn't laugh in training, couldn't play cards, couldn't have carbonated water – still water was fine, but not fizzy. You couldn't drink anything before a meal or twenty minutes after. You were given a bag of tablets and you had no idea what they were, but you had to take them three times a day. You had to have Creatine. I was really suspicious of that stuff, because there were quite a few cases of it being contaminated with steroids, but no, you had to take it no matter what your fears. There were injections of vitamins and minerals too, and you didn't know what they were, but you had to have them. There were other people around the squad too – not just Eileen Drewery – who were a bit weird. They were described to the press as psychologists, but it seemed like other forms of spiritualism to me. Then there was 'Snowy White', and 'Bird of Paradise', the song he always played to soothe the players. What the hell was that about?!

I didn't get Hoddle, and neither did the rest of the players, which is why he went, no doubt. But I have to hold my hand up and admit that I didn't help myself with him. I was a smart, street-wise kid, but I wasn't good at that time at working things out and making them work for me – maybe because I didn't have to as I scored so many goals, and that forced people to take me for what I was. Hoddle couldn't do that, and I think sometimes he looked at me like I was from another planet ... while I knew he was on one!

There were two incidents that cemented my fate under him, and ensured that I never got any sort of chance, even before I was injured, which ruined any faint prospect of going to the World Cup finals in 1998. The first came just three games into his reign, when we went to Georgia right at the end of 1996 for a qualifying match. With all the rules and no chance of having a laugh or even any entertainment, it was like a living nightmare, a four-day trip that seemed to go on for four years.

The night before the match, he named his team and I was on the fringe again, out of his plans. I hadn't been involved for the first two games against Moldova and Poland, which was fair enough because he stuck with Alan Shearer. But big Al was injured for Georgia and I thought I must be in the reckoning after the two seasons I'd just had, and the season I was having this time. But he put Teddy and Les Ferdinand up front, and then brought Ian Wright on, and I knew then he didn't fancy me, even though I had fought my way in as first change under Terry Venables. I was twenty-one, and I sat on the bench in Tbilisi thinking there was no point me being there.

On the plane on the way back, it was about a five-hour journey and I got smashed. I was sitting there moaning with Macca because he'd been dropped after Hoddle said he wasn't suited to the rough pitch! I was getting more and more agitated, and eventually, I said to him, 'Right, that's it, I'm going to tell the fucker what I think of him.' Macca was going, 'No, no, you dope, don't be stupid, it's suicide,' but I was adamant. I got up and waltzed down the plane to the front, with a brandy in one hand and a huge cigar in the other. I got by Hoddle, puffing on the cigar, and took a swig of the brandy for courage, then I let him have it. 'How come I'm not playing, you soft get, I want to know why' – that sort of intellectual argument! He was looking at me like I'd just shat on his food tray. He spluttered a reply about me not being quite ready, and this wasn't the place to talk about it, and I don't think even he could believe what I had just done. The rest of the lads were pissing themselves, it was better than the in-flight video. Needless to say I didn't get selected for a while after that.

I did get in eventually though, for my first appearance under Hoddle against Mexico at the end of March in 1997, just before I got sent off in the game at Everton. I was alongside Ian Wright in an 'experimental' line-up because it was a friendly. Nothing much happened until fifty-five minutes, when Wrighty escaped his marker to get a header off. It was blocked but I was steaming in and put the loose ball away. Dead easy, but it was my first goal for my country in only my second start. Me dad was there, and he was so proud afterwards he was almost in tears. I rang me mum and she was the same. She always said she wouldn't come to matches to watch me because I was so small she was terrified I would get hurt! But she wished she had been there that night.

Scoring a goal for your country, it's the pinnacle, and just before my twenty-second birthday I did it. Even if I guessed Hoddle didn't rate me, that was the ultimate for me and I thought then that I must have some hope of getting a regular place. Bob Hope more like. I only played for Hoddle twice more, and one of those was in his very last game. It was such a scratch side, he had Paul Merson and Dion Dublin up front, and he still didn't start me. The funny thing was, he gave me two starts and I scored two goals. No other player had a better strike rate for him! When it came to it, he never played me in a competitive match, not even one minute, and that showed he didn't trust me. Venables put me on in the quarter final of a European Championship and trusted me enough to give me the fifth penalty in the shoot-out. But Hoddle didn't, and that was based more on his own blinkered way of thinking, because while he was England manager there was only Shearer whose record compared to mine domestically, no one else even got close. Not that I'm bitter like!

What did it for me was the operation I had on me hooter in the summer of 1997. If you ask me, Hoddle was a bit of a control freak, something I didn't know too much about at that time, but I was to become all too familiar with later. It was the end of the season and England were playing a qualifier against Poland before they went to France for 'Le Tournoi', a friendly tournament that also had Brazil, Italy and the home nation in it. It was his big build-up thing, where he wanted to produce the conditions that we would be playing in a year later. So two hours after naming his squad, when he got a fax in his hand from our gaffer Roy Evans, pulling me and Macca out, he was fucking livid. He didn't see me as central to his plans anyway, so I reckon when he believed I had crossed him, he thought he could make an example of me. And he did. He held a press conference especially, and went on about one door closing for us, and another opening for someone else. Effectively, he said that we'd done our chance of playing in the World Cup next year.

It was obvious he reckoned we pulled out of the trip to have a bit of time off. He thought we'd bunked off, basically. I can't speak for Macca, he had a bad knee and he needed an operation, although I'm not sure whether he ever had it or not. I really did need an op, desperately. I have always had problems with my sinuses, and they had got a lot worse over the previous year. I tried those strips that open your nostrils up, and they were pretty good – they definitely weren't a fashion statement as people said, because I looked a right knob-head – but the doctor had told me that the only way to cure it was to have the operation. We knew that it would open me up to the inevitable rumours about drugs, with people saying it was something to do with snorting coke, but I honestly never dreamt Hoddle wouldn't believe me. The only time Liverpool would let me have the op done was in the summer, when I had two months to recover, which was understandable because they paid my wages. And I needed time to recover. With all the fuss that Hoddle's comments caused, the club was furious and they wanted to release pictures of me after I'd had the surgery. I refused, though, because I looked like the Elephant Man and I didn't want pictures circulating for the rest of my life of me with a face like a car crash. I was in a bad way.

Later that summer, I was given an offer to go to Canada by Molson Beers, to do a few appearances with the Superstars Champion of Champions, Brian Budd. Ally McCoist eventually did it, and he got paid about twenty grand for two days' work, but they were desperate to get me. We went back to the surgeon and asked him whether I could make the flight. He thought about it for a bit, and said it probably wasn't wise but it was up to me. So I goes, laughing, 'Well, what's the worst that can happen?' He shot back, all deadly serious, 'Your nose will explode and you'll bleed to death on the aisle floor.' Hmmn, think we'll give that one a swerve then.

Hoddle stuck to his word, and I didn't get in a squad for seven months. Then he called me up pretty much out of the blue for a friendly against Cameroon, and I got my third

England start. I got my second goal, too, right on the stroke of half time. I was thrilled. I'd missed the start of the season with the injury I picked up in Norway, and Michael Owen was the new kid on the block. But when I came back I scored eight goals in eleven games and even Hoddle couldn't ignore me. Funny thing was, I was suspended when he picked me because I'd been sent off at Bolton, which was un-Hod like. I scored against Cameroon, and I was thinking, That'll fucking teach ya. Except that I was completely wrong again. By my standards, I had a bad patch after that international. I scored four goals in seven games in December, which wasn't hopeless, but not great for me. Then I got one in nine, which was worrying.

It wasn't helped by the fact that in the middle of it Hoddle named a squad to play against Chile at Wembley, and I wasn't in it. I had scored for England in the previous game less than two months before, and now I wasn't good enough to even get in the twenty-two. He came out saying that I had to work harder, improve my form. But my form for England was fucking marvellous! That didn't make sense to me, but then not much under Hoddle did. It was a bad time, and I felt let down by the England manager. Two weeks later, I was called off at Anfield and my World Cup was over. He mouthed all the right things about me still having time to get on the plane to France, but we both knew there was no chance. In the end, I guess that we just didn't understand each other. When he was sacked for saying those things about disabled people, what he came out with didn't surprise me, because it wasn't that far removed from all the other strange stuff he went on about that I couldn't get my head around. And I suppose he couldn't get his head around me either, a headstrong young lad from a council estate in Liverpool – although someone once told me that he came from a similar background, so you'd have thought that might have given him a clue.

It wasn't quite the end of me and Glenn Hoddle actually, because when I got myself fit the next season, I just happened to be called into his final squad before he got the boot. I had worked really hard to get fit all over the summer, and I was back within seven months, which all the doctors said was unheard of. I gave it everything to come back from that injury, went through agonies at the time and suffered terribly, because your mind is a real dark place when you have an injury like that and you're left working on your own all the time. I was injured at the end of February 1998, and I made my first team return in a game in Kosice in Slovakia by the middle of September. In November, I got the surprise of my life when I was put in the England squad to face the Czech Republic. I got on late in the game, but only after he had tried Wrighty, Dion Dublin and Paul Merson up front. Still, it was nice to be there to wave him off. I may sound bitter, but I'm not really, it's just that I felt my England career stalled under Hoddle, when I was at the right age and in the right form for it to have taken a giant leap forward, and I never recovered from that.

It was only when Kevin Keegan arrived that things looked up for a while. Many things have been said about Keegan – most of them true as far as I can see! – but, seriously, I'll always have loyalty towards him, because when he was England boss he always had a great deal of loyalty to me. I have never been convinced that his management style could work at international level, but he suffered some unfair criticism during his reign as boss of the national side. No one deserves to be crucified for trying to do a job as impossible as that. Not Glenn Hoddle, and not Kevin Keegan. They do it to the best of their ability, even if they are not suited to the job. I think Keegan had too many limitations to be a success with England, but he was also desperately unlucky, and no one ever takes that into account.

After Hoddle, the FA wanted someone the players could get along with, and Keegan was the obvious man. Except that he wasn't up to it tactically. I think it's fair to say that, given those are his own words not mine. Under him, we hardly ever planned for anything, there was not much tactical work on the training ground, no planning for certain scenarios during a game, even when we knew what the opposition were likely to do. Keegan had the old Liverpool philosophy of playing off the cuff, of the team being fluid and just adapting out there on the pitch to what was happening. But at international level when it is nuances that win matches, you need to be better prepared than that. His final game summed it up, really. We played Germany at Wembley in the last match before it was redeveloped, and we went with Gareth Southgate as a marker in midfield, because they used to play Mehmet Scholl behind two strikers and Keegan wanted him picked up. Fair enough ... until we kicked off, that is. Because Scholl played off only one striker in a more conventional role, so Southgate was redundant in that role. We were completely overrun in midfield, but it took Keegan until beyond half time to change it and by then we had lost the match.

I was in the squad that game, but not stripped, and it was a bit like watching a car crash from a distance. Afterwards, he came into the dressing room and held his hands up. 'I can't take it any further, it's time for someone else to have a go, lads,' he said. And that was it. He went out to face the media and – fair play to him – he admitted he wasn't up to it, that he'd had a crack and came up short. You'd have thought people would have applauded him for being so straight and doing the right thing by his country, but not a bit of it. He was slaughtered. And the strange thing was, it was the same sort of stuff that was thrown at Roy Evans. Keegan was hammered because he tried to generate a bit of team spirit in the England squad, which was so clearly lacking under Glenn Hoddle. He was hammered because he let his players be grown-ups and decide for themselves when to go to bed, when to have a drink, how to relax. If you had believed all the hysteria then England under Keegan was a group of players who were boozing, gambling wild men who were completely out of control, and all because the manager used to let the players relax by having race nights and playing a few hands of cards.

England under Keegan was a sensible group. The senior players like Shearer, Adams, Sheringham, Keown and Seaman set a great example, and there were no wild nights, nothing out of the ordinary. When we went to Euro 2000, we were stuck in this tiny hotel in the most boring town in Belgium, which has got to be the most boring country on earth. So to relieve the boredom, a couple of the lads acted as bookies, and the rest would bet with them. It was usually Shearer and Sheri, and they'd take bets on the matches that were being played in the tournament, and also race nights that Keegan set up. You'd have video tapes of races and have a bet on the outcome. The money gambled wasn't crazy, but the fun was trying to take it out of Alan Shearer's pocket. At various times during the tournament, we'd calculate his losses in the thousands, but by the end you knew he'd be up because he was such a shrewd operator.

Nobody had to bet, so can anyone tell me what the hell was wrong with it? The same with the cards. There is not a football club in the world where players don't play cards, and yet with England it was as if it was a crime. There were stories about boozing too, but again, with the senior players we had in that squad there was never a chance of excess. It was as if the media couldn't cope with the idea of footballers relaxing, and they would do anything to have a go at the manager for allowing it. Yet if Keegan was anything, then he was good at getting a spirit going, making playing for England fun, and making the players feel as though it was something to play for their country. In those days, he was a great motivator and a really decent man. He did his best to create the conditions for a winning England side.

What worries me is that the way the media is now, they don't seem to allow managers to build any sort of team spirit, because they find anything designed to get players together as outrageous. So you end up with squads that turn up, don't even say hello and go straight off to their rooms, where they stay until they go to training or to the match. I can remember reading an interview with Chris Powell, who was given a surprise call-up into the England squad by Eriksson, and he had this awestruck tone that David Beckham actually spoke to him and knew his name.

When you go and play for England you are supposed to be in it together. Under Venables, and to a lesser extent Keegan, you'd be together all the time building spirit, and everyone would be equal, everyone would know each other. Yet now, after all the furore during the Keegan era, Eriksson has to play it safe. There's no bonding, no team-building, no spirit of togetherness . . . and it shows. Look at what happened in World Cup 2002. We went out against Brazil with barely a whimper, because when it came to it, when the chips were really down, there was no team spirit to see us through. After well over a decade in top-flight football, I can tell you the one thing that is absolutely necessary to become winners is incredible team spirit. The side has to be together. That is why managers like Sir Alex Ferguson and Arsene Wenger and just lately Jose Mourinho are always trying to suggest there's a conspiracy against their sides. They want the 'us and them' scenario, because it generates the mentality they require. The media almost disallowed that under Keegan, and because everything has to be so bland under Eriksson, it's a real problem. The only chance England has of winning anything is if the quality players we have available now are allowed to bond together to become a real team. But I'm not sure that can ever happen, especially under Eriksson.

Keegan picked me. I don't think I was ever truly fit during the whole time that he was manager of England, but he picked me anyway. It is a huge regret I suffered so many injuries before major tournaments, because I have never been able to play a real part in any of them. Euro '96 turned out to be the peak of my international career, which was effectively on the decline when I was twenty-one. I don't think Hoddle gave me a fair chance, largely, I felt, because of his prejudices about my character, and his inability to judge on talent alone. But as it turned out, I was knackered for the World Cup in 1998 anyway, so it was irrelevant. Keegan, for all his faults, was always good at seeing a player by the most important criterion – how he performed out there on the pitch. He'd coached me when I was with the under-21s and seen some ability, and then I had helped turn his Newcastle sides over a few times, so he rated me. He gave me every chance before Euro 2000, because he knew there was a goal-scoring ability inside me.

But I had been injured for nearly all of the 1999–2000 season, and I wasn't even a quarter fit when I went out there with the squad to Belgium. I had picked up an ankle injury at

the start of September, and didn't come back until the penult-
imate game of the season. I had played one full game for
Liverpool, and he gave me three games for England before the
Championships started. But I wasn't ready, despite the show
of faith he gave by selecting me. I went out there, and I knew
I wouldn't play, knew it was a waste of time me going really,
because there wasn't much value in even putting me on. I
watched it in a detached way, interested but not involved.
Bored mostly, because I was away from home for more than a
month, and I knew there was hardly any chance of me playing.
From a distance, I think Keegan was unlucky. He was three
minutes away from reaching the quarter finals, and it was only
a bad mistake at the end of the game against Romania that
stopped him from taking us through. He was also deprived of
key players. Keegan never had a central midfielder to dominate
the game. Incey had come to the end of his time with England
then, and Steven Gerrard – who was the natural successor –
was maybe a little too young, and anyway he got injured when
he played so well against Germany as a substitute in the game
we won 1–0 in the group stage. Michael Owen suffered a lot of
injuries under Keegan, and so did I, so he didn't always have a
partner for Alan Shearer, who was also coming to the end of
his international time, as were Tony Adams and Martin Keown.
Keegan had his failings, that was for sure. We used to ask the
people who worked with him, What is it with Kevin? Why
doesr 't he do more tactical work? And they just shrugged and
said that was him, he'd had success doing it his way, and there
was no changing. He was instinctive, impulsive, and that was
that. There was no depth to his management approach. Also,
he wasn't the great communicator everyone thinks. He'd try
and talk to the lads where Hoddle didn't even bother, but
Keegan was a bit of a biff when it came to dealing with us.
He'd hang around the pool room at the team hotel and try to
strike up a conversation, chatting away, but it was like having
your maiden aunt there when you're a kid, long awkward
silences punctuated with embarrassed chit-chat as you desperately tried to edge away. It didn't work with Keegan, but he
wasn't as bad as the reputation he left behind.

Eriksson on the other hand has, for me, a reputation vastly inflated beyond his actual achievements. He was a safe pair of hands after Keegan, but he wasn't the first choice of the players. When Germany beat us 1–0 in October 2000 and Keegan quit, the FA took the unprecedented step of asking some of the senior players who they thought should be the next manager. Quite a few were asked, although not me because I was struggling with an injury – again – and Howard Wilkinson thought it would be better if I went back to my club to get treatment. But everyone who was canvassed, almost to a man, came up with the name that I would have offered – Terry Venables. He was the unanimous choice, but there was a feeling within the Football Association that he was damaged goods and they wanted to bring in a foreign influence, so the second choice was Arsene Wenger. But one of the people doing the soundings was the Arsenal vice-chairman David Dein, who was on the international committee, which made it a non-starter.

It came to Eriksson next and I think he got the job largely because of the reasons Sir Alex Ferguson astutely outlined when it seemed Sven was going to succeed him at Manchester United. When I read what Ferguson said, I nearly spat out me Frosties, because it was almost word for word what was said in the dressing room about him. Fergie blew Eriksson's chance of getting the Old Trafford job out of the water when he 'let slip' that a deal had been done with the United board even though Eriksson was still in charge of England, and he said: 'I think Sven would be the nice easy choice for United's directors because nothing really happens, does it? He doesn't change anything, he sails along, nobody falls out. He says, "The first half we were good, the second half not so good. I am pleased with the result." He is the acceptable face. Carlos Quieroz knows him from his Benfica days, and he says what Eriksson did so well was not to fall out with anyone, the press like him, he is best pals with the president – I think he does that a bit.' Ferguson also scorned him for being so responsive to public opinion, and I always thought that was a problem with him.

His choice of captain always seemed to be based on who was popular with the public, not who was influential within the team. Come to think of it, that could describe his team selection too. If Eriksson had been manager in Euro '96, then I would have played, because there was a real bandwagon rolling in my favour before the tournament . . . there was even a bit of a concerted newspaper campaign to get me in the side. But Terry Venables was right to stick to his guns, and sometimes with Eriksson you feel that he blows a bit too easy with the wind. Maybe he doesn't have a strong enough opinion of his own. Or if he does, he hides it well.

To be fair to him, he played me a few times, and in a couple of games I thought I struck up a real understanding with Michael Owen. We played a World Cup qualifier in Greece in June 2001 after we won the treble at Liverpool, and I won the Man of the Match award that day. I drifted off the front behind Michael and created one of the goals for Paul Scholes, and came within a whisker of scoring myself. Afterwards, there seemed to be surprise that we could have played so well together, when there was a feeling we couldn't forge a partnership at Liverpool. I always thought we could, and that game in Greece showed it. We took apart a very good team that day, Michael, me and Scholesy in a little forward triangle, and for one of the few times in my England career I felt the team was set up to play around me and accommodate my talent.

For the large part though, Eriksson was a long-ball merchant, and he obviously thought I didn't fit into that pattern. He wanted pace up front, no matter what the standard was. Darius Vassell won far more caps under Eriksson than I could ever have dreamt of, and that's because the manager was obsessed with lumping early long balls for quick fellas up front. It's the modern disease, and for me it is the preserve of the bankrupt coach. You don't see the top teams playing like that, very few of them rely purely on pace up front. They pass the ball, intelligently create openings for strikers who are in the side because they can finish, not because they can catch pigeons. When we lost in the World Cup quarter final in 2002, our Brazilian opponents didn't have any pace up front at all, but it didn't matter to them because they wanted to play football. We didn't.

That game against Brazil turned out to be my last involvement with England, and I had guessed as much at the time. In fact, when I flew back from Japan I decided on the plane that I was going to retire from international football because it was a waste of fucking time flying all the way around the world when you know that you've got no chance of playing. It's just that Eriksson beat me to it, and stopped picking me before I could say I didn't want to be picked. Sums up my career under him, really. I've got nothing against him, and I've got no real complaints about not being picked. Apart from that brief time around the game in Greece, I don't think I would ever have fit into one of his teams.

He seems a perfectly nice bloke, although even though I played for him for three years I haven't got a clue what he is like. Do you know what? In all that time, I never had a conversation with him once. If the stories about his private life are anything to go by, he's obviously a bit of a rascal, so he can't be all bad! There is clearly a bit more to his personality than he ever lets out when he's with the England players. To me, though, he's not a particularly good manager. He's a half-decent coach who has got himself a massive reputation. He is typically Scandinavian in his approach in that he is an organizer, and a thorough one at that. England play like Swedish teams now – we are organized, defensive, fit and direct. But we have no imagination in our tactics, no style, no real flair and most importantly, no Plan B to fall back on when Plan A fails. For what my opinion is worth – and clearly it's worth little to Eriksson – we should have done much better than we have in recent years, because we have the players to win trophies . . . but not necessarily the right approach or system to get the best out of those players.

I played my first game for Eriksson as a sub in the qualifying game at Anfield against Finland, when we beat them 2–1. I almost scored as well, came really close with a good chance late on. That was in March 2001, and later that year, I scored against Mexico and then played well in Greece. Early the next season I started in a friendly against Holland, but we were woeful that day, outplayed by a decent footballing side. It should have set the alarm bells ringing. Soon after though, we went to Germany and thrashed them 5–1. I was on the bench and didn't get on, but it was an incredible night because my three teammates from Liverpool scored, Michael, Stevie G and Emile. There was a proper party when we got back to England. No matter which way you look at it, that was a fantastic result. Yet I think it probably did us more harm in the long run, because it deceived people – and maybe even the manager himself – that the long-ball approach can work in international football.

If you look at the sides that win things, then the stats say categorically it doesn't. We beat Albania three days later and I scored what was probably my best goal for my country. Again I came on as a substitute, into a difficult situation because we were only winning 1–0 when everyone expected us to thrash them. Late on, I turned on the edge of the box inside a defender and lifted the ball over the keeper with a delicate chip from a difficult angle. Eriksson described me as 'a fox in the box', and there was a bit of a groundswell towards me as the finisher that England needed. It was probably enough to get me into the side for the crucial qualifier against Greece at Old Trafford in October 2001, when we needed to win to be sure of reaching the World Cup finals, depending on the result in Germany's game against Finland. I partnered Emile up front but we never got any service, and I never had a chance. I got neck ache that afternoon there were so many high balls launched forward. The only other thing I remember is having a bit of a squabble with David Beckham over a free kick on the right of the box, which was perfect for a left footer. He'd taken quite a few already and not come close, so I fancied me chances. He wouldn't give it up though and pulled rank. Missed it as well, but I suppose it was the right decision and he was just getting his range, because he scored eventually, with just about the last kick of the game, to sneak a draw . . . which was good enough to take us to Japan and Korea because Germany didn't beat Finland.

It's funny, because I felt I had a chance to do well at that World Cup. I bowed to the inevitable and moved to Leeds in November of 2001, just after the Greece game, and I was flying at Elland Road at first. When I got there, after I got match fit, I couldn't stop scoring and my form was back to the level it had been before I did me ligaments against Everton in 1998. I kept getting word that Eriksson was pleased and I had to keep it going, that sort of thing, but I never got picked. He left me out of a squad to face Holland in Amsterdam, and then I was a sub at Elland Road for a game against Italy at the end of March 2002.

It was my home ground, I was playing really well, scoring goals and Leeds were still challenging at that point. Soon after, I did me back and me Achilles and I wasn't quite right all through the rest of the season and the summer, but I should have started in that game against Italy. Instead he stuck with Michael and Emile, even though it was a friendly. I was annoyed, but not surprised. What did surprise me was when I came on in the second half David Beckham came off, so someone had to take the captain's armband. As it happened, I was one of the most experienced players left on the pitch and as it was also my home stadium, Eriksson gave me the captaincy. It might only have been for forty-five minutes, but it was a proud, proud moment, especially because all the family – with the exception of me mum, obviously – were there to see me, and when I saw me dad in the lounge afterwards, his first words were: 'All right, skip.' I scored as well, so it was a perfect day for me, a fairytale. I scored again in the last minute of a friendly against Cameroon in a World Cup warm-up, but even though there was a bit of a clamour in the media saying I should be in the side because I was the only natural goal scorer in the squad, I knew that day it was going to be another big tournament where I wouldn't get the chance to bother the scorers. The friendly was in Korea on the way to the finals, and

Eriksson chose Vassell to partner Michael Owen up front. What was the sense in that, unless he was going even more long ball?

Inevitably, it turned out that way. We started the tournament against Sweden, he kept Owen and Vassell together, and it was a typical Scandinavian derby, which ended in stalemate. Against Argentina we did okay, defending brilliantly and caught them on the break with Michael and Emile preferred up front and Teddy Sheringham brought on as a sub.

Nigeria in the next game was even worse than Sweden, we needed a draw and that's what we got without creating a real chance. What bugged me was that Teddy and Darius both got on, and I was ignored again. It did me head in, and I thought about going to see Eriksson, tell him straight that I'd had enough, that it was bollocks the way we were playing this long-ball rubbish, not creating any chances, and what was even more bollocks was that I hadn't even had a minute on the pitch when I had scored for him regularly in the rare opportunities I was offered.

I was a bit smarter this time though and bit me tongue, might have wondered quietly if I would get a chance, but didn't get the cigars and brandy out! Eriksson had said that it was difficult for him to play me because I had been struggling with a back injury. It didn't stop him playing Michael though, or David Beckham, when they were clearly unfit. In the knock-out stage we won well against a very, very poor Denmark team, and he put me on in the second half because Michael's injury had got a lot worse. Problem was, we were already 3–0 up so it was game over. We shut up shop and I didn't get a kick. Agghh! When we got to the quarter final, I did the usual interviews and I was asked about Michael's injury. I said that I was ready to step in if he didn't make it, that Geoff Hurst had taken his chance when Jimmy Greaves was injured for the quarter final in 1966, and look what happened to him. The usual stuff, being positive and suppressing the instinct to say Michael was knackered and the manager needed to start with eleven fit players, not nine. You know what, he slaughtered me for it. He said it was disrespectful to my teammates to suggest I should be playing if Michael wasn't, that I shouldn't have said that sort of thing. Disrespectful, was he having a laugh?

It was exactly the same stuff Houllier always came out with when you said – in private – you should be playing, and I wondered if Eriksson had been having some sneaky chats with my Liverpool boss. I hadn't even said I should be playing, I'd said I was ready if needed, which is what I should have been saying. Any respect I had for Eriksson was gone after that. Not that I had much after the way he treated Macca – just bombed him out without even the courtesy of a phone call, when it was obvious with Beckham injured that he would have added to the squad massively. I felt it was a wrong decision not to take a player who had won so many medals with the best team in Europe, and could have provided something we desperately required in Japan. As far as many members of the squad were concerned it was a decision based on personal animosity and not sound footballing logic.

Everything I had suspected about Eriksson was shown in the quarter final against Brazil. He needed to take some brave decisions because Michael and David were clearly not capable of playing in the game. Of course both wanted to, but as a manager he had to take the decision away from them and be strong. That wasn't his style, because he was more worried about the reaction if he dropped two big-name players, no matter what the circumstances. I'm not saying I should have been playing here, but I do think you need eleven fit players if you are going in against a side like Brazil. In the game itself, Michael scored early after a bad mistake from Lucio, and after that he played on one leg.

We did okay, defending deep and hanging on until just before half time, when Rivaldo scored a damn good goal from an incisive passing movement that maybe would have been cut out at the start if the skipper had been properly fit. At half time, you could see on the faces of the players that they were shell-shocked having conceded a goal to a very good team, and they thought that was it. But it was still only 1–1 and it was time for the manager to get to work, change the tactics and instil some belief in the team. How we could have done with Terry Venables that day. Even Kevin Keegan would have done, for goodness sake. But Eriksson is not a passionate man, he's not a talker at all in fact. He hardly says anything to the players, prefers to let his coaches do the work while he stands back and observes from a distance. He said nothing in the changing room at half time, absolutely fuck all, just stood there with a startled look on his face like he too believed we were fucked. And that's the way it turned out. We went out of the quarter final of the World Cup without even a whimper, just rolled over and died because we didn't have a clue what we were doing out there against a side who played decent football, and because there was no team spirit, no fight, no togetherness. And the manager didn't say a word.

All those days when we met up and went straight to our rooms, all those nights when everyone was stuck in their room on their PlayStation or mobile, the lack of identity under Eriksson, it all came home to roost. He didn't shout, he didn't inspire, he didn't encourage and he didn't offer any tactical insight or switches. As far as I could see, he said a silent prayer and that was that. Ronaldinho scored, of course, and even when he subsequently got sent off, we didn't have a clue. Against ten men and with the chance to control the tempo of the game, we weren't up to it, and the match drifted away from us like it was a bad dream. Predictably enough, I didn't get on, even though if they had got the ball into the box I would have fancied my chances of scoring. I was gutted, not because I hadn't played, but because we were so pathetic, so lame in the way we just accepted defeat, and I think Eriksson has to shoulder part of the blame for that.

What makes it even worse is the fact that had we won the quarter final, then the route was wide open for us to win it, because all the decent sides had gone out already. But we blew it. When you think about it, it's no big surprise. We had a direct style, but we didn't have any real team spirit. The only way long-ball football is successful is when you have a team of scrappers who are prepared to fight for everything. But Eriksson's style is calm, detached, and the complete opposite of all that. England are an organized team and there won't be any slip-ups in qualifying. Get to the finals, though, and when we come up against a proper team, that won't be enough – and that's a shame given the talent we have available.

When I left Shizuoka that night, I knew that was the end of England for me. I had mixed feelings. My England career lasted only six years, I got only eleven starts, and I was probably better than that. But I have had the misfortune to be playing at the same time as some incredibly talented strikers. Add to that the fact that I was injured for just about every major championship, and I can't complain. I never really had a chance to string together a run of games when I've been sharp and healthy. In fact, the most I've ever played is three games on the run, which isn't nearly enough for a striker to get his rhythm.

I have won more caps than some players far better than me, and I have scored goals for my country, which are priceless. I have also been captain of England, which I think I might just have engraved on my tombstone. Whatever else happens to me, I can say that I have followed in the footsteps of Billy Wright, Bobby Moore, Emlyn Hughes and Bryan Robson and captained my country. It's not bad. Perhaps the worst thing that could have happened to me was Glenn Hoddle, because he didn't believe in me at a time when I believe I was ready to make an England place my own. Maybe I've been unlucky to have played under some managers who didn't understand me, or just weren't up to the job. But then, I was lucky to have been part of the incredible events at Euro '96. I think those weeks in June, when the sun was shining and the whole country was behind us, will always go down in most people's memories as great times for the nation. Every time I see Terry Venables I always tell him the same thing – he should have put me on in extra time against Germany, if only to take the penalty that Gareth Southgate missed.

As a chapter, I guess my England story is finished because Eriksson was never going to pick me again. Still, if he needs a goal scorer to take to Germany, then he's always got my number. I reckon as I approached thirty, I finally got back to something like the form I had enjoyed earlier in my career . . . and if the player I was – who burst onto the scene in the mid nineties – was around now, then you could be sure Eriksson would play him.

There's one final word on my England career, by the way. The eagle-eyed amongst you will have noticed that I claim eight goals for my country when the record books show seven. The disputed one was in the game against Paraguay in the build-up to the 2002 World Cup, when I made my first appearance back at Anfield after moving to Leeds. I shot from wide on the right, it skimmed a defender's head and went into the net. It was put down as an own goal, but believe me, I'm claiming it. Danny Murphy was credited with a goal in that game when his shot was going nowhere near the goal until it got deflected. At least mine was going in anyway. I've not had too much luck in my England career, and I reckon I deserve a bit, so if anyone from FIFA is reading this, that goal was mine . . . please change your record books accordingly!

10) HOULLIER

I've got a Liverpool programme in my drawer at home, from Saturday 8 December 2001. It was an unremarkable match, Liverpool played Middlesbrough and won 2–0. In his notes for the game, Phil Thompson spoke of his pleasure in winning the Manager of the Month award in the absence of Gerard Houllier. And he also spoke of the team spirit that the two of them had created at the club. That apart, there was little else of interest in there, except maybe for a short sentence tucked away on page ten. Next to a much bigger piece asking Emile Heskey what it was like to score in the previous home game against Sunderland, there were a few words with the tiny headline that stated rather blandly, 'Farewell Robbie'.

It was two weeks after I was forced out of Liverpool, and this was the first chance they'd had at Anfield to acknowledge my departure. Clearly, it wasn't big news. After a fifteen-year association with the club, after joining them as a schoolboy for nothing, scoring 171 goals in 330 games and being sold for a profit of more than £12 million, I warranted the briefest of sentences hidden away deep in the bowels of the match-day programme. That, more than anything, summed up the behaviour of the people who made it impossible for me to continue playing for the home-town team that was in my blood, the club that is still closest to my heart. The sentence read: 'Robbie Fowler completed his move to Leeds United last week after fifteen years with Liverpool.' It went on to attribute a quote to me – which I never said – indicating that the move was amicable and in the best interests of both parties. Then there was a sentence from Thompson that apparently wasn't important enough to have been contained in his notes at the front of the programme. 'I know there are a lot of disappointed fans, but I hope they will have belief in the club. When you look at how the club has developed under Gerard's leadership I don't think anybody can complain.' That was it. Eight years in the first-team squad, sixth-highest goal scorer in the club's history, one goal behind the legendary Kenny Dalglish, fastest ever to 100 goals and only Ian Rush with a better goals-to-games ratio, the biggest fee Liverpool had ever received for any player, and the thanks I got was a sentence in the programme two weeks after I left. Any complaints?

It's easy for me to point the finger and blame Houllier for what happened, easy for me to look back and say that I made a huge mistake in allowing his underhand campaign to force me out. Easy for me to say that if I'd somehow seen him off, fought harder to stay at the club where I believe I belonged, then things would be very different now. But I didn't, and they aren't, and that's that. Houllier did what he thought he had to do, I guess he did what he thought was in the best interests of the club, and I suffered, but hey, I'm not the first person in football who believes he's been treated like a disposable commodity. It's a rough business, and if you don't learn that from day one, then you are going to be fucked good style. There is no such thing as loyalty, no such thing as dignity, not from clubs when they think you've come to the end of your shelf life. I could be bitter towards Houllier and Thompson, but I'm not on a personal level. I actually played alongside Phil Thompson during a charity game at Anfield not too long ago, and I got on well with him. He seemed a really decent bloke, totally different to the knob-head who told me I'd been at Anfield too long and should fuck off out of there. That's the problem with football, it's ruthless, and so are the people involved in it. Everybody is out to screw everyone else and they don't care in the slightest about you as a person. You are a commodity and you can be treated in the most Godawful manner if they think it can help them in the slightest way. Away from football, away from his job as assistant manager of Liverpool, Thompson is fine, and I'm sure Houllier is exactly the same. However, I still wish he hadn't walked in that door at the start of the 1998 season.

We'd heard rumours all summer that Roy was getting a new assistant, that it was some top-class French coach who would shake things up as his number two, after Ronnie Moran had retired at the end of the previous season. Then we heard his name, Gerard Houllier, who was the technical director of the French Football Federation. He was supposed to be the architect of France's World Cup win that summer, the man who put it all in place. Impressive. Surely he'd make a decent number two. But then the stories got confused. We began getting tales back from some of the French lads at Arsenal that he wasn't a genius at all, he was the Howard fucking Wilkinson of French football, a long-ball merchant who had failed as national team manager and was moved aside into a penpusher role. He'd only won one French League title with Paris St Germain, and then moved on. He was the manager who couldn't get France to the World Cup finals even though they needed a single point from their final two group games. He'd never played professional football. And he wasn't coming as an assistant at all . . . he was going to replace Roy. That set the alarm bells ringing, but as it turned out it was only half right. In one of the most ludicrous decisions ever taken by the board of Liverpool Football Club, Gerard Houllier was appointed as joint manager alongside Roy Evans on 17 July 1998. That decision was to have a profound effect on the future of that great club.

And on me. I was injured when he arrived, still in a knee brace after my ligaments exploded during the game against Everton in March. I had been working with the physios all summer and had hardly left Melwood. Judas was great with me. He's called that because he supported Bolton but worked for Burnley, and they never let him forget it where he comes from. He went to Bolton after he left us, and then Sunderland,

and he's undoubtedly one of the best guys I've ever worked with. He fell out with Houllier and was left with no option but to leave the club in the end. It was over Michael Owen's hamstring injury a year later. Judas spent all his time with Michael helping him to get back to fitness. He even took Michael on holiday to Cornwall with him, so he could keep an eye on him twenty-four hours a day. He got Michael back doing work in training, but alone, away from the rest of the lads, because he needed strengthening work with weights. Houllier wanted him back playing and said that Michael needed to join in at the end of sessions with the lads in the five-a-sides. Judas argued that he wasn't ready, it could do him long-term damage because his hamstrings wouldn't be strong enough for the rigours of the season.

Houllier argued that he needed to get a feel for the ball and join in with the other players to help morale. They kept arguing, but with Houllier at Liverpool, there was only ever one winner. So Michael went back to playing without the rehab, and Judas went to the job centre. Well, he went to the Reebok Stadium. Over that season Michael kept breaking down, and Houllier was forced to admit that he had got it wrong. He didn't give Judas his job back though. I got some incredible treatment from the physios at Liverpool – Dave Galley and Mark Browse were so dedicated – and they helped me get back far quicker than the doctors thought was possible. They reckoned I'd be out for a year, but I was back playing again by the start of September, only six months after I got injured. When Houllier arrived, I was in the middle of that work, and he was impressed with the effort I was putting in. He came to see me in the gym early on and had a brief chat. Explained what he expected and how he saw me progressing with the injury, and he was quite thorough. No problems with that at all, we got on well together and I was quite impressed on first meeting. You know what they say about first impressions.

Some of the other lads weren't so impressed. Training changed as soon as he arrived, and the first thing they noticed was that there was no enjoyment allowed in training . . . it was a deadly serious business. Razor Ruddock took the piss out of

Houllier on the day he introduced himself to the squad, and that was him finished. I don't think he stopped to pick up his coat. It soon became clear that even smiling was frowned upon, and there were plenty of rules that were suddenly pinned up on the changing-room walls. Stupid stuff like being allowed red wine with dinner, but not white. Nobody was too bothered about the changes in training, Houllier brought a coach with him called Patrice Bergues, a fantastic man who the players liked, and even though he made us do a lot more running than they were used to, it wasn't a problem. He did other things like change the menu in the canteen, and everyone expected that too. There were new watches that checked your heartbeat and various new routines, but it was the seriousness of it all that grated, as though we were all back at school. Of course that filtered through to me, and everyone was saying the same thing: 'Hang on a minute, I don't like the look of this.'

The biggest problem was the relationship with Roy Evans, because we weren't stupid, we knew what Houllier was there for, and it wasn't to help the gaffer ... except maybe find the exit. As I've said, the players had a lot of respect for Roy. There was a real feeling that with the young kids coming through and with so many young internationals developing – and with Stan out of the way and Incey settled in – there was a real chance of something happening at Anfield. No one could quite get their head around the reason for bringing Houllier in as joint manager. Coach, yes, that made sense. But joint manager? That would cause problems. No one knew who made the decisions, who was in charge. I don't think either of them knew, and it was fucking stupid. We all thought that it was an easy cop-out for the board – they wanted to ease Roy out but didn't have the nerve to sack him, so they took the soft option and waited for him to walk away. From day one, most of us were waiting for that to come about, and we didn't have to wait long.

Things happened like the gaffer would announce what time the bus was leaving for an away game, and then Houllier would change it by fifteen minutes. How daft was that? On

White lines, don't do it: my infamous celebration.
Note Macca anticipating the trouble it would cause and trying to get me up.

You can't take your ball home
on international duty.

You looking at me?
Me, Macca and mischief,
as ever.

A goal for England,
celebrating with guess who.

He's behind you . . .
on England duty.

I'm not letting go mate
— me with the UEFA Cup
and the third part of
a historic treble.

Where did you get that hat?
Happier times with Houllier.

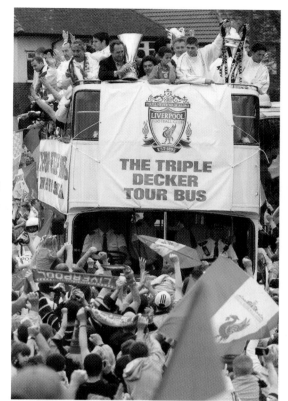

The greatest day of my football life.

Madison and me with the FA Cup, and a fella with a dodgy barnet who's become one of the best midfielders in the world.

Thank you and good night.
Taking a bow at Anfield.

Yesterday's news.
The headlines as I join
Leeds United.

Above. Swap shirts mate?
Michael and me, opponents now.

Above right. A one to one
with Gazza.

Right. Leeds, Leeds, Leeds.
Rare appreciation at Elland Road.

Scoring *against*
Liverpool for once.

Goal for City. Must have been
against Arsenal, surely.

the pre-season tour too, the lads said that after the final game in Scandinavia against Rosenborg, Roy told them they could go out and have a drink as we had always done when the work was finished, but then Houllier overruled him and refused permission. That didn't go down well, no matter what the logic in it. Then he sacked our fitness coach Andy Clark, who was really popular with the squad and did some brilliant work with me and the rest of the lads. He was always there for me, helping me get my strength back, and then working on my muscle speed. Overnight he was gone, and there was no one to do those things for me, which was a blow. I later learnt that Roy had been told by the board they wanted to bring someone in to replace Ronnie Moran, and asked Roy to run the rule over Houllier. He went into the meeting thinking he was looking at his assistant, but it quickly became apparent that wasn't the case. Then they dropped the idea of joint managers on him, and he was locked into a corner that he couldn't get out of. We all realized within a few days of pre-season that Roy Evans knew he'd made a terrible mistake.

I've often thought about the reasons for Houllier wanting me out of Anfield. Some were pretty obvious to be honest, and I was to blame, no doubt about it. More on that later. But beyond those, I've always wondered whether those early days when he was joint manager with Roy Evans had something to do with it, because there was a lot of suspicion of him amongst the players then, a distrust that never really abated. Houllier cleared out the squad he inherited from Roy Evans so comprehensively, and you have to wonder if he did it because he knew he'd lost that group of players when Evans was undermined in the few months they worked together. As a theory, it makes sense, because when you look at who he got rid of, only three kids in the squad – Michael Owen, Jamie Carragher and Danny Murphy – survived the transition from joint to sole manager, and like me when Souness went, they probably didn't have a clue what was going on. Just those three, Steven Gerrard, who was on the verge of the first team when Roy left, and me, although it felt like he was trying to get me out almost from the start. Maybe Houllier felt he could never win the trust of the rest of the players after what they had seen in the early days.

There was one incident during those three months they were together that summed up the feeling of the players towards Houllier. There had been problems that became more and more visible, and generated quite a bit of unrest. I had worked very hard to get back, had a reserve match at Leicester where I scored, and then I was in the first-team squad. My comeback game was in Kosice in Slovakia, a low-key UEFA Cup tie which we won 3–0, and I got half an hour at the end. Next game I started and scored twice against Charlton, and I thought I was up and running. I should have known better under Houllier though. Apparently he and Roy had a dispute about whether to play me in the next game against Manchester United, and Houllier won, which meant I lost. So did Liverpool, 2–0. Already, there was tension between the managers, and it was getting visibly worse. They'd already rowed just before my comeback when Houllier dropped Karlheinz Riedle after two wins, and the lads were going bonkers about the team being changed for no reason when we were on a winning streak. I came back again and scored two more in the home leg against Kosice. But I was dropped again, twice, and what did me head in was the fact that he never told me beforehand, he just dropped the bombshell on the bus on the way to the ground in front of all the other lads, and then expected me to smile about it. It caused a lot of bad feeling, and serious questions were already being asked.

Then came the moment when Houllier lost a great deal of respect from the players. We went to Valencia for the second leg of our second-round UEFA Cup tie. We had drawn the first leg at Anfield and no one gave us much of a chance for the return. In the first half we'd done pretty well, and had the upper hand, but right on the stroke of the interval we gave them a soft goal. In the dressing room, Houllier was like a rabbit in the headlights. He didn't know what to say or do, just stood there with his mouth opening and closing like a goldfish. Roy sized up what was going on and took command, brushed

Houllier aside and gave this inspirational speech that said we were the better team and we weren't going to lay down and die. We went in the dressing room crushed, but went out ten feet tall. Macca scored and then Paddy Berger got one right at the end. In the dying seconds though, Macca got involved in a bit of pushing and shoving with their full back, and Incey joined in. It was nothing, but the referee incensed everyone by flashing his red card at both of them. Down to nine men, we conceded a goal immediately, but clung on into a lengthy injury time to go through on away goals.

We were fucking livid, and surrounded the ref on the whistle, protesting like mad that he had tried to cheat us out of the game. In the dressing room we were all still fired up by the victory and the antics of the ref. Then, in the corner of the room, our assistant manager Dougie Livermore saw Houllier – who had stood back and not joined in at all – rooting around amongst the kit dragging some of the shirts out. We had refused to swap shirts at the end because it had kicked off in the game and we were pretty disgusted with Valencia's behaviour. So Roy asked him what the fuck he was doing, and Houllier said he was taking a shirt each for the referee and his two linesmen, who all happened to be French. Roy went ballistic and so did the players, because the ref had almost cost us the tie, and he told him to fuck off. Then Houllier changed his story and tried to say that the shirts were in fact for the French players in the Valencia team. Again, he was told to fuck off, and it was wondered loudly why he was out there cavorting with the ref when he should have been in the dressing room celebrating with his team. He chucked them down in a strop and walked out, and as he did every one of the players looked around at each other and just shook their heads in disbelief. Never mind alarm bells, it was time for a full-scale evacuation.

Roy resigned eight days later. In fact, he decided that night he had to go, because there was no chance he could make the relationship work with Houllier. How could it work? Who had the final say in team selection? Who was in charge? The players didn't know, and straight away that made it unworkable. If you're dropped, like I was, then which one has dropped you? Who do you discuss it with? In my first month under Houllier, I was dropped more times than I had been in the previous five years. But who did I take my frustrations to? Nobody spoke to me, nobody seemed to want to. I was told later by the gaffer that when he and Houllier decided to drop a player they always agreed to tell him together. But when the time came for the news to be passed on, Houllier always seemed to be missing.

In those early days, the players formed the opinion that Houllier was just waiting until he got the job on his own, and it was difficult to read the situation any differently, even if it wasn't the truth. I have a great deal of respect for Roy Evans in holding his hand up, saying it could not work, and walking away. He could have scratched along, he could have taken another job at the club, but he walked away because he was a big man, and he thought it was best for Liverpool. If it was bad enough the gaffer leaving then two things happened immediately that got those alarms clanging even louder. First, Houllier appointed Phil Thompson as his assistant, or rather, he had the appointment made for him by the board, who wanted to keep a link with the boot-room tradition that had been lost when Houllier walked in. What a nightmare that was, for all of the younger lads in the squad who remembered him from his days as reserve team boss.

As I've said, I've got nothing against Phil, he's a decent bloke away from the job, but when he came back he obviously bought into the idea that there was no discipline at Anfield, that the players were acting like wild men and were out of control. Tommo wasn't exactly laid back at the best of times, so given a mandate to get tough he really was fucking impossible. Fair play to him, he has got incredible passion for Liverpool, and even though he's been sacked twice by them he will always be a fan and always wear his heart on his sleeve. But for me, he was the wrong character to have brought in at that time because Houllier had enough rules and regulations, and enough prejudices and strange ways, without having a ranter on the staff.

The other disturbing aspect of Roy going was the stuff Houllier came out with when he took over as sole manager. Honestly, it was as if Liverpool were in the same position as Newcastle, on the verge of relegation to the second division when Keegan took over. The season before he arrived, we finished a strong third and there was only one direction we were going – upwards. We had a fantastic young side, but Houllier was going on and on about the players 'not being able to kick the ball in the right way', and the need for massive funds to reinforce the team right the way through the squad. He also said something that puzzled everyone. 'The job is so massive that it will take at least five years to turn this club around and become genuine contenders again,' he pronounced, to the amazement and disgust of the entire squad.

Okay, hands up, we had under-achieved the previous seasons, but we had the England goalkeeper, an England centre half and full back, an England captain and England play-maker in midfield, an England winger who was the star of Euro '96 and two strikers who were described as the future of England for the next ten years. Plus, we had twelve other internationals in the squad, and all bar a couple of them were under the age of twenty-five. Add to that at least six kids coming through who would go on to play for their country, and that wasn't a massive rebuilding job, it was the solid foundation for a bright future. There was work to be done, of course there was, and Roy was the first to recognize that. We needed strengthening in defence desperately, and he had tried to sign about a dozen centre halves in his time as manager, but was frustrated for one reason or another. But I reckon Houllier was wrong to implicitly criticize the man he had worked alongside in such a terrible way, and he was wrong about the job he needed to do.

I have spoken to someone very high up in the Anfield organization who was instrumental at the time in bringing Houllier in. He told me that their view was simple: Houllier wasn't the architect of the France World Cup win, but he was the architect of their fantastic youth production line, so if he was anything then he was good at helping develop young players. The board knew we had many prospects at Anfield, a fantastic young squad that needed guiding through, and he said their clear idea and clear instruction to the new manager was to make that happen. Instead he spent well over a hundred million on bringing in foreign players, and systematically sold off nearly all the young internationals and prospects that he inherited. Roy Evans had overseen the building of Liverpool's brilliant youth academy, which was finished when Houllier arrived and was functioning so well that Roy brought through six players who went on to become England internationals. All that stopped after Houllier arrived and not one kid was developed under him who went on to become a first-team regular. When I spoke to the man involved in his appointment, he admitted that the board had got it wrong. They made a big mistake, because they thought he was a coach who was brilliant at developing young talent, and instead he turned out to be the worst kind of chequebook manager, spending many millions, much of it wasted.

Things changed at Melwood, and no complaints, a lot of it was for the better. Houllier developed the training ground so that we ended up with fantastic facilities, and he quickly addressed the problems at the back. There was no doubt we needed strengthening in that area, and he made Liverpool a difficult team to beat. But in doing that, maybe he also laid the foundations for my departure from the club, because we became a side who played on the counter, with one striker up front chasing behind opposition defences. Obviously, to do that it helped if you had pace, and both Michael and later Emile Heskey when he signed were quicker than me. I've always joked that I was unlucky to get John Beck – the notorious long-ball merchant from Cambridge – as my manager at both club and international level. But there was probably some truth in that humour. They were John Beck with knobs on. Both of them have a touch of the exotic about them, largely because of the mystique of foreign managers operating in the English game. But dissect both their approaches and they are pretty similar, and pretty basic. Effective too, up to a point.

I must confess, I didn't enjoy playing in their sides because it was always a struggle as striker. You don't get too much ball to work with, even fewer chances, and obviously that makes it difficult. In Houllier's first season we could already feel the change, because even though we were as leaky as ever at the back, the signs were there that we were not going to be as adventurous going forward. I was in and out of the side early on, but then things settled down as I began to improve my fitness, and after the Valencia game I got a regular run. I scored eighteen goals that season, which wasn't too bad considering that I was recovering from one of the worst injuries a professional can get, I'd had no pre-season, had missed the first six games of the season, and didn't really start playing regularly until November. Oh, and I also missed the last month of the campaign.

That was my own fault, and perhaps was another significant development in the deteriorating relationship between me and Houllier. I wasn't happy with what had happened at the club. Training was fucking miserable and I didn't enjoy going in any more. Driving into work you'd be thinking that it was another slog, another day when you're told off for laughing or whatever – another day when you weren't even allowed to talk during training. Even though I knew I shouldn't let it happen, it began to affect me on the pitch and my performances dipped a little. Then we went to Chelsea and I got involved in a bit of an exchange with Graeme Le Saux. There was some history from the season before because he had got into a punch-up with Incey in the tunnel after the game. Apparently they'd been at it during the match and when they came off, Le Saux started saying stuff about Incey's missis, and he wasn't having any of that. There was a right commotion with punches flying everywhere, and lots of the lads from both sides joining in. It was like the wild west, and the police had to wade in eventually to keep the warring sides apart. Incey was screaming blue murder about revenge, and I don't think Le Saux was very happy either.

It was against that backdrop that we visited Stamford Bridge on 27 February 1999. Only a few minutes into the game, and it was clear Le Saux was up for it. He was snapping into challenges and running around like he was possessed. I was chuckling because on the pitch Incey's a horrible bastard and he wasn't going to stand for any of that. It was fireworks all right, but mostly going off inside my head. I jumped for a ball with Le Saux and he caught me right on the side of the head with his elbow. As far as I was concerned he did me, and I was boiling. The next time the ball was near I jumped at him . . . and he did me again, the fucker. That was it. I was off on one. Under Houllier, one of the big things he preached was discipline, and he would go ballistic if one of us got sent off. I knew I couldn't retaliate physically, so I laid into him verbally. To my mind he'd done me twice and I wasn't going to let him get away with it. You get it all the time in football, opponents winding each other up, trying to make them lose control by finding a weakness.

If anyone finds that shocking in any way, then they obviously don't know much about football. I've had it through my career, defenders giving me all the smackhead gibes, and I usually respond by saying they've had too many smacks on their heads, given how ugly they are. Recently, my old mate Gary Neville was giving it to me about me not winning any medals while he's won millions. I had some ammo that day, though, because his missis had been in the paper over something or other, so I just referred him to the previous week's article. That soon shut him up, and his bottom lip was going. The same happened with Le Saux. I knew he could be wound up about all the gibes over his sexuality, which had started when he was called a poof by his own teammate David Batty, and the two of them had a punch-up on the pitch during a game for Blackburn. So I gave it to him. As far as I was concerned he was fair game, because he'd done me twice, and so I was giving him down the banks for being a poof. His lip started going massively, and he was really whining, so that made me lay it on a bit more. Then, his voice rising, he shouted, 'But I'm married.' And I responded quickly, 'So was Elton John, mate.'

That was it, the red mist came down and he did me again for a third time. I thought I'd got him then, and so I started bending over, showing him my arse and asking whether he'd like a bit of it. Look. I've played in England teams with Graeme, and he's a really decent fella. I have never had any problem with him at all, and I knew his wife when we were on internationals. I know that he's not gay, and I'm not bothered in the slightest about his or anybody else's sexuality. It was just a bit of childish winding up because he'd done me so badly. Even the referee Paul Durkin was laughing about it when he booked me for 'taunting Le Saux'. I told him I wasn't fucking laughing when he twatted me three times. I got booked, we all calmed down, the game went on, we lost 2–1 and we all went home. End of story. Errr, not quite.

It all kicked off. You'd have thought I'd taken a machete to him and cut him into little pieces. The incident was shown on the telly, and I have to say it doesn't look great! Of course they didn't have any footage of me being done, and the press went mad. The thing was, it was the broadsheet press that led the way. For the first time in my life, I was of interest to the *Guardian*, who couldn't believe that this horrible little oik from the inner city had the temerity to do something as obscene as make a gesture to one of their favourite footballers. Graeme Le Saux read the *Guardian*, for goodness sake, so he must be intelligent and sensitive. And I must be some sort of caveman. How dare I be homophobic? They all lined up the usual suspects, saying what a disgrace I was, and how I should be banned for life. Ken Bates, the Chelsea chairman, was apoplectic, and he said it was the end of football as we know it.

What had the game come to? he wondered. It wasn't the brightest thing I have ever done, I'll admit, but in the context of football it's not the worst thing that has ever happened. Ken Bates seemed to conveniently forget that football is a sport based firmly in the working classes. It's a tough sport, and to get to the top you have to be incredibly thick-skinned. A bit of name-calling never hurt anyone, and the truth is I wasn't being homophobic, I was merely trying to exploit a known weakness in an opponent who had done me a number of times. When you look back now at the outrage it caused – a bit of name-calling, for fuck's sake – then it's laughable. I was just giving Le Saux something back for what was pretty terrible behaviour on his part . . . and I'm sure he'd be the first to admit that now. Houllier, of course, went fucking crazy at me, said I'd let the club down, that I didn't know how to behave, all that stuff. When I pointed out that I'd been caught with an elbow and hadn't reacted physically, he just ignored it and kept chuntering on about his image. By then we knew he'd been courting all the broadsheet writers, taking them out to lunch to get favourable treatment for himself, and I reckon he was worried about me ruining the intelligent image he liked to project. Inevitably, with such a campaign against me, I was hauled up before the FA, even though the referee had seen the incident and dealt with it accordingly by booking me.

In the meantime though, before I could attend my personal hearing, we played Everton at Anfield on 3 April and I produced another classic image for the television companies. It was the line sniffing, and again it obviously didn't go down well with Houllier, but not for the reasons you may think. When I did it, it really was supposed to be a humorous response to all the terrible stick I'd been getting. I got in the changing room afterwards, and quite a few of the lads were laughing, saying that it was hilarious and only Robbie Fowler could dream up a stunt like that. I'd scored twice and we'd beaten the enemy 3–2, so Houllier was pretty happy because it was something positive in a difficult season, although he did ask me, just before he went to do the press conference, how the hell he was going to explain that one to the waiting media.

I could tell him exactly how not to do it – make up the fucking fantasy that he eventually came up with! He went into the tiny press room at Anfield, that used to be the boot room before they developed the facilities in the main stand, and he came out with this incredible stuff about 'eating the grass'. Apparently, Rigobert Song – our Cameroon international centre half – had brought this celebration with him from Africa. It was common over there in Cameroon, the players would get down and eat the grass after they scored, and I had seen him do it in training. It was, Houllier said with a completely straight face, my tribute to Rigobert. I spoke to one or two of the press lads later, and they told me they had to stuff their fists in their mouths to stop themselves laughing out loud. People had tears in their eyes it was so funny. Nobody could ask another question because they had to run outside and break down in gales of laughter. And Houllier stood through it all blinking, without a flicker of a smile. He thought it had been a fantastic excuse.

Of course the papers mullered him. They really went to town on how ridiculous his explanation had been, and what a fool he had made of himself. I've got to say, if my actions were stupid, then his handling of it wasn't exactly inspired. He made a bad situation worse, and there was general hysteria around the country for the next two weeks while the debate raged about my behaviour. Houllier was hurt by the criticism he received, and he blamed me for it. Really blamed me. It must have been fully two years later when he told a mate of mine how I was finished that day, when he had been ridiculed for defending me. Houllier had rung this guy, a journalist, to give him a volley about criticism of Emile Heskey. He knew the reporter had contact with me and was a supporter of mine, and he laid into him, saying he was just slagging Emile off to get me in the team. Then he referred back to the 'eating the grass' incident, and he let rip. 'I tried to defend your mate, I tried to fucking defend the idiot and what did you do? You ridiculed me. I was made to look ridiculous because of Fowler, and I defended him. I tell you, I will never make that mistake again. You fucking ridiculed me, you tried to destroy my reputation, because I was loyal to your mate. Don't think I will ever forget that.'

It was that sort of stuff, basically pointing to the fact that he was made to look stupid because of me. And I don't think he ever forgave me for that. It was my fault, of course, but I hardly asked him to come up with something as fucking stupid as he did. I always got the impression Houllier had a big ego, and it was bruised badly by that incident. From that day I was damaged goods as far as he was concerned, and I suspect he was working out how to get rid of me from that moment onwards. Of course, the FA threw the book at me. They considered both cases at the same time, and they gave me a six-match ban. I don't think my defence helped. The club used their own solicitor, Kevin Dooley, who has sadly passed away now, and he came up with this explanation that was almost as bad as Houllier's. He said that the Le Saux incident was merely expressing a common Scouse phrase, 'you're my arse', which hasn't got any gay connotations, but just means you're rubbish. I was sitting there with my head in my hands when he came out with that stuff, off the cuff. Fuck me, I thought, I'm doomed now. I was right, but it was bollocks.

Six matches for a bit of verbals in the heat of the moment with an opponent who I felt had tried to knock my head off, and for a joke that was intended to show that I wasn't on drugs and how annoyed I was at the allegations that were always hurled at me. It just shows how far removed from reality they are at the FA. Six games for that. It was a fucking disgrace and I should have taken them to court for restraint of trade or something. Apart from the fact that they were just two minor humorous incidents – however childish – that did no harm to anyone, both matters had been witnessed by the officials, Paul Durkin and David Elleray. Both were very experienced referees who were regarded as the best in the Premiership, and both had taken appropriate action at the time. I reckon we had a fair case for saying the FA had acted beyond their jurisdiction, and had punished me beyond their powers. I was determined to appeal, but Houllier refused, he said we had to consider the image of the club and we would take it on the chin. So that was that, I was really annoyed, but we would not appeal. It was the end of my season.

We finished seventh that season, and Macca left for Real Madrid. Houllier got rid of Jamo, Incey, Trigger, Harky, Jason McAteer, Mark Wright, Phil Babb, Karlheinz Riedle, Tony Warner, Stig Bjornebye, Bjorn Kvarme and Oyvind Leonhardsen overnight, and then completed the job by bombing out Steve Staunton, Brad Friedel, Vegard Heggem and such good young players as Dominic Matteo, David Thompson, Stephen Wright and, eventually, Jamie Redknapp and me. Things went from bad to worse when I was the victim of that unprovoked attack in the Moat House Hotel on the evening after my last game of the season against Villa. Houllier got me in and read me the riot act, slaughtered me in front of everyone, and said I had to change my attitude. Fair enough, I'd been in a bit of bother that season, and I knew more than anyone the time had come to get my head down and keep out of the limelight. The whole club had been turned on its head in the summer, and there were so many new faces I needed *Championship Manager* just to keep up.

They called George down to talk, and I realized that no matter how hard done by I felt, there was no use feeling sorry for myself. So I knuckled down, got a great pre-season under my belt and scored a few goals. For the first time since my knee injury I felt properly sharp, and almost back to the sort of level I had when I was tearing up the Premiership. I scored a hat-trick against a German XI and then a really good goal on the opening day of the season at Sheffield Wednesday. Then we played Arsenal at Anfield, and again I scored, another good goal and a decent performance. I was told that Arsenal had been in for me that summer with a serious offer, but Liverpool wouldn't consider it. I never got a direct approach, but if I had then I think I'd have considered it at that time, as much as I loved Liverpool. I'd taken a bit of a pounding over the trouble I'd been in, and also from the media, and I was sick to death of it. I was also sick to death of the training, of how fucking miserable everyone was, and it was getting more and more desperate with all the new faces, every one a foreigner who seemed soooo serious.

The biggest problem for me was the stick I'd been getting in town. I'm a Scouser through and through, and proud of my city. I'd defend the people of Liverpool against anyone in the world, and I don't think there's any better people. There is always a minority though that make your life hell, and I was getting that big style. The incident in the Moat House was just the tip of it, and it really knocked the stuffing out of me. Everywhere I went, I'd have kids shouting smackhead at me. It got to the stage where none of the kids even thought of me for my football, it was always the druggie thing. I hesitate to say it, but it drives me nuts around Liverpool now. I see all these kids and they talk about Wayne Rooney as this incredible footballer, and then when they talk about me, it's, 'Fowler, isn't he the smackhead?' It's not big-headed to say that when I was Rooney's age, I probably had a bigger impact than he's having now. He got away from Liverpool, and that has probably helped him. I was miserable at the start of the 1999–2000 season, and I was thinking about my position. Deep down, though, I felt I couldn't turn my back on the club and the city because it just meant too much, no matter how much Houllier got to me.

As it happens, injury did for me again anyway, so I never had any decision to make, and this time it turned out to be worse than the knee ligament injury that almost ruined my career. I was feeling pretty good at the start of that season, and I felt I could pin down a place under Houllier, and with Keegan in charge of England stake a claim for that too. I played against Manchester United, but I'd had some pain in my ankle, and I didn't feel anywhere near right. As a striker, you need to feel sharp, you need 100 per cent to get the edge over defenders, and even if you lose just one or two per cent it can make a massive difference. The United game was the one when Carra doubled his Liverpool goals tally . . . but in the wrong net. We got beat 3–2, and it was also the match when Massimo Taibi had his one and only decent game for United. Just our luck, and just mine when I limped away from Anfield later that evening. I tried to play on, but it wasn't working. I struggled through an hour against Everton, but really I knew there was something badly wrong. The physio confirmed it, and I was whisked off to a clinic in Leeds that specialized in ankle problems for X-rays and scans. They said because of the fracture I had right at the start of my career there was calcification on the joint, which was rubbing and causing the pain and tenderness. It wasn't a problem, it could be resolved by surgery, but it meant at least two months out. That was all I needed, because the knee injury had already robbed me of playing time. Two months was very bad. What transpired was much, much worse.

I was out with that ankle injury for the entire season. It was a fairly straightforward procedure and I was back in rehab almost immediately, working hard to get fit and get back playing. There is nothing worse than being injured as a professional footballer, because you become a non-person. The manager isn't interested if you can't play for him, he doesn't know you exist. You don't train with the team, don't get changed with them, don't eat with them in the canteen, don't go to matches, don't feel part of it in any way. You trudge in early in the morning, go and see the physio and report for treatment. You might spend all morning working on one exercise, then all afternoon in the gym, and your only company is the tea lady. You go home and kick the cat, and then it all starts again the next day. You can have months and months of that, and never seem to be any closer to fitness, and it kills you.

Being injured for such a long time can scar you mentally, because it is such a demoralizing experience. At times with that ankle injury, I didn't think I could take much more of it, after suffering so badly with the knee problem. I'd put so much into getting back quickly from that, and here I was again, going through exactly the same thing. You have moments when you think, Fuck it, I'm gonna jack this. I struggled along, wrestling with my demons, working every day with the physios at Liverpool, who were brilliant, trying not to think about my problems too much. Eventually, the two months were up, and I was back playing for the ressies, scored a hat-trick at Barnsley and in two more games, but things still weren't right. It felt as bad as ever, the movement more restricted than before I had the op. The doctors at Leeds were telling me everything was fine, it was in my head, so I played on, came on as a sub in a Premiership game against Wimbledon with Houllier putting pressure on me to play, just like he did with Michael Owen. I scored as well, but I was about 25 per cent, and I looked and felt terrible. In the end I went for a second opinion, and they said that the cut from the original operation had been too deep, and so the bone had calcified again. It was three months on from the original operation, and I was back to square one. I could have cried. In fact, I could have chucked meself off the Liver Buildings. This time, it was four months. Four more months of my career down the drain because the op went wrong. God knows what Glenn Hoddle must have thought I'd done in a previous life.

More torture, more pain, more endless struggle. And more worry, because Houllier announced out of the blue at training one day that he had spent a club record fee of £12 million on Emile Heskey. Believe me, there is no sentiment in football. It had been a strange season, Houllier had brought in ten foreigners, and we had struggled for the large part, losing in the Worthington Cup at Southampton and at home to Blackburn in the FA Cup. In the league we had hovered around fifth place for much of the season, but went on a bit of a run after Christmas. Manchester United were the runaway leaders, but we sneaked up to second, and needed one win from our last five matches to be sure of a Champions' League place.

It was a good effort, but as we got close to the finish line things started to go badly wrong. I'd worked so hard, almost driven myself into the ground, and I knew I could help even if I wasn't 100 per cent. I'd scored for the reserves at Manchester United and Houllier called me back into the squad for the visit to Everton, but he wouldn't play me. Half a game, half a kick and we were desperate. Chelsea away, again I was on the bench and again we were desperate. But we had Leicester and Southampton at home so no worries. I thought I must play against Leicester, but yet again I was on the bench and again we lost. Finally, I got the call and I was back in from the start. After all that hard work, I had the chance against the Saints to put that season's demons behind me. I did for an hour anyway. We were playing okay, slightly better than the previous three matches, and drawing, but Houllier dragged me off. I was gutted. Just destroyed. He had played me up front on my own in such an important match on my first game back, and I felt as though he was somehow trying to show me up, trying to humiliate me by making it so hard I looked stupid. It was a terrible way to treat me after everything I had given him to get back and try to help the cause. I went off down the tunnel boiling, unable to speak. I got showered, still livid, still feeling cheated, and as soon as the match was over I left the dressing room and went into one of the lounges.

Then Phil Thompson came in, started bawling at me, said Houllier was furious that I had left the dressing room when he had things to say, and I had to get my arse back there sharpish. I told him to pass a message on to Houllier from me: 'Fuck right off.' He skulked away, but then Joe Corrigan our goal-keeping coach came in and said it wasn't worth the hassle, I should get back in there and listen because I was only doing harm to myself. I really didn't care because I felt cheated. In training on Monday Houllier never said anything, ignored me completely. Later in the week he announced his team for the final game at Bradford where we still needed a win, and surprise, surprise, I wasn't in it. Later still, he announced the subs, and my name was missing again. He never said a word to me about it and so I went home and planned my weekend off.

I hate not playing. It does my head in. I am a footballer, I have done it all my life and it is what I am trained to do. I overcame the drawbacks about my size and strength, I reached the top of my profession and captained my country because I have a desire that burns inside me. When I am denied the chance to play, it is an insult that feels like a dagger plunged into me. Houllier hated players showing any kind of emotion when they were not playing. He hated confrontation. He couldn't deal with players expressing any anger or questioning any of his decisions. He was always right. And if you challenged him in any way, showed even the slightest dissent when you were dropped or substituted, he thought it was a lack of respect for him.

Even if you were treated abysmally, left out of the most important game of your career, he seemed to expect you to accept it without a murmur, because otherwise you wouldn't be showing respect for his management skills. You were not allowed to show any emotions, any pride or desire. These days with the number of games we play, it's obvious players have to be rested sometimes, have to be rotated. But surely it's also obvious that you need drive and commitment to play at the top. If you have a player who accepts being dropped without a flicker, who doesn't mind being left out, then do you really want him to play for you? What Houllier ended up with at Anfield was a squad with too many players who didn't mind being dropped, because they were the only players he could work with. Other managers, they want to see players hurt when they are left out, they want to see character and a winning mentality.

I didn't show Houllier any respect at the end of that season, that much is true. He had every right to take against me after the way I reacted, because I reacted badly. Very badly. I didn't go moaning to the press, but at the same time I couldn't believe that he wouldn't even put me on the bench for one of Liverpool's most important games in years. Didn't he remember the Sheffield Wednesday game where our lack of strikers cost us a place in the Champions' League? Even if I pissed him off, surely he should put aside personal differences for the good of the club's European ambitions. Nope. I didn't even travel to Bradford, and instead I got a day off to go to my nephew's christening.

After the year I'd had, the darkness of all those days chasing my fitness and struggling to return to where I'd been, my head was a mess. So I acted stupidly again. Made another mistake. I was at the party, getting bevvied, and listening to the score. David Weatherall got above the Liverpool defence and it was 1–0 to Bradford after twelve minutes. So I rang Houllier's mobile, and didn't speak when it went to message. As the game wore on, Liverpool couldn't get near to breaking them down, and when they did there was no one there to put away the chances. We lost 1–0 and we had missed out on the Champions' League. In my mind I had been denied one of my biggest ambitions because the manager appeared to want to embarrass me rather than put the interests of the club first. So I rang him again and this time I left a message. It was short and to the point: 'I'm gutted you cost me the Champions' League. I hope you're fucking satisfied in leaving me out now.' Not necessarily my wisest move.

He called me in on the Monday, and George too. He asked me what I wanted to do, whether I wanted to play for Liverpool or move, because he was happy to ship me out tomorrow.

I said I wanted to stay, explained my frustrations and the problems I had endured with the injuries, the nightmares I'd suffered and what it had done to my state of mind. People don't know this, but my dad was really ill during that time, and it affected me badly. It's funny, but the fans watch you play on a Saturday and they think you must always be at the top of your game. But just like everyone else, you get affected by the problems going on around you. You have a bad night with the children, but you can't be tired the next day. You have a family problem and you have to put it completely out of your mind. My dad had been ill for a long time, and in 1997 when the tournament that Glenn Hoddle caned me for missing was on, he underwent several operations on a bowel problem. I try not to show it, but I do worry about my family, and my dad's health, and it got to me that summer, which is another reason why I didn't want to travel to France with the England squad. In 2000–01, me dad had serious problems and he suffered a series of strokes, which was worrying me quite badly. I told all this to Houllier, and I also explained that I wanted more than anything to play for Liverpool, that I was determined to work as hard as it took to get into the side. So we shook hands, and he said that as far as he was concerned the chapter was closed, I had a future at Anfield and he would forget what I'd done. He said he wanted me to be central to his plans, and he said he would give me 100 per cent backing.

He lied to me. Before then, I'd suspected he wanted me out. From that very day, he made it fucking obvious he wanted to see the back of me. He tried desperately to sell me to anyone who was interested, while at the same time attempting to undermine my reputation with the supporters. It was a proper campaign too. Houllier used the local paper, the *Liverpool Echo*, to feed stuff to the fans, questioning my form and ability. There was a reporter called Chris Bascombe who was a mad Liverpool fan and was new to the job, covering the club for the paper. He was reliant totally on what the manager gave to him, and obviously keen to make an impression. So Houllier fed him stuff about me all the time, and used the fact that Bascombe was a bit raw and inexperienced to get the paper to stick the knife into me. From the start of the 2000–01 season, there was a pretty concerted campaign against me conducted by Houllier.

I now know Chris quite well, and he's a decent bloke who was just used a bit early on in his career. He's told me since what Houllier used to do, how he would get him to criticize me, just having little gibes all the time. They used to give marks for each player in the paper, and if ever Chris marked me up then Houllier was on, asking why he'd given me that rating. He'd always ask Chris how he felt I was performing, always putting into his mind that I wasn't doing well. I wasn't the only one either. Towards the end of his Anfield reign, Houllier did the same thing with Michael Owen. He couldn't just bomb him out because of the fans so he started questioning him, started trying to undermine him, and attempted to disrupt his relationship with the fans, just like he did with me. Chris wouldn't have it by then and stuck up to him. Every time he gave Michael a decent write-up, Houllier would go mad and have a go. One day, when Chris had supported Michael again there was a row, and Houllier blurted out, 'If Michael pissed on your hands you'd say it was Lucozade.'

I now know it was the same with me, and I know he couldn't just bomb me like he did most of the rest of that fantastic young squad he inherited, and then rubbish them after he'd done it. That was his problem, he wanted me out but he knew I was popular with the fans. They called me God, so he couldn't come out against me dead straight. I think I would have had more respect for him if he'd come out and said what he felt, that he didn't rate me and wanted me gone. But he wouldn't. In public, he always, always claimed he had supported me, had gone out of his way to stand by me, and claimed that he had given me more chances than he should have done. In private, he was working out how best to see the back of me. I know that he used to brief a couple of other reporters on the local paper, and they came out with some terrible stuff about me.

What really got me was that one of them used to be paid to write my personal website stuff . . . and then in his other work he was backing Houllier against me every chance he got. Sneaky twat. One of the favourite tricks was to support the other strikers at my expense, even if they were rubbish. It was laughable at times. According to the two reporters Houllier used, Titi Camara was the greatest striker to have ever pulled on a Liverpool shirt, and the campaign behind him was incredible. I think he scored about ten goals in his whole Liverpool career, and yet they worshipped him as though he was Rushie or Roger Hunt. That was until Houllier tired of him, of course, and then bombed him out of the club, complete with the outraged condemnation of the reporters who had canonized him only weeks earlier.

You can imagine the stick I got after I was dropped for the final game at Bradford. I thought the time had come to fight back, and give Houllier less ammunition. That summer, I put everything into getting fit after I'd lost a second year through injury. I worked hard, maybe too hard, and got my weight down to below the level when I first got into the team as a kid, which was actually a bit of a problem because I was so light I was easy to push off the ball. But then I got my weight right, and in pre-season I was flying, I felt great and sharper than I had done for a while. It all went well on a training camp and we went to Belfast for a pre-season tournament. We played Glentoran on a Thursday night, 3 August 2000, and I was thrilled because I was captain. I had been made vice captain in the summer of '99 – a promise Houllier had made when I was ready to sign a new contract earlier in the season – but because of the injuries, I had never got a game when Jamie Redknapp wasn't playing. This was my first chance because Jamie, unfortunately, had a bad injury and was ruled out for the whole season.

So I was looking forward to the game, hyped up a bit because I would be skipper for the first time, and me dad would be out there watching me. It was an easy enough game, a warm-up against a bunch of part-timers that was a stroll really, a 4–0 win that could have been a lot bigger. There's always a but though, isn't there? For me, my whole career was becoming one big but by that stage. It was as though I was cursed. You get there at the top, everything goes so well that you almost start believing it must be a dream, and then bam. Reality intervenes and you get smacked around the head with a great big stick. It's hard to work out sometimes as a footballer whether you are charmed or cursed. I have achieved so much in my career, got so far and had the most fabulous life. But I have always felt it could have been better, I could have won more trophies and I could have had better luck with injuries. I've lost so many years through injury, and they have taken something away from my game, that much is obvious. Yet most of them have been sheer bad luck.

What happened to me in the summer of 2000 was so bloody typical. I went in for a challenge and their keeper came charging into me, just smashed right into me and bowled me over. I was fucking done again, and straight away I knew it was a bad one. It was me ankle, the same one that had caused me to lose a year of my career, and I was fucking livid. The Glentoran keeper was a bloke called Alan Gough, a part-timer who turned out to be a Manchester United fan. Whether he meant to hurt me or not, I obviously don't know, but Liverpool were angry enough about the incident that they said they wouldn't be playing in Ireland again after that. There was some talk in the papers of the keeper trying to injure me because he was a United fan and hated Liverpool, but that seems a bit fanciful. I wasn't happy, though, done again by a keeper and yet another start to the season ruined. What the fuck had I done to deserve that? It was all the ammo Houllier needed, though, it was as if I had brought the injury on myself. From that day on at Liverpool, I was never given a real chance.

I came back after a month of yet more rehab, but he wouldn't play me. I scored five goals for the reserves, but the best I got was a place on the bench for the trip to Bucharest for the UEFA Cup tie. Eventually, Emile got injured and he had no choice but to play me for the return leg. We stacked the defence, did fuck all going forward, and then he criticized me afterwards for not scoring. I was out for the next two games, and came back again for the next round against Slovan Liberec. Kerrie was expecting our second child at that time, and she went into labour the night before the game. I was up half the night and through the next morning, and finally our beautiful daughter Jaya was born on 26 October 2001. Later that day I went back to the team hotel and Houllier asked me if I was up to playing, and I was in the side. I had a bit of a 'mare, missed a penalty and we scraped a 1–0 win. Houllier coated me afterwards, but never mentioned that I'd been in the hospital with Kerrie. One of the papers picked up on it, and said at least I had an excuse for playing shit, but what about the other ten players, because we did have a shocking night. Houllier went ballistic again. He rang the reporter, coated him and said he was just trying to get Fowler in the side. I was gobsmacked. That wasn't just strange behaviour, it was fucking weird. If anyone defended me, they were coated, if anyone criticized Emile, say, they were coated again. There was another time when Emile had a bad game, admitted himself that he'd had a real stinker, and he was laughing about it when one of the reporters took the piss out of him a bit for being shit. Yet Houllier rang the press guy, swearing like mad down the phone, banned him from the club, accused him of campaigning to get Fowler in the side and of being racist to boot!

As the season wore on, it became increasingly obvious that he wanted me out. I hardly played, and when I did I was taken off. I couldn't get any sort of rhythm, and as a striker that is so important. Every time I played and scored a goal, I was dropped the next game. It happened after Chelsea, Spurs and Arsenal. I played in a Worthington Cup tie at Stoke, scored three goals and had a hand in four others, which suggested I was getting there. Straight after the game, Houllier went into the press room and he was boiling, really animated. He absolutely tore into me, said I was unfit, overweight, out of shape, and not up to it. After I had just scored a hat-trick in our best performance of the season to take my tally to four in three matches!

I was dropped again. It was painful, unfair and despicable really, and I knew it was leading somewhere, although I couldn't quite detect where because Houllier, remember, had said he would support me. I think I got the answer when I was on the bench yet again, for a visit to Aston Villa. I was warming up, running down the touchline and the fans were chanting my name, really giving me some great support, which always cheered me up. Then, Nicky Barmby came along to me and said the gaffer wanted me to go and sit back down on the bench again. Why the fuck would he do that? Apparently, he had heard the fans singing my name, and turned round to Phil Thompson and said they couldn't have that, they'd have to get the fucker to sit down quick, and ordered Nicky to get me back on the bench. He didn't even want the fans to support me.

To say the least I was pissed off. He had been so two-faced it was frightening – saying he was supporting me when he appeared to be trying his best to undermine me. But that was just a mere appetizer for what was to come. Just before Christmas we went to Old Trafford and beat Manchester United 1–0, with a goal from Danny Murphy. At the end of the game, Houllier raced onto the pitch like David Pleat in that white suit, celebrating as if we had just won the European Cup. He and Phil Thompson were going round hugging the players, and then got them to go around the pitch like it was a lap of honour. I was on the bench as usual and didn't get on, but I couldn't believe my eyes. The manager and his assistant were leading the players in the sort of celebrations that are normally reserved for historic, legend-making results. I merely picked up me shin pads and walked down the touchline towards the tunnel.

On Monday morning I got called into the office. Houllier tore a strip off me, wanted to know why I didn't join in the celebrations with my teammates, why I wasn't prepared to support them in their victory. I swear, he said that to me and I was looking at him wondering how the captain of Liverpool could be in the manager's office being slaughtered for not celebrating on the pitch at Old Trafford just because we had beaten Manchester United. So I let him have it. Why the fuck should I be celebrating on the pitch? Would we do it if we'd won at Derby or Stoke or Bradford? Would we celebrate as if we had won the Cup Final if we beat Everton, who were bigger rivals than United could ever be? Of course we fucking wouldn't.

Celebrating at Old Trafford was fucking embarrassing, humiliating even, because it showed that we didn't think we were on a level with United, that we thought beating them was an incredible achievement. It was the sort of thing some tin-pot lower league club would do, not Liverpool, not a club that had won four European Cups and eighteen League Championships. I told him all that, and in the end even he had to agree with me. Grudgingly, but he told me that I was right. It was an episode that said an awful lot about his way of thinking towards me.

A few days later I found out exactly what was on his mind. George rang me in a state of shock. He'd just had Colin Hutchinson, the Chelsea Managing Director, on, saying that Liverpool had agreed a £12 million fee for me, and did I want to move to Stamford Bridge? George thought he was pulling his leg, but he had a great relationship with Colin, who was a decent, honest bloke – a rarity in football – and was straight down the line. He told us that Liverpool had even sent him a copy of my contract . . . detailing what I was on and what I was due to earn over the next few years. He'd had talks with Rick Parry, his counterpart at Anfield, and there was an agent who had spoken to Houllier and said he had cleared the whole thing. Chelsea were really keen to sign me, and between Colin Hutchinson and the agent who was dealing with Liverpool, we were kept completely up to date about exactly what was going on. It was incredible. George went in to find out what the fuck was going on, and he was given this half-baked story about Chelsea making an offer and the manager not being interested, but if Robbie wanted to leave then they wouldn't stand in his way. Then we would get the story from the agent, who had spoken to Houllier and Parry, and been told in no uncertain terms to make the deal happen.

Colin Hutchinson was straight with us. He could have used the situation to help persuade me to sign for his club, but I think he was so amazed by the actions of Liverpool that he simply wanted to make sure we received an honest picture of what was really happening. This dragged on for a few days until the press got wind of the story, and then Houllier was forced to come out and deny he wanted to sell me. He gave it the usual stuff of saying no one had supported me more than him, but I had to sort myself out, show the right attitude, get fit, blah, blah, blah. I might have a chance of getting properly fit if I fucking played. I came out and said it wasn't a problem, there was lots of speculation but the manager and me knew what was happening, and I was happy with the situation. Yeah, I knew what was happening all right, they were trying to get me out of the club, that much was fucking obvious. And I knew where I stood with him too – with my back to him, fearing that I'd be feeling a sharp pain at any moment. Colin Hutchinson said that in the end he was ringing up Liverpool and not getting an answer. He couldn't get through and no one would ring him back. Fuck knows what they thought that would achieve, but he lost his patience with Liverpool, because they were messing him around so much and using Chelsea.

I knew I could have gone, and I knew Houllier would have loved it if I did, but that Christmas the Liverpool fans made me realize how important the club was to me. Every time I warmed up, they would sing my name and give me the most incredible backing. Sometimes, it would bring tears to my eyes. I also got support from some important people to me. Kenny Dalglish rang me and said he realized exactly what was going on, and I had to be strong, had to see my way through it and it would all work out. So did Rushie. He said that no matter what they did to me, they could never destroy me. John Aldridge also rang and spent a long time talking to me, telling me how to deal with it, not to lose my rag and give Houllier something else to attack me with. That backing meant so much to me from three Liverpool goal-scoring legends, three of the greatest strikers who have ever played for the club. Eventually Chelsea went away in a huff, vowing never to do business with Liverpool again, but almost straight away it all started again, this time with Aston Villa. Again, it was the same agent used, the same style of contact and eventually the same type of denials. All the time I wasn't playing, and it was obvious they were hoping I would crack. No chance.

Things got much worse though, and I wondered if I had

the strength to fight them off. Over Christmas we had such a busy schedule and there was no time to even have a proper Christmas dinner. There was no party, and no chance to take Kerrie out. So after the New Year was out of the way, Houllier said we could go out for a quiet Christmas celebration. It was Tuesday 2 January 2001, and we didn't have a game until the Saturday. Kerrie and me went out with Calvey and his wife Lisa for a meal to let our hair down. Afterwards, we went to a bar for a few drinks, and to this day I don't know why we bothered.

It was after midnight, but nowhere near 3 a.m. as has been suggested . . . the place didn't even stay open that late. As we were leaving, some girl came up to us outside the bar on Slater Street with a camera and started taking pictures. She pushed the camera right into my face and caught me in the eye. So I put my arm up to protect myself, and the camera dropped to the floor. She started screaming, and two doormen walked out of the bar. They grabbed me, held me by the arms and started smacking me. I took a pounding and I couldn't believe it. Calvey tried to intervene, and he got dragged inside by some other doormen and started getting smacked. The police were quickly on the scene, and they arrested one of the doormen. Then another doorman came out and gave me another smack. They wanted me to press charges but after all I had gone through with the previous assault, I didn't think it was worth it, especially with all that fuss for very little at the end of it.

Strangely enough, the bar had a CCTV, but the tape just happened to go missing. It was an unprovoked attack, and for the life of me I can't understand why it happened. I heard later that the first two bouncers were connected to the blokes that had assaulted me in the bar in the Moat House, and it was some sort of revenge. The bar clearly had vigorous employee-vetting procedures. Houllier was in his element of course. Straight away he was asking everyone what I was doing there in the wrong place at the wrong time, even though he was grudgingly forced to admit that it was a totally unprovoked, senseless assault. I was dropped from the FA Cup tie at Rotherham on the Saturday, and then left out of the squad to travel to Crystal Palace for the first leg of the Worthington Cup semi final and a trip to Villa. I was slaughtered by Houllier's stooges in the press, and he milked it for what it was worth. Then he went straight out and bought Jari Litmanen, which really rubbed it in.

Of course, I was smarting like mad about giving him such an opportunity, but even though this sounds like a whole load of excuses, the fact is I was out for a quiet post-Christmas night with my wife, best mate and his wife, and just happened to be a random victim. It could just as easily have happened at midday, if I had walked past the wrong people then. It wasn't late, and I wasn't pissed in a wild club or anything. I was left on the bench for a game against Middlesbrough when we really bombed, but Michael was struggling with an injury so Houllier had to bring me back for the second leg against Palace. We had misfired in the first leg and lost, but we stuffed them 5–0 at Anfield and I scored a good goal. I even struck up an instant rapport with Jari, and the crowd were singing both our names afterwards. You should have seen Houllier's face.

We went to Leeds in the cup and I had to play because Jari wasn't registered in time and Michael was injured, and I created both goals and was given Man of the Match on Sky. Fuck me, we can't have that, so I was dropped straight away, even though I'd only played two games in a month and was star man in both. The thing was, I was on a roll by then and the fans could see that my form was there, along with my appetite. For all Houllier's criticism of the circumstances surrounding the assault, he knew I was totally innocent, and the fans knew that if he left me out it was personal and not professional. I came back and scored twice against West Ham, then started in the Olympic Stadium against Roma, when me and Michael gave them a torrid time and we got probably our best result – and performance – of the season by winning 2–0. So he left me out again for the next two. Cheers, boss.

Anyone who knows about strikers realizes that we have to play a run of games to get in a groove and have the right sort of mentality and confidence to score goals. So I was played for one game and rested for three, then brought back when my sharpness had gone. I kept playing well when I was given the chance, and scored goals even though I had barely started two consecutive games all season. In spite of the obvious problems that caused so much unrest in the camp, we got past Palace and got to the Worthington Cup final, and then following quickly on we had quarter finals in the FA and UEFA Cups against Tranmere and Porto. My form was so good that Houllier had to play me, and we did really well. We held Porto over there, and beat them easily at Anfield. In between we went to Anfield, and interestingly Houllier decided that for a tough, physically demanding, pressure-laden FA Cup tie at a lower league club, he would go with the eight fit British players left in the squad, and I scored a good goal, as did Michael, Danny and Stevie, and we were into another semi, against another lower league club. If my luck was out, then Houllier's was well and truly in that season. I wonder if he ever did the lottery.

It was a bizarre season. It seems obvious to me what was happening, it was hard not to notice when they were so unsubtle about it. Yet to my face Houllier continued to say that he wanted me to stay and be a focal point of his team. Fat chance. There was one incident with him that summed up our relationship perfectly. We had hit a bit of a bad spell, and he reckoned that team spirit wasn't what it should be. I could have pointed out that with all the rules designed to stop any spirit, it wasn't a surprise, and his treatment of players didn't help either. But he came to me, said I was good at getting the lads together and making them feel a group. He wanted me to organize a night out for everyone so we all became a bit closer, bonded better. Fair enough, the manager actually saying we could have a night out, we weren't going to turn that one down. I asked the lads what they wanted to do. We organized a bar where we could have a few drinks without being disturbed, we had a meal and then there were a few dancers to relax the evening a little. It wasn't outrageous, merely a pole-dancing type of thing, the sort of stuff that groups of blokes who work together get up to every week.

Everyone seemed to enjoy themselves and it was quite a success, no wild behaviour, and we all packed off home pretty early. Problem was, one of the lads had got a phone call from his missis halfway through the evening asking what he was up to. He said we'd had a bite to eat, were having a few drinks and there were a couple of dancers, fairly quiet really. She went ballistic, drove round to drag him out of there, and then she rang Houllier to complain! It was funny really, and we gave him plenty of stick for being so hen-pecked, but the next day Houllier called a meeting. In front of all the players he got me in the middle and laid into me. Asked me what I thought I was doing, embarrassing all the players by arranging something like that, bringing the name of the club down, all that kind of stuff. Then he got me to apologize to them all. It was fucking ridiculous and every single one of the lads said how embarrassed they were about Houllier's behaviour. So what had started out as a relaxed team-building exercise, suggested by Houllier himself, was eventually turned on its head by him to somehow undermine the whole spirit in the squad ... and take me another step closer to the exit door.

Yet he needed me. That season I scored eighteen goals from only twenty-eight starts. Given that I was fucked about so much and never got into a rhythm, never really got a solid run of matches together to help my sharpness and fitness, that was a decent return. Emile had fifty starts and got twenty-two goals, Michael got twenty-two from thirty-five starts. The manager will argue that he rotated us to keep us fresh, but the reality was that I only played when the others were injured. I knew that, I knew they were his first-choice partnership and he wanted me out of the club. Even the tea lady knew that. But instead of burying me all the time, maybe Houllier should have had a closer look at the stats, because they do tell a story.

For everything he threw at me, I always remained professional. I never once criticized him and I even praised his handling of me in the media, despite thinking privately it was an absolute disgrace. I also scored goals consistently for him, despite never being picked consistently. That season, I scored in two semi finals and two cup finals. I also scored the two goals at Charlton that got us into the Champions' League on the final day of the season. I scored important goals against

Manchester United, Arsenal, Everton and Chelsea, and I captained the side in the most successful season Houllier ever had. All that with the certainty in my mind that he wanted me out of the club, and he had an assistant manager who felt the same and made it patently clear. If either of them had ever stopped and considered what I actually offered during that season, would they have been quite so keen to see the back of me? When I eventually couldn't take it any more, they brought in a succession of strikers to replace me. In their eyes, I was too much trouble. So they went out and bought Nicolas Anelka, Milan Baros, El Hadji Diouf and Anthony Le Tallec. None of them were any trouble at all, were they? None of them scored any goals, that's for sure.

In many ways, it was amazing that I lasted so long, and it was only the love I had for the club and the support of my family and friends that saw me stick it out. I didn't like being left out, but I could handle it – sort of. I know you can't play fifty or sixty games a season these days, it's just not possible, and I understand perfectly that a striker needs to be rested. However, by the end, I even suspected they only put me in the team when it was severely weakened, as if they were making sure I failed. For all the decent people I've met at Leeds and Manchester City, for all the wonderful fans at those two clubs, I know I should still be at Liverpool now. Who knows what would have happened if I'd stayed? They did well that season I left, but at the end when it came down to the pressure games they didn't have anyone to put the ball in the net for them. If they'd had another striker who didn't moan or go running to the press, and remained professional enough to score goals in semi finals, finals and the biggest games, despite being messed about, then maybe they would have done even better.

Hey, who knows? Maybe Houllier and Thompson wouldn't have been sacked. They did what they felt they had to do, and as the management they had the power and the right to do that and I had no comeback. That's why I made no complaints. Regrets, yes, even though I know they are pointless. Regrets not just for myself either, but for the club I have given so much of my life to, because those years after Roy Evans proved to be wasted years in many ways. Liverpool were on the verge of challenging when Roy was eased out, close to competing with Manchester United and Arsenal. When Houllier was sacked, they were a million miles away from those two and Chelsea. The question is, have Liverpool slipped too far behind in those intervening years to ever get back on the level of the top three? At least they have a decent manager in Rafael Benitez now, who seems to be able to work without big money, so they've got a chance, and you have to say his Champions League triumph was incredible, miraculous, even. But whichever way you look at it, after spending so much money they were a lot further behind the leaders when Houllier left than before he arrived.

Had Houllier proved to be the type of manager the board thought they were getting, then Liverpool, with all the quality young players he inherited and the riches at his disposal, would have been up there with the big three, that is certain. He's not a bad man, and he has a decent side to his nature, a compassionate side. I think it was that flaw in his character about not being able to accept confrontation or criticism of any kind, that prevented him from being a great manager. He fell out with so many players that it was hard for him to get any team spirit or atmosphere going for very long, without having to bring new players in. If I felt hard done by, then at least I was in good company. He rowed with Titi Camara, Sander Westerveld, Christian Ziege, Markus Babbel, Gary McAllister, Nicky Barmby, Jari Litmanen, Abel Xavier, Nicolas Anelka, El Hadji Diouf, John Arne Riise and even the likes of Didi Hamann and Michael Owen. Nicky Barmby was forced out because Houllier didn't think he had a cheery enough attitude around the place; Gary McAllister and Jari Litmanen because they made a few comments about team selection. Sander Westerveld was public enemy number one for having the audacity to make a few comments after Houllier, overnight, brought in not one but two keepers to replace him. I heard a story that after Sander left the club he returned at Christmas as a guest of Markus Babbel. When Houllier saw him there he went ballistic and demanded to know who had invited him. Coincidentally, Markus didn't have much of an Anfield future after that. And as for Michael, it hardly seems possible that he could have tried to undermine him, but he did. Michael had questioned a few things, and even dared to say that the style of play had to change, that he wasn't prepared to keep toiling on alone up front with so few chances coming his way. That was never likely to go down well, even if it was his star striker saying it.

Houllier bought more than forty players for Liverpool in his five and a half years, at a cost of around £130 million. Of those, five were British or Irish. Almost half the players he bought were recruited from the French league, which was supposed to be his area of expertise. Of those, two – Traore and Riise – could remotely be described as first-team regulars when Houllier left. Arsenal's dominance in the Premiership was built on the back of outstanding talent recruited from France. Liverpool are still waiting. His first signing was Jean Michel Ferri, a midfielder who cost £2.5 million and played precisely fifty-one minutes for the club. In defence of Houllier, he made some good signings. Players like Sami Hyypia, Stephane Henchoz, Nicky Barmby, Didi Hamann, Emile Heskey and Jari Litmanen were all top class, and added to the fine local talent he inherited. The 2000–01 season showed that we were a decent side, even if we enjoyed some good fortune on the way to the treble.

It's just that he fell out with so many of us, there was often an air of discontent around the place, simmering just below the surface. It seemed to me that he wanted to get rid of every last trace of the Roy Evans era, a mistake – especially when you look at some of the players he replaced them with. I remember he bought Gregory Vignal, a young French lad who looked an okay player. One day, he was sitting in the car park blubbing. He was supposed to make his debut that night in a Worthington Cup tie, but he'd got a bit of a cold and they decided he couldn't play. So he sat there crying in front of his teammates. The rest of us were going 'Uh-oh, what the fuck have we got here?' It was the same with Houllier's first buy, Ferri, which always makes a big impression. Everyone else was thinking that he was just a spy, and we'd joke that he must have a tape recorder in his bag, which he took back to Houllier every night.

It was a crazy time, we played twenty-five cup games that

season, and loitered around fourth place in the Premiership for virtually the whole campaign. I'm pretty certain most of the lads weren't very sure about Houllier, or some of his methods, but at the same time we were getting results, so no one was complaining too much. I was in a terrible position. I knew they didn't fancy me, they wanted me out, and they made that clear almost every step of the way that season. And yet I was still involved, still playing games and still contributing when I was given my chance. I found myself torn all the time. I knew I wasn't being treated entirely fairly, but I wasn't completely shut out either. Most of the season Houllier decided that Michael and I couldn't play together – even though we had proved we could for England – so we were competing against each other for a place alongside his first choice, Emile Heskey. One game towards the end though, he dropped the pair of us and played Vladi Smicer up just behind Emile, which had everyone scratching their heads.

There was no point trying to second-guess Houllier. At the end of it all, we reached three cup finals and had a game on the last day of the season we needed to win to make the Champions' League. It was the greatest season of my career, and also one of the worst. Perhaps my most appropriate memory was going on an open-top bus tour around the city with three shining, glittering silver trophies to show to half a million fans who had lined the streets. It should have been the best day of my career, and in some ways it was, because when I was a kid I used to sit on the pavement clapping as my heroes paraded by, dreaming of being up there, and now here I was as one of the heroes waving from the top of the bus. It was wonderful, but flashing through my mind for most of that incredible journey around my home city was the thought that some of the people standing on the bus beside me, holding the cup aloft with me, would be happier if I wasn't actually there. That was my treble season summed up in one image.

TREBLE (11)

It's funny, but whenever I think of the painful relationship I had with Jekyll and Hyde – or Houllier and Thompson as they were slightly better known at Anfield – that doesn't completely detract from my memories of the treble season in 2000–01. That was the most painful year of my career . . . and also the best. At the end of that season 500,000 people came out in the city of Liverpool to cheer their heroes as they rode around on an open-top bus. Half a million people standing at the side of the road just as I had done as a kid, staring up in wonder, the little ones hoping that one day it will be them. And it was me on the top of that bus, holding up a trophy, laughing, waving and taking in the most incredible experience of my life.

It is hard even now to put into words what that meant to me, to see people that I knew in the crowd, to go down from Anfield through the city centre and on to the edge of Toxteth where I used to live. I was the man who lifted all three of those trophies that we paraded around the city, and now I was showing them off to my home crowd. It was sublime, would have been the most perfect moment of my football life, but for the two people standing behind me, clearly already plotting their next move. When I think back now, I realize that no matter what happened that season, the treble year at Anfield was undoubtedly the high point of my career. Yet there is still a tinge of regret that it could have been even better.

It was a schizophrenic season for me. In terms of trophies, I have never had a better year, and it is unlikely to be matched by very many people. In terms of my mental state, it got worse and worse as the season wore on. You want to win things as a footballer, you want to be there holding up the trophies and playing your part. I did that, I lifted all three trophies and I felt I had every right to do so, because I had contributed in all three finals. But at the same time I didn't start in two of them and a part of you is always niggling away, saying that you weren't really part of the team, the manager doesn't really rate you, the fans know you are a bit of a fraud going wild celebrating when you were only on for a few minutes or so. I did contribute, even in the FA Cup final when I was only on for a short time, but I could have contributed an awful lot more. See, even now I'm schizophrenic about it.

The game in Roma, when Michael scored twice and I played really well supporting defence and attack, was my third start in a row, which was virtually unheard of under Houllier. I was playing well, the team was winning and we had produced some big performances in big matches. So it was only natural that I would be dropped for the next two games in the lead-up to the Worthington Cup final. We beat City in the FA Cup, but then lost at home to Roma, sneaking through only because the referee gave a penalty and then changed his mind to award a corner instead. That was on the Thursday, and the Sunday, 25 February 2001, was the day of the final, the first final under Houllier, and the first since we had played Manchester United in the FA Cup final at Wembley back in 1996. Naturally enough, I assumed I would be on the bench, that Houllier would find some way of not playing me. But when we trained the day after the UEFA Cup tie, there were indications that I might be in the side, and as we travelled down to Cardiff for the final at the Millennium Stadium, there was a buzz around that said I might be starting. I was so anxious to be in that side, and so determined to play well if I got even a sniff of a chance.

There is so much money around in football now, the top players do earn ridiculous amounts, but the real players, those that have desire and heart, they might like the money but the only thing they care passionately about is winning something. I was at the Champions' League final in Istanbul in 2005 when Steven Gerrard lifted that fantastic trophy above his head, and I must admit that even though I'd been gone from Liverpool for three years, I felt a tinge of regret because I was thinking it should have been me, I should have still been at Liverpool under Rafael Benitez, playing in the European Cup final, which was probably the biggest dream of all when I was a kid ... except for maybe playing in the World Cup final. Not that I'm greedy or anything.

In 2001, the Worthington Cup final would do very nicely thank you. With Jamie Redknapp injured – God bless him – I was captain of the team when selected, and that meant if I started in Cardiff I would be lifting the cup if we won. Houllier never told us the team beforehand, he used to announce it in the dressing room when we got to the ground a couple of hours before the game, but we could tell from the routines in training whether we were in or not. And from the way the staff treated you. It's a strange thing, the psychology of a team, but if you are not playing then the coaches tend to treat you slightly differently. They can't look at you, and they speak to you a little more quietly. They just don't engage you in the same way. If you are playing then they seem to like you a little more, be a little more positive towards you. So even when the team isn't announced, players tend to know who's in and who's not. On the Saturday night before the final, I knew I was in. It was a great feeling after the problems I'd had that season, and when I rang me dad he was overjoyed. The whole family had come down to Cardiff, even me mum was there, and they were really excited about it. I think me mum had brought a book, just in case, but this was one of the first games she had ever actually come along to watch me in, and me dad said afterwards that she kept saying all afternoon, 'I hope he doesn't get hurt.'

We played Birmingham City, and before the game Jamie Redknapp had a word with me. Jamie is the nicest man on earth, and the worst thing about that treble season was that as club skipper he didn't get to play in any of the games. He was there at Anfield when I arrived as a YTS, promoted from the youths that trained on a Tuesday night, and we have always been firm friends. When someone new came into the club, Jamie was always the first to have a word with them, welcome them and make them feel like they belonged. He can talk to anyone, and his presence around the club is fantastic.

Jamie was always a fabulous player of course, but even if he wasn't an England international midfielder with a pass to die for, you'd still have him around because of the influence he can have over a club in bringing everyone together, and in understanding the dynamics of a group. He said to me that he would be sitting on the bench, and if I could, would I get him involved in some way, because he'd love to be part of the final in just a small way. No problem, I said, I'd sneak over and rip his kecks off, that would get him noticed. On the bus on the way to the game there was the usual chatter, and everyone was excited because this was what it was all about. Michael wasn't too happy, because he was the one left out, and Houllier never brought him on that day, which was a bit unfair. He deserved to be part of that game, he had contributed a lot along the way that season, and I don't see why he wasn't put on, because in the end we had a full extra-time period to play.

It all started so well for us. Some days, you know it is going to be your day. I went on to that pitch feeling ten feet tall, leading out my home-town club into a major final, with 75,000 fans there cheering me on. I knew I was going to score. As I led the team out, I looked to my right, and out of the corner of my eye I spotted this massive fella, lumbering up alongside me. It was Dele Adebola, my old teammate from the Liverpool Schoolboys team, who was centre forward for Birmingham that day. I turned round to him and said that we'd come a long way from Penny Lane. He laughed, and said he wouldn't have minded doing the journey on my wages rather than his. That was a great moment for me, to walk out at the Millennium Stadium to play football against one of the lads I used to kick around with in the old days, when we were starry-eyed kids dreaming of a football career. Incredibly, I was the only player in the starting team that day who had survived from the last time we had won a trophy for Liverpool, in the Coca-Cola Cup final against Bolton in 1995. Jamie Redknapp was the only other one in the entire squad. All this was going through my head as we sang the national anthem, and as the game got under way I knew it would be my day. I had a chance early on and came close to scoring, and created problems for the Birmingham defence who didn't seem to be able to pick up my runs. It was easy for me to find space, and on the half hour, when we launched a long ball forward and Emile knocked it down about twenty-five yards from goal, I had a couple of yards as the ball bounced in front of me.

At the time I said I just closed my eyes and hit it and hoped. You always try to be modest after scoring, otherwise your mates will just pull you down for being a big-headed biff, but in fact I meant that goal against Birmingham. Even as Emo jumped I could see the keeper had strayed off his line a little and the ball bounced up at the perfect height for me to get a proper contact to smash it over his head. It was one of those that if you connect with it properly, it goes in. If not, it ends up on me dad's lap in row H. I knew it was in, the moment I hit it. I was turning even before it had gone in, and I was off down the touchline. I ran towards our bench and charged into the group of them standing there, all going mad. As I got closer and closer I could see Houllier standing with his arms out waiting for me. So I dropped me shoulder, did a swerve and ran straight past him. I think he imagined I was going to hug him or something, but there was no fucking chance of that.

I was mobbed by the players, but I was trying to lean across to grab Jamie and celebrate with him, which was my way of saying that he was as much a part of it as anybody, that he was an important member of our squad. Afterwards Houllier said it showed the incredible spirit in the squad, that I wanted to include the club captain in things, and that it showed just how together we all were, and what a sense of purpose we all had. Bollocks really. I just wanted to include Jamie because he was a mate and he deserved the recognition, but the biggest reason I ran to the bench was because I scored at the Birmingham end, and when I set off to celebrate, I started running towards these big ugly bastards in blue, who were screaming abuse at me, their faces all screwed up like they wanted to kill me. So I thought I'd better go off in search of our fans, and the closest point where they were congregated was behind our bench! It was a special goal to me, one of the best I've ever scored, and one of the most important. Me mum and dad were there to see their son captain the side and score a goal, and as the game went on it began to seem like it would be the goal that won the cup for Liverpool.

As it happened, I had a couple of other chances to kill the game off, and only a couple of great saves from their keeper Ian Bennett stopped me. Then, with the game in stoppage time at the end of ninety minutes, Stephane Henchoz – who was my friend and neighbour – managed to fuck things up for me by giving them a penalty with the last kick of the game. Darren Purse put it in, and we were into extra time. I still felt good, but we began to tire and they had another decent penalty shout when Stephane again fouled, but this time it was turned down. With about five minutes to go, Vladimir Smicer floated in a cross and I got a great contact with my head, and again I was wheeling around because I thought I'd scored. But this time Bennett got a hand to it, God knows how, and we were into penalties.

I was down for the fifth, just like in Euro '96, and I was hoping I'd get the chance to score the winner in the shoot-out. They missed their first so it looked like I would get the chance, but then Didi Hamann blasted his penalty at Bennett – who said Germans were good at penalties – and I had to score to keep us in it. I was a bit cheeky, chipped it in the top corner to the keeper's left, and we were in sudden death. Jamie Carragher converted a great penalty and Andy Johnson missed theirs, and I was climbing onto the small podium to collect the cup as captain, and also the Alan Hardaker Trophy as Man of the Match. We danced around the stadium that afternoon, relieved really that we had brought some silverware back to Anfield after a six-year gap, and I spotted me mum and dad in the crowd. Mum was all tearful, she said she couldn't look when I was taking the penalty and was so relieved that I had scored it. Me dad was proud, and I gave him the medal and the trophy, with express instructions not to throw them down the nearest drain. Apparently, they were stuck in traffic for hours after the final, and so they were passing the trophy around the nearest cars in the jam to entertain a few of the fans. At least nobody nicked it.

I was satisfied with the way I'd played, mostly because it showed a few people that I wasn't finished. We had a party at the team hotel with wives and girlfriends invited, and we were even allowed a few beers. Michael was really pissed off that he didn't even get on, and he wasn't afraid to show it to Houllier. Strangely enough, it didn't count against him, even though normally if you showed dissent like that it meant an automatic lecture on disrespect to your teammates, and a step closer to being kicked out of the club. But we had a bit of a party anyway.

It was the start of my best run of the season. I played five games on the bounce, and I almost got a nosebleed. We did well too, knocked a good Porto side out of the UEFA Cup quarter final, and went to Tranmere for that incredibly tricky FA Cup quarter final and made light work of that too. Then it was the visit of Manchester United to Anfield. Against United, I played my best football since the knee injury in 1997 that stopped me in my tracks. I scored what was a proper striker's goal, and I thought I led the line really well against a strong United defence. Yet when Danny Murphy got sent off, I looked up with resignation to see my number up on the board and I was off again, even though I was captain.

On the Monday, I went to see Houllier and told him that he might as well take the captain's armband off me, that a captain should be a leader, should be the man you want out there when things go against you to rally the side, to fight for them and see it through, not the first man to be hauled off when things go a little wrong. I explained to him how much it meant to me to be captain of my home-town club, to lead Liverpool, and how hurtful it was to have the captaincy treated like it was just a badge they gave out at school. Predictably enough, even though I had played my best football for some years and scored a really good goal against the Champions, I was on the bench for the next game, the UEFA Cup semi final in Barcelona. Man, it did my head in. We bored our way into the final, didn't get into their half, and when I came on I played the last fifteen minutes at left back, which was a fairly unique experience. I did try playing left wing for a short while when I was a kid, but you didn't get any chances out there. Maybe my career had come full circle under Houllier.

Next game up was the FA Cup semi final against Wycombe, and I scored what proved to be the winner with a free kick from outside the box, but as we got to the sharp end of the season I got fewer and fewer chances to play. In fact, the best I managed in the final two months of the season was a run of two games on the bounce . . . once. It didn't make sense to me, but I knew there was no point complaining, because if you did that to Houllier, even in private, then you were done for. I got my head down, sat on the bench and waited. And waited. When I played we did well, but as the season got more and more serious he went with Michael and Emile, and didn't consider playing the three of us, which had happened a few times earlier in the season, and which had happened quite a lot for England.

There has been an awful lot of rubbish said about my relationship with Michael and Emile. Both are brilliant guys who I always got on well with, and I enjoyed playing alongside both of them. They are both top class as well, there is no question of that, and the fact that all three of us played for England at the same times suggests that Liverpool weren't badly off for strikers. Never once did I think I should have been playing ahead of either of them, and I would never dream of suggesting that I'm better than either of them. It doesn't work like that in football. I would like to think that people will look back on that time and say that we all offered something, and we could all play together. When I moan about being dropped, it has nothing to do with my opinion of other players. It's all about my own drive, my own voice inside my head, the one that has brought me to the top of my profession and never allows me to settle for second best, to coast or cheat. The top players, the ones you want by your side, they can never accept being dropped, no matter who replaces them.

With Michael, I've heard all the stuff that we didn't get on, but that's just not true. When Kerrie and I married, he was one of the few guests from the football club. We were a different generation, so we weren't best buddies – Macca was my close mate and Jamie Carragher his. But when Houllier brought all the foreign players into the club, the English lads always stuck together. Michael is quite quiet and private but we always got on, and it's a myth too to say that we couldn't play together. One of the best performances of the Houllier era was the 2–0 win in Rome, when we were up front together. One of the best performances of Eriksson's England side was the 2–0 win in Greece, when we were up front together.

There's an interesting theory that when I'd established myself in the Liverpool side, Michael came along and stole my thunder, and I was never the same player. The fact is, I got injured just after Michael arrived, and we hardly played together for two seasons. When I came back from injury, Houllier had arrived, and he never really gave me the chance to get my sharpness back, never really gave me the run in the team I desperately needed to establish myself again. If I had a problem, it was with the manager, and not Michael. It's true that when he first came into the side he was a pace merchant who didn't look up much, purely because he was so young, and that didn't help my style of play particularly. But it was the same when I came into the side with Rushie, my play wasn't the best at bringing people in around me. You develop. After the injury I got against Everton, I think that I lost half a yard of pace, and so I had to adapt anyway. I've shown over the later stages of my career that I can be a creator as well as a goal scorer, although I like to think that I can still do both. As I developed other aspects of my game, I was able to combine with Michael a lot more, and we became a far more effective partnership.

By the treble season, I think we were a handful, because we could both score goals and we could both bring people in around us. Maybe we lacked a little height as a partnership, but we worked well together, and if we'd had the right type of service I think we could have been devastating. Maybe the long-ball way Houllier played didn't suit either of us too much. I have no bitterness towards Michael, nothing but admiration for his ability, and he has always been supportive of me, always complimented me and said what a good player I am. It's a tiny bit like the way things were with Stan Collymore. I thought Stan was a terrific player, incredibly talented, and when he arrived at Anfield I thought we were a fantastic partnership. We weren't best mates, but we got on fine together – no matter what he says! – and I appreciated his talent. In fact, I think he could have been a world beater, and it's a shame his career ended like it did. I wasn't jealous of him, and one thing I can say is that in my whole career I can't remember one player I didn't get on with. I've been incredibly lucky that wherever I've been, I've always fitted in and been quite popular with the lads – maybe I've always been one of the jokers that got the team spirit going. Even Houllier acknowledged that, because when we were struggling he did turn to me.

Towards the end of the treble season, though, things went against me. Michael had gone a long time without a goal, but in the two league games before the FA Cup and UEFA Cup finals, he was on fire. He scored a fantastic hat-trick against Newcastle, and I can remember thinking that wouldn't be too good for me. In the build-up to the FA Cup final in Cardiff, my emotions were all over the place. I desperately wanted to play, if for nothing else than to erase the memory of my last FA Cup final appearance against Manchester United, when we were woeful. Yet I could sense that I was going to be left out. The usual signs were there, people like Joe Corrigan and Sammy Lee, who were great blokes, stopped looking me in the eye, and Thompson was even more negative than usual. We travelled down to the same hotel in Cardiff, and things were pretty tense around the camp. The worst thing about managers who have all those rules and regulations is that they tend to crush the life out of their squads. When there is no room for fun, then you don't really appreciate the good times as much, don't enjoy the build-up to finals as you should do. That is what it was like before the FA Cup final, most of the players were subdued when they should have been flying. I think you could see that in our performance, because apart from the last fifteen minutes or so, we didn't play at all against Arsenal.

We didn't know the team, but in my heart I knew I wasn't playing. I spoke to me dad and George and Calvey, and I tried to be upbeat because even when I know I'm not in the side I tend to hide it. Even me dad could sense I was down, and he knew I wasn't in. On the day of the game, we travelled to the Millennium Stadium early, and there were some great scenes. It was a boiling hot day, and as we approached the ground we could see our fans out on the streets having a beer, enjoying themselves and even mixing with some of the Arsenal supporters. I wasn't feeling too good about the whole day, but that gave me a bit of a lift. Until we got in the dressing room and Houllier read the team out. Up front, Michael and Emile. Bench, me. I knew I wasn't playing, but when he told me I was still gutted. Devastated. I was thinking that I was captain and I should be out there with the chance to lift that trophy.

The FA Cup, it's the stuff of dreams, isn't it? When you're a kid, you kick the ball around in the streets, and it's the World Cup, the European Cup or the FA Cup. Cup final day when we were little used to last about nine hours. They'd show the teams at their hotel in the morning, eating their bloody breakfast. The build-up was magical, the suspense mounting as they went through all those rituals, had all those stupid things on the telly like cup final *It's a Knockout*. Then they were on the coach with the players as they drove to Wembley, and on to the pitch. I always liked that bit, when the players were walking out on the pitch in what always seemed to be glorious sunshine. They'd wander around waving at their mates in the ground, soaking up the atmosphere like kings.

Yet that afternoon when I walked out on the pitch I felt nothing. I was numb. My mates later told me that they knew I wasn't playing the minute they saw me come out on the pitch to have a walk around. Apparently, my face was like death, and I looked truly gutted. I'm not sure what I was feeling, because I could barely think straight. I considered walking out for a few seconds, but that would have been stupid. And I was thinking that I needed to get myself together because I might still have a chance. It was impossible though. All I kept thinking was that I was captain and I should be out there. It was one of the worst moments of my life. When the game got under way, I sat there almost disinterested in what was going on. Except that we were getting stuffed. We didn't turn up for that match, and the only reason that Arsenal didn't have the game wrapped up by half time was that the referee didn't spot Stephane Henchoz doing his Michael Jordan impressions. I swear he knocked the ball away with his hand about twenty times. Well, at least twice.

In the end, we couldn't hold them any longer and Freddie Ljungberg scored with about twenty minutes to go. They could have had about eight by then, but when they took the lead, it was as if they settled for one. As the game was going on, I was thinking that Houllier must give me a chance because nothing was happening for us. Then the call came out to warm up, and they called the linesman over to make a substitution. This was it, this was my chance to make an impact on the FA Cup final. Fat chance. He put Gary McAllister on. I was left down one end of the stadium, warming up behind the goal. Then, suddenly, I could see Thompson waving wildly at me. So I waved back. Well, I've always been a polite person. I trotted over and I was on. There were fifteen minutes left, we hadn't had a kick in the second half, and I had the chance to help turn things around.

I'm not saying for a second that me coming on changed the result. Michael did that with two great goals, but I contributed. With eight minutes remaining we had a free kick from out on the left that Gary McAllister swung in. Markus Babbel flicked it on, and the ball was dropping to Michael, but Patrick Vieira was definitely going to get to him. So I did what any decent striker would do, and stepped in front of him to block him off. My contribution to the FA Cup final victory wasn't massive, but it was significant. I fouled Vieira to allow Michael to score. That one will go down in the Cup Final annals. Not my most positive contribution to a game ever, but afterwards Michael was pretty happy with me. From there we were a different side. It was as if Arsenal couldn't believe they could have dominated for so long, had so many off the line – I think it was about eight – and yet still be level going into the last five minutes. We scored again when Michael broke away from an Arsenal corner and finished brilliantly with his left foot. After that we had a couple more chances, and I've received a bit of stick because there were one or two moments when I could have sent Michael in again. But each time, his run was right across the defender in front of me, and there was no way I could get the ball off without it being intercepted.

When it came to the presentation, I knew I had to get my hands on that cup. Sami Hyypia had been captain on the day because I didn't start, but I was on the pitch at the end so I was entitled to pick it up. But Jamie Redknapp was the club captain, and after the terrible time he'd had that season, not playing one game through an awful knee injury, I thought it was only fair he got to pick up the FA Cup. I went to him and told him my plan, and at first he was having none of it, refused point blank. But I told Sami and the two of us eventually persuaded him. We all went up together, and for the only time in FA Cup final history three people picked up the trophy. I don't want to be all smarmy about this, but I think that was a great moment because it showed what all the lads thought of Jamie, and how respected he was around the place. I've still got a picture of that moment at home, because for me, that was the best memory of what had been a horrible day. Even so, I felt I was entitled to join in the celebrations, to go and pick up that cup, because at least I'd made a contribution, even if it had been one that few people noticed. I didn't let go like I would have done if I'd been on at the start, but I had offered something. With fifteen minutes to go we were dead and buried, but after me and Paddy Berger came on, things had changed. I could cling on to that as some consolation.

I had to over the next few days too, because we were straight off to Dortmund for the UEFA Cup final, and things looked gloomy again for me. There was a bit of a campaign in the media for my inclusion in that match, because Emo was showing signs of weariness after playing so many games that season. Michael had missed the Worthington Cup final, me the FA Cup final, and so if the manager was being true to his claims over rotation, then surely it would be Emile's turn to sit it out in Germany? The thing about Houllier, though, was that his rules only applied when it suited him. Even though the game against Arsenal showed we needed a bit of a shake-up, I wasn't confident of starting in Dortmund. In fact, I knew I'd be fucked over. We were playing Alaves, an exciting Spanish side but not a powerful one, and it was obvious we were going to try and overpower them, which meant Houllier would go long ball, and stick with Emo up front no matter how he felt.

In some ways, being left out of the UEFA Cup final wasn't as painful as the FA Cup final, and the numbness, the darkness that had engulfed me in Cardiff, didn't resurface. I was prepared for it, was almost immune to what Houllier always seemed to throw my way, and I also managed to stay positive, reckoning that if things remained pretty close then I had a chance of getting on. If I did then I would show him all right, and show the fans what I could really do. The Liverpool fans that season were incredible. In Dortmund, there must have been 40,000 of them, even though we only got about 15,000 tickets. God knows how they did it, but they were out in force for days before the final, and during the match itself I've never heard anything like it. When I was warming up on the sidelines, they chanted my name for ever, this incredible noise greeting my every step, and I felt that even if the manager didn't appreciate me, then the supporters obviously did. I took great strength from that, and when I was getting ready to go on, I had one thought in my mind – to do something for the fans. It was a weird game. We pissed it early on – Markus Babbel got a header within four minutes, Stevie G smashed one in from the right-hand side, and even though they got one back, Gary McAllister converted a penalty before half time to give us what seemed like an impregnable lead with our defence.

Javi Moreno had other ideas. He scored with a header and

then a free kick within six minutes of half time, and the game was level. If anything, they were ahead on points at that stage, and Houllier started mumbling furiously to himself on the bench, which was a very curious habit he developed during that season. I was sitting there trying to telepathically send a word for him to keep mumbling – Fowler. Not sure if it worked, but after sixty-five minutes I finally got the call for Emile, who was absolutely knackered. We got back into the game again immediately, and I just missed a header when Danny Murphy floated one into the box.

On seventy-three minutes, Murph sent one out to Gary McAllister, and he found me with a good ball as I drifted in from the left. It opened up in front of me, as I skipped past one defender, and then as another one dived in, I could see a shooting chance. I had to whip it past the defender onto my right foot, and there was space for a shot. No backlift, not much to aim at, but if I got it accurately into the corner ... It was an incredible feeling when that one went in. Many Liverpool fans voted it their goal of the season, even ahead of the Worthington Cup Final goal and the one I scored against Manchester United. I caught it just right and it curled into the corner. Even by that stage of my career, I hadn't sorted out a goal celebration, so I just ran to the Liverpool fans and screamed at them. They went ballistic, and Nicky Barmby jumped on my back, closely followed by the rest of the Liverpool bench. Houllier and Thompson were the only two who weren't going mad, but I guess they were thinking about how they could close out the game. We did that quite easily, and I was going to be the man who had won the UEFA Cup final for Liverpool, just as Michael had done in the FA Cup four days earlier. One minute left, forty seconds left. We were counting down the time when they got a corner and chipped a hopeful ball into the box. It was an easy one for Sander Westerveld, but somehow he misjudged it, Jordi Cruyff got in ahead of him, and incredibly, we had conceded a goal in the last minute in a cup final again. There must have been a conspiracy against me. I couldn't believe my eyes, and I wanted to go over to Sander and shake him by the throat. Houllier had taken Michael off before extra time, and replaced him with

Vladimir Smicer, but he still made me play behind Vladi, as an extra midfielder, even though he was a winger who didn't know how to hold the line. I almost scored anyway. I was sent through by Murph and put the ball into the net, only for it to be ruled offside. I was onside, and the goal should have stood. I know that because I've watched a video of the game recently, and was amazed that I scored another because I have no memory of it! I didn't recall that 'goal' at all, and when I saw it, I couldn't believe how unlucky I was because when the ball was played, I was level.

I had one more chance in extra time when Stevie's cross just went over my head, and then minutes later Gary McAllister sent in a free kick, which was headed into his own net by an Alaves defender. It was a bizarre moment, because the Golden Goal rule was in place for that final, and none of us quite realized we had won the game when it went in. It took quite a few seconds for it to sink in, though the sight of everyone running off the bench onto the pitch to celebrate in the middle gave it away. This time, I had made a proper contribution, a match-winning one until the final seconds of normal time, and I was determined to enjoy the moment.

You'll see pictures of me wearing various hats thrown down to the pitch by our fans, each one even more ludicrous than the one before. I had this blue cricket hat on that grandads wear, and then a pork pie hat straight out of the Specials. When we went up to get the trophy, I was last on the podium to greet Johan Cruyff, who was the guest of honour, handing out the medals. He'd criticized Houllier quite strongly for his long-ball game in the build-up to the final, and clearly wasn't a fan. When he shook my hand, he told me I was a star for the goal I scored, and then he kind of leant in and whispered: 'Don't let him drag you down, you're too good.' I assumde he meant Houllier, and to hear that from such a legend as Cruyff was a real moment for me, one that I will treasure. I had raised a European trophy, and I didn't want to let it go. When I was a boy, Emlyn Hughes had done it for Liverpool, as had Phil Thompson and Graeme Souness. Peter Reid had done it for Everton in the Cup Winners' Cup final. Now it was me. Heaven.

We didn't celebrate that win, or the cup final win, because the fixture list was so fucked up we still had a final league game to go. It was at Charlton, and we needed to win to qualify for the Champions' League. We were in a straight fight with Leeds for third place, and whoever got there got to play in the big one next season. In terms of money, it was our most important game of the season, because it meant so much to the club to be in the Champions' League for the first time. I knew what was coming – after the glory of the two finals I knew Houllier would start me at Charlton. He had to this time, after the way I'd played in Dortmund, and I didn't let him down either.

I scored twice that Saturday afternoon, 19 May 2001, one of them an overhead kick that I was proud of, and I put Liverpool into the Champions' League. Considering all I had gone through, I was happy with my contribution that afternoon. I had showed Houllier that when it came to it, he could rely on me, that I was a goal scorer when it mattered. Even after the kick in the teeth of being left out of two cup finals, I had got back up and shown my bottle, and my ability. I went away at the end of that season, after that emotional bus ride around the city of Liverpool, feeling that I was returning to my best form, that the old Robbie Fowler was on the way back. Despite all my anguish and disappointments, I went away feeling happy.

You'd have thought that after scoring in two cup finals and two semi finals to help Liverpool lift an historic treble, and after scoring the goals that got them into the Champions' League, I'd have been guaranteed a future at Anfield. I did. Houllier didn't. That summer, in June I played for England in Greece, and had what was without question my best game for my country. I was on fire that day in Athens, we won 2–0 against a very good side that went on to win the European Championships, and I got the Man of the Match award. I had played alongside Michael Owen and we struck up a really effective partnership, with me dropping in behind him to cause them a real headache throughout the game. I went back to Anfield for the start of pre-season with my confidence at the highest level it had been since Houllier arrived. I had been hurt about not starting in the two finals at the end of the 2001 season, but I reckoned that with the form I was in, and with the backing of the fans, he couldn't ignore me, especially because on the international stage I had shown Michael and I were a real partnership.

Within days of getting back I knew I had no chance under him. He'd had a press day for the new season, and some of the local reporters asked him about my performance against Greece, and how well I'd combined with Michael. He said he hadn't seen it. This was a man who claimed he watched every game in Europe, watched tapes all night long of every international game that was played, and he hadn't seen a major World Cup qualifier where three of his leading players were alongside each other, because Emo had been on the left wing as well. He also said he doubted we had played that well together, and then started questioning my work rate.

One of the press lads rang me and told me what he had said, and straight away the alarm bells were ringing again. What the fuck did I have to do to prove to him that I was worth a place? By then, deep down, I knew my number was up at Liverpool, even if I didn't want to face the truth because I couldn't bear the idea of moving away from the city. I was also told that the only reason Houllier hadn't got rid of me with the rest of the squad he inherited was because the chairman refused.

David Moores is a fantastic fella, and one of the best chairmen a club could ever wish for. I was so pleased for him when Liverpool won the Champions' League in Istanbul, because he deserves it so much for everything he has put into the club. Ask any player at Liverpool and they will tell you the same about Mr Moores, he is a lovely guy who lives for the club and has a genuine passion for the city. He has suffered so much since he took over as chairman, because the club went through a barren spell after he came in and he was desperate to bring back success to Anfield. He has taken some fearsome stick and at times I've heard it's made him quite ill with the worry of it all, but he stuck with it and took it all because he wants so much to see Liverpool getting back to the level they were in the seventies and eighties. By winning the Champions' League, he has fulfilled one of his dreams, and maybe proven a few people wrong along the way.

I've always liked and admired him, and I know that the chairman was one of my biggest supporters. I was told that he refused point blank when Houllier suggested very early on I should go, and he backed me throughout all the problems I had with the manager, and with the attacks that I suffered in the city. He spoke to me a few times and told me to keep going, told me how much of a hero I was to the fans, and how every fan – including him – was behind me and willing me to do well. He is such a relaxed, down-to-earth bloke to be a chairman of a club, and the players at Anfield loved him. When I see him now he's always brilliant, although I do tell him how much of a mistake he made in letting Houllier force me out. You can imagine he must be great to work with if you're a manager, because no one loves the club more than him, and who knows, maybe one day I'll get that pleasure . . . I still think I've got a bit of unfinished business at Anfield.

Back in the summer of 2001, I started to think my business was well and truly finished at the club. When you know the manager has a grudge against you there are two choices. Either you stick it out and hope he goes, or he gets rid of you. That's the way it is at football clubs. Looking at my position then, it was obvious my choices were limited. He'd just won a treble – thanks partly to me – so he was fire-proof and things were suddenly stacked against me. What I think happened that summer was that he also sat down and evaluated the situation, and realized that if there was ever a chance to get rid of me, then it was that season. Even if it would be an unpopular move to force me out, he knew he could get away with it then – in my view, that's what happened.

Within days of reporting back for pre-season, I'd worked out what was going on. I spoke to George and me dad, and told them that I was finished at Liverpool and we'd have to look at another club. Me dad was heartbroken, and he kept saying to me to stick it out, that I was too good to get rid of, that the fans loved me so much they'd never let it happen. But I knew that those things wouldn't come into play. George went in to speak to him, and he came out with all the usual guff about no one supporting me anymore, and George just quietly replied by asking if that were the case then why had he tried to sell me to so many clubs? That didn't go down well either.

From there it was really a question of time, and exactly how he could get me out. It was funny standing back and watching him in action, coming up with all these incredible scams just to try and put pressure on me, trying to engineer a situation where he could turn the fans against me and get rid of me. The funniest thing of all, though, was that he needn't have bothered with all that rubbish, because the one weapon that would work was quite simple. All he had to do was not play me, because that more than anything would force me out. As you know I have always hated being left out, always hated being taken off, and nothing fucks with me head more than that. If he had come to me and said that he didn't fancy me, that Emo and Michael were his first choice and Jari would play ahead of me as well, and it was better if I looked elsewhere, then I would have gone right away. There is no chance that I could have sat there drawing my wages on false pretences as fourth choice not playing. We could have sorted it in seconds.

It was so obvious it was amusing at times though. We went on a pre-season to Holland to play in the Amsterdam tournament, and the night before we played Ajax he launched into a tirade against me, saying I had picked up another injury and that I wasn't fit enough, that he couldn't afford to have a striker who was injured all the time, that he would have to go out and buy another if I was going to be so injury-prone, that I was stretching his patience, and hinting that it was all to do with my lifestyle. Thing was, there was nothing wrong with me. I had no injury (I had been injury-free for about a year) and I played the next night. In fact, I scored and was just about the only player in the team who performed, as we were totally blown away by the Dutch side. It was pathetic really, because the papers were full of this stuff about me being injured and him having to replace me, and then that very night I played. In fact, over the previous season after missing the first four matches, I'd only missed one more game with a proper injury.

It didn't stop him signing Milan Baros though. That was his next tactic. He'd gone on and on about how a top-class side needed four strikers, and how pleased he was with the blend he had now with Michael, me, Emo and Jari. So then he went out and signed a fifth striker. He also announced that at the Amsterdam tournament, as though he was trying a different tactic every day. Again, I knew what that meant, because if anyone was going to make way then it was obviously me. Houllier said Baros was one for the future and he wouldn't be joining immediately, but he was already a full Czech international at that point, and it didn't take a genius to work out what was going on.

After the incident the previous Christmas where I was the totally innocent victim of a violent attack, I had kept my head down, kept my side of the bargain. In the summer I thought I was entitled to a bit of respect for what I had achieved, despite having it rammed down my throat that I wasn't first choice. Houllier never gave me any respect. One day right at the end of the summer, I got a message on my mobile from Gary McAllister that really puzzled me, because I didn't have a clue what he was going on about. He was gibbering on about Liverpool, and he said, 'The gaffer wants to know whether you are coming or not. Can you ring him?' Coming where? For what? I rang Gary, who was a great fella who had a couple of brilliant seasons with Liverpool, and asked him what the fuck he was going on about. He was dead embarrassed, didn't know what to say, and started muttering an apology. I told him he'd lost me completely, and I didn't have a clue what he was saying. He said, all embarrassed: 'Robbie, I'm really sorry. I rang you by mistake and left that message. It should have been for Robbie Keane at Leeds. Houllier had got me to ring him to talk to him about Liverpool. I was told to ring him up and try and find out whether he was coming or not, because he was delaying things.' Apparently Robbie and Gary had played together at Coventry and they were mates, and Liverpool had used that link.

It made me laugh when all that stuff about Chelsea tapping up Ashley Cole came out, because every club does it all the time. Gary McAllister's approach to Keano is typical of how it happens. There is always someone at a club who knows someone connected to the player that they are interested in, and they make secret contact, sound him out, and if he's interested they then work out a plan of how to get him out of the club he currently plays for. Deals can be done, wages agreed, stories leaked to the press and pressure put on before a club has any idea that their player is on his way somewhere else. They can even agree that the player will kick up a fuss to keep the price down. The only surprise with Chelsea is that they were so stupid to do it in public with Cole. Why the hell did they need to do that, when he's friends with half the Chelsea players and staff anyway? We used to do it on England duty on behalf of Roy Evans – sound out players he might be interested in and try to sell the club. It goes on all the time and is impossible to stop. It seems illogical and arbitrary to try and enforce a rule that 99.9 per cent of clubs can get around with ease. In fact, it would be 100 per cent if stupidity or recklessness didn't sometimes take over.

Keano was a Liverpool fan as a kid, and was interested, but in the end he wanted to stay at Leeds because he thought he'd moved around too much after playing at Coventry, Inter Milan and then Leeds in the space of a couple of years. He turned them down, but it confirmed how sneaky Houllier was. He'd told me that he wasn't interested in bringing in another striker, that he would give me a fair chance to make a stake for the first team, and there was nothing in the rumours about Robbie Keane. I'd rewarded him with some important goals, and that was how he showed his gratitude. The same had happened before Emile Heskey arrived at Anfield. The *Daily Mirror* had done an exclusive saying he was coming, and had even revealed details of his contract. I went in to see Houllier to find out where I stood, and he told me it was rubbish, there was nothing in the story at all. Two days later he had signed. You had to laugh.

The funniest thing I ever heard was when he was sacked by Liverpool. Again the *Mirror* did the exclusive, saying he was about to be axed, and they even named his successor, Rafael Benitez. But he went into work the next day, and when everyone rang up, he said it wasn't true, he was going nowhere, it was rubbish. That was on the Tuesday, and it wasn't until the Thursday that he finally got around to admitting that he was, in fact, sacked. I've heard stories from some of the staff at Melwood that weeks after he was sacked he kept ringing up the press office, asking what was happening, what was in the papers – which was an obsession of his – and when they said nothing, he said in that case they could take the afternoon off.

There is a funny story of him ringing Rick Parry's secretary up, demanding to know why his company credit card had been stopped, to be told that he had ceased being an employee of the club weeks ago. I don't know if it is true, but there are a lot of people at Anfield who would like it to be, because believe me, he wasn't popular with the staff at the club, never mind the players.

One of the worst things he did was to the lovely dinner ladies at Melwood, Paula and Anne. Everybody loved them when I was at Liverpool, they used to really look after us and pamper all the players, cooking us our special dishes. Houllier treated them terribly though. One Christmas, we were all in as usual for training and he made Paula and Anne come in for him, give up their own family celebrations so that they could cook Christmas dinner for Houllier and his family, who he'd invited to the training ground for their meal. So he had a nice family day at Melwood, enjoying a slap-up Christmas dinner, while the kitchen staff had to sacrifice their day with their family. Even the players were outraged by that one, because it was a really unkind thing to do, especially on that day of all days.

What happened just before the start of the season confirmed all my worst fears, and again it was almost comic it was so contrived. It was just before the Charity Shield against Manchester United on 12 August. We'd already played a Champions' League qualifier on the Wednesday against FC Haka of Finland, and, surprise, surprise, I was on the bench again. What was an even bigger surprise was the fact that Houllier told me after that game I would definitely be playing against United at the Millennium Stadium in Cardiff. He rarely told us who was playing, and we had to work it out ourselves, so I was taken aback when I was told I was in. The day before we were due to head down to Wales, we were training as usual at Melwood, and I was practising my shooting, firing balls into an empty net. As I was doing it, Phil Thompson tripped over to stand behind the goal. As I shot, the net billowed out a bit, and the ball went near him. It couldn't have hit him, because there was a net in the way, and I would have had to have a radioactive shot to burn the net away to actually get the ball through to him. But in typical fashion, he took off. He started screaming that the ball could have hit him. He was giving me down the banks in front of all the players, and I just told him to fuck off and stop being a baby, because the ball couldn't have hit him even if I'd wanted it to. He went into an even bigger rage, and then he came out with all the stuff that they were clearly saying behind my back.

Thompson said that I'd been at Liverpool too long, that was my problem. Now what kind of comment was that from a man who had served Liverpool for so long, and wanted to stay at the club all his life? He ranted on a bit more, and I just said that only at Liverpool under him and Houllier could they get annoyed about strikers practising shooting at goal. He stormed off, all the lads had a right laugh, and we forgot about it. Until the day of the Charity Shield.

I knew I was playing and I would be captain, and on the way down it was a far happier journey than the last time I went to Cardiff. Thompson blanked me a bit, but that apart nothing was said. Then, on the day of the game, Houllier hit me with an incredible bombshell. He hadn't even been at the training session where I'd had the row with Thompson, and he hadn't said anything at all about it. But just a couple of hours before the kick-off, after we got to the stadium, he said I wasn't playing. He said I wasn't even on the bench. No explanation, no apology because he'd already told me I was playing, just kicked out of the team and not even involved. I was amazed, just astounded that they could do it like that, and wondering why the fuck it had happened. I never imagined for a second that a training-ground spat that was straight from the play-ground could be behind it.

I found out it was, though, on the Monday. Houllier called me into his office, and told me that I was dropped because I had been rude to Thompson, adding that I wouldn't play again until I apologized. This was a multi-million-pound business based on the playing talent available, and they were excluding the captain from playing because he had kicked a ball into a net and it had billowed out a bit when someone was standing within a few metres of it. How fucking stupid is that? It's a disgrace really, and I can't believe that the board allowed the manager to behave like that. I suppose they had no choice, because he had been so successful the previous season, but that was a criminal waste of resources they surely should not have tolerated . . . unless there was an underlying motivation they were aware of.

Houllier said I needed to apologize, and I said I didn't feel any need to. I asked him exactly what I was supposed to apologize for. He said Thompson had claimed I had tried to hit him deliberately, the big fucking girl. How could I have tried to hit him deliberately, there was a net in the bleeding way? The only way I could deliberately have tried to hit him was if I had kicked a pair of scissors at the net first, to make a hole for the ball to go through. Even Houllier had to suppress a little smile about that one, because he knew as much as me that this was all a big sham. I went away thinking what a bunch of wankers they all were, and for the life of me I couldn't understand why they didn't just come straight out and say that it was their ball, and they didn't want me to play any more. But even if they had the ball, they didn't have the balls to front up to the fans and tell them they wanted me out. So we had to do this stupid fucking dance where all of us knew it was bollocks.

The most stupid thing of all was that I didn't play any football of any sort for two weeks, and I missed the opening game of the season as well as the Charity Shield. Things got worse, because Houllier obviously decided his plan was going well, and he was a master of media manipulation. He called a meeting between me and Thompson, saying that we had to get it all sorted out, and I said fair enough. When I got to the training ground, instead of going into the manager's office, where Houllier always held meetings of any sort (especially discipline), he led me out to the middle of the training pitch. Then Thompson came out and stood there mumbling away for a bit. Suddenly, he threw his arms into the air for no reason, and I was thinking this was a strange fucking do. The next day, there was a picture in all the newspapers of me standing there looking sullen, while Thompson apparently pleaded with me.

The story was pretty easy for the tabloids to write ... I was being pig-headed when the management were trying their best to sort it all out. Jamie Redknapp came in pissing himself laughing, saying that I'd been caught in a sting. He went through it with all the lads and they said the same thing: the manager just by chance happens to call a meeting not in his office, but for the first time ever in the middle of the training pitch, and just by chance there happens to be a photographer waiting with some step-ladders to snatch a picture over the twenty-foot-high training-ground wall. You couldn't make it up.

I made an apology – of sorts – after George came down and told them what a right load of tossers they were looking. I said I was sorry for kicking a ball near to Phil Thompson, even if there was no way it could ever have hit him. He accepted my apology with a smile like he had won the lottery, the wrong 'un. They put me back in the side for the return game against FC Haka, where I scored, but I was dropped again for the Super Cup final in Monaco against Bayern Munich. In a way I wasn't too bothered about that – although I was always gutted to be left out of any match – because it was a Mickey Mouse game where the Germans played their sixth team, but Houllier seemed to take it seriously enough, and later claimed it was one of five cups he won in a year. What was the other, the Arkles Dominos Cup?! The Charity Shield doesn't really count, does it? He actually brought me back for two matches after that, but it was as though he only ever played me when we had a really weakened team out, so as to make me look particularly bad.

There were several things that made it even more ludicrous. He came out and said he would have to sell me if I didn't sign a new contract. I was the only one he was faintly bothered about being near the end of their contract, even though there were about seven players at the club who had less time to go than me. Michael Owen had less time than me, and he was dragging his heels over a new deal, yet Houllier never once said that he would have to be sold if he didn't sign. Even more funny was the fact that they never once came to me offering a new contract. All that time Houllier was banging on about me not signing a new deal, I was never, ever offered one. He singled me out from the summer of 2001, and it was on the agenda until I left at the end of November, and yet in all that time, nothing was put on the table, nothing was said to me, and nothing was ever discussed with George. The only contact we ever had was a conversation between Rick Parry and George to discuss a meeting. Every time we mentioned that the lack of an offer for us to even consider was a tiny flaw in Houllier's argument, the club would say that they wanted to get Michael's deal out of the way first. They could have spoken to me that summer of 2001 about a new deal, after I had led the club as stand-in skipper to an historic treble. Instead, they were happy not to even broach the subject and let me get down to eighteen months and counting . . . presumably because they never had any intention of renewing.

When I did leave to join Leeds, Thompson even had the audacity to raise that as an excuse for selling me, and early the next year Houllier spoke at the AGM at Anfield and said the time was right to sell me because I was getting too near to the end of my contract. You've got to hand it to him, that is some nerve. The funny thing is, Houllier never once mentioned that contract stance of his again, even when he later allowed Michael to get down to within less than a year of the end of his contract. Because of that, Real Madrid were able to come in and steal him for less than £8 million, which considering that he was a former European Footballer of the Year and the current England centre forward, was a pathetic amount of money. The only reason that Madrid were able to rob Liverpool like that, the only reason that Liverpool were cheated in the transfer market, was because Houllier had allowed the contract to get dangerously near to running out. That meant Michael could become a free agent, and Madrid could dictate the price. All this when the manager had said he would never allow the situation to arise again.

You know when your number's up, and I was looking around at my options, wondering where I would go, when the inevitable happened. By the end of September, I'd started just three matches, which was fucking stupid considering my record the previous season. I've said before, I understand perfectly that there is no sentiment in football, and when the manager wants you out, you've got no chance unless he goes first. It was just the manner in which he did it that upset me, and still upsets me now. After all I had done for the club, after the service I had offered as a young striker, and as captain, I thought I was entitled to at least a little respect. I was kidding myself though. Steve Staunton was a fabulous servant to the club who had been there since the Kenny Dalglish glory days, and he was treated like a dog who needed to be kicked by Houllier. So was Paul Ince, when he had given everything for the club during his time at Anfield. Sander Westerveld was given the same treatment just months after he turned in a fantastic clean-sheet record during the treble season. And I was no different. I had to go, and the question was, when? For me that was important, because the summer of 2002 was World Cup year, and after missing France 1998 I didn't want to miss out on another.

I had become established alongside Michael as the front-line pairing for England, and yet with Houllier not playing me I was fast slipping out of contention again. I had played three games on the bounce over that summer for my country, but was on the bench for the game in Germany that really mattered at the beginning of September, because Houllier had refused to pick me at the start of the season. I sometimes wonder whether Houllier had left me out at the start of the campaign, just so I wouldn't feature for England and give him even more problems. Four days after we beat Germany 5–1 in Munich, I did get on against Albania and scored one of my best-ever goals for England. But Eriksson spoke to me afterwards and said it was hard for him to pick me when I wasn't playing regularly for my club. He said that I should have been first choice, but I would seriously have to look at my position at Anfield if I was going to start regularly for England.

There was an offer on the table from Chelsea still, and there was also talk of interest from Manchester United and Arsenal. George investigated both of those, but the answer was that while the managers admired me, they didn't think the time was right. I just wasn't sure about Chelsea. Everyone in the game knew they were broke, and while they had some great players and they were a glamorous club, there was a real chance it could all fall apart. As it was the only offer on the table though, I was left seriously considering it. Out of the blue, Houllier put me in against Newcastle when we played well and won. Then he put me in again against Leeds. That turned out to be a momentous day in Anfield history. It was Saturday 13 October 2001, and it was the day that Houllier almost died. David O'Leary told me later that when he arrived at Anfield that day with his Leeds team, he took one look at Houllier and thought something was seriously wrong. The two were friends and he even commented on it, and Houllier admitted to him that he felt terrible, and had done for a couple of months. O'Leary, apparently, had wanted to sneak in a few questions about me, and my situation at the club, because it looked from the outside like I would be on my way. But when he saw Houllier, his only thought was for our manager's welfare. How right he was.

It was an unremarkable game. We were a bit sluggish, I struggled in the first half because it was only my second start in about a month, and I was only playing because Michael was injured. Leeds scored before the break, and Emile was limping around, so everyone was looking to get into the dressing room at half time to shake things up. Houllier told Jari Litmanen to go and warm up because he would be replacing Emile, and then he gave us a team talk. I look back now, and it was unusually short for him, only a few seconds before he let Thompson take over to give it the old 'c'mon, lads, c'mon' pub football stuff that he specialized in. While he was talking, Houllier slipped out with the club doctor, Mark Waller – who is an absolute legend for all the help he gives you; nothing is too much for him – because he was feeling a bit faint and sweating a lot, but none of us noticed it because we were going through the changes and Tommo was giving his speech. When we went out on the pitch after the interval, not one of us knew what had happened.

It was funny, because a couple of times during the second half I glanced at the bench and didn't see the manager. He used to stand there quite a lot in the technical area, watching the game without saying anything, but it never crossed my mind to wonder where he was. In the second half of that game I was pushed further forward when Jari came on, and I played really well. I beat a couple of players on the edge of their box and chipped the keeper. It glanced down onto the line off the cross bar, and Danny Murphy headed it into an empty net. My first instinct, after celebrating the goal, was to wheel around to the bench to have a look at Houllier and see how he felt about me making the equalizer with a decent bit of skill. But again, I couldn't locate him.

It was only when we got into the dressing room afterwards that we discovered the truth. I was quite keen to get in there to hear what Houllier had to say about my performance, because I thought I had done all right. When we got in the dressing room, Thompson was deep in conversation with the physio, Dave Galley. Then he called us together and told us, in a grave voice, that the manager had been rushed into Broadgreen Hospital suffering with chest pains. No one knew at that time what the problem was, but everyone was assuming it was his heart. It was a sickening moment, because nobody had any information, and nobody knew how serious it was. Emile had been treated by the physios in their room at half time, and Houllier was taken in there. He saw how bad it was, and he told us all about it. Everyone was in a state of shock, and we all feared the worst because of what Emile had seen. Then people started giving their diagnoses, saying that if it was a heart attack the next twenty-four hours would be critical, and that the manager wouldn't be able to come back to work for months, if at all.

It was a crazy time, with everyone offering an opinion, and with the press clamouring outside in the corridor to speak to us about what had happened. Gary McAllister was detailed to go out and express our shock and sadness, and Tommo went down to the hospital to find out the latest. We were due to assemble at Speke Airport the next day, to fly out to Kiev for a

Champions' League game, and they said we would be told then exactly what was going on. I heard stuff on the news that night, and in the morning O'Leary was on the telly being pictured on the steps of the hospital in Liverpool, after visiting. He said that Houllier had undergone a massive operation on his heart, but that he had come through it. Then we were at the training ground, being briefed by Tommo on what had happened, and warned not to say anything more in the press. He told us the manager had suffered an acute dissection of the aorta, which meant nothing to me except that it wasn't a heart attack.

Apparently, the main artery that carries the blood from the heart had split, and it was leaking. He had just hours to live before they did the operation, and they had to put him into a coma to carry it out. There was no guarantee that he would survive the op, and because they had to stop the blood-flow to his brain, there was a chance of brain damage.

The operation took eleven hours, and that morning of the 14th, they rang Rick Parry and Tommo to tell them that it had been a success, and the manager had come through it all right. At that stage, though, as we flew out to Kiev, there was no knowing what condition he would be in after he was brought out of the coma, and that wouldn't be for another few days. There was relief that he had survived, but still confusion over whether he would be able to continue, and how long before he would be back. Parry told us that it would be three months, that he should be back after Christmas, but there was no way of telling for sure. There was talk even at the airport of Kenny Dalglish being brought in to take temporary charge until Houllier was fit to continue.

For me, it was a difficult time. I had spent days and months agonizing about my future because the manager was trying to force me out, and now he was struck down with a terrible illness. Like everyone else in the squad, I was really sad and worried for him and his family, and I felt genuine sympathy. But at the same time, I couldn't help but think about my situation. Who would be in charge until he came back, and did that mean I would be given a fairer chance? Parry had said that

Tommo and Sammy Lee would be in charge for the time being, but it seemed that Thompson was the one pushing himself forward, doing all the press interviews and acting like he was the boss. If that was the case, then it wasn't much use to me, because he clearly had the agenda against me like Houllier. We beat Kiev well, and everyone went out there wanting to do it for Houllier, me as much as anyone. But I was on the bench again despite playing well against Leeds and Michael being injured, and any thoughts I had that I would have to reconsider my position evaporated on the long flight back from the Ukraine.

The next game up was at Leicester, and Thompson pinned a note up in the dressing room that said simply: 'Do it for the boss.' So I did. I got a hat-trick. By then, Houllier was already ringing players to congratulate them or just talk to them, but I never got a phone call after I scored a hat-trick for him. All I got was the axe. I must be the only player in history who has scored a treble and then got dropped for the next game. I scored against Leicester and the fans were going mad, and yet for the next Premiership match at Charlton I was on the bench again, as I was for the next three matches too. It was clear by then that nobody was coming in to take charge, and that Houllier was picking the team by phone, relaying messages to Thompson.

I didn't play. We had massive games against Manchester United and Barcelona, and even though I'd done really well against Leicester and at Boavista in the Champions' League, I didn't get a look-in, so it was clear Thompson was just going to carry on with the same policy. We played Barca at Anfield, and they stuffed us out of sight, playing some incredible football that made us look stupid. We were getting hammered by three goals when the call finally came for me to warm up, and Tommo asked me to go on and change the game. Thanks for that! We were playing a team that had their own ball they were keeping that much possession, and he wanted me to turn things around. So I went on, and as I ran past Frank De Boer, I shouted out, 'Hey, mister, can we have a kick of your ball please?!' It made both of us laugh, but I'm not sure Tommo was too amused.

I'd really had enough, and I was considering the Chelsea option again. I had a family to consider by then, and moving to London seemed a big move. There didn't seem to be too much interest from elsewhere, and I was in a real dilemma about what to do. So I asked a friend who was a journalist to have a ring round to see what he could find out. I was particularly intrigued by what was happening at Leeds, because they had a fine young manager in David O'Leary, and a brilliant young side that seemed to be stacked full of British players. I reckoned they were really up and coming and could be the side of the future, and I liked the football they played. At Anfield it was sterile stuff really, all safety first and long balls, with the strikers doing most of their work defensively, and hardly getting any chances.

Leeds were so much more exciting and exhilarating, and to me they seemed an almost exotic prospect in comparison to Liverpool. My mate knew one of the directors there, a guy called David Walker who was in charge of communications at Elland Road, and who used to be a journalist. He was great. He went to O'Leary and discussed it, then went to Peter Ridsdale, the Leeds chairman, and told him I was available. They spent about a week working it all out to see if they could afford me, and from there things happened pretty quickly. In hindsight, though, maybe what happened over the course of that transfer should have got the alarm bells ringing a little, because throughout my deal Leeds didn't really seem to pursue sound business practice.

Ridsdale contacted Liverpool and asked if I was available. I reckon Rick Parry spat his coffee out when he got that call. I bet he couldn't have agreed quickly enough. The call went in to Houllier, who was convalescing in France, and he immediately sanctioned the deal. He probably immediately sanctioned a fucking great party as well. But the fee was a different matter. Leeds were prepared to pay £8 million, and I thought that was plenty considering that Houllier had failed to offer me a new deal and I only had eighteen months left on my contract.

In fact, George reckoned Leeds should have screwed Liverpool into the ground, given that they were desperate to get rid of me and my time was running down. Every week that went by was just wasted money and time at Anfield, and in the end I believe they would have cracked and let me go for whatever Ridsdale was proposing. Incredibly, though, he allowed the fee to rise and rise until it got to £12 million. George was livid. He told Ridsdale to tell Liverpool to go fuck themselves, and he wanted nothing more to do with it. O'Leary said exactly the same. What happened next perhaps suggests why Leeds got into such a state financially. Instead of following George's advice, and then planning a strategy to put pressure on the board at Anfield to allow me to leave for the right price, Ridsdale instead appointed an agent to negotiate on his behalf with Liverpool. So the agent got paid for doing a deal that was already done, and which both parties were desperate to complete. And instead of getting the price down, it actually went up. In the end, it was £12 million plus loads of add-ons if Leeds did well in the Premiership and in Europe. If they'd have been a bit tougher in the transfer market, then they could have got me for half that. It was crazy, and maybe typical of what was going on at Elland Road around that time.

All that went on while I sat on the bench at Anfield, wondering whether I was doing the right thing. Being stuffed by Barca showed that maybe we weren't as good a team as people thought, and then the next match confirmed everything about Liverpool for me, and why I had to leave Anfield even though I loved the club and the city. It was to be my final game for the club. We played Sunderland at home on 25 November, and I started even though Michael had returned to the side. That was unusual, but at least it gave me the chance to captain Liverpool for one last time. It was an uneventful enough game, we scored early to take the lead, but then, just before half time, Didi Hamann got himself sent off. Trudging to the dressing room for the interval, I knew exactly what was coming next. Sure enough, Thompson starts blathering on about changing the style, strengthening the midfield, showing resilience . . . and of course taking me off to bring on an extra midfielder. So my epitaph at Anfield was to be sacrificed at half time to strengthen the midfield and go all defensive. Kind of sums up my time under Houllier.

If there were any lingering doubts, then they disappeared that wet afternoon as autumn turned into winter in the back end of 2001. No matter what I did, how hard I tried and how well I played, I was always going to be the fall guy under Jekyll and Hyde, and there was no escaping it. I went home that night and rang George, and asked him what the fuck was holding up the move. The next couple of days, with Leeds going mad and Ridsdale chomping at the bit to tell everyone what a great coup he had pulled off, there was a snag holding up the deal. No one could get hold of Parry. Apparently, he had taken himself away to some lonely retreat in Wales somewhere without a phone, and his mobile didn't work in the mountains, so there was no contacting him. Probably didn't have enough ten-pence pieces for the call box either. By Tuesday it was finally sorted, and I was given permission to travel over for talks with Leeds. I was driven over there by a mate who had this knackered old Montego Estate that was falling to bits. Even Ridsdale did a double-take when he saw that one. My mate picked up me and me dad in Liverpool, and we went to the chairman's flat in the centre of Leeds. As we arrived, the first person we bumped into was Dom Matteo, who was a little surprised to see me. 'Fuck me, I've travelled two hundred miles to get away from you, what the fuck are you doing here?' I told him I'd come to sign, and he said he'd better dust down his tin hat because the bullets were about to start flying again. Cheeky bastard. I met Ridsdale and David Walker, and also the agent who made so much money out of the deal, even though I'd never clapped eyes on him before. George went away into a side room with Ridsdale and twenty minutes later they emerged shaking hands, the deal done. They gave me a four-year contract and I was a Leeds player, subject to a medical.

And subject to surviving the journey home. My move to Leeds almost didn't go through because we were inches away from a major pile-up on the M62 on the way back to Liverpool that night. It was pissing down, and the old Montego wasn't very good in the wet. I was sitting in the back and you couldn't see a fucking thing because it was so misted up. Suddenly this car in front brakes, swerves and goes into a spin. It did two laps of the lane in front of us before smashing into the crash barrier. Me mate stepped onto the brakes but they weren't exactly modern and we just kept going forward towards the car. Then we went into a bit of a skid ourselves. We were skidding closer and closer to the car right in front of us, and my life flashed before me at that moment. All of us in the car were gulping and bracing ourselves, but just as we thought we'd better start saying our prayers, the brakes kicked in and we slowed, stopping about two inches from the car. The car behind us went through the same routine and missed us by inches, and the one behind had a bit of a skid too. It caused a massive traffic jam and even got onto the radio traffic reports. We had to get out and push the car in front onto the hard shoulder, because it had bounced right out into the lane in front of us. Its wheels were at right angles, and we couldn't get it off the motorway for ages. It was comical, because everyone was doing a double-take as an England footballer got out of this old banger and tried to push another old banger onto the hard shoulder, with the people he was with standing around pissing themselves at the sight of it.

The next day we went back in a slightly newer model of car, and there was a bit of concern about the medical because of the injuries that I'd had in the previous four years. But I sailed through. The physio there at Leeds was a fantastic guy called Dave Hancock and he gave me a real going over. I did all the fitness tests over two days, all the cardio-vascular stuff to see how fit you are, and at the end of it he said the only person at Leeds who had ever done better was Lee Bowyer, and he was a freak of nature! So that was it. On the Friday they had a press conference where I was unveiled. After fifteen years at Anfield, after that journey from Toxteth to Anfield Road, I was on the move once more. I was a Leeds United player. At the press conference the questions were obviously about Houllier and our relationship. I didn't want to sound bitter because there's nothing worse than a player leaving a club and then slagging them off straight away, so I glossed over most of it. It hurt though, to have been treated in that way, and it hurt more when I heard some of the things that Thompson had said. At the press conference Liverpool held, he tried to make out that they didn't want me to go, that they tried to keep me but I insisted, and the only reason they relented was because I had so little left on my contract. Apparently, all the assembled media people just burst out laughing when he said that.

After the press call at the Leeds training ground, I was driving home to get my gear and sort out a few things when I got a text message from a photographer I know called Bradley Ormesher, who does all the football stuff in the north of England. It just said, 'You looked so lost there at Leeds, and so out of place in a white shirt.' I knew exactly what he meant. After so long at Liverpool, the club where I believed I belonged, I was like a lost soul in those first few days with my new club. I was thinking, What have I done letting Houllier beat me like that? But then, when the games start, you just get on with it. And I can honestly say that for all the problems that arose at Elland Road, for all the mess the club was in, the year I had there was one of the most enjoyable of my career.

TAKE THE MONEY AND RUN, SON (13)

Sometimes, your life turns on one decision. It might be fate, but I don't really believe in that. Or I didn't until I saw Liverpool win the Champions' League in Istanbul. If it wasn't fate that took me to Leeds, then it was a simple decision-making process that ruled out the other options available. Those options were pretty simple really. Either I stayed at Liverpool and endured yet more torture under a bullet-proof Houllier or I moved on. No contest. I had to go. So where? Again it was a simple choice: Leeds or Chelsea. Look at what happened to the two clubs over the next few years, and it would be pretty easy to say I fucked up, to put it mildly. With Roman Abramovich's money, Chelsea became the richest club in the world, buying whichever player they fancied, and their dominance of English football was virtually guaranteed. Leeds, on the other hand, became a pub team. In the space of little over a year, they went from being the next great team in the Premiership, to being a side that were doomed to relegation. It was a pretty rotten choice on my part then.

The thing was, at the time it was Chelsea who looked doomed. Everyone in football knew about their debts, and towards the end of 2001 everyone in football was holding their breath, waiting for the big crash. George took some soundings and it was clear they didn't have a pot to piss in. There was a real feeling that they could be the biggest club ever to go under, that they would go bust, and their creditors would use their prime stadium location to recover the debts. Going to Chelsea would have been a massive gamble at that time, and Leeds seemed the much safer option. After all that has happened at Elland Road, it is hard to imagine even whispering that sentence today, but that really is how it was back in November 2001. I don't think it was fate that took me away from Stamford Bridge to Leeds, but sheer bad luck. And a bit of fantasizing from Peter Ridsdale.

He persuaded me to go to Leeds when really, they were in a terrible mess already. More of a financial mess than even Chelsea were. I've since discovered that the club was in the shit and massively in debt long before I arrived there. The warning signs were there the previous summer, in fact, because after a great couple of seasons when they had got in the Champions' League and then got to the semi finals, they didn't buy anyone. It was all there for them to kick on and dominate English football with a fabulous young side, but they didn't, because they were broke. More than broke. Piecing it all together since, it seems obvious to me that by November when I suddenly came on the market, Ridsdale was willing to gamble to stave off what became inevitable. If I came in and scored the goals Leeds were lacking, then they might just win the Premiership, and that might just have got them out of the shit. So Ridsdale spent money the club could not afford on me and Seth Johnson, closed his eyes and crossed his fingers.

Of course, there was no hint of that situation when I signed. After going to the chairman's flat, we went on to a hotel in the centre of Leeds to meet some of the directors of the club, and as we sat around chatting away, they painted this incredible picture of financial strength and exciting prospects. They told me a deal had already been done to build a new 70,000-seater stadium, and the money was virtually in place. They said that would generate all the funds the manager needed to allow the club to dominate English football for years. They said I was just the start of even more spending, that Leeds would be a force that even Manchester United couldn't reckon with. They pointed to brilliant young players like Rio Ferdinand, Alan

Smith, Harry Kewell, Jonathan Woodgate, Lee Bowyer, Dom Matteo, Mark Viduka, Erik Bakke, Danny Mills, Seth, me and Paul Robinson, and said it was the basis of a side that could take on Europe.

It was a heady, intoxicating image, and everything tallied up. The board were as excited as me, and it was only later that I was told not all of them knew the full picture. Ridsdale was in a position to know – obviously should have known – and if he did, he did a number on me. And he did it big time. There was no way of knowing any of that when I joined, and no way I could have even guessed something was wrong. I was just unlucky, because if I'd joined Chelsea, then who knows? I might have been there when Abramovich saved them, and took them to places none of their players ever imagined. It didn't happen because if Ridsdale was anything, then he was plausible. He might have liked the sound of his own voice a bit much, but I have got nothing against him. What he did, he did because of his love for the club, and his desire to see them succeed. He's a nice enough fella, if not a brilliant businessman. And even after all this, it's hard for me not to like him.

It's tough to know where to start when telling the story of my one year at Leeds, because so much happened in that time. But I think the manager is the best place to begin. David O'Leary has received plenty of stick for the way he handled the team, and there were loads of stories around about massive dissent in the dressing room and fights with the players, but it just didn't happen. Most of the players liked him and respected him. You always get some mutterings in the dressing room from those who are not playing, that's normal, and it happened at Elland Road when I was there. But the gaffer was very popular within the dressing room. I liked him, and I don't have a bad word to say about him. He was good to me, he helped me and in the short time I worked for him I could see he was a very, very good manager. I know nearly all the rest of the lads in the squad felt the same way.

A week after I arrived, the trial of Woody and Lee Bowyer ended. Jonathan Woodgate was found guilty of affray, and given 100 hours of community service, and Lee was found not guilty on all counts. It was a relief, and the manager said to everyone that they should look forward, not back, and not go over old ground. Only trouble was, a book he had written about Leeds during the time of that trial, and the time of the Champions' League run when the team got to the semi final, was serialized in the *News of the World*. He also had a weekly column in the *Sunday People*, and he was honour-bound to talk about the end of the trial in that. People made a huge deal about that book, which he wrote in conjunction with David Walker, our communications director. A lot of people said it really pissed all the players off, that they were told not to rake all that stuff up again, and then the manager made money out of writing about it. But here's the truth: in all the time I was at Leeds, I never once heard any player even mention the gaffer's book, or his newspaper column. Nobody was pissed off.

If you know anything about a dressing room, then something like that would never have an effect on players' performance, or the level of the team. Day to day, we are interested in the racing results, each other's latest haircut or fashion disaster, any new cars or any new girlfriends, and how well or badly we are doing on the training ground or on the pitch on a Saturday. If you listen to the media, then we must be sensitive lambs who are affected by the slightest nuance of politics or intrigue. But at clubs like Liverpool and Leeds, there is always rumour and comment, always someone saying something, and you become immune to it. A manager saying don't talk about something and then talking about it himself, not one of the players will give a monkey's about that. They might get pissed off if he tries to force them out or if he bare-faced lies to them. It might affect the team as a whole if one of the lads is treated really diabolically or if the manager acts particularly ruthlessly, but even then, it will only be for a few days or so. I reckon hardly any of the players even read that book, probably not one of them. We read a few lines in the newspapers about it, but it was pretty boring really, just saying no one was to blame and we all pulled together. No one was even interested in it, never mind getting steamed up about it.

O'Leary was also criticized heavily because he was supposed to have lost the dressing room with his lack of discipline, and his constant criticism of the players. Which one was it? Too much discipline or not enough? Yeah sure, he might have had a go at a couple of us from time to time, but players aren't daft about football. We might be pretty stupid in other areas, but believe me, deep down we know when we're crap, even if we might try to hide it, or blame someone else. If you're crap then the manager knows it and you know it, and if he says anything about it, then fine, he's entitled to. You just hold your hand up and try to do better. As for a lack of discipline, that was bollocks too. Apparently, we were outraged when he didn't fine Robbie Keane for mouthing a few swear words at the gaffer after he substituted him. Do me a favour.

Something like that, it happens every single week. If you're taken off, you're gutted, and it's a working-class sport, so people swear. Jesus, if everyone was fined every time we swore, we'd all be fucking broke. I can assure you that players just think something like that is funny. O'Leary was also criticized because apparently he upset the players when Danny Mills gave him a bit of a barrage during training, and he didn't fine Millsy. Rubbish again. We were all killing ourselves. It's hilarious when a player loses it in training and has a bit of a go. We all give him stick about it for weeks afterwards. The boss could be tough when he wanted to be, but by and large he was pretty relaxed, which created a great atmosphere at the training ground, and around the team. Most players love that, they prefer to be treated like adults, they want to enjoy their work, just like anyone else doing their jobs. Our training was good, we had great coaches in Brian Kidd and Eddie Gray, and it was always interesting and varied. For me, it was a damn sight better than under Houllier, because there was a bit of enjoyment around the club and we weren't treated like kids. There weren't a thousand rules that said 'thou shalt not laugh'. There was just a mentality that said we were professionals, and we acted like it.

O'Leary got sacked because he stopped getting on with Peter Ridsdale, I'm sure about that. There was stuff put out about him losing the dressing room to try and justify the sacking, but that was just a bit of PR flannel as far as I'm concerned. There was no dressing-room rebellion, hardly anyone was against the manager amongst the lads and most of them were right behind him. When he was sacked at the end of the 2001–02 season, I rang up a mate of mine on the newspapers and asked him to write a story saying how shocked I was and how unfair all the players thought it was. We finished fifth that season, even after all the problems we had, qualified for the UEFA Cup and we still had a fantastic team full of very young full internationals. It was a team that could have gone on from there to much greater things, if it had been kept together under David O'Leary, but the club was in so much financial trouble there was no chance of that. I get asked all the time what happened at Leeds, how it all managed to fall apart there, and for me, the reason is the same one that got the manager the sack. The club was going bust, and there had to be a scapegoat. He was that scapegoat.

O'Leary didn't like what was going on, and apart from Ridsdale himself, probably the manager was the only other one who realized there were financial problems. He must have realized that it was all going tits up at Elland Road, and he just tried to put his finger in the dam. When he stood out against selling all the players, kicked up a bit of a fuss and asked a few questions so it threw the spotlight on what Ridsdale was doing, he was moved aside, and someone was brought in who would agree to the plan, and put the best gloss on it. That was it, as simple as that. The club was falling apart, and the chairman wanted someone around who would try to make it look less disastrous than it was. But believe me, it was a fucking mess.

I arrived at the start of December for a fee of £12 million. We also signed Seth Johnson for £8 million. So the chairman spent £20 million before Christmas, saying that the club was going places, was the next major force in English football. By the start of January, we were top of the Premiership, and yet by the end of that month, the chairman was warning that we would have to sell at least £30 millionworth of players to reduce the debt and balance the budget at the end of the season. So what happened in two months when we were top of the table? Nothing happened, it was just that the financial mess got so bad the other directors started asking serious questions. Allan Leighton, the club's deputy chairman and now chairman of the Post Office, began looking more closely into the books, and didn't like what he saw. He realized the club couldn't go on carrying such massive debts. I don't know how bad they were at that time, but the talk around the club was that they were over £100 million. It was clear they didn't have the money to buy me or Seth, and it was a bad move. I can see even now why they did it, because earlier in the season Leeds had not scored enough goals, and by bringing me in, the chairman thought it might be the missing link. Leeds was so much in debt, a gamble of £20 million hardly mattered . . . and could have paid off. But the day of reckoning always comes, and by January, just a couple of months after I signed for Leeds, it arrived at Elland Road. The club was virtually bankrupt, and it was a question of how they settled the debts. I can tell you, two months after signing for a club I assumed was loaded and going places, that came as one hell of a shock.

From about the end of January, there were stories of Rio Ferdinand being sold to Manchester United. There were also stories about Olivier Dacourt being sold to Juventus or Roma, and of a massive bid for Mark Viduka. In fact, when I arrived I'd heard that one of the reasons Leeds were prepared to spend so much money on me when they could have got me cheaper was because they had received a bid of over £20 million for Viduka from Real Madrid. He had almost signed for them the summer before, and the offer was supposed to still be on the table. It never materialized, but if there is one thing that does unsettle players, then it is stories about the club going bust and everyone being sold off. We are far more likely to read the back pages of the tabloids than any book. Every week it was another of the players, Kewell to Italy, Woody to Newcastle, Rio always to United, Bowyer to Arsenal or Liverpool. It went on and on, and in the end I was a bit pissed off that the only name never mentioned was mine. You do block most of it out, because at big clubs there is always rumour and speculation, but this was different. There was no doubt there was truth behind it all, because the bloody chairman himself kept coming out and saying it. So every week we went out knowing that no matter what happened, the team would more than likely be broken up at the end of the season, if not before.

That has an effect in the end, it is bound to. It undermines morale more than anything, just niggles away all the time, nothing too obvious, but taking its toll in the end. It didn't take a mathematical genius to work out that even winning the Premiership and getting into the Champions' League wouldn't go anywhere near covering those debts, so nothing we did would keep the team together. Even that doesn't really explain why our performances tailed off so badly in the New Year, after we had done so well to go top of the league on New Year's Day. I have my own explanation, which will disappoint a lot of conspiracy theorists looking for the dark secrets behind the decline of Leeds in the first few months of 2002. We were plain unlucky. Sorry to be so boring, but it happens in football sometimes.

I made my debut for Leeds against Fulham at Craven Cottage on 2 December 2001, which is a bit of a coincidence, because I made my Liverpool debut there too, eight years earlier. It didn't go quite so well as when I was eighteen and scored, because Leeds only drew 0–0 in a terrible game, and I never got a kick. Things looked up pretty sharpish though, as I settled into my new club, and got some match fitness behind me, after months of being stuck on the bench. What a great feeling it was to be first choice again, to be wanted. And what a great squad it was to be part of. At Liverpool, everything was so disjointed because there were so many foreign players in the squad. Nothing against them at all, some of the lads Houllier brought in were magnificent, Stephane Henchoz was a great lad, so was Didi Hamann, and they joined in lots of things. But when you have so many different nationalities and inevitably so many different cliques based around countries, then you lose a bit of identity and a bit of spirit.

At Leeds, most of the players were British, and most of them were brought up on the spirit of English football. I loved it at Elland Road, people like Woody and Michael Duberry,

Jason Wilcox – one of the funniest men ever – Dom and Lee Bowyer, Rio and Bats, Smithy – everyone really, they were all top class. Everyone liked a laugh and everyone mucked in together. The spirit was incredible, and the team ethic was magnificent too. There was never a dull day, and after being there just a few weeks, I felt like I'd been there all my life. Even the fall-out from the trial didn't cause problems. I can honestly say that I never noticed any tension between Michael Duberry and Lee Bowyer or Woody. They all spoke to each other, all got along, and me, Woody and Michael used to have a brilliant time together.

I'll never forget when we were on tour in China in pre-season during the summer of 2002 after the World Cup. We'd played a game and were given the night off, and every single one of the lads went into the bar together for a few drinks and a laugh. We found a karaoke machine and got everyone up singing. Terry Venables had just been appointed as manager, but wasn't due to join us until we got to Australia, and so Eddie Gray was in charge. Eventually, he sent the physio Dave Hancock and masseur Clive Brown to tell us it was time to go to bed, but we just got them up singing as well. It was getting late and the barmen were falling asleep, so we decided to move on, but Woody, Michael and me decided that we were up for a proper night by then, so we retired to my room, and started some card games. Whoever lost three games on the spin had to do a forfeit, and they were the usual pranks – press-ups, then sit-ups. Then when you did a sit-up you had to kiss someone's arse cheek as you came up. Woody had to do it to Michael first, and so on. If people thought there was a problem between those two, then they might have rethought that night when they saw Woody kissing Michael Duberry's arse! Believe it or not, I never had to do it, because I never lost all night. After that, we decided on another game. The corridors on each floor of the hotel were in a figure-of-eight shape coming back on themselves, and we decided it would be fun to have a race around them. In the buff. So we timed each other racing around the hotel corridors at about four in the morning, completely starkers. Woody did twenty-two seconds, so did I, and Michael did twenty. We reckoned he cheated, so we had to do it all over again, and he still won.

We had the same sort of laugh the night after. I roomed with Woody and we tried to order a Chinese, but the hotel didn't have any! So we went out to look for something to eat. It was a busy area, and we didn't know which way to go, but just across the way was this old fella with a rickshaw, so we hailed that. He took us around to look for something to eat, but it was a roasting hot night, and after a while the sweat was pouring off him. The poor old fella was shattered, so we told him to stop and have a rest. We got him to sit up in the back alongside Woody, and then I jumped down, and got in front to pull it. I dragged the rickshaw along for a bit, but the fucking thing was incredibly heavy, and I was weaving from side to side smashing into stalls all down the street, with people and dogs diving out of the way to take cover. Eventually we built up some speed, and I lost control completely and I had to dive for cover myself as the thing crashed straight into a stall, with Woody and the mad old fella pissing themselves in the back.

They were happy days at Leeds, none better than when I scored my first goals for the club against Everton (surprisingly enough) on 19 December 2001. It was a strange night, because I was really pleased to have opened my account, we got into a 3–0 lead and then we almost threw it away. Eventually we won 3–2, but my contribution was overshadowed a little by what was happening off the pitch. The trial of Woodgate and Bowyer had finished on 14 December, and Woody was unavailable because he had to do his community service. He had been fined eight weeks' wages by the club, and had asked for it to be donated to youth projects in the inner city. Lee had also been fined four weeks' wages, but he refused to accept the punishment because he was found not guilty on all charges. Ridsdale immediately put him on the transfer list, and all hell broke loose. He was left out of that game against Everton, but he was up on the TV gantry, doing some radio work. When we scored, the players ran over to salute him, and the fans started going mad, chanting his name. I wasn't at the club when the incident happened that caused proceedings to be taken against the players, so I am not in a position to go into the rights and wrongs of the whole thing. But if the players got some stick for supporting Lee that night and through his dispute with the club, then they would argue that we were very much a united team, all together and all behind each other, and he was a terrific player we wanted in the squad. In the end, he accepted the fine and came back into the team, and said he was ready to sign a new contract. I believe he would have done too, but by the end of that season when negotiations got under way, every single one of us could see the writing on the wall, and there were plenty of people looking to get out of there in the summer of 2002. You can't blame Lee for doing that, because things had gone belly up by then, so why would anyone in their right mind commit themselves long term to a club that was obviously going bust? Even Alan Smith, who was a massive Leeds fan and had a real affinity with the club, wasn't going to do that.

The previous Christmas, it had all looked so different. After scoring against Everton, I got a hat-trick at Bolton on Boxing Day, and then I scored a pretty good goal against West Ham on New Year's Day, which pleased me, because Jamo was in goal. Mind you, he did make an incredible save from me later on, so it was honours even. We won 3–0, and we played some fantastic football. Mark Viduka, me and Harry Kewell struck up a great understanding, and it was a joy at times to play the intricate, exciting football that Leeds produced at that time. It was light years ahead of what Liverpool had produced under Houllier when I was there, because there was a desire to entertain at Elland Road, and give the fans some real excitement. It was our undoing at times, though, because we threw away big leads, like when we were 3–1 up against Newcastle and somehow lost 4–3. Our biggest problem, though, was injury and suspension, and that was why I said some plain bad luck did for us. After we beat West Ham, which seriously suggested we could win the Premiership, we didn't in fact win another league game until March.

During that time, the messages from Ridsdale about selling

players and cutting debts got more and more serious, and that is hardly the thing you need when you hit a bad patch. But we also had to deal with an unprecedented string of injuries and suspensions that ripped the heart out of the team. Woody was injured for long periods, as were Rio, Dom Matteo, Erik Bakke, Olivier Dacourt and Harry Kewell. I got a terrible hip injury in March that just got worse and worse, and really I was in no condition to play, but I struggled on because we had no one else. Some of the injuries were self-inflicted, mind. Woody, the stupid sod, broke his jaw pissing about with his mate on a night out, and was ruled out for the season, and also missed the World Cup. You can't legislate for injuries like that, when an entire team is ruled out for weeks, and, on top of that, we had these incredible, debilitating suspensions. You could argue, of course, that was our own fault, and yeah, I'll hold my hand up and say they didn't help. At times we were lacking discipline, and we had quite a few players who seemed to go looking for trouble a bit too much.

But I think Leeds were also a victim of the image portrayed by the fall-out from the court case. There was this perception of the players all being out-of-control thugs, and I think the FA decided they needed to show they were being tough with us. Lee Bowyer got a six-match ban for an incident that had happened over a year previously, but couldn't be pursued because of the court case. Normally, it would have been a three-game ban. Alan Smith got a five-match suspension when he was sent off in a horrible, intimidating FA Cup tie at Cardiff, and he didn't do anything. That was shameful really, he shouldn't have been punished so severely when all he did was hold a bloke off who was trying to kick lumps off him. Danny Mills got a seven-match ban for two incidents, and my memory was that they weren't too serious ... although you never know with Danny, he could start an argument in an empty house. With all those players out, even the strong squad the gaffer had built up at Leeds was stretched beyond breaking point, and I'm slightly puzzled why people find it hard to work out the reason behind our decline after the turn of the year. In many ways, with so many people out for so long, we did bloody well to get to fifth and into the UEFA Cup, and keep our season going for so long.

Questions were asked, of course, and a lot of people preferred to believe that we failed because we were a wild bunch who were always out partying, fighting with the manager and never training. They preferred to believe that we were ripped apart by petty jealousies about books and spats and newspaper columns, and not because the club was falling apart about our ears because of gross financial mismanagement. I have to hold my hand up once more, and say I didn't help by getting myself arrested, which again was used in evidence against the whole club. What people don't know is that I was arrested not once, but twice during my time at Leeds.

The first was very high profile, and came after our Christmas party in the city centre. It was a fancy-dress do, and everyone turned up in outrageous costumes. Me and Calvey went as commandos, complete with camouflage paint and hats, and some little plastic guns. It wasn't a particularly wild night, we had a few beers and got a taxi back to the flat that I had bought in the same block as Dom. The driver seemed to be going a long way round, and I nodded off in the front. Then he pulled into a petrol station. I was still asleep, but Calvey thought it was a bit unusual, because when do you ever get a taxi that hasn't filled up on petrol before it gets a pick-up? The next thing, this car pulled up out of nowhere alongside us, and a photographer got out. He's a bloke I saw quite often later at Leeds, and is a professional snapper, not just some punter with a disposable camera. He started taking snaps of me kipping in the front of the cab, the paint streaked down my face and my cap slipped down over my eyes.

Calvey went berserk, because it was obviously a set-up, the cabbie had tipped the wink to the photographer, and we were being stung. He screamed at the cabbie that he was a cheating bastard who had set us up, and the bloke just squirmed away, because he was bang to rights. So Calvey jumped out of the car and set off at the snapper, shouting at him, 'Give us the camera or you're dead' – that sort of persuasive, sensitive argument. The bloke told him to fuck off, and then legged it towards the shop at the petrol station. By this time I'd woken up, and I was trying to work out what all the fuss was about, and I could see Calvey in this army gear aiming his plastic shooter at the snapper, trying to gun him down! Calvey followed the photographer into the shop, and he was hiding behind the counter with the attendant. So he went over and said to the bloke who worked there, give us the camera, and good as gold he handed it over straight away! Calvey took the film out and dropped the camera, but we were fucked because the taxi driver had scooted off out of there to avoid a bit of a slap.

Fortunately, a couple rolled up in a car just at that moment, and I leant in and asked if there was any chance of a lift. They took us back to the hotel, but the photographer, the cheeky bastard, only had the nerve to go and report us to the police. They came round and arrested us on suspicion of criminal damage or something like that, but even they were saying that the snapper had a fucking nerve after setting us up like that. Nothing came of it, but the press had a field day anyway, and it was used as the perfect example of how immoral the players at Leeds United were. The funniest thing of all was that it was me asleep in the taxi because I swear, whenever we go out, Calvey always, always falls asleep at the table. No matter where we are, what we're doing, if it gets after midnight then his head hits the table and he's snoring. To this day I can't believe that he managed to stay awake on that journey.

The other time I got arrested was a bizarre one. When I say I was arrested that might be gilding it a bit far, because I think I was only cautioned with the threat of being taken in for questioning. It all came about at Filbert Street, one of my more favoured hunting grounds. That season I had already scored a hat-trick for Liverpool there, and I scored for Leeds when we visited in March. I had one of my better games for the club, in fact, created the other goal in a 2–0 win and could have had a few more with a bit of luck. I left feeling pretty satisfied with myself, not least because that win had put us back on track a bit, gave us an outside chance of still making the Champions' League. On Monday at the Leeds training ground at Thorpe Arch, one of the office lads came running over, saying there were police in the complex waiting to interview me. What the fuck for? was my first thought. Surely it couldn't have anything to do with when I'd shown my arse there, eight years earlier.

When I got in, they sat me down and, with a real sense of gravity, they said they had to caution me they were investigating a claim of serious assault, committed by me at Filbert Street at approximately 2.35 p.m. on Saturday 23 March 2002. My head was popping now, and my eyes were as wide as saucers. Serious assault, Jesus, this was heavy stuff. For the life of me, though, I couldn't get my head around it, because nothing had happened there for once, nothing at all. So I got a bit panicky, and started to shout, 'What the fuck's all this about? Who am I supposed to have assaulted? Who has made these trumped-up accusations against me?' The policemen, who had driven all the way up from Leicester, looked at each other, and then said, even graver still, 'Filbert the Fox.' I couldn't help laughing out loud, and then I blurted: 'But he's got a three-foot-thick stuffed head, how the fuck could I ever have assaulted him?!' When we had been warming up, I was messing around, kicking some balls at the Leicester mascot, chasing up behind him where he couldn't see me. And then, as I ran past him, I clipped him on his three-foot stuffed furry head, and then ran away. That was it, a little tap around his big fat head! But the bloody idiot had complained to the police, and they were duty-bound to travel all the way up the motorway to interview me. Suffice to say it never went any further, but I'd love to know what the press would have made of that one if they had got hold of it.

I managed to get to the end of the season without further incident, but the hip injury that had troubled me was badly aggravated at Derby in April. I went to the World Cup with the problem and struggled through, even though I knew I wasn't right. I scored a goal in a warm-up game against Cameroon and told Eriksson that I felt fine, but really it was still bothering me. I got through the tournament all right, largely because he didn't play me, but when I went on the pre-season to China and Australia, it flared up again. Under the circumstances, that was the worst possible thing that could have happened to me. By then, Terry Venables had replaced

David O'Leary, and the big clear-out had started. Rio went to Manchester United as expected, Lee Bowyer was sold to Liverpool (only for the deal to collapse), Olly Dacourt went out on loan to Roma, Robbie Keane went to Spurs, Danny Mills went out on loan to Boro, and deals were set up all over the place for what seemed like most of the rest of the squad.

I was sat there kicking my heels on the treatment table, wondering what the fuck was going on as the club went into meltdown, and what the hell was to become of me. History has me down as being a failure at Elland Road, and when I went back there with Manchester City, the fans booed me, which really hurt. But I played some pretty good stuff when I was there, after I got myself fully match fit, and I would have done even better if it had not been for that hip injury. I scored twelve goals in eighteen games after I arrived, and I would have got more, but I was restricted for the last few games of the season. At times, we played some really special stuff, and I combined brilliantly with Mark Viduka and Harry Kewell who were probably the partners best suited to my style of play that I've ever had in my career. We might not have won the Premiership that season, but if we had not endured so many injuries, then we would have come pretty damn close. It is a shame for English football that such a good young side with so many talented British players never had the chance to come to maturity.

It was a depressing place to be that summer after I got back from the World Cup, and even though Venables actually started off 2002–03 pretty well and briefly topped the table, things got worse and worse as the full implications of the financial mess became clear. The chairman said the players we lost in the summer would be the extent of the clear-out, but every one of us knew that wasn't the truth. Dressing rooms are a strange place. No one will discuss money outright, so nobody quite knows what everyone else is on, unless they read it in the papers. And transfers are the same. You'd think that with being in the same dressing room day in day out we'd know each other's business inside out, but it doesn't work like that. Maybe the person closest to the player the rumours are about will know what's going on, but these things don't often spread around, and when a transfer happens, it can come as a big surprise to the lads. When I left Anfield, most of the other players didn't know, even though the negotiations went on for a couple of weeks. When we lost Rio in the summer, even though it was all over the papers not many of us really knew what was going on because we were away on holiday after the World Cup. Mind you, in Japan me, Rio and Millsy would discuss the situation at Elland Road and always come up with the same conclusion: whatever happened in the summer was just the tip of the iceberg. It sounds mercenary, and it smacks of rats leaving a sinking ship, but get real, when everyone is bailing out, you don't want to be the last man standing.

It was the first season of the transfer window, and I reckon that saved Leeds. Any longer to sell players and we wouldn't have had a squad left. As it was, we did okay early on, won the first few and beat Manchester United on 14 September to flirt with the top of the table. We only won once more in the Premiership between then and Christmas. The stories in the papers were getting worse and worse, and I knew it would be me next. Madrid had lost interest in Mark Viduka by the summer and Roma didn't come in either, so he was stuck on the books, and we had a forward line of me, Mark, Harry Kewell and Smithy, as well as Michael Bridges, who was still injured. Given I'd only been there five minutes and hadn't established myself, it was fairly obvious that at least one of us had to go, and that one would be me. It was probably only the fact that I was injured in the summer that kept me at the club as long as I was, although there was hardly a stampede beating its way to my door for a signature. The hip injury was a nightmare, because we kept thinking I could play through it, but by the end of pre-season I knew I needed an op, and it took months to recover. In fact, I didn't come back until Bolton in December where I scored but struggled like mad with my sharpness.

I think that injury did more damage to my career than any other, because it robbed me of a pre-season when I desperately needed one. Because of the circumstances, that injury set me back two years when I should have been at my prime. I know I sound like a scratched record, but I have always needed games, and plenty of them, and when I'm out for a while I'm always the first to admit I struggle. I struggled like an arthritic grandad when I finally came back for Leeds in December, but I'll fight anyone who says I was a failure there, because the goals I scored until I got injured in my first six months were as good a ratio as they have seen at Elland Road. When I came back I was laboured, though, and Terry Venables said that he wanted me to concentrate on getting fit, even if it meant missing a few games.

I was happy enough with that, but as Christmas approached, he called me into the office and said he had a problem. He said that as much as he had tried to resist, Ridsdale insisted on more sales, and the only ones he thought he could clear out in the January transfer window were me and Woody, because he'd be able to get decent fees for us. There was no interest in Mark Viduka, Harry Kewell was waiting for a summer move, Lee Bowyer was getting towards the end of his contract after his move to Liverpool fell through so he was worth nothing, and even the chairman realized he'd be lynched if he tried to sell Alan Smith. What did I think? I thought like everyone else in the squad: if there was an interesting enough offer I was off. In the words of my next manager, Kevin Keegan, it wasn't how it was described in the brochure. I had come to Leeds to win the title and play in the Champions' League, not scrabble around fighting relegation and worrying about who was next for the tap on the shoulder. The club tried to cover it up for a few weeks over Christmas, but they had the feelers out for some time before the window opened, and they were putting a lot of pressure on me to accept a move if one came up.

I had the feelers out myself, and there was a flicker of interest from Old Trafford. Sir Alex Ferguson had made enquiries through a third party years before when I first arrived on the scene at Anfield, and I heard suggestions a couple of times after that. Going from Liverpool to Old Trafford is impossible, and I could never have done that. But I had a call saying Manchester City were interested.

What happened next perhaps summed up more than anything the mess that Leeds were in, and the way that things were being handled. When I said I was interested I expected George to do all the negotiations, but Ridsdale said he had appointed the same agent who was involved in my move to Elland Road, the one I had never met until the day I signed. What was all that about? When we spoke to City, just before the New Year, their offer was about £15,000 a week less than I was already on, and I still had three years left on my Leeds contract. So there was no chance. I knew I had to leave Elland Road, but how could I take a million pound a year pay cut? Leeds were panicking, because they needed the cash, and they needed me off the wage bill. The agent rang George and offered him a cut of the deal if we reconsidered, but there was no way. George would only consider my best interests, and he told me about that straight away. Then Ridsdale rang George, and came up with this incredible plan. If Leeds made up the difference in my wages, would we reconsider? I couldn't see how that could work, but George spoke to Keegan and he said he was happy that he could work his way around it. I don't know the intricacies of the deal even now, but the plan was that Leeds would pay City monthly, and they would give me the same amount I was on at Elland Road.

It rumbled on for a couple of weeks, and we were troubled that an agent we didn't really know was apparently going to get so much money out of the deal . . . George went to Ridsdale and said it wasn't on, because in the end the money that goes to agents is just money that goes out of the pot. These days in football there seems to be an awful lot of money that goes outside the game. We said no deal unless there was no agent involved. We didn't need him, the club didn't need him because George was talking to Ridsdale and Keegan, and the City manager was also in touch with a close friend of mine to keep me updated. The ultimatum to Ridsdale was that the agent should back off, we didn't want him involved in any way, and if there was any payment to be made, then it should come to us. He agreed, and he gave us his word that there would be no payment to the agent, and the bloke would not contact me, George or Keegan. So it was back on, although I did still have my doubts.

I always got on well with Kevin Keegan, he was good to me as England manager and he tried to make international squads fun to be around, which was a big plus point. He may admit himself to being a bit lacking in the tactical side of the game, but he is a great motivator, and at least he's not one of those managers who have a million stupid rules that say when you can and can't cough. I wasn't sure about City though. When I was at Liverpool, we were always in the chase for the title and European honours, even if we didn't always deliver. I went to Leeds because they had been in the Champions' League semi final and had such an exciting young side they were bound to be Premiership contenders. Or so I thought. City, on the other hand, were a side that had only recently been promoted, and were consolidating their position in the top flight. There are some fantastic players at Manchester City, but looking at the team then, I could see that it would take a few years for them to be genuine contenders, and at my age I wasn't sure if I could afford to be part of another building process. At the same time, I had to get out of Leeds, because by the Christmas of 2002 I was sure they were heading out of the Premiership. George had spoken to Ridsdale and a couple of the other Leeds directors, and the soundings were all the same – they were struggling to survive. They wanted me out even though it meant they had to give another club's player £15,000 a week, and also take a £6 million loss on the fee they had paid for me just twelve months earlier, because City were only offering around £6.5 million. Woody was also going, and we were told that it was only a matter of time before Viduka, Kewell, Bowyer, Smith and Robinson were all sold. So, in the middle of January 2003, I went over to City's training ground to meet Keegan and have a medical.

From the off, it didn't feel right. I met Keegan for about five minutes and some of the players for lunch in their canteen. But I didn't get the chance to speak properly to the manager or any of his staff, and then I was whisked off to Leighton Hospital near Crewe to have what was the longest medical of my life.

We were there for about twelve hours, and the tests were exhaustive. I was with the City physio Rob Harris, and their PR guy, and because of my history with injuries they went through the works. All the time I was feeling that it didn't fit. And in the back of my mind, I was thinking that there was a chance I could go back to Anfield. I know a lot of people will be shocked by that given everything I've said about Houllier, but my heart was at Liverpool, and even though I never got on with him, I realized I'd made a mistake allowing him to force me out of there. The thing was, I think Houllier realized he might have made a mistake as well. They were going through a really difficult patch by that point, and he was getting a lot of stick.

One of their biggest problems was goal-scoring, because Emile had gone through a really dry patch, and Michael had struggled with injury. If you look at my record under Houllier at Anfield, the one thing I had always done for him was score goals, even with the problems we had. I believe Houllier also realized that I had a decent effect on team spirits too. I've always got on with everyone and brought the squad together a little, no matter which club I've been at. The new signings he had brought in to replace me hadn't hit it off yet, and they hadn't helped team spirit either, because I heard there was a lot of muttering about them. Nicolas Anelka had done something to piss him off and he wasn't signed on a permanent basis, and neither Diouf nor Baros had scored any goals. It looked as if the problem was really going to cost him, and Houllier was looking around for a solution ... any solution, even me! It seems mad now, but the same friend who had spoken to Leeds for me went to see Houllier at the team hotel before they played in the first leg of their Worthington Cup semi final at Sheffield United. They spoke about me coming back, and Houllier was interested. The fee would be as low as £5 million, and I was prepared to take a pay cut. Houllier said he'd have to get it past the board, who had stopped him spending any money after the failure of the guys he'd brought in during the previous summer. On top of that, he said he was in a weaker position with them now, because things had gone so badly. It wouldn't be easy for him to force through something as controversial as this. But he was happy to think about it, and he wanted some time. Time was the one thing we didn't have, because if I didn't get out before the transfer deadline at the end of January, then I would be stuck at Elland Road until the summer, and then there would be a proper scramble to get out. By the time I had travelled to Manchester for my medical, all this was swirling around in my head, and I hadn't been given the brush-off by Liverpool at that point.

From the medical, I was given a lift back to Liverpool by my mate, and Kerrie rang to ask me to get some milk. It was late, eleven o'clock at night, and we stopped off at a big Sainsbury's on the M53, just before the Mersey Tunnel. I wasn't happy and my head was pounding. I went into the shop to get the milk, came out and sat down in the car and said, 'I can't do it, I can't go through with the move.' My mate told me to sleep on it and speak to George in the morning. But there was no point, because I knew I couldn't go through with it, and no matter how much thought I gave it, I'd come to the same decision. So he rang George there and then, and told him that the deal was off. George said he'd contact City in the morning and tell them.

The next day, all hell broke loose. Apparently, late at night, the City chairman David Bernstein had used one or two minor things brought out in the medical to have another crack at Ridsdale and bring the price down even further. The two had rowed into the night, but eventually a deal was agreed where City would only put about £2 million down, and then pay another £3 million over the next few years. It was a shocking price and a bad way to do business, but I knew nothing of it when I had made my decision. George rang through the next morning to tell them, to be greeted by an apologetic Keegan saying that he was sorry about the chairman's approach to the negotiations, and he'd kicked off about it. George just said that the deal was off, and that was that. But somehow, the media got hold of the idea that I had pulled out because of the way that City had tried to do business with Leeds, and the way that the chairman behaved. I heard later that Keegan had really kicked off with him over it, and it had caused a major split at the club. But I can honestly say I never knew a thing about that.

There were three reasons why I turned the move down at the eleventh hour. One was because, in the back of my mind, I felt I hadn't done myself justice at Leeds, and it was nagging away at me that I would be seen as a failure at Elland Road even with the record I had there, which with my personality and insecurities is something that I could never accept. Two was the fact that I hadn't even spoken to Keegan about the way he saw the club going, that I'd had so little contact with anyone at the club, and yet it was a major decision I was making here. Three, of course, was the fact that Houllier hadn't ruled out a move back to Liverpool, and in my mind while there was still a possibility of going to Anfield, then I had to hold out for it.

The next few days were hell, because at Leeds they went into meltdown, while there seemed to be some pretty bad fall-out from City as well. Houllier made contact to say he was still working on the deal, and hadn't ruled it out completely, but after that we heard nothing from him at all. Ridsdale was in constant touch, and we told him that one of the problems had been our unease with the agent's part in the deal, because we had heard from Keegan that he was still involved, even though they had given their word he wouldn't be.

You don't know what happens behind the scenes, but it staggers me how much agents can take out of football these days. Players have their own agents, and they get paid for their services, which is fair enough. But why the hell should a second or sometimes even third agent be appointed? Apparently his job is to 'facilitate' the deal, but what does that mean? He rings one chairman and then passes a message on to the other? Why can't they just ring each other? As Gary Lineker said, it's all a bit 'murky', and to me it's not right that they can profit so much for doing so little. When Ridsdale found out about the interest from Liverpool, he got straight onto the phone to Rick Parry himself, and tried to sort out a move. He said that Parry had said the board wouldn't sanction it, even though the manager wanted it. He didn't need to pay an agent millions for that, did he? By the end of that week, it was clear that there was no chance of moving to Anfield before the transfer deadline because Houllier was told there was not another penny to spend. He eventually said that things might change by the summer, but he couldn't offer any guarantees. In the meantime, Keegan had been back on apologizing for what happened, and explaining that he thought he had made a great mistake by not talking to me personally about selling the club. He asked for a chance to meet me, just to have a chat about things, and to explain what he felt. If I still didn't want to move to City after that, fine, he would shake hands, respect me totally and walk away and not bother us again. When he put it that way, I thought the least I could do was to give him the courtesy of a meeting, even if I still didn't think I would go to City.

I'd done a few media interviews and said that I wanted to stay and prove myself to the Leeds fans. I meant it too. I knew I could score goals if I was fit and sharp, and I didn't want to leave a sour taste behind. It was obvious that if I left after just one year for half what they'd paid for me, I'd be slaughtered, and I didn't want that because I went to Leeds to win things. It wasn't my fault it turned out the way it did – I always thought they were a club with real financial muscle, and if I'd known the truth, then I wouldn't have gone there in a million years. Since then, people have pointed the finger at Ridsdale, saying that he blew things by spending £20 million on me and Seth Johnson, but believe me, that was a drop in the ocean. It's like saying you went bankrupt owing a hundred million because you bought a couple of lightbulbs. It still hurts me now that the Leeds fans boo me, and that they believe I was somehow to blame for their demise.

Two things happened to change my mind about slugging it out at Elland Road. One was Keegan. You've got to hand it to him, he talks a damn good game. He came over to my flat and stayed for about three hours, chatting about his vision for the club, and how he saw me developing. He apologized for not having more contact with me before, and he talked about me being the top-class striker who could help take Manchester City into Europe. Then he talked about his racehorses. It turns out he breeds his own horses and that impressed me as well. We shook hands when he left and I promised to give it a couple of days' thought, because in my mind I was still torn between staying and getting the hell out of there. When I went in to work at Thorpe Arch the next day, though, my mind was made up for me right there on the spot. After training, I was putting my bag in the boot of my car, when one of the directors drove into the car park. He jumped out of the car, greeted me warmly, and then came up close to whisper in my ear. 'Take the money and run, son,' he said, 'because believe me, this club is going under.' I could see in his eyes he wasn't joking, or just saying it as a ploy to move me on. He was deadly serious, and I knew right there what I had to do. So I got on the phone to George, and told him to ring Ridsdale. We were going to City. Leeds, on the other hand, were going into the Championship, and the director was right. They nearly went under, and people were almost crushed in the stampede out of there during the summer.

Much later, I heard that even though we had received promises no money would be paid to the agent Leeds had parachuted into the deal, even though we had demanded he have nothing to do with it and didn't contact me or Keegan, he got paid. God knows what was happening there, but it all made me even more relieved to get out, and reassured that I got the decision right to leave when I did.

We had the agreement that Leeds would make up the shortfall on my contract, but they even managed to go back on their word on that one. Ridsdale shook hands with George over the arrangement, and confirmed it with our solicitor, but when I made the switch to City, surprise, surprise, the paperwork was missing. We had to write solicitor's letters and threaten legal action to get them to honour their word. Ridsdale didn't take any calls for a couple of weeks after I left, and then he stepped down as chairman himself. That left us in an even worse position, because he was the man we had the agreement with, and he had scarpered out of there without settling everything.

Then Trevor Birch took over as Chief Executive, but before

we could get close to sorting it out, he had walked too. We got to the stage where we were about to file bankruptcy proceedings against Leeds United plc, with a genuine threat to wind them up. We resolved it in the end, and eventually we managed to have it assigned as a football debt, which meant Leeds were obliged to pay up, even if they did go bankrupt. We never got to find out what had happened to the fee that Ridsdale said would be paid to us instead of the agent we tried to freeze out, though. You'd have thought both clubs would have been happy with our actions because, in a way, we were making a bit of a stand. But football doesn't seem to work that way any more.

At Manchester City, the fans hated me. Fucking hated me. I arrived with this big price tag and a big reputation, and I was hopeless. I don't mind admitting it either. I was crap when I first got there. You don't mean to be crap of course, you don't think, Right I'm going out there and I'm gonna be fucking shit today. With me, I think every game that this is the one, I'm going out and I'm gonna be brilliant, score goals and everyone will be chanting my name. But for a long time at City, it didn't happen for me. I've got excuses, plenty of them if you'd like them. Injuries, problems with my confidence and mental state, and yet another strike partner who was a selfish bastard who just played for himself. But the fact remains that I was crap, and there's no use blaming anyone else for that.

I arrived in the winter of 2003, and it wasn't until 2005 that I really started to play at the City of Manchester Stadium, really showed the fans there that I wasn't the cabbage they thought I was. Y'know what, one of the proudest achievements in my career was coming in the top three in the Player of the Season awards at the end of 2004–05, voted for by the City fans. I know it doesn't sound much, and I didn't even win it, Richard Dunne – who had a fantastic season – did. But it really meant something to me, that I had finally won around the supporters who had ridiculed me, and who had hated me – in my mind really hated me – at times. There was a season and a half at

City when I felt as though my football world was falling apart, when I felt for the first time in my life that I didn't want to play, that maybe my career had come to an end and I should look for something else. For all the trouble I had with Houllier, for all the nightmare of Leeds, the early days at City were amongst the lowest moments of my life, and it was only the support of my wife and family that kept me going and saw me through it.

Throughout this book, I have purposely skipped over my family life. I have always tried to keep that separate from my football career, because it does my head in when I see certain players milking the media by using their family – their kids – to get publicity and make them money. I have always thought that if you want to protect your kids, to keep them away from the media, then you can't wheel them in and out when it suits you. You can't say to the media, 'You can have bits of us, but not all of us.' The way it is these days, it's all or nothing, and that's that. We all know that, but it doesn't stop some people moaning like mad when they think their privacy has been invaded – the same people who sell themselves to the glossy magazines. I've got no time for them, and I think Kerrie and me made a decision early on that we were never going to get caught up like that. Mind you, there's no chance of that ever happening with Kerrie anyway, because she's the most down-to-earth girl you could ever meet. I feel so lucky that I met her when I did, because's she's everything anyone could ask for. Down to earth, great fun, fantastic character, a wonderful mum, and of course she's beautiful. Me mum and dad love her, which is always a good recommendation.

She is the world to me. And my three girls. As a family, it is perfect, and I count myself so lucky to have them. It makes me laugh when I see the perception people have of me, and the idea that I'm some sort of wild man who is on the slide to oblivion. Because I was described as a world beater early on, but then never quite reached the heights predicted for me, just about everyone seems to assume it's because I have wasted my career with booze and partying. Yep, did that when I was younger – when I was scoring all those goals. But I am married with three wonderful children and I have a stable, loving environment around me, from Kerrie and the kids, my mum and dad, to all my aunties and uncles and cousins and nephews and nieces and me nana. I have strong family support that would never let me get out of hand.

Kerrie is the rock of all that. She was born on Merseyside in a place called Whiston near St Helens. We met first in a bar called the Retro in Liverpool in December of 1996 . . . but I was too shy to even speak to her. I saw her there surrounded by this massive group of girls, and I thought she must be on a night out with her mates. It turned out they were all her sisters – because she's got hundreds of them! Four actually, Lorraine, Mandy, Camille and Vicki. Anyway, they were far too intimidating to approach, but I was desperate to talk to her, so I stood there like a biff, staring at this gorgeous girl but not having the courage to actually speak to her, because I'm a shy lad. Then she walked out. I was gutted, I thought I'd lost my chance to speak to this incredible-looking woman, who had flitted in and out of my life. Thankfully, I went on to a club with Calvey and Gordon, and there she was, with her sisters still, and looking even more gorgeous than before. (Well, I'd had a few more drinks by then!) This time I managed to pluck up the courage for a chat, we exchanged numbers, and then I spent the next few days worrying about when was the right time to call. When I did, I arranged a date, and being such a romantic fool we met down me local for a pint! We got on really well from the start, and it was funny, because straight away I knew she was the one for me. Kerrie is not your typical footballer's wife, she's not one of those characters off the telly, and she would never want to be associated with anything like that. She's an independent, fiery, feisty character, but she's not pushy or interested in being in the limelight.

We have a quiet home life, we're not bothered by the media like some footballers and their partners, and that suits us. Kerrie is the love of my life, and there is nothing I enjoy more than being there at home with my family. Our first daughter, Madison, was born on 26 August 1999 in the Liverpool Women's Hospital, which is actually on the edge of Toxteth and just a mile away from Sefton General where I was born. She was born on a Thursday, and to celebrate, I went out and scored my usual goal against Arsenal!

Jaya was next. She was born on 26 October 2000 in the early hours of another Thursday morning. We had a European game that night against Slovan Liberec, and I had phoned Houllier to say that I had been up all night with Kerrie, because she had gone into labour on the Wednesday evening. He said I should go in and train, so I did at 11 a.m., went back to the hospital and then reported for the match. I had an absolute stinker, missed a penalty and got slated in the press, and yet I hadn't slept for twenty-four hours so it was hardly surprising I was rubbish. I did ask the lads in the dressing room later what their excuse was.

It's strange that even though I've come a long way in my life, the girls are Toxteth kids, born a short distance away from where I was born, even if their lives now are a million miles away from the childhood I had.

Mackenzie was born on 27 September 2002, so there is not too much of a gap between all three of them, which is good for the girls, but maybe not so good for Kerrie who has her hands full! Madison and Jaya were christened in the Metropolitan Cathedral in Liverpool, the Catholic one they call Paddy's Wigwam, because of its unusual design. Mackenzie, though, was christened at St Patrick's in Toxteth, where I was christened, which again is an important link for the girls to where their family originally comes from. Me mum got to know Father Kenny very well at St Patrick's, as did Kerrie and me. We both thought he was a really nice person, and the perfect man to christen Mackenzie, and to offer some guidance as the girls grow up. I also think that it is good to keep them grounded in where the family is from. I'm proud of my Toxteth roots, and I want them to be too. We live on the Wirral now, in a fabulous house with lots of grounds. The girls are driven around in Kerrie's four-wheel drive, and they go to a very nice private school. It probably couldn't be more different from my own upbringing, but I don't want them to forget where we come from, and I don't want to ever turn my back on Toxteth.

I go back there a lot, and I still do things around the area with youth football and stuff like that. As I come towards the end of my career I would like to put more back into Toxteth, and into Liverpool in general, and I definitely want to keep my links there.

The children have changed my life, that is for sure. They are a bundle of energy, on the go non-stop from the moment they wake, which is usually very early. And there are no concessions for the fact their dad is a footballer, in fact, I don't think they even know. They are my pride and joy, and every emotion I've described in this book, every high and low through football, is nothing compared to the emotion I feel when I think about them, when I see them do things for the first time. First steps, first words, first day at school, turn on the taps. They are the world to me, and my future is based around the idea of being able to spend time with them while they are still growing up, which is not something you can always do when you are playing football.

Kerrie married me on 9 June 2001, and it was the happiest day of my life. There were around 250 people who travelled to Duns Castle in Scotland for the service, which was held under a marquee in the grounds. It was a wonderful day. We had a pipes band to lead us into the service, and a string quartet playing through the ceremony. Even some of my hard-bitten family from Toxteth were moved by it all, and we had a fantastic time at the party afterwards. The whole day went off without a hitch, apart from the small problem of the castle security having to chase some photographers across this wild parkland in the grounds, when they had scaled the walls to try and get a sneak picture of the service! The thing was, we were releasing pictures to all the papers anyway because there was no way we would ever sell our wedding to one of those glossy magazines, so they didn't have to bother with all that Andy McNabb SAS style stuff. Funny though.

We have been through a lot together, Kerrie and me, and perhaps the most difficult thing was when we moved to Leeds. At first, I stayed in a flat out there on my own, because of the children, and then we lived in three flats before buying a house in Alwoodley on the outskirts of Leeds. It was a beautiful place in a nice area, and you'd have thought it was the last place to get any trouble. One night though, I went to bed tired, and obviously forgot to put the alarm on. In the morning when I came down, I went to the table by the front door where we usually kept all the keys and stuff like that. No keys, so I shouted up to Kerrie to ask where she'd put them. As I did so, I glanced out of the window and thought it was a bit strange that Kerrie's car was missing, but assumed it was parked further up the drive. Kerrie, though, said she'd not touched the keys and they were definitely on the table, and that's when I started to panic. I went into the living room, but didn't notice anything different. It was only when I went into the kitchen and saw some of the drawers had been pulled out that I realized something was badly wrong. It turned out they had cut a pane of glass out of the patio doors in the living room and got in that way. The thing was, it was raining the night before, but there wasn't a mark on the carpet, no other sign of entry and no damage in the house at all. Because it was pissing down, they took their shoes off and nicked my trainers to walk around in. And they had cleared us out. I'm normally a very light sleeper and I didn't hear a thing that night. We were all in the house asleep, and they were downstairs robbing us. It was terrifying really, especially when you consider the girls were asleep in the house too.

The police said there was a spate of burglaries in the area, targeting houses with big cars outside, and they were a very professional gang who knew what they were doing. When we moved back to Liverpool later, I saw a piece in the paper saying that there had been a robbery in the same area, and the person who had been broken into disturbed them, and was murdered. Now that is terrifying, and shows you what can happen. They had taken all our stuff, put it out of the front door and then taken Kerrie's keys, loaded it into her car and driven away with it, without anybody noticing. The thing was, they had locked the door on the way out, and taken the keys with them. They had also nicked our mobile phones and the handsets from the telephones, so we were stuck in the house, without any way of alerting anyone. All my numbers for Leeds were in my mobile, so they thought I'd gone AWOL for a day, until I could get in there and explain what had happened. I think I did far more damage getting out than they did getting in.

It unnerved us both, and Kerrie said she couldn't live there any longer. The thought of what might have happened if we'd woken up was just too bad to contemplate, with such a young family living there. So we went back to Liverpool with the girls, and I tried to commute most days. It took me three hours each way, and nearly bloody killed me! I think that journey was another of the reasons why I left Leeds, because I knew it would be hard to ever settle there, after the experience we had. For me, my family and their happiness are the most important thing, more important even than football, which consumed me when I was younger. Kerrie has been there through everything with me, all the hard times I have had, and she has always been such an incredible influence on me. I look at what we have got, and it does make me laugh the image people have of me as this yobbo, some sort of scally who is bound to piss it all away. I think we're pretty secure, and even if I haven't thought too much into the future because I still believe I have a present playing at the highest level for some time to come, I know the future will involve working closely with Kerrie. Management may be interesting at some stage, but again, I want to put that off for as long as possible, because I'm not finished playing yet, not by a long chalk. Kerrie has her own business, a lingerie shop on Cavern Walks called Bardot, just down from where the Beatles used to play all those years ago, and I'm pretty certain we'll look to expand it in some way. That could be my next calling, a businessman ... and if it's got a golf course attached, then so much the better. Whatever happens, I'll have my family, and a stable, loving background, so there's no need to worry I'll be another football statistic!

I needed my family when I first got to City, because my head had gone. I know that sounds rubbish, I was a £6 million signing who was a professional footballer and I shouldn't have any excuses and I'll hold my hand up and admit my attitude was all wrong. Looking back, I don't think I adjusted very well to the move to City. Whichever way I looked at it, it seemed that I was moving further away from challenging for honours, and that may have affected me a bit. Again, I know it sounds crap from a professional, but I had got the idea in my mind of a move back to Liverpool. At that time they were close to taking the final step towards the top, and I honestly thought I could have offered something extra that would have helped them do it. They needed goals that season, and I think I could have popped up with a couple at the right time for them. After the experience of being burgled in Leeds, too, I just wanted to be back in Liverpool, with my family around me. When it didn't happen, I was crushed. Keegan sold me the idea of City being in Europe, qualifying for the UEFA Cup that season, and I think we probably should have done it too. But for the whole of my career, apart from a few months at Leeds, I was used to being up there at least challenging, or believing we could challenge, for the title, and being an automatic guarantee for Europe. Being contenders. The difference in mindset to what I was used to and what I had come to was a real eye-opener, and I obviously didn't handle it well.

Things got so bad for me, that for the first time in my life I didn't want to play football. It seems incredible, I know, but I was on the verge of giving it up and walking away. I'd had enough. I was frustrated with my form, frustrated with life at City, devastated by what was happening to me. I hated playing football, really hated it. I used to come off after games – usually during games when I was substituted, and I would almost be in tears. I'm not just saying that either, I really was coming into the dressing room unable to speak, unable to unscramble my mind, and almost unable to hold back my emotions. It got to the stage where I couldn't carry on, and I told Kevin Keegan that too. I spoke to him a couple of times and told him how much I hated it all, and that I wanted to quit.

We had a big meeting, Keegan was there, Derek Fazackerly and Stuart Pearce and I poured my heart out. I told them plain and simple that I hated football and I wasn't going to play any more. Looking back, I couldn't handle it, my mental state was very frail and I couldn't cope with being such an ordinary player. Again, I know that sounds crazy because it is down to me how I perform, but I had lost my sparkle and my hunger and I was getting hammered by the fans. I used to dread going to work, I hated training and I hated playing matches. In my mind, it got to the stage where I really felt I had no other option but to retire. I have to say it was only the kindness and the support of the management that got me through it. They were great with me, and I appreciate the way that they backed me up and brought me back to near my best form. They listened to me, let me work it all out of my system, and then they said they knew how I felt, and they would help me get through it, they would do what it takes for me to come out of it. I remember walking away after I said I hated playing and didn't want to do it any more, and Stuart Pearce followed me. He put his arm round me and he said that he didn't believe a word I had said. He explained that he knew what I was like, he knew the player I was and the determination I had, and he knew that I loved football, that it was my life and I would never walk away from it. He also said that he understood perfectly the frustrations I felt, the feelings I had, but he would get me through it and I would be back to the player that I was. He talked about the faith he had in me, and the ability I had, and he made me feel a damn sight better.

How had it come to that? How I had got to the stage where I felt my life was falling apart, and my best days in football were just a distant memory for me? It was just before Christmas 2004 when I went to see Keegan and the coaches and told them how I felt. I had basically had two years of hell at Maine Road and the City of Manchester Stadium, and I had lost all faith in my ability. I knew I was rubbish and I knew the fans were right to criticize me, and I couldn't handle not being at the level I knew that I should be at. I look back on my career, and without being too big-headed I know I was bloody good. There were times when no one could touch me, and even now, at the time of writing this book, I know I can play at the very top level. Sure, I've lost a bit of pace, there's no doubt about that, and I curse that ligament injury I picked up against Everton, because that was a shocking blow to my career. That edge of pace is crucial to a striker, because it gives you a split second to get in front of the defender, and that split second is crucial in goal-scoring. It hasn't detracted too much from my abilities though. I know I can score goals if I get the service, and I know as well that I can provide the service. After my heart-to-heart with Keegan and the coaches at City, they helped rebuild my confidence, and they helped me ease back into the level I am still capable of. After that miserable Christmas, I started playing again, and the last five months of the 2004–05 season I started to get the old confidence back. I scored a few goals, set up a few more and the fans got behind me. By the end of the season I was flying, and apart from a brief spell at Leeds when I was on fire, it was the best I've played for a long, long time. Consistently, over a long period, in some ways it was the best I've played since that injury way back in 1997. What I did was get back to the form that made me a top-class striker, and proved that there was still life in me yet.

But for nearly two seasons at City, I was nowhere near that class, I was nowhere near the player I knew I should be, and as time drew on, things just got worse and worse inside my head. My confidence crumbled, I began worrying about the fans and resenting what they were saying about me. I became bitter about my football, and I became one of those players I have always hated in my career, a moaner who never appreciated what he had, and never made the most of his talent because he was too busy feeling sorry for himself and finding excuses. I had plenty of them, mostly related to my fitness. When I arrived at City in early 2003, I think I'd played about three games in the previous eight months, because of the hip injury I suffered at Derby. I wasn't match fit because I had missed the pre-season, and I wasn't right mentally either, because of the drama surrounding the move. I almost arrived in time to make my debut against Fulham, but the delay in the transfer robbed me of an interesting little hat-trick. Instead, City beat them 4–1 without me in what was apparently their best performance of the season, and I arrived the day afterwards.

My debut came on 1 February 2003, at home to West Bromwich Albion. I didn't get a kick, and we got beat 2–1 against a side everyone knew would be relegated. The fans weren't happy, and it was obvious who the fall guy was going to be: me. Straight away, people were saying they didn't need me, that I would only unbalance the team. To add to the problem, I wasn't fit, nowhere near fit enough. People were having a go about my weight, about my attitude and my fitness, and the truth was I needed a decent run of training to get something like a pre-season into me. But of course we were playing and Keegan was picking me, so I didn't really have the chance to work as hard as I would have liked. We played Manchester United next, and I didn't get a kick again. When I was taken off, Shaun Goater came on and scored the equalizer, and almost won the match. He is a hero at City and the fans love him, and that hardly helped endear me to them! It took me until 16 March to score my first goal, a decent chip over Ian Bennett to beat Birmingham, but in the very next game I picked up a back injury against Chelsea that ruined my season. It was my own fault really. We were messing about in training and I went in goal. I tried to do one of those scorpion kicks that the Colombia goalkeeper did at Wembley, and I landed on my shoulder. I looked a right prat, and I got up sharpish, pretending that nothing was wrong, while the rest of the players were slaughtering me. But when I played at Chelsea the next day I stiffened up so bad that I couldn't move at half time, and had to come off. Try explaining that one to the press. We were stuffed by Chelsea 5–0 and we were woeful in the first half, so people assumed I was simply taken off for being crap. I hardly trained for the rest of that season because of that fucking shoulder. I used to have an injection to play, and then have to rest for much of the week after the game. That didn't help my fitness at all, and the fans started to get really restless about my form, because obviously they didn't know about the injury.

It didn't help either that Nicolas Anelka and me never hit it off as a partnership. In fact, I can't think of a worse partner for my style, because even though he's a brilliant player, there is only one thing he plays for ... and that's himself. When I arrived at Maine Road, Keegan came out with all the gumph about him asking Anelka to name any striker in the Premiership that he'd like as a partner, and Nico was supposed to have said me. That cheered me up no end, until I actually got there, and found out it was a right load of bollocks. I think I was the last striker on earth he wanted alongside him, from the way he was with me. The day I arrived, he was due to play in this big charity match at Bolton the next night, where a lot of the star players from across Europe were involved. I tried to get a conversation going about it, tried to engage him a little, but he just grunted at me, turned on his heel and was off. Charming. But that's Nico for you. In the end I got used to his attitude. I think he's a really quiet bloke, and he doesn't like mixing. Fair enough, if that's the way he is, it's no skin off my nose. Keegan told me I had to help him, that I must try to engage him, just speak to him to try and bring him out and make him part of the team. So I tried. And tried. And got nothing back at all, so I thought, Fuck that then.

I think maybe he was a little jealous, or just threatened by my arrival. He was used to being the big star after his move from Arsenal to Real Madrid, and maybe he looked down on a lot of the City lads because he had been places they hadn't. When I arrived I was a big-name striker who had played at the top level and had a big reputation, and that seemed to put his nose out a bit. I thought he was a great player, a real striker, and all top goal scorers can be a bit selfish at times so it wasn't unusual he was playing for himself. At other times, when you're in an impossible position and somebody else is obviously better placed, you have to do what is best for the team. He never seemed to do that, and it became infuriating in the end, not just for me, but for the whole team. He seemed to ostracize himself by the end because of it, and there were one or two fights. He smacked one of the kids in training one day, which was bang out of order, and the other lads let him know about it. Joey Barton also had a go at him at half time during one match because he was being so selfish and lazy.

For me, it was difficult, because in those early months with no match fitness and with real problems of my own, the last thing I wanted was a selfish bastard alongside me, who let me do all the running, and just stood there smashing everything that came his way at goal, no matter what position he was in. There was one game, and I can't even remember the opposition now, but I remember the sinking feeling I got when he scored. He was at this ridiculous angle out on the touchline, with the keeper at the near post, and two or three of us unmarked so it was an easy tap-in if he pulled it back. But he smashed it again even though it was impossible to score . . . and somehow the keeper fucking missed it, and it crawled into the net. He was off celebrating while the rest of us were standing there with our heads in our hands, thinking, that's it, he'll never fucking pass now. That first few months when I arrived, I didn't get one pass off him, and after the goal against Birmingham, I didn't score again until 21 April when I scored another good one with a lob against Sunderland. That was it for me right until the end of the season. And Nico didn't do much better. He only scored one right at the end when we got stuffed by Arsenal, and then two against Liverpool at Anfield, when we beat them to stop them from getting in the Champions' League . . . which might not have happened if they'd signed me!

We were both subbed in a game against Boro, and on the final day of the season against Southampton – which was the last ever match at Maine Road – I was on the bench as the manager gave Shaun Goater a start in what was his last game for the club. That was fair enough, and I think the manager was good like that in thinking about players, but when I came on we were losing 1–0 and I had a chance to score what would have been a big goal in a very important game for the fans. It was stopped brilliantly by Antti Niemi, we lost 1–0 and the fans went away moaning about me again! We were this so-called £20 million striking partnership, and in almost four months we had scored five goals between us. He'd scored plenty before I arrived, and I looked unfit and sluggish because of the shoulder injury, so it wasn't hard for the supporters to point the finger, blaming me for his poor form and our poor return.

I guess I'm not that good at accepting criticism, because it hurt me – the whole situation caused me a lot of pain. I went away that summer wondering what I had done, what had happened to my career. We won four games after I arrived, and we finished a poor mid table. I thought there would be more signings and money available in the summer, but that proved to be something of a mirage. It was difficult for me to make that adjustment to a team with slightly lower expectations and ambitions, but that was nothing really compared to my own inner problems. I spent most of that off-season dwelling on what had gone wrong, tormenting myself about my shocking loss of form, and the stick I was getting off the fans. I knew I deserved it and I knew I was a better player than they had seen, but the injuries and my low confidence made things worse and worse, and it affected me badly.

I began to think I'd made the wrong decision, and I began having really bad regrets about leaving Liverpool, which was pointless, and made me even more depressed. By this time we were still living in the flat in Liverpool while our house on the Wirral was being finished, and even the bloody commuting was getting me down. It didn't help that Keegan was forced to make a series of free transfer signings to flesh out the squad. At least he bought some decent players, though, and some great lads. He got Macca from Real Madrid, which for me was a real coup, although as things have turned out, he never got a chance at City because of the injuries he suffered. He also signed David Seaman and Trevor Sinclair, two friends of mine from England duty who are great characters as well as being great professionals. It improved my mood to be joined by some good mates, but the fact was that the vision the manager sold to me was nowhere near the reality, just as it turned out at Leeds, and I let it get to me.

I was depressed, and things didn't get any easier when we learnt that summer of 2003 that our midfielder Marc Vivien Foe had tragically died playing for his country Cameroon in a Confederations Cup semi final against Colombia. I didn't know him too well because I hadn't been at the club long, but he was clearly a decent guy who was well liked in the dressing room, and he was an incredible athlete, a formidable warrior on the pitch who seemed naturally fit. So it was such a shock to turn on the radio and hear that he had suffered a heart problem during the game and, despite the best efforts of the medics, died before he could even reach the hospital. It puts into perspective my own grumbles and problems that summer, but at the time it was a devastating blow that hit every member of our team badly. Devastating things like that happen, and as a professional you are supposed to shrug them off and get on with things, yet it doesn't always work like that, because how can you just switch off about a guy that was there in the dressing room only a few weeks before, part of all the banter, the jokes and the bonding that goes on? Again, I let my mind be overtaken by thoughts of how wrong it was, how difficult it all was.

I look back now and I realize quite clearly that I shouldn't have reacted as I did, I shouldn't have let myself descend into the state I eventually got into. I wasn't professional enough, but my mind was so clouded I couldn't see that simple fact. I moped around too much, had a lousy pre-season where I didn't work hard enough on my fitness, and after starting the season badly and after just two games I was on the bench, where I stayed for two months. I didn't score my first goal until 1 November, and that, unsurprisingly enough, only came when Anelka was out injured. Things between me and him got worse and worse in terms of our partnership, and we went through the whole of 2004 without both of us even once scoring in the same game, which says it all I guess. We didn't hit it off, simple as that, and to be fair to him, he was still scoring plenty of goals, twenty-four that season, so it was only natural that it would be me who made way. I had a little run around the turn of the year when I scored in three consecutive games, but I got only seven league goals all season, and ten in total, which wasn't good enough by a long way. What was even more depressing, even more humiliating really, was the fact that in thirty-one games in the Premiership that season, I was substituted fourteen times and was a substitute myself in another eight matches.

So in the entire season I played the full ninety minutes only nine times. I had a few niggling injuries, but for the large part I was out of the side or taken off because I was nowhere near good enough, physically or mentally. Only three games that season stand out for me as moments that temporarily lifted the gloom. At Christmas, I scored the last-minute goal that gave us a valuable point against Liverpool, which was satisfying. Soon after, I was also involved in one of the most incredible games I have ever experienced, when we went to Spurs in an FA Cup fourth-round replay. We were 3–0 down just after the half-hour, and Joey Barton got himself sent off as we were leaving the pitch at the interval. The manager's instruction as we left the dressing room for the second period was to play for a bit of pride and don't get humiliated. We did that all right, with one of the best comebacks I have ever had the pleasure to be involved in. With ten men we clawed it back to 3–3, and then with the last touch of the game, John Macken produced a quite outstanding header to give us victory. That gave us a tie with Manchester United, and although we lost that, we did stuff them at our place in the Premiership game a few weeks later, and I scored a very good opening goal. I also got into a bit of bother after an exchange with a few United fans who gave me some stick, so I counted four fingers up at them, just to wind them up over the number of European Cups Liverpool had won. Next time, I can just stick my hand up!

The 2003–04 season, though, was a complete wash-out, for the team and for me personally. Keegan had talked about us making the Champions' League that year, but that was just a joke. The only way we would have done that was if we'd sneaked onto the Manchester United team bus. We went nearly four months without a league win, and got knocked out of the UEFA Cup – which we only got in via the fair-play league – by some God-awful team from Poland. At one point it looked as though we would be relegated, and even though we eventually finished sixteenth, it was a fucking miserable season, where we were in danger until we beat Newcastle two games from the end. For me, it finished like it started ... on the bench and questioning my position, my form, even my future. By then, I was having serious doubts about whether I could ever become again the player I was, and I was constantly questioning whether I still had the desire to continue.

Things couldn't go on like that, and it all came to a head early into the 2004–05 season. I scored on the opening day against Fulham, but was then given the substitute treatment again, and I began to really hate myself and my job. We played Everton at the City of Manchester Stadium early in September and, true to form, I was taken off again, on sixty-three minutes. I was in tears as I reached the dressing room, tears of rage that I had let myself down again, that the fans had the opportunity to boo me again, that I was just a shadow of the player who had scored all those goals earlier in my career. I walked into the dressing room, got changed in five seconds flat, and I was out of there, still burning about it all, still fighting back the anger with myself and the tears and the humiliation of it all. I walked straight out of the stadium, and as I did, I thought to myself that I'd just keep walking and never come back. Fuck it, I thought, why put myself through this every week when I hate going out there, hate even going into training?

A few days later I was called into the office and asked to explain myself. I had a bit of an exchange with the manager, who said it was disrespectful to my teammates to walk out like that. He got it completely wrong, though, because it was nothing to do with being substituted, and all to do with my frustration and despair at my form. I'd had a terrible game and I knew it. And it killed me. I tried to explain all that, and eventually it all came out. Keegan called his coaches into the room and I told them how much I hated football, and how I didn't want to play any more. They were so good to me, and the manager said I just had to go away to get my head right and work on my fitness. He told me that there would be no pressure on me, and I could go away until I was right, and physically up to playing again. For all the complaints about Keegan at City, I appreciate what he did for me then, because he probably saved my career. I was at such a low ebb at that point, I really could have turned my back on the whole thing, and walked away. It was a moment when my football career could have been over, at the age of twenty-nine. From that moment, though, the support I got seemed to take a huge weight off my shoulders, and I felt a different person. When I eventually did get back playing my form started to return, slowly, slowly, until, by the end of the season, I was playing my best football in a long, long time. In my mind, I was back, or at least almost there.

I will always thank Kevin Keegan for that, but there is a postscript to the incident, which left a sour taste in the mouth. In the press at the time, the manager was quoted as saying that I would be fined, but in private he told me I wouldn't be.

Months later, I was checking my wage slip when I found I'd been deducted the money. I went ballistic, and had a real up-and-downer with the manager. How the hell could they tell me I wasn't being fined, and then sneak it out of my wages without even bloody telling me? It turned out that they had sent a letter informing me of the fine . . . but they'd sent it to my flat, which I hadn't lived in for sometime. I'd been living on the Wirral for years, but instead they sent the letter to Liverpool, and I thought that was sneaky and underhand. I refused to accept the fine, and we had a bit of a stand-off for a while, until I backed down. I know it was out of line getting off like that before the end of the game, but I wasn't the only one who'd done it, just the only sap who'd been fined. Others had done it and got away with it, but when it came to me, I was the one who had an example made of him.

It sums up my relationship with Keegan really. It sums up the way he was towards the players when he was manager at Manchester City. On the one hand, he was a decent fella, who didn't want to upset anyone. On the other, he went about things in the wrong way by hiding away and not taking important things head-on. There are people at City who dislike him intensely, but I would never put myself in that camp. There are players who complain that he never spoke to them, never communicated, but again, he wasn't like that with me. He was very good with me, even though we had a few disagreements over time. He talked to me, but I know he started losing a lot of respect from a lot of the players because he didn't talk to them. I think it was sad what happened to him, but I do believe it was time for a change when he left. It always struck me with Keegan that he was very similar to Terry Venables in that they were both very, very good at dealing with players as international managers, very good at relating to players in an international squad, and giving them an identity and a spirit. But when it came to being club managers they were both almost a totally different person, and as club bosses, whether they were good or bad at their job, I'm not sure.

I think it's fair to say that there was a feeling against Keegan by the time he was sacked as manager at the City of Manchester Stadium. Again, I wouldn't count myself in that group, but maybe I was in the minority. I was glad that my form came back before he left, and I could contribute towards the City cause under him, that I could justify some of the faith he had shown in me, and that I could show the fans that every time he came out and supported me, he wasn't talking a load of tripe. People have already made that lazy mistake of saying that my form picked up after Keegan left, but the truth is that after he helped me through the worst time in my football life, I started to play again. It's perhaps no coincidence that when Anelka was bombed out and then sold to Fenerbahce in the January of 2005, my form really took off. I think the City fans can draw their own conclusions from that. I know there are a lot that still idolize him, that still believe the club was wrong to sell him, and you can't argue against the fact that he scored goals for Manchester City. If Nicolas wanted to cut himself off from the rest of the squad and do his own thing, act in his own way, then that's his right. There's no mileage in me slagging him off and no point either, but for me there is more to a successful football side than individuals with ability. You have to be a team, and you have to create an environment for that team to thrive. When you get characters like Nico, then it can disrupt that atmosphere, and sometimes it can fuck you up. That probably happened at City, just like it happened at Liverpool with Stan Collymore. Look at both players, and you can see a pattern with them, it wasn't a one-off at a single club. Sometimes, I think managers are so desperate to find talent at a reasonable price they are prepared to overlook the bleeding obvious and take a chance, against their better judgement. I'd like to know how often it works though.

Keegan maybe lost a little respect over his treatment of Anelka, because he seemed to indulge him a bit. The players were outraged when he smacked the kid in training, but nothing got done. There were mutterings about him turning up late or doing a bunk, but nothing much got done about that either. Then that turned the spotlight onto the training itself, and whether it was good enough, or serious enough, or whether the manager bothered enough. Some of the lads moaned that we weren't doing enough work, but I thought his training was fine, it was just like we had at Liverpool, and Macca said it was pretty similar to the stuff they did at Real Madrid, so it couldn't have been that bad. I wanted to do well for Keegan, I really did, and I wanted to show him that I was putting it in for him, even if like the rest of the players I thought the time had come for something to change.

After the goal against Fulham on the opening day, I didn't score again until 6 December. But in January, when I was used as a lone striker after he finally left Anelka out, I started to do the business for him. I'd been left out for five games after that incident against Everton when I walked out, and I had worked hard on my fitness. There were about four or five games on the trot in the New Year when I was given the Man of the Match award, and under Keegan I reached a major milestone in my career. At Norwich on 28 February 2005 when I scored the first of two that night, it took me to 150 goals in the Premiership. I was only the third player in the history of the competition to do that, behind Alan Shearer and Andy Cole, and to be in the top three all-time Premiership scorers means something even to me, a cocky little Toxteth lad who never gave a stuff about records. I've had so many setbacks since 1997, and I've missed far too much football through injury, so to have got into the top three when there were so many amazing strikers around English football, it gives me intense pride. When I scored that goal, the lads went mad in the dressing room afterwards, and the manager was dead pleased for me too. He went out to the press and gave me a wonderful tribute, put me up there with some of the best strikers of all time, which was decent of him, and an honour, considering that he was one of the greats himself as a player.

Within a fortnight of that game, he was gone. There were always a few problems with Keegan not relating to the players, and sometimes coming across as if he was just winging everything when it came to matches. I understand there were a few problems with him in the relationships he had with the staff at the club too.

But the biggest problem, for me, was that he announced his retirement a long time before he was due to go. He said he would step down at the end of his contract in the summer of 2006, but how the hell could that work? Once a manager says he's going, then it gives everyone a licence to piss around. You can't have the same respect for a man who isn't going to see the job through, because you know he has immediately lost all authority. It's almost a subconscious thing, players just ease back a little because the manager has got no hold over them. It happened to Sir Alex Ferguson at Manchester United when he announced his retirement, and it was only when he changed his mind and said he was continuing that results picked up. Maybe when a manager decides he is going, in his own mind he just slacks off a little too, hasn't quite got the same motivation. A lot of the players at City thought that, and things got worse and worse as the season progressed. By Christmas, some of the players were openly speaking out against him, although I can say hand on heart that it was never me.

It's no real secret that David James came out and said the situation couldn't go on as it was, and I think there was some communication to that effect to the board. Jamo wasn't the only one to go to them and speak out, and the chairman, John Wardle, did the only thing he could do, which was to thank the manager for all his incredible efforts and let him go. As I've said, I wouldn't argue with that decision, because it was time for a change – and the results we had after he left prove that. When Stuart Pearce took over as temporary manager, we were desperately unlucky to lose our first game against Spurs, but after that we didn't lose again until the end of the season. It was an incredible run, and we played some very good football. We were unbeaten in our last eight matches, and I started to really enjoy my football again, to the extent that the old belief came flooding back ... and maybe it wouldn't be too big-headed to say that some of the old ability came back too. I did it for Keegan, but under Stuart Pearce, I would just about dare to venture that I am reaching a new level.

I think Stuart Pearce is good for Manchester City. It is not hard to see his passion for the game, and his commitment to the club. But don't be deceived into thinking he is just a motivator, because he's also a bloody good coach who knows the game inside out tactically. He has worked under some of the best coaches ever in Brian Clough, Bobby Robson and Terry Venables and you can see that he has learnt a lot from all of them. We go back a long way, to when we were in the England squad together for Euro '96, and he was a fantastic man to have on your side. I'll never forget the courage he showed in taking that penalty against Spain in the quarter final, when a lesser man would have bottled it, after his miss against Germany in the semi final of the World Cup in 1990. He will never shirk a challenge, and even though when he took over as full-time manager at City there were plenty of odds stacked against him, who would bet against Stuart Pearce being a success as a manager? Not me, not after what happened at the end of the 2004–05 season. He took us from looking down at the fringes of another relegation scrap, to within one kick of getting into Europe. Sadly, it was me who missed that kick.

It seems an appropriate end to my story so far, the penalty kick I had to put City into the UEFA Cup, at the end of the season when I nearly walked away from football for ever. It was 15 May 2005, and we met Middlesbrough at the City of Manchester, with the winner taking the final European place. A draw, though, was enough for them to sneak it. It was a mad, mad game. They scored early on, we equalized when Kiki Musampa scored a great goal, and we were set up for an incredible finale. Never in my whole life have I seen anything like it. A couple of minutes before the end, Nicky Weaver starts warming up, and the gaffer is shouting over to Jamo. I didn't have a clue what was going on, but then the board goes up, and Jamo is racing over to the touchline. It flashed across my mind that it was the stupidest fucking substitution I'd ever seen, because why change one keeper for another when it's goals that you need? But my jaw dropped with the penny as it dawned on me that Jamo was staying on and our midfielder Claudio Reyna was going off, and that he was just going over to change his goalkeeper's jersey for a blue shirt.

There had been some talk earlier in the day of Jamo getting an outfield shirt, but nobody took it seriously, and in the heat of the battle it never crossed my mind that the boss could actually be mad enough to try it. What the keeper did next was the funniest thing I have ever seen. I almost couldn't play for laughing, even though it was such a serious situation. Jamo is a massive fucker, six foot six and built like a brick shithouse. Every single ounce of his huge frame went into smashing the Boro defenders around like they were skittles.

You should have seen the looks on their faces! They were wondering what the fuck was happening, and you could tell they were desperate for the final whistle. Then, just as it is about to be blown, the ball flies across the goal and there is Jamo, ready to tap it in. Only a hand from Boro full back Franck Queudrue stopped him scoring the most remarkable goal of all time, I swear. But it was a penalty, and everyone is looking around, seeing who's gonna take it. I was looking round too, but all I saw was everyone staring at the ground, so I thought, Why not? I've never bottled a challenge, might just be a chance to give something back to the fans.

I said afterwards I had a premonition I was going to get a moment like that, and fuck it up. That's putting it a bit strong actually. During the build-up to the game, I did get a feeling in my bones that something dramatic would happen, that I would get a penalty and I might not score it. It wasn't a premonition, just a bit of idle speculation about all the possibilities that could happen in the match. I've done it before, lots, thought about the worst that could happen in a game. It never normally does. This time, I was staring at Middlesbrough keeper Mark Schwarzer from twelve yards, knowing that I had one kick to put us into Europe.

The fans were quieter than they are at Old Trafford, and the tension was hanging on the air like static electricity. Almost 50,000 people in the stadium, and every single pair of eyes on me. I put the ball down and thought I had to place it to the keeper's left. Then I thought I'd be better off smashing it, but immediately I dismissed that idea because it meant changing my mind, and you always fuck up when you change your mind on penalties. So it was Plan A, and I turned around without looking at the net, kept my eyes on the ball as I approached, and then hit it with a good clean strike where I intended. You could hear the crowd sucking in their breath as I hit it, and what seemed like an eternity before a huge, anguished growl swept around the ground. He saved it. The fucker saved it. It was a good penalty but he chose the right way, dived well and got a strong hand to it to keep it out.

It was a horrible, gut-wrenching moment, and I could hardly take it in. After all that happened to me, all the pain I had been through in the previous eighteen months or so, I thought I deserved some luck. I thought the City fans deserved something back from me, after they had stuck by me and given me such support, even after I had been so crap for them. But no, it wasn't to be. It was one last boot in the bollocks even after all the blows there I'd already suffered. Stuart Pearce was magnificent afterwards, he reminded me of his penalty in 1990, and he said I had to get my mind right, I had to understand that it is one of those things that can happen to the very best, there's nothing you can do about it, and you have to be strong and move on. And you know what? I have. It hasn't affected me in the slightest, I know that there is no point at all dwelling on it, that I have to use the experience and make myself stronger. I don't want to sound as though I don't care, but I've dealt with it, and I'm already looking to the future.

And what of the future? Well, the end of the 2004–05 season took me to within a year of the end of my contract at Manchester City, but I've no plans to retire just yet. I was thirty just before the end of the season, and when I reached that birthday, I sat down and looked closely at myself. Yep, I've lost a lot of pace, but I was never lightning anyway. I've gained a bit more guile, a bit more experience, and my technique has improved out of sight. For the past few years, I've always had some barbed comments about my weight, with people suggesting I'm too fat to play top-class football. The truth – the God's honest truth – is that I'm only a few pounds over the weight I was when I first started. It might sound like a good excuse from a fat lad that likes doughnuts, but I need to have some weight on me, to hold off defenders. I'm not the biggest, and believe me, they are. You get centre halves who are like brick walls, and when they kick you up the arse, you keep going all the way down the tunnel unless you've got some strength to hold them off. When I came back from the knee injury, I slimmed right down, got to my lightest weight ever. But I was too weak, too small and I got pushed off the ball too easily. Weight is not an issue for me.

I am playing as well now as I have done for a very long time, and I know that I've got three or four more years left in me. I know I can carry on in the top flight, and in my mind, I still think I'm good enough to play for England, even if I'd have to wait for Eriksson to go to have any chance. I got to the milestone of 150 goals, but it was never my intention to stop there. Andy Cole is next up. He's about twenty or so goals ahead of me, and I'm already doing the calculations. Shearer may be out of reach on 250, but hey, I'm an optimist. You have to be where I come from.

There's a funny story from my friendship with Macca. In all the time he was out in Madrid, I never got the chance to go out and see him play, because our schedules always clashed. Finally, right at the end of the 2003 season, I got the chance to go and see him. It turned out to be Steve's final match for Real Madrid. It also turned out to be a game they needed to win to lift the Spanish title. It was an electric night, and they know how to hype it up out there. They won easily on the night, and the party began. I was with my cousin Paul out watching the match, and after the celebrations were all over on the pitch, we went down to see Macca in the players' bar. He was in a right lively mood and he had hatched a plan. 'Sneak on the bus with us when we parade around the city,' he whispered. So we did. We each put on one of the official T-shirts the players had to celebrate their millionth title win or whatever, and there's me, a Manchester City striker, and me cousin who's a painter and decorator, standing on an open-top bus parading around the city with all the Real Madrid squad, waving the trophy around, and celebrating a title win at last! As we got into the main square when the players get off the bus and dive into the big fountain in the middle, a group of English lads standing by the roadside recognized me, and started chanting my name. It was quiet at first, and then got louder and louder until it was ringing around the whole square. 'Fow-ler, Fow-ler,' they sang, and I couldn't help but smile. All those years I dreamt about lifting the Championship trophy, and now here I was finally doing it, even if it was the wrong fucking one, and the wrong fucking team. Maybe that was my only chance, but I'm not giving up hope just yet. After what has happened to me so far, anything is possible.

I was in Istanbul when Liverpool won the Champions' League at the end of the 2004–05 season, and I had to wipe away a tear from my eye at the end. I did think for just a few seconds that it could have been me, holding up the trophy, and dancing away into the night.

A lot of that team were there when I was captain, and I spoke to a few of the lads afterwards. Each one said the same. 'Sorry, Robbie lad, if it hadn't been for Houllier, you'd have been out there too.' You never know. It might just have happened. Probably not, but it is nice to think that something as incredible as that experience, which was truly awesome and had me standing on me seat just like I was a ten-year-old kid again supporting Everton, could have happened to me . . . could still happen to me. But regrets? No chance.

I'm reminded of that story about George Best – the one where he's in a hotel room with Miss World, thousands of pounds in readies and loads of champagne, and the guy bringing room service asks, 'George, where did it all go wrong?' Sometimes, people ask the same sort of question about my career. They ask me where it all went wrong. I became the third top scorer in Premiership history, I have played twelve years at the very top of the English game, played for my country in the biggest tournaments, played in finals and chased titles, and I'm still proving that I'm up there with some of the best even after reaching what some people regard as the veteran stage. I've got years left in me, and I look around, and I don't see too many strikers that would embarrass me when it comes to finishing. Plenty that would beat me in a foot race of course. Me nana might do that. But I've got something left still. So no, it hasn't all gone wrong. For a lad from Toxteth who came from nothing and dreamt only of playing football, it's all gone rather spectacularly well, actually.

EPILOGUE

Flicking back through the pages of this book, as I write the epilogue, one sentence stands out for me. Speaking about Liverpool and my love for the club, I suggested that I still had a bit of unfinished business at Anfield. Bloody hell, move over Derek Acorah. No one thought that I would ever go back to Liverpool as a player, not one person. Except me. Oh, ok, two people actually, because me dad always said I would as well, and I can't even begin to tell you how happy I am that he was right. When I think back to that day at the end of January when I signed a six-month contract to play with Liverpool until the end of the season, it still makes me smile. I honestly don't believe that I have ever been happier in my football life than the moment when I sat in my car outside Anfield, a minute after I had put pen to paper to bring me home.

I think it's pretty obvious throughout the course of this book that I was devastated to leave Liverpool. Regret is the wrong word to describe how I felt about leaving, because I was forced to leave, and there is no point wasting such energy and emotion over something that was, sadly, inevitable. What killed me, though, was the manner in which I left Anfield. My last game was against Sunderland, when I was captain, but was taken off at half time because Didi Hamann had been sent off, and – predictably enough – I was the one who was sacrificed to go long ball and defensive. When I sat in the dressing room as the other players went back out onto the pitch, I knew it was my last game before I was sold to Leeds, and I knew it was a shitty way to go out. I sat there with my head in my hands for an eternity, wondering how it had come to this, and muttering a thousand curses against those people at the club who I felt had tried to destroy me. Over the years that followed, throughout my time at Leeds and Manchester City, the one thing that hurt me more than anything else was the fact that I never got the chance to say goodbye to the fans. Replacing me to bring on a defensive midfielder was a logical decision I guess, one that ignored emotion and sentiment. But it didn't help me, and it left me with that feeling of unfinished business. In fact, it has always gnawed away at me, and if there was any bitterness, it was over that. It was a shocking end really, and I have always thought it was despicable treatment. I am the luckiest footballer alive in that the Liverpool fans have given me the most incredible support throughout my career. Words can't even describe the relationship I have with them, so to not even be able to say thank you to them and show my appreciation? That hurt, and was possibly the most painful of all the thousand cuts they inflicted on me.

When Rafael Benitez told me that he wanted me to come back, one of my first thoughts was that at least now I could say goodbye properly. But believe me, that wasn't the reason I went back to Liverpool. The final chapter of this book talks of how I felt I could still compete at the top level. I'm not stupid, I know that people talk about me as some great lost talent, as a player who wasted his career. I know too, that when I left Liverpool I lost the chance to win the honours that would have silenced that talk. Like all players, I want to win things, I have a desire raging inside me. I want to sit down at the end of my career and look at the medals that show I achieved something. As it was with Leeds and Manchester City, that wouldn't happen and the doubts would always linger. Going back to Liverpool, I knew that under Mr Benitez they would compete at the highest level, and I would have the chance to end my career on a high, challenging for real honours. If anything annoyed me during my last six months at Manchester City – incensed me, to be accurate – it was the suggestion that

I had no desire, that I was coasting out my time until my contract was up and I could disappear gently into retirement. I have one word in response to that suggestion: bollocks.

By Christmas 2005, it was pretty obvious that Stuart Pearce didn't fancy me . . . in a footballing sense, of course! There was no way through for me into the starting line up at the City of Manchester stadium, and little chance of me being given a new contract, so it seemed I would be on my way in the summer, if not before. There was plenty of speculation about clubs being interested in me, and I seemed to be linked with just about every side in the Championship. One of the clubs was Norwich, and the question of signing me was put to their manager Nigel Worthington. Apparently, his response was that he wouldn't be interested in someone like me, because he wanted someone who was hungry, who had a desire for success. I must admit, I was bloody angry about that. Apart from the fact that I'd never go to Norwich anyway, I thought back to the previous February, when I had become the third highest scorer in Premiership history, and passed 150 goals into the bargain.

Who did I score two goals against that day? Norwich. I was hungry enough then, and had not changed over the following ten months. I can honestly say that I have not lost my hunger to play and score goals, even at this stage of my career. I hate not playing, and I love scoring goals. In only my third game back at Liverpool under Rafael Benitez, against Arsenal, I was substituted in the second half, and I was gutted. It was as much as I could manage not to throw my shirt down in disgust. It was the perfectly correct decision to bring on a fresh pair of legs, but I was still distraught that I had been taken off, because I am so desperate to play. That desire will never leave me.

That is why I managed to get so upset with Stuart Pearce in my final few months at Manchester City. I started to dislike him, because he didn't play me. I have nothing against him, and in fact, he did me a big favour when it came to negotiations between the club and Liverpool, for which I'll always be grateful. But if anyone leaves me out when I feel I should be playing, I'll hate them. And I always feel I should be playing! After missing that penalty against Boro, which cost City a place in the UEFA Cup, things got worse for me over the summer. When I reported back for pre-season I had discomfort in my back, which seemed to get worse and worse. Eventually, I went for a second opinion, which ultimately revealed that I had fractured one of the discs in my spine. It is so typical of my luck that every time I get an injury it seems to take an age to discover the real cause. With a back injury, as well, people think you are chucking in a sickie, but this was very real, and I had to spend most of my time lying down to rest my spine. It was horrendous – the disc had virtually exploded and caused me an awful lot of pain, and yet people were still darkly suggesting that I was trying it on. I have my suspicions that even the gaffer had some doubts, and maybe that was one of the reasons why I was pushed out into the cold, even when I was fit. I've since heard from a few people close to Pearce that he was less than impressed that I had returned in the summer with a back injury and that he had been muttering about me playing too much golf. But the fracture in the disc had nothing to do with golf.

There was also a suggestion that he didn't like my attitude in training, but I can't believe that because when we spoke he always told me that I was doing exactly what he wanted and if I kept it going I would get my chance in the first team. I eventually did in early January, after being out of the side for six months. It was in the FA Cup against Scunthorpe, and I scored a hat-trick. It wasn't a bad one either, even if it was against a lower league side. City had gone through a bit of a barren patch before that game, so naturally there was a bit of a groundswell for me to be in the team, and even a few questions asked about the manager's selection policy. The next game though, I was on the bench, and it was against the old enemy Manchester United. We took them apart, and I came on and scored a goal at the end that I'm proud of. As it turned out, it was my last goal for City, which I suppose is not a bad note on which to have ended my relationship with the club. The fans there were always good to me, they supported me through some bad times, and I am glad I got the chance to score that goal and offer them a little bit of happiness.

Mind you, even then people could tell where my heart lied. When I scored it was at the United end of the ground, and as I celebrated, I got the usual pile of objects thrown at me. Bradley

Ormesher, the Mirror photographer, was sitting taking pictures at that end and he said he picked up almost £10 in loose change afterwards! He also got a mobile phone smack bang on the back of his head, so it wasn't all profit. Anyway, as I sensibly wheeled away from them I couldn't resist the chance to stick up five fingers on one hand, to remind them of the number of European Cups Liverpool have won. I got some stick off Gary Neville, just for a change.

The next game, I was on the bench again, but by then I had already made up my mind that I would be on my way. I knew that I didn't want my career to simply fizzle out, I didn't want to hang around on the bench for the rest of the season and then find myself without a contract. I know that I still have something to offer at the top level, and I knew then I had to find a platform which would allow me to prove that. George, my advisor, had spoken with Stuart Pearce, and discovered that there had been a couple of enquiries from lower league sides, and some intriguing contact from Premiership clubs. One was Wigan, and the prospect of playing for Paul Jewell was a pretty good one. But Pearce had turned them down flat. The other was even more interesting. A friend of mine knows Bill Kenwright pretty well and he said that Everton were desperately looking for a striker. I was asked about how I would feel going to Goodison. To be honest, I was torn, because on the one hand it was the club I supported as a boy and followed everywhere, but on the other, they had thrown pies at me and mullered me for twelve years. It would have been an agonizing decision to have had to make, but again, when the Everton manager made his approach, he was told that City were not interested in letting me go because they needed cover. That was a depressing situation, because it meant I wasn't playing but couldn't get another club, so George went in to ask what the hell was going on.

Pearce said he wouldn't accept an offer for me, but at the same time, if I had an offer I was interested in, then I should talk about it. Reading between the lines, that meant City didn't want to accept an approach because they would have to pay up my contract, but if I went in with a club, it meant I would forsake a pay off. All this time, even though people probably thought I was mad, I was holding on to the idea that Liverpool would still come in for me. It wasn't just some wrong-un's fantasy, because there had been a little sniff of interest the previous summer, until the back ruled me out. I still had plenty of contacts amongst the players at Anfield, and the likes of Carra and Stevie Gerrard had spoken to me, and suggested it wasn't out of the question. Apparently, Benitez was impressed by my movement and thought I was the sort of intelligent player he could use, but he naturally had doubts about my fitness. Around October, another mate told me that Mr Benitez had said that I had a chance of going back, if I got myself fit. Nothing happened though, and I was beginning to despair that I would never get my wish. People ask me why I was so desperate to go back, and they openly wonder why I clung on to the faint hope, even when it seemed so impossible. The truth is – and I don't want to make this sound too sentimental, but it is the way it is – my nana Mary's dying wish was to see me play for Liverpool again. Like all the family, she was gutted when I left, and whenever I saw her she would always say, 'Eh, Robbie lad, isn't it about time you went back where you belong?' She died in the winter of 2005 and the last time I saw her, she said the same thing. She whispered to me that she wanted to see me in the red shirt one last time before she went. You can tell in the pages of this book how much she meant to me and if I didn't have enough motivation of my own, then she had made me even more determined to somehow return to Anfield, one day, in whatever capacity I could. Christ, I would even go back to clean the terraces.

When it happened it all came very quickly. One of the scouts at Anfield had kept in touch with me, and one day he mentioned that the scouting department had agreed to recommend me to the manager as an extra body to the forward line, where they had been a bit short.

When I met him, I was impressed immediately. He knew exactly what he was looking for, exactly where I could fit into his style of play and he asked me whether I could do the job he wanted. He admitted he was worried about my fitness and said that some people had suggested I had got a little bit lazy. I assured him that I would run half way around the world to play for Liverpool again. I knew that if I could get my condition right I could still do the running and I knew if I got the chance, I could prove I could do it even at the top level, and I told him as much. He must have been impressed, because the next day Liverpool's chief executive Rick Parry contacted George and said he wanted to talk. There was only a six-month contract on offer initially and the money was far less than if I'd have stayed at Manchester City, so it very definitely wasn't a financial decision. I can say with my hand on my heart that I never considered the money. I would have played for nothing had they asked me to.

When I eventually went in I didn't read the contract, because I was just thinking, I'd better get it signed before they took it away again. I didn't want to let me nana down. I think I broke the speed limit every inch of the way into Liverpool and I dashed into the office with the biggest grin on my face anyone has ever seen. I walked through the door and Paula, the lovely girl on the reception at Anfield, who I've known for a long time, almost broke down in tears. That almost set me off, too. Afterwards, I went and sat in my car for a few moments to consider what had happened. That moment the phone rang and it was me dad. I said that I had just signed and I told him that I couldn't wipe the stupid grin off my face. For days and days afterwards, I went around smiling like a complete dope. But I was back and I couldn't help it. I had never lost hope it would happen and I think now that I wanted it so much, it eventually came true.

As I have said, it was only a six-month contract, with no promises. But I was happy enough to sign that. The final chapter of this book, written just after Liverpool had won the Champions' League in 2005, suggested that I still considered I could play at that level, even thought I wasn't much worse than some strikers who have represented England recently. And that was how I felt when I signed. I knew that if I could get fit, I could prove I was worth a new contract. Nothing has changed in my mind.

I started matches much earlier than anticipated, when I came back, and people said some very nice things about me. For me, going back to Liverpool wasn't the end . . . it's only the beginning.

Acknowledgements

Thanks go to everyone who gave their time, and so much of themselves, to help this story be told. In particular, Bobby Fowler was a valuable and entertaining source of information, as was Marie Ryder, the nicest person on earth. Without them, of course, there would be no story. Kerrie Fowler was supportive and interested ... and yes, we do remember your shop is called Bardot. George Scott was honest, helpful and revealing, which is a unique attitude in the world of football. Stephen Calvey is not only Robbie's friend and protector, but also a loyal, funny and interesting fount of all knowledge. Gordon Gotham, too, has offered support and friendship. Bob Lynch was courteous, instructive and helpful, just as he has been throughout Robbie's career. Thanks from Robbie must go, too, to all his family and friends – too numerous to mention – who have contributed so much to his fascinating tale. In particular, he wants to remember the important role played in his development by his nana Mary, Grandad Johnny and uncle Alan.

Roy Evans, a decent man from a world not renowned for such people, was patient and informative, and to his eternal credit always willing to see the best in everyone. Roy, Graeme Souness, Kenny Dalglish and Ian Rush require thanks for their contribution, both to the success of Robbie Fowler and to the creation of this book. Tony Grant is different among footballers in that he has a perfect memory and is willing to share it. He is also a top man, who should have won many caps for England.

Many people have provided important source material, but without three in particular, life would have been much more difficult. Matt D'Arcy, once of the *Daily Star* and now of the beaches of Portugal, offered his time, help and massive cuttings library in support of the research required. He even entered the technological age to make it easier. Richard Tanner of the *Express* was equally helpful and informative, his records providing the facts on which this book is based. He is not known as Statto for nothing. Chris Bascombe of the *Liverpool Echo* was another key contributor. Thanks go to him for endless observations, and his willingness to act as a sounding board. We are grateful to the following journalists for their knowledge, guidance and support at important moments: Ian Whittell, Phil Thomas, Andy Hunter, Paul Joyce, Dominic Fifield and John Edwards. To Dean Morse, Bob Blair and Mike Allen of the *Daily Mirror*, sincere thanks for your support and patience through difficult times, and your ability to provide a calming insight when most required.

Several people have provided support and assistance throughout the life of this epic endeavour. Without David Luxton, our agent, this book would not have been possible. Sorry we didn't return your calls. We would also like to thank Richard Milner at Pan Macmillan for his many qualities, not least patience ... which they do say is a virtue, and was desperately required. Thank you. Sarah Edworthy was indispensable from day one, providing the encouragement to get the project off the ground, and the crucial knowledge of how to go about it. Throughout, she provided a steady hand and a steely red pen, to keep us focused and away from the edge of despair. Brendan Wignall, too, was kind enough to offer his immense insight and knowledge. Further gratitude must be offered to Brian Naylor, Colin Christie and Rob Sinnott for their help, and yes, it is finished, or rather, abandoned.

Last, but most importantly, thanks and an apology must go to Amanda James, who has the patience and beauty of a saint, and has endured far too much in the painful months of this book's construction. Without you, it would not have been possible, nor without the support of Josh, Joel, Isaac and Ellie. Now, we can spend quality time together. Honest.

David Maddock

Index